Japan's
Cultural
Code Words

Other Books by Boyé Lafayette De Mente

Japan's Cultural Code Words

233 Key Terms That Explain The Attitudes and Behavior of The Japanese

Boyé Lafayette De Mente

TUTTLE PUBLISHING
Boston • Rutland, Vermont • Tokyo

Published by Tuttle Publishing,
an imprint of Periplus Editions (HK) Ltd.
© 2004 Boyé Lafayette De Mente
All rights reserved
LCC Card No. 2003116861
ISBN 0-8048-3574-8

Printed in Singapore

Distributed by:
Japan
Tuttle Publishing
Yaekari Building, 3rd Floor
5-4-12 Osaki, Shinagawa-ku
Tokyo 141-0032
Tel: (03) 5437 0171; Fax: (03) 5437 0755
Email: tuttle-sales@gol.com

North America, Latin America & Europe
Tuttle Publishing
Airport Industrial Park
364 Innovation Drive
North Clarendon, VT 05759-9436
Tel: (802) 773 8930; Fax: (802) 773 6993
Email: info@tuttlepublishing.com
www.tuttlepublishing.com

Asia Pacific
Berkeley Books Pte. Ltd.
130 Joo Seng Road, #06-01/03
Singapore 368357
Tel: (65) 6280 1330; Fax: (65) 6280 6290
Email: inquiries@periplus.com.sg

10 09 08 07 06 05 04
10 9 8 7 6 5 4 3 2 1

CONTENTS

The Two Faces of Japan

WESTERNERS have traditionally been intrigued by Asian attitudes and behavior that have been perceived as ranging from cute, quaint, and seductive to strange and sometimes savage. To Western eyes there was something alien about a people who could change from being exquisitely mannered, gentle, generous and philosophically sophisticated at one moment to what could only be described as barbaric a short time later. The extremes of such behavior among Asians were especially conspicuous because these sudden transformations in character often seemed to deny their humanity.

In part at least, the traditional dual character of Chinese, Koreans, Japanese and other Asians was a product of cultures that denied them the inherent human aspirations for individuality and personal freedom, and forced them to think and behave in ways that were unnatural. This enforced behavior was an unending source of conflict between their natural instincts and what they had to do to survive and remain members of their societies.

In the case of Japan, this dual-nature culture permeated every aspect of society, leaving virtually nothing to either the personal preferences or to the conscience of the individuals concerned. Life was totally structured. Religion, politics, and economics were inseparably meshed. The only acceptable behavior was strict conformity to the standards set by the ruling powers, and to sanctified custom.

As long as there were no disruptions in Japanese society, it functioned smoothly on the surface. But when the system weakened and began to change, people did not know how to conduct themselves in a rational, principled manner because they had no understanding of, or experience with, inner-directed behavior. The introduction of any unsettling element, from within or without, generally resulted in some kind of violence.

Japan's history is filled with destructive behavior resulting from the over-restrictive, tunnel vision of its traditional culture. Some of this destructive behavior was directed against perceived competitors or enemies, and some of it was directed toward the Japanese themselves.

But while Japan's conformity-oriented culture was the antithesis of personal freedom, it nevertheless provided both the framework and the impetus for extraordinary competition between groups, and once this group competitiveness was harnessed to national goals, it gave Japan one of the world's most dynamic societies. Unfortunately, the dynamism created by Japan's unique blend of philosophies and cultures was not tempered by any universal moral obligation to preserve and protect the weak, or any clearly defined sense of fair play. In the Confucianism-based Japanese context of things, the proper order was that the powerful made and enforced the laws and the weak obeyed them.

The speed with which the Japanese accepted the ideals of democracy and human rights, introduced into the country by the United States following the end of World

War II in 1945, was a remarkable demonstration of the inherent affinity that people have for freedom, regardless of their history. As the programming of Japan's traditional culture gradually weakened from 1945 on, individual Japanese began to exercise some personal choice in their private lives. But the newly mandated freedoms had a minimal effect on a number of key institutions. Japan's educational, economic, and political systems remained hidebound bulwarks of traditional behavior. The politically guided economic system in particular was able to generate enormous power that could be directed with the precision of a laser beam.

During the intervening decades, the traditional conditioning and orientation of the Japanese have continued to diminish, and ongoing influence from the West has wrought fundamental changes in the attitudes and behavior of the Japanese, especially in those of the younger generations. Nevertheless, Japan's traditional culture is still so powerful that it continues to be the prevailing force in molding and tuning the national character of the Japanese, with the result that they still have two faces—one modern and rational, and one traditional and emotional.

The best and fastest way to an understanding of the emotional and traditional side of Japanese attitudes and behavior is through their "business and cultural code words"—terms that reveal their psychology and philosophy in far more depth and precision than any Rorschach test.

Boyé Lafayette De Mente
Tokyo, Japan

揚げ足
Ageashi
(Ah-gay-ah-she)

Tripping on Your Own Tongue

The Japanese have traditionally been wary of people who were good talkers, equating the habit and demonstrations of such ability with unprincipled, untrustworthy behavior. While this attitude toward loquacity is also common in the West, in Japan the negative response to people who talk a great deal has been much more deeply ingrained in the culture and far more important in the overall scheme of things—particularly in the past.

The distrust and dislike of verbosity in Japan had its origin in Buddhism and Confucianism, both of which called for a quiet, contemplative demeanor and held that actions spoke much louder than words.

Historically in Japan, self-restraint in expression was equated with cultural attainment, morality and wisdom, and a great deal of all communication was therefore silent—a function of cultural intuition rather than words.

Another key factor contributing to the importance of verbal restraint was the nature of Japanese etiquette itself. In formal situations, saying exactly the right thing, at the right time, and in the right way, was an absolute requirement. In encounters with superiors, the authorities, and government and court officials, including samurai warriors, speech standards were especially strict, and the consequence of not adhering to them precisely could literally be fatal. Because of this obsessive concern with a precise protocol in verbal communication, it became characteristic of the Japanese to say as little as possible in order to avoid *ageashi* (ah-gay-ah-she), or "being tripped up by their own tongue."

Occasions when "slips of the tongue," *ageashi wo toru* (ah-gay-ah-she oh toe-rue), could have serious, even fatal, consequences were so common in Japanese life that avoiding them was a never-ending challenge. Thus, verbosity in itself was dangerous, because the more a person talked the more likely it was that he or she might make some kind of error in the choice of vocabulary, use the wrong tone of the voice, or try the patience of the listener—all of which could trigger a negative reaction from the other party.

In present-day Japan, committing an *ageashi* is still a serious breach of etiquette, and with some exceptions people still react negatively to big talkers—including politicians. People who are permitted a certain talkativeness include entertainers—particularly comedians whose stock-in-trade is their wit and facile-tongued newscasters, professional commentators, educators, and increasingly since the early 1990s, a few of the country's leading businessmen who have achieved the status of *sensei* (sensay-e), "teacher" or "master," and are no longer looked upon only as businessmen.

The Japanese, however, are a long way from accepting and being comfortable with the fast-talking, free-for-all kind of verbal behavior that is common among Americans and other Westerners, and as a consequence, an appreciation of talkative behavior is one of the handicaps that adversely affects the ability of Westerners to communicate effectively in Japan. It is an ironic cultural twist that while the Japanese prefer verbal restraint and periods of silence, Americans regard reticence to talk as a weakness, and periods of silence as a vacuum that must be filled up.

Japanese negotiators almost always take for granted that Westerners will commit any number of *ageashi* during the course of meetings because of their propensity to talk, and the Japanese encourage this by keeping quiet most of the time. The Japanese custom of reticence in speech thus contributes to the American habit of talking too much—of literally engaging in *sekkyo* (sake-k'yoe), or "preaching," at every opportunity. This factor becomes even more significant when it is combined with the Japanese custom of deliberately interspersing time gaps into their negotiating sessions that are especially stressful—periods of one, two, or more minutes when they simply stop listening and take impromptu breaks.

There is nothing malicious about these breaks. Formal encounters in Japan have always demanded extraordinary attention and concentration and were therefore stressful. It became customary to insert such breaks into formal situations so the participants could relax for a short while. But all too often when the Japanese side tunes out, inexperienced American negotiators presume that they are not getting through to the Japanese; the Americans then panic and redouble their verbal efforts to break down what they perceive as a barrier.

Generally speaking, the foreign side in negotiating sessions cannot speed up the flow of the meetings by changing the built-in behavior of their Japanese counterparts, so the only rational course is to adapt to the situation at hand.

See *Kosho.*

Age Tsurau
(Ah-gay T'sue-rah-oh)

Finding Endless Fault

The Japanese, like many other people, take perverse satisfaction in criticizing their politicians, businesspeople, educators, doctors and just about every other category of people in the country—despite the fact that they often go to extremes in praising Japan's accomplishments and generally see themselves as superior to other people. The Japanese behave in this seemingly contradictory manner because they have much higher expectations of their compatriots which are not usually met.

When it comes to the level to which expectations are met, however, the Japanese are in a class by themselves. While other people are generally satisfied with a degree of skill, efficiency and quality that is far below the maximum possible, the Japanese were traditionally conditioned to strive for perfection in everything they did. Anything less than perfection was subject to being criticized.

Although most of the attitudes and practices that created and sustained Japan's perfectionist syndrome have weakened or disappeared altogether, perfectionism was so deeply rooted in the culture that it is still a significant factor in the character and behavior of most of the people.

Present-day Japanese who are involved in international business regard this cultural characteristic with mixed emotions. On the one hand, they are proud of their high standards; on the other hand, they recognize that their standards are sometimes too high and that overly high standards may be a serious impediment to business. It is becoming more and more common for Westernized Japanese to apologize to their foreign counterparts for the fastidiousness of their own colleagues, many of whom seem to be more dedicated to *age tsurau* (ah-gay t'sue-rah-oh), or "endless fault-finding," than they are to actually doing business.

The immediate reaction of these *age tsurau* people to anything new is to look for faults—to dissect every product and every proposition from every angle to see if it meets their cultural expectations. Where Western-made products are concerned, these built-in concerns cover the overall appearance of a product—the design, size, color, material, finish, touch and other features. If any one of these factors is "culturally incompatible," which is not always the same as saying it is not well made, the product is generally turned down, or it is suggested that the product be redesigned to fit Japanese expectations. There is a growing facet of this cultural barrier, however, that works in favor of the outsider trying to get in. Japanese importers or buyers who decide on what will sell and what will not sell in the Japanese marketplace, especially those who are older, are often behind the times.

I have personally been involved in numerous attempts to introduce products into Japan, been told by potential importers and distributors that the products would not sell because they were culturally unsuited to Japan, and then seen the products become runaway sellers within a year. But the foreign businessman wanting to establish a relationship with a Japanese company, and especially to sell a foreign-made product in Japan, must still be concerned about every imaginable detail of the product.

From the Japanese viewpoint, it is the small things that make the difference between success and failure in any enterprise.

Perhaps the only practical way to reduce the amount of time it takes to implement a business deal with Japanese companies is to provide, on the first approach, written answers to every question they might reasonably be expected to have, along with a generous number of other answers that are only indirectly related to the product or project.

愛想笑い
Aiso Warai
(Aye-so Wah-rye)

Beware of Fake Smiles

One of the denigrating stories that Westerners used to tell about the Japanese, and about other Asians as well, was that they had so little respect for human life that when a member of their family or someone else close to them suffered a serious tragedy or died, they would laugh instead of cry.

In reality, when faced with tragedy and death, the Japanese suffered the pangs of sorrow just as much as anyone else, but they had been conditioned by their culture to repress their emotions in public in order not to upset or embarrass other people.

16

The smile that they showed to the outside world was their way of both hiding their own feelings and protecting others.

The cultural conditioning responsible for this traditional behavior has virtually disappeared from Japanese society. The display of strong emotions in public is no longer taboo and is seen often. Older Japanese who respond to sad events with stoicism are no different from their counterparts in other cultures.

There are occasions, however, when an *aiso warai* (aye-so wah-rye), or "fake smile," is an important aspect of contemporary Japanese behavior, and *aiso warai* provides a lesson in how serious many Japanese businessmen are in creating a positive atmosphere for their customers.

Most Western visitors to Japan are struck and deeply impressed by the attitude and behavior of employees in department stores and other large places of business catering to the general public. There are few if any dour expressions, and as a rule, the employees act friendly and are eager to help customers. Their smiling, friendly expressions are not always natural ones, however, and wearing a pleasant demeanor is not left up to the discretion of employees. Japanese operators of public service businesses such as hotels, restaurants, cabarets and retail outlets have traditionally instructed their employees in the art of making their customers feel good by keeping a happy, grateful look on their faces. In the employee instructional materials of some companies, the right kind of facial expression is described in specific detail, pointing out that employees should continuously strive to maintain a look that expresses love for their customers and gratitude for their patronage.

This aspect of human relations has been developed to a high art in Japan's nighttime entertainment trades, particularly in cabarets and other drinking places that feature the company of hostesses. Here, where customers come specifically to enjoy themselves and to forget their problems or worries, making the customer feel good is the first priority of the entire staff.

The most successful hostesses (successful in terms of how much their customers spend and how long the hostesses survive in the highly competitive atmosphere of the cabaret world) invariably include those who have good-natured, smiling faces and who are expert at combining this with a sensual, tantalizing behavior that keeps attracting regular customers. Hostesses who do not naturally have these personality traits must depend instead upon a well-practiced *aiso warai* manner, often combined with sexual availability, to keep them in the business.

Because of the traditional role of *aiso warai* in Japan, the Japanese recognize an artificial smile when they see one; but because a smile is unnatural does not detract from its value if it is used in a traditionally accepted manner and place. Under these circumstances, *aiso warai* is recognized as a legitimate type of role-playing that not only contributes to better business, but also to the emotional well-being of all who are involved.

Foreign businessmen and politicians should be wary of going too far with an *aiso warai* approach to their Japanese counterparts. Typical Western behavior often strikes the Japanese as being too shallow and insincere in the first place. In formal situations, overdoing a warm, smiling, joking manner results in a decidedly negative reaction from the Japanese.

相槌
Aizuchi
(Aye-zoo-chee)

Synchronizing Your Movements

In feudal Japan there was a precise way to perform virtually every daily activity, from tying one's shoes and holding chopsticks to bowing and presenting a gift or other article to a person.

This preciseness in the way things were done was the only accepted form of behavior, and over the centuries it came to be equated with morality. The moral person behaved in the prescribed manner. Anyone who behaved differently was regarded as antisocial and un-Japanese. Japanese culture therefore had an especially powerful homogenizing influence on the members of the society.

Despite the great deal of casual and personalized behavior that one sees in Japan today, the cultural conditioning that took place over many centuries is far from gone, and it continues to add a distinctive color and flavor to life.

In traditional settings, whether in the home, in *ryokan* (ree-oh kahn) inns, or in business offices, the Japanese still automatically follow most of the age-old patterns of behavior, because the customs remain a part of their identity as Japanese.

Part of this Japanese identity includes a custom that involves positive reinforcement in oral communication. When the Japanese hold informal conversations, as well as when they engage in formal discussions, they are conditioned to constantly encourage the person who is speaking by what is known as *aizuchi* (aye-zoo-chee), or "chiming in," meaning that they nod at regular intervals, say *hai* (hi), "yes," or make an affirmative "uh" sound.

The custom of *aizuchi* is deeply ingrained in the Japanese, and the habit often misleads foreigners who are not familiar with it, because they presume that the Japanese are indicating that they understand, that they agree, that they want the speaker to continue, and so on. As it happens, none of the above may be true, and in formal negotiations there is always the chance that interpreting *aizuchi* as an affirmative may be erroneous. In most cases, the person "giving" the *aizuchi* is simply obeying a cultural impulse to signal to the speaker that he or she is listening—or at least pretending to listen.

At the same time, the custom of *aizuchi* is an important courtesy that is expected as part of overall Japanese etiquette. Failure to respond with a suitable *aizuchi* nod or sound clearly indicates that the listener is in an unfriendly or unreceptive mood, or that something else is preventing communication.

This kind of personal interaction is part of the intimacy that the Japanese share in their efforts to achieve and maintain harmony. Ostensibly, *aizuchi* keeps the Japanese on the same cultural wavelength and help make things go smoothly. Of course, Westerners have their own *aizuchi*, but it is far less vital to Western communication and harmonious relations, even though the signals are just as often used in a noncommittal way to avoid agreeing or disagreeing with someone.

The use of *aizuchi* presents a special problem for foreigners who are not familiar with Japanese behavior, because most foreigners tend to automatically accept the signals at face value. It is important for foreigners to realize that neither a nod nor a "yes," or *hai*, necessarily mean that they are being understood by the Japanese, or that anyone is agreeing with them; it is often necessary to take other steps to determine where the Japanese really stand on a proposal or on an issue. This is particularly vital when the linguistic ability of the Japanese party is weak or in doubt. The Japanese habitually give "affirmative" signs when they do not understand someone because they consider it rude to stop the speaker, and, generally, because they would be embarrassed by admitting that they do not understand.

Conversely, foreigners dealing with the Japanese get caught up in the same cultural trap and behave exactly as the Japanese do—indicating that they understand when they do not, and thereby allowing many things to go over their heads. This kind of behavior from both sides is a primary source of the frustration, misunderstanding and extra time that is involved in discussions between the Japanese and foreigners.

When foreigners are on the receiving end of discussions, virtually the only strategy that assures comprehension is to take notes during the conversation and later to apologize and ask the Japanese to clarify the points they were making—more than once if necessary. If foreigners are making the presentation and have any indication that their Japanese audience might not fully understand their comments, they should pause frequently during their discourse and ask if there are any questions or if anyone would like a point covered again. Generally, there are a few Japanese in any group that will ask questions. Ultimately, if the Japanese audience is not truly bilingual, the only solution is to have the main points translated into Japanese and given to the Japanese participants as advance information or as a follow-up memo.

There is still another aspect of the *aizuchi* trap. Foreigners who study the Japanese language and spend much of their time associating with Japanese, and who otherwise immerse themselves in Japanese society, soon find themselves behaving like the Japanese, bowing and giving other characteristic nonverbal signals. This makes the Japanese feel more at ease, and facilitates the flow of communication. But such behavior typically misleads the Japanese into believing that the foreigner not only understands the Japanese language, but will also accept their viewpoint. Foreigners whose verbal communication skills in Japanese are not on a par with the much easier nonverbal skills must be especially careful not to fall into this trap.

垢抜けした
Akanukeshita
(Ah-kah-nuu-kay-sshtah)

The Power of Polished Manners

Having been intimately involved with Japan since the late 1940s, I am forever wondering what it is like for Westerners, especially Americans, to experience present-day Japan for the first time.

I have witnessed such experiences thousands of times, have made a point of asking hundreds of individuals to describe their experiences to me, and have traveled around Japan with dozens of people from the moment of their arrival in the country—and still I have the same intense sense of wonder. The problem is that I want to be them—to have the experience myself, over and over, and that, of course, is impossible.

Over half a century of observing the reactions of Westerners to Japan has taught me a number of things—one of which is the extraordinary impact that traditional Japanese manners have on Americans. While Americans generally take great pride in their casual, informal ways—in effect, in their lack of manners—their reactions when they encounter the formal, highly stylized etiquette of the Japanese suggest that they are suddenly embarrassed and feel awkward. This reaction is partially valid; a lack of a relatively high standard of manners often relates directly to one's character and attitude toward other people. But some foreigners go overboard in their praise of Japanese etiquette because they cannot see beyond its facade.

The problem with Japan's traditional etiquette is that it went too far and was eventually divorced from moral or humane feelings; etiquette alone became the standard of morality, making it an end unto itself and often masking the most inhumane and immoral behavior.

Traditional Japanese etiquette had its origins in ancient Shinto rituals, in court ceremonies adopted from Korea and China between the years 300 and 700, and in the ritualistic practices of Buddhist priests. Japan's samurai warrior class, which rose to power in the late 1100s and which drew its spiritual and practical philosophy from Zen Buddhism, was to put the finishing touches on Japan's traditional etiquette, spreading it among the general population by example and edict, and thereby preserving it down to modern times.

The essence of Japanese etiquette is described in the term *akanukeshita* (ah-kah-nuu-kay-sshtah), which literally means "what is left after all of the dirt and grime has been removed" and in practical terms refers to refined, elegant manners and speech.

Few Japanese families today have the motivation, patience, or time to condition their children in the physical facets of traditional Japanese etiquette, much less its underlying philosophy. Most young Japanese first encounter aspects of the country's traditional etiquette in a structured and disciplined setting in school, where it is imposed upon them as part of the educational system. But because it is no longer the foundation for all interpersonal relationships, much of the etiquette they learn in school is ignored outside the classroom.

The weakening of Japan's traditional etiquette between 1945 and 1965 resulted in a dramatic spurt in the crime rate and in social disturbances in general. By the 1980s, corporate managers had become deeply concerned about the lack of manners and discipline in their new employees, and many companies began sponsoring intensive training programs designed to "remove the dirt and grime" from them. Since that time, behavioral standards set at the workplace have played a more significant role in preserving Japanese etiquette than the home and school combined. Businesses that serve the public directly are especially strict in their standards for employee behavior.

Most Westerners continue to find Japanese etiquette both impressive and intimidating. Americans in particular are uncomfortable in the presence of *akanukeshita* people who also speak a different language. All too often Westerners go too far in their attempts to accommodate the Japanese and not appear ill-mannered; they praise the Japanese too highly and lower their expectations of what they originally hoped to get from the Japanese.

Not surprisingly, however, many present-day Japanese feel inhibited and abused by the etiquette demands they must live up to in their homeland, and envy the casual manners of the West. They often note that both sides will be better served when the Japanese are subjected to a little less *akanukeshita* scrubbing and Westerners to considerably more.

諦めが悪い
Akirame ga Warui
(Ah-kee-rah-may gah Wah-rue-ee)

We Don't Know How to Quit!

Japan's defeat in World War II was the most significant and most traumatic event in the country's long history. In the early spring of 1945, by which time it had become more than obvious that the country had lost a war for the first time in its history, there was a flurry of activity among a number of internationally minded Japanese to end the fighting and to save the main islands of Japan from further bombing raids and from being invaded by the United States and its allied powers.

By June of that year, the situation had become so desperate that some of the most militant and nationalistic officers in the armed forces began acknowledging that there was no way Japan could win, and if the fighting were not stopped soon, the very existence of the country could be in jeopardy. Dozens of meetings were held and all kinds of suggestions for ending the war were endlessly discussed. Finally, in desperation, a ranking military officer blurted out, "We don't know how to surrender!"

This soul-wrenching cry spoke volumes about Japan's formalized and process-oriented feudal culture, which had conditioned people to behave in such precise patterns that flexibility and individual innovation were almost always taboo. Once a course of action had been officially approved, the only acceptable approach was to follow it to the end, regardless of how bitter the end might be.

Many of the more turbulent events in Japanese history, including acts at the individual and at the national level, have been made inevitable by the demands of a system that did not allow deviations from programmed behavior and official plans, regardless of the circumstances or conditions existing at the time, or how circumstances or conditions might change. These events included wars, acts of revenge, ceremonial suicides by samurai warriors and military officers, and mass suicides by civilians caught up in the madness of a system that took precedence over people.

Soon after the end of the Pacific War in August 1945, Japan's political and business leaders began focusing on rebuilding the nation with all of the considerable skill and energy they had previously devoted to the war effort. Workers and managers were programmed to succeed. There was no such thing as an eight-hour workday or a 40-hour workweek. The whole country became a beehive of incessant activity. The people worked with what has been described as a "hot fury," in part to expiate the shame of having failed at war, but also to satisfy an obsession to prove that they were a superior people.

By the 1980s, the Japanese had succeeded so well in their drive for economic power that they again came under attack, this time by foreign politicians and businessmen who criticized them for saving too much, for working too hard, and for giving no quarter when it came to taking over foreign markets and protecting their own markets. In addition to long hours of work, many Japanese managers never took their authorized vacations, and as a result they lost touch with their families, becoming strangers in their own homes.

Once again the Japanese were faced with the need to change, this time from robot-like "economic animals" to a less intense, less work-driven behavior that would not only improve their life-styles, but which would also cut back on the avalanche of Japanese-made exports that was smothering the United States and other countries. But just as in 1945, the Japanese were unable to change their behavior because they were still locked in the same *akirame ga warui* (ah-kee-rah-may gah wah-rue-ee), or "I/we don't know how to quit" syndrome, that prolonged World War II for months.

The situation ultimately became so serious that the government, even though caught up in the same feudalistic time warp of blindly pursuing its goals, began to exhort company managers and employees to reduce their working hours and to develop social lives.

Today most workers in Japan are on a five-day workweek schedule, and the leisure industries are booming. But the majority of Japanese managers continue to suffer from the *akirame ga warui* conditioning that makes them work like drones.

諦めない
Akiramenai
(Ah-kee-rah-may-nigh)

Do or Die

There have been innumerable incidents in Japanese history in which people found themselves in life-or-death situations and chose to die rather than live. Many of these incidents involved samurai, ninja, or soldiers; others involved just ordinary people.

There have also been numerous historical incidents in which the persons involved chose to die—often by their own hand—although their predicaments were not life-threatening, or even desperate from the Western viewpoint.

Some of the most famous anecdotes in Japanese history have to do with individuals killing themselves in order to attract attention to some issue or to some fault in their superiors—a custom that is also common in other Asian countries; in Vietnam and elsewhere in Southeast Asia, monks have drenched themselves with gasoline and set themselves on fire in a form of protest.

Of course, being willing to die for a principle or for the sake of others occurs in other cultures too, but the willingness of the Japanese to sacrifice themselves has traditionally gone well beyond the ordinary. Historically, Japanese culture as a whole has generally been one of self-sacrifice—of individuals repressing and denying their individuality in service to their families, communities, employers and country.

Another facet of this cultural conditioning in self-sacrifice occurred at a purely personal level. The Japanese have been programmed to persevere in whatever they set out to do, regardless of the obstacles and hardships they encounter. This conditioning was so thorough in the past that perseverance became automatic. Broadly speaking, every Japanese was programmed to the point that once they had set out to do something, they could not turn back or give up. *Akiramenai* (Ah-kee-rah-may-nigh), or "I can't give up," became a byword, and not being able to give up became a part of the fate of the Japanese. It permeated their psyche.

The characteristic persistence of the Japanese, whether in pursuing artistic or martial skills, in war, in business, or in seeking revenge for any insult or slight, is partly rooted in the *akiramenai* syndrome—though unbounded pride also plays a key role in this persistence.

Another aspect of this "do or die" syndrome in Japanese culture was that attempting to achieve goals directly and quickly, and directly confronting challenges to these efforts, invariably resulted in a severe backlash that could be fatal. This prompted the Japanese to generally approach their goals in a subtle manner, concealing both their actions and their goals, to avoid attracting opposition.

The degree and power of Japan's "do or die" cultural conditioning has been steadily declining since the end of the feudal system in Japan in 1945. But it was so strong and pervasive for so long that the legacy lingers on, and this characteristic of the culture is still a readily discernible factor in the behavior of most adult Japanese today.

Descriptions of Japanese attitudes and behavior today invariably note that rather than trying to achieve major goals quickly and openly, the Japanese will typically take small, subtle, incremental steps. Said one expatriate businessman in Japan: "Instead of dashing straight up a mountain they want to climb, the Japanese way is to circle it slowly, gradually working their way to the top. That way, nobody pays much attention to what they are doing." Applying this principle often allows the Japanese to reap the benefits of many economic and political situations by staying out of the public spotlight.

悪循環
Akujunkan
(Ah-kuu-june-kahn)

The Great Runaround

One of the great frustrations of life in Japan, and one of the things that contributes to an unbelievable amount of inefficiency—despite the country's reputation for high productivity—is the practice of dividing various functions into their smallest parts, and requiring that each one be done separately in a different place, by a different person. Until the 1990s, virtually all local and national government offices, post offices and banks were notorious examples of this divide-and-complicate syndrome.

In post offices, for example, one had to go to one window to have a letter or package weighed, to another window for stamps, and to yet a third window to mail the item. If something else was required, such as a tax stamp, it could mean visiting a fourth window.

The worst aspects of the traditional Japanese custom of *akujunkan* (ah-kuu-june-kahn), which translates as "vicious circle," or "evil runaround," have finally been eliminated from the more mundane activities of daily life, but the custom continues to persist to varying degrees in government agencies, in commercial companies, and in professional organizations. Foreign businesspeople most often encounter bureaucratic government *akujunkan* when they are trying to get approvals or licenses to import or manufacture a product. In some cases, the process may require action by half a dozen or more agencies or departments, and must be completed in a required order.

Having to circulate documents to several different control centers is in itself not the problem. The problem is that this system offers virtually unlimited possibilities for abuse, and can be turned into a costly or insurmountable unofficial barrier that petitioners can do nothing about if they do not have any political clout that can be applied in the right place.

In commercial enterprises, *akujunkan* can be used in the same way to slow down or otherwise thwart business proposals or projects that are already underway. The process of getting a proposal through a large Japanese company can be so complex and time-consuming, however, that foreigners are likely to regard themselves as victims of an "evil runaround" even when there is no such intent by the Japanese side.

One way to determine if a proposal is being subjected to an *akujunkan* is to develop a personal relationship with a member of the company who is involved with the process; take the person out for an evening on the town, and subtly inform him or her that you would appreciate hearing the real truth, *honto no koto* (hohn-toe no koe-toe), about how the proposal is faring. This kind of relationship is generally essential to get a proposal off the ground floor and circulating in a Japanese company in the first place, so developing close contacts is part of the modus operandi in dealing with Japanese companies.

Another way of determining if a project is being stalled and if *akujunkan* is involved is to have a highly placed Japanese contact with connections at the company make an unofficial inquiry on your behalf.

Where commercial and professional organizations are concerned, the Japanese are not nearly as likely as foreigners to being victimized by runarounds because they may be tipped off by cultural nuances or signs that are often undetectable to foreigners, but are very conspicuous to the Japanese. In some cases, these signs are the vocabulary and the tone of voice that is used in discussing the proposals. If a section manager, department manager or director says that something is *muzukashii* (muu-zoo kah-shee), "troublesome," or "difficult," for example, it almost always means they are not interested in a particular proposal or proposition.

Since the 1980s, a movement has been underway in Japan to eliminate the reluctance of the Japanese to say "no" directly and quickly when they are not interested in a proposal, but no progress is being made. The more Japanese have been exposed to Western influence, however, the more likely they are to be candid and forthright in their responses to overtures from the outside.

It is advisable for foreign businesspeople approaching a Japanese company to make it very clear up front that they want their Japanese counterparts to be frank and forward in their responses, and if a business process continues for an unreasonable length of time, it is good to repeat this request. If the Japanese are genuinely interested in the proposal and are still considering it, they will explain the delay.

甘い、甘く
Amai / Amaku
(Ah-my / Ah-mah-kuu)

Spreading on the Sugar

During most of its history, Japan was noted as a paradise for children. Until the early 1950s, mothers habitually slept with their infant children, and carried them on their backs for several hours each day while they did housework or shopped; or they strapped them to the backs of older siblings who carried them around while they worked or played. Young children were almost never put down and left alone.

One of the results of this constant body contact and interaction was that Japanese infants and young children almost never cried. During my first decade in Japan in the 1940s and 1950s, I was very conscious of this "unusual" infant behavior, and many times I made note of it.

Another thing that I noted almost daily for several years while living in Japan was that Japanese mothers let their very young children play alone along the edge of a nearby canal that had a vertical embankment of some ten feet, and no barrier between its edge and the children's makeshift playground. The mothers, whom I never heard shout at or even quietly caution their children in any way, were obviously not worried that their children would fall into the canal, and to my knowledge none ever did. Why? I still do not know.

I did become aware, however, that Japanese mothers traditionally treated their young children with an extraordinary degree of *amai* (ah-my), which can be translated as "loving indulgence." Children who misbehaved were seldom if ever admonished, and boys in particular were allowed to have their way. I also learned that, where males were concerned, the *amai* syndrome was an integral part of Japan's traditionally male-dominated, sexist society, and that for males this *amai* continued for life. Young boys were first indulged by their mothers, then by their wives and by public women in the nighttime entertainment trades.

One of the reasons for the extent of *amai* toward children in Japan apparently derived from the fact that once they reached the age of seven or eight—and in upper-class families at an even earlier age—they were forced to leave most of their childhood behind, assume serious responsibilities, and be subjected to strict discipline.

Child-raising in Japan has changed remarkably since the 1960s. Mothers seldom if ever carry infants on their backs anymore, and crying babies are now more common. More and more parents now both verbally admonish and physically punish misbehaving children, and teenage delinquency is growing steadily. Mothers still cater to their young school-age sons, however, because of the self-imposed pressure the mothers are under to see that their sons pass very demanding tests required to get into the more desirable schools.

While Japanese wives generally no longer cater to their husbands' every whim or remain quiet about extramarital affairs, *amai* has not disappeared from the adult male scene. There are still several hundred thousand bars, cabarets, clubs, bathhouses and discreet assignation houses where men can go and be indulged to their hearts' content.

There is another side to this cultural coin that is called *amaku* (ah-mah-kuu), which has perhaps even deeper implications for Japanese society. Japanese men have been and still are conditioned by the culture to *amaku* women—that is to look down on them, to denigrate their abilities and worth, and to treat them like playthings or like children. Japanese men also have a tendency to view foreigners, both men and women, with a certain amount of *amaku*; Japanese men feel that their education, discipline and spirit are superior to that of foreign men.

飴と鞭
Ame to Muchi
(Ah-may toe Muu-chee)

Candy or the Whip

In war and in the administration of the laws of the shogunate, torture during Japan's feudal age was routine. When government agents dispatched common people, the methods were designed to be especially cruel in order to instill fear in the public. Samurai who fell into disfavor and received death sentences were given the right to kill themselves rather than suffer the ignominy of death by one of the other more gruesome Japanese methods of killing. Although this right was deemed a privilege, the samurai way of immolating themselves, *hara-kiri* (hah-rah-kee-ree), or "stomach-cutting," was anything but humane and painless.

The cultural contradictions demonstrated by the dual attitude of the Japanese toward harmony and peace and the means to achieve them were not limited to matters involving rivalries between clans, or issues of shogunate law, public security, and so on. Contradictions permeated Japanese society in general. Just behind the facade of Japan's exquisitely refined etiquette, the extraordinary hospitality extended to guests, and the gentleness and generosity of the common people, there was a hard core of cruelty lurking in the background.

This cultural conditioning in cruelty accounted for the excesses of the samurai during Japan's feudal age, as well as the killing orgies Japanese soldiers inflicted upon people they captured during World War II.

There has never been a universal quality to Japanese behavior, however. It has traditionally been selective, and it so remains today. How the Japanese treat people depends on the category of the person involved, and whether or not any personal relationship exists.

Examples of overt physical cruelty are rare in Japan today, but there continues to be an element of mental cruelty in present-day Japanese society—cruelty in the sense that, generally speaking, people are not allowed to honestly or candidly express themselves; they are required to suppress their individuality in most professional and public situations.

Japanese society still operates on the principle of *ame to muchi* (ah-may toe muu-chee), "candy and the whip," a not-so-subtle reference to the fact that if anyone breaches the rules of established conduct, they will be punished. Government agencies, corporations, professional organizations, and the like maintain a public facade of treating the public, employees, members of groups, and so on, with *ame*, "candy"—with the kindness and gentleness of a mother caring for a child, but behind that facade is *muchi* or "the whip," and the threat of serious punishment if anyone steps out of line.

In spite of its emphasis on *wa* (wah), "harmony," and *heiwa* (hay-e-wah), "peace," Japanese society has always been impregnated with a broad streak of cruelty and a penchant for violence that has been regularly inflicted upon people in order to ensure harmony and peace. In fact, Japanese history has been characterized by an almost infinite number of incidents involving cruelty and violence as an official and routine practice; furthermore, cruelty in Japan was traditionally not only an instrument of the government. It was also something that the people, particularly the samurai class, often inflicted upon themselves.

Rather than a flogging with bamboo whips, which was one of the practices during Japan's long feudal period, punishment in contemporary Japan most often consists of social and economic sanctions which include expelling people from their groups, removing them from consideration for promotion, refusing to cooperate with them, disallowing licenses, and similar kinds of ostracism.

Foreign employers in Japan must be very cautious about using the *muchi* part of the *ame to muchi* approach to management, because Japanese employees will normally not accept disciplinary action from foreigners. Generally speaking, the Japanese carefully distinguish between foreign behavior and Japanese behavior, and they resist foreign efforts to punish them with Japanese methods.

The Japanese do not like the indigenous system of punishment, but there is no way they can avoid it, as long as they are members of a Japanese corporation or organization. When foreign organizations are concerned, however, they know that *muchi* can be avoided; furthermore, Japanese employees often dispute the right of a foreign company to discipline them in the first place.

The only practical solution to this problem of employee discipline by foreign employers is to have the forms of punishment that the company can impose clearly detailed in comprehensive articles of employment that all employees are required to sign as a condition of their employment.

暗黙の了解
Anmoku no Ryokai
(Ahn-moe-kuu no Rio-kie)

Unspoken Understanding

The relatively small size of the Japanese archipelago and the virtual isolation of the Japanese from the rest of the world throughout most of their history has led to an extraordinary degree of homogenization of Japan and its culture. This homogenization process became a matter of government policy following the ascendancy of the Tokugawa Shogunate in 1603, and the policy was continued until the end of World War II. By that time the government's efforts to mold all Japanese into the same pattern had become so pervasive that anyone who did not look like the "standard" Japanese, and think and behave in the manner approved by the government, was in serious jeopardy.

There were good and bad points to this government policy. On the positive side, it contributed greatly to social harmony for the simple reason that the vast majority of people both thought and acted very much alike; also, people were equally conditioned to obey the laws of the land and their superiors, and people were therefore not exposed to the kind of friction that grows out of diversity.

From the traditional, authoritarian viewpoint, the Japanese thus became ideal workers, soldiers and organization people; they were obedient, loyal and dedicated, and therefore capable of achieving remarkable results in whatever they were organized to do. The negative side of this remarkable program to homogenize the whole nation played a vital role in the recent history of Japan, including the seizure of political power by the military in the 1930s and the ensuing Pacific War.

Probably the main handicap of the herd-like mentality and behavior that still prevails to a significant degree in present-day Japan is that, by its very nature, conformity limits individuality, personal responsibility and personal aspirations, creativity, and basic political and social reform—witness the ongoing efforts to reform the government, and the difficulty the Japanese have in communicating with the outside world.

The Japanese are very conscious of both their homogeneity and of the social etiquette and customs that make them different from other people, and they consciously use both of these factors in their relations with non-Japanese, sometimes as a tactic in achieving their goals, and other times as an excuse for delaying things or not doing anything at all.

Because of their homogeneity, the Japanese have a set of common values and a body of common knowledge, sometimes referred to as *anmoku no ryokai* (ahn-moe-kuu no rio-kie), or "unspoken understanding," that gives them an advantage in their dealings among themselves as well as with foreign businesspeople and politicians.

Generally speaking, this *anmoku no ryokai* means that in any encounter with foreigners, a group of Japanese presents a solid team front, unified by their cultural conditioning that makes them formidable opponents. At the same time, however, this group cohesion and need to act together generally results in Japanese groups being inflexible, a negative trait which sometimes cancels out the benefits of the team approach in business and in negotiations.

Foreigners dealing with the Japanese are often handicapped because they have been conditioned in the opposite way—to think and behave as individuals. It goes without saying that when facing a well-trained team in sports, business or politics, the only recourse is to field a team that is equally if not better trained, which is a lesson that many Western companies and countries have yet to learn.

安心感
Anshinkan
(Ahn-sheen-kahn)

Building Peace of Mind

Almost immediately after the forced opening of Japan to the Western world in the 1850s and the subsequent industrialization of the nation's economy, the Japanese became famous for copying Western products—products that were originally brought into the country by American and other foreign businessmen who had learned that they could be made much more cheaply in Japan. Furthermore, the Japanese often improved the products.

For the next century and more, critics continuously accused the Japanese of never having made a single significant invention, which was true only in relative terms.

Throughout most of their early history, the Japanese concentrated their intellectual prowess and their energy on improving the simple patterns of life they had synthesized from the arts, crafts and philosophies developed in China and India. The Japanese focused more on aesthetics and on emotional and spiritual contentment than they did on changing the way things were done. In the process, they developed a culture that was extraordinarily sophisticated and filled with the beauty of paper, wood, stone and metal products handcrafted by masters.

During the long pre-industrial age, the Japanese spent a great deal of their time with festivals, religious rituals, aesthetic practices, and the development of a variety of physical skills, a life-style in which *anshinkan* (ahn-sheen-kahn), or "peace of mind," played more important role than the production of material wealth or excessive consumption.

The shogunate government of elite warriors that ruled Japan from around 1185 to 1868 eventually adopted the policy of keeping the population at a near-subsistence level of existence in order to make it easier to control them.

By the 1970s, much of this traditional culture of the heart and spirit had disappeared from Japan, buried under an avalanche of Western ideas and the rush to create a totally new life-style based on ever-changing technology. But enough traditional culture remains that *anshinkan* is still a high priority in virtually all relations, private and public.

Virtually all Japanese still bow to the concept of "peace of mind" as an important part of life, and most still regularly go out of their way to expose themselves to the arts, crafts, and environment of traditional customs and culture—indulging themselves in hot baths, eating traditional dishes in inns and restaurants that have not changed for hundreds of years, wearing *yukata* (you-kah-tah) and kimono at home or at hot-spring spas, and following stylized manners that came into being in the ancient courts of emperors.

The desire for *anshinkan* in Japan still has a direct impact on all areas of public life today, and in particular on business relations. Businesspeople prefer not to do business with others until they know them well and have confidence in their ability, honesty, goodwill and dependability, and feel "peace of mind" in dealing with them. To succeed in doing business in Japan, foreign businesspeople must be aware of *anshinkan* and make it a significant part of their approach and ongoing relations with Japanese companies.

It also helps for the foreign side to publicly state to its Japanese counterparts that a relationship based on *anshinkan* is desired, and that all of its efforts will be designed to achieve that goal. Among other things, the Japanese will be surprised that foreigners know the term, and the Japanese will be even more gratified to learn that foreigners view it as a desirable part of a relationship.

洗いざらい
Araizarai
(Ah-rye-zah-rye)

Letting It All Out

Japan's law enforcement agencies have traditionally had, or assumed, the right and the authority to use beatings and other forms of torture to obtain confessions from criminal suspects. Historical movies and television dramas typically show local samurai authorities stringing suspects up by the hands and whipping them with strips of bamboo lashed together. Contemporary movies show detective and police heroes beating suspects.

In earlier times, the beatings generally did not end until suspects confessed or died, or until someone, usually other than the police, brought in proof that the suspects were innocent—which sometimes happened.

There have been recent exposés about conditions in Japanese jails and prisons which indicate things have not changed much; the requirement that prisoners sit on the floor for long periods of time is an additional torture for foreign prisoners not accustomed to this posture as the Japanese are.

Another characteristic of Japanese justice that is as true today as it was in the past is the importance of confessing to guilt and expressing remorse. As far as the Japanese are concerned, refusing to confess to a crime is as bad as and sometimes worse than committing a crime. During Japan's feudal age the penalty for a variety of crimes was death, regardless of how much remorse one might express. But there were also occasions when expressions of remorse would result in treatment that was extraordinarily lenient by the standards of the times.

In today's Japan, *araizarai* (ah-rye-zah-rye), "washing everything" or "telling everything," when confronted with accusations of wrongdoing is regarded very much like a sacred obligation that no one can refuse to honor. The *araizarai* custom is especially important where white-collar crimes are concerned. Company executives, politicians, and the like who are arrested and accused of criminal acts typically tell all, and they receive reduced sentences for their contrition and cooperation.

The Japanese naturally expect people who have been arrested to *araizarai* without the use of force of any kind—which is apparently a holdover from the old days when the only way to avoid heavy torture was to confess quickly. The tendency of foreign suspects to claim innocence and refuse to admit guilt strikes the Japanese as both arrogant and irrational. Having been forced to live with the arrogance of the shogunate and samurai for many generations, the Japanese are exceptionally sensitive about this kind of behavior.

Generally, suspects and prison inmates who refuse to admit guilt are treated more harshly than those who have followed the *araizarai* custom. When foreigners doing business with Japan make honest mistakes, it is naturally best to admit them and to explain the mistakes quickly and thoroughly. This includes acknowledging and apologizing for bad judgment—something that is especially common when foreigners first become involved in the Japanese business world and are inclined to do things according to their own business customs.

Foreigners can also get mileage out of adopting another very common Japanese custom: apologizing in advance for any errors that they might unintentionally make in the future. Another worthwhile habit for foreigners to adopt in their business dialogue with the Japanese is to avoid speaking in absolutes, and to leave some room for "adjusting things"—an expression and a custom that is near and dear to the hearts of the Japanese.

粗探し
Arasagashi
(Ah-rah-sah-gah-she)

A Nation of Nitpickers

When Westerners first encountered the Japanese writing system, which is an adaptation of the much more ancient and complex Chinese system, they reacted in a variety of ways. Some of them were awed by the aesthetic aspects of the language when it was written, or more accurately, drawn, in stylized calligraphy. Others were overwhelmed by the complexity and enormity of the system, and shied away from any attempt to learn it. Still others looked upon the Japanese with a degree of arrogant superiority for having adopted such a difficult way of writing, certain in their own minds that the system was a handicap that would be impossible to overcome.

The Japanese way of writing has indeed been a mixed blessing, but the passing of time has, I believe, swung the pendulum in favor of the system so that in many ways its advantages now outweigh its disadvantages.

The fundamental advantage of the Japanese writing system derives, in fact, from its complexity, and the degree of effort and the long period of time that is required to learn to write and read it. This effort, which naturally begins in childhood, has an extraordinary influence on the mental attitude, manual skills as well as the character of the Japanese.

All young Japanese must learn patience, perseverance, a considerable degree of manual dexterity, appreciation of graphic harmony, and some familiarity with aesthetics in order to master the ideograms used to write their language. This discipline and the training that the Japanese must undergo to learn to read and write their own language is enough to set them apart from many other people, and give them advantages that continue throughout their lives.

When the Japanese system of writing, which is obviously very precise and demanding, is combined with other traditional activities that require equally precise forms and processes, the overall influence on the Japanese character is profound. To the Japanese, the making of anything requires extraordinary attention to the finest detail—a factor that makes them among the world's most discriminating people. The Japanese have been conditioned to be compulsive about forms and processes, and about identifying and labeling everything according to its status and role, and the word for this characteristic in Japanese is *arasagashi* (ah-rah-sah-gah-she), which translates nicely into English as "nit-picking."

In earlier years, many foreign products failed in the Japanese marketplace because they were below the quality standards acceptable to the Japanese, or because they were not neatly "finished"; threads were left hanging from apparel, or the insides or bottoms of products were left rough and unattractive.

The design and finishing standards for products in Japan evolved centuries ago through the apprenticeship system in the handicraft industries. This approach demanded virtual perfection regardless of how mundane the product might be, with the result that ordinary kitchen utensils were typically works of ceramic and lacquer ware art.

While the cultural conditioning that turns all Japanese into moderate *arasagashi* has waned considerably in recent decades, enough of it still remains in the educational system and in the overall acculturation process that even the youngest generation has a critical eye that distinguishes its members from their counterparts in most Western countries. Anyone presuming to sell anything in Japan should be aware of the *arasagashi* nature of the Japanese before starting out, to avoid learning about it the hard and expensive way.

有り難迷惑
Arigata Meiwaku
(Ah-ree-gah-tah May-ee-wah-kuu)

Too Much of a Good Thing

It is widely recognized that the Japanese are an exceptionally clever people. In fact, all adult Japanese have had virtually enough "on-the-job" training to qualify for doctorates in psychology and sociology, and to use these skills with professional flair in interacting with other people. The Japanese owe much of their education and experience in these fields to their traditional etiquette, which was not only an exercise in self-discipline, but also provided skill in manipulating people to behave in an expected or desired manner.

In addition to legal sanctions used to enforce minutely prescribed manners, the Japanese were also guided by deeply ingrained moral beliefs based on Confucian principles, and these beliefs were used to justify programming personal behavior down to the smallest detail.

Another factor that conditioned the Japanese in the art of manipulating people was the competitive nature of their society. There was competition between individuals and between groups in every aspect of Japanese life, and to survive and succeed it was essential that people learn how to get the most out of their relationships by influencing the behavior of others.

One of the key requirements in the Japanese notion of morality was the importance of fulfilling one's obligations—those that were inherent in one's sex, age and position, as well as those that occurred because of circumstance. And there were many obligations—so many, in fact, that the Japanese were extremely cautious about putting themselves into situations where they would acquire new ones. Not surprisingly, however, it was common for some to take advantage of the well-known disposition among the Japanese to return favors by subjecting people to *arigata meiwaku* (ah-ree-gah-tah may-ee-wah-kuu), which translates as "misplaced kindness" or "unwelcome kindness."

Arigata meiwaku is more common in Japan today than in earlier times because there are far more opportunities to give and receive favors, whether or not they are wanted. As a result, the Japanese have become very experienced at avoiding these unwelcome kindnesses—primarily by ignoring them and pretending that they never happened. But foreigners dealing with Japanese generally do not distinguish so clearly between wanted and unwanted favors, and they are very reluctant to ignore kindnesses regardless of whether they are welcome or unwelcome. Because of this, foreigners in Japan often find themselves and their professional skills being taken advantage of by people they hardly know or by people they do not know at all.

Over the decades, I myself have ended up "donating" hours and days of time to advise and assist Japanese acquaintances whom I had only just met, simply because I did not want to contribute to the "ugly American" image.

Another factor that results in foreigners going out of their way to help the Japanese is the traditional Japanese character itself. By Western standards, the humble, passive and sincere behavior typical of the Japanese makes them appear so naive, so helpless, and so deserving of help that most Westerners cannot resist the impulse to help them. Of course, a great deal of this motivation to "help" the Japanese is an exercise in egoism and is nothing more than showing off; the Japanese are very much aware of this, and they exploit it to the fullest.

Some foreigners who are in Japan long enough to discover the power of obligation turn the use of *arigata meiwaku* into a profession, deliberately building up "social debts" with the Japanese in key positions in order to further their goals. Again, the Japanese recognize a "misplaced kindness" instantly, and whether or not they accept one depends on their own agenda—which may be no more than to get what they can from the people concerned, and then ignore them.

The accepted Japanese way of avoiding undesirable obligation is to regularly repay any obligations so that one is not put in the position of not being able to turn down a request for some major favor.

足きり
Ashikiri
(Ah-she-kee-ree)

Cutting Off the Legs

The role that swords played in Japan's history is remarkable; there are few if any equivalents in other cultures. Guns and other kinds of weapons have, of course, played key roles in the histories of other countries, but in no case did any of these weapons become so revered and so vital as swords did in Japan, where they took on the essence of religious icons. The number of words based on *kiru* (kee-ruu), "to cut," seems to reflect the importance of the sword in Japanese culture.

Among the most culturally pregnant of these terms are *hara-kiri* (hah-rah-kee-ree), literally "belly-cutting," which was the samurai way of committing ritual suicide; the word *kiru* itself, which also came to mean "to kill"; *kirimakuru* (kee-ree-mah-kuu-rue), "to mow down an enemy"; *kirimawasu* (kee-ree-mah-wah-sue), "to manage or control"; *kirimori* (kee-ree-moh-ree), "management or administration"; *kirimusubu* (kee-ree-muu-sue-buu), "to clash with"; *kirikaeru* (kee-ree-kay-rue), "to change, renew"; and so on.

Kubikiri (kuu-bee-kee-ree), which originally meant "decapitation" or, literally, "cutting the neck," is now a common colloquial term meaning "to fire" or "to dismiss from a job." Another expression with *kiri* that became vogue in the latter part of the 1980s was *ashikiri* (ah-she-kee-ree), literally "leg-cutting," in reference to "cutting off" candidates for schools or jobs on the basis of test scores.

In 1979 Japan introduced a standard achievement test for high school seniors and graduates interested in attending national or public universities. Those who scored well in the examination were then allowed to take the entrance examination of a single public or national university. This meant that if they failed to score well enough in the university entrance examination to gain admittance to the university of their choice, applicants had to wait another year before they could retake the test or sit for an exam at another school. As a result, each year many of the hundreds of thousands of high school graduates who failed in their initial attempt to enter a university, began to study for their second chance at an entrance exam the following year. These young people became known colloquially as *ronin* (roe-neen), the traditional name for a masterless samurai.

Naturally enough the entrance exams, which covered seven broad categories, were very unpopular with students and their parents, and the tests resulted in thousands of students simply giving up and not taking the tests in the first place.

In 1987 the entrance examination system was shortened and revised. The number of subjects covered by the tests was reduced from seven to five, tests were held on different days for national and public universities, and students were allowed to take the exams for two universities instead of just one. The reforms resulted in huge numbers of students taking the new, shortened entrance exams, making it necessary for unprecedented *ashikiri* to reduce the number of students allowed to enter a university. This meant that the reforms did not help more students get into universities, and because more students took the entry tests each year, there were more who failed and ended up as *ronin*.

Japanese corporations have traditionally practiced *ashikiri* in their hiring practices, generally employing only those candidates who score well in the company exams they are required to take. The exams are not the only method for selecting employees, however; companies also regularly hire candidates who come highly recommended by their professors, and applicants who had outstanding athletic careers during their school years are favored by companies—regardless of their test scores.

During the early post-World War II decades, foreign companies in Japan generally had to be satisfied with candidates for employment who had experienced "leg-cutting" by any number of Japanese companies. By the 1980s, however, a number of foreign firms had become well established in the Japanese marketplace, and had adopted the Japanese system of nurturing close relationships with university professors, allowing them to attract more able candidates.

Today, *ashikiri* continues to play a primary role in separating Japan's educated elite from the rest of the population, offering them employment and social advantages that are not available to others.

あしらう
Ashirau
(Ah-she-rah-oh)

The Diplomatic Brush-Off

The first foreign government representative to be stationed in Japan, Townsend Harris of the United States, was kept by the country's shogunate government at arm's length for nearly two years in the remote village of Shimoda at the tip of the Izu Peninsula.

Even after Harris was finally allowed to travel to Edo, now Tokyo, to present his credentials to the Court of the Shogun, he was put off week after week and month after month by a variety of techniques the Japanese had perfected over centuries.

One of these techniques was to try to distract Harris from his mission by providing him with female companionship. An attractive geisha was ordered by the government—ostensibly as a servant—to take up residence in Harris's makeshift home, which was an old temple. If Harris's own account of what happened afterward can be believed, he was so ill from the Japanese diet and so upset at the continuing delays that he paid no attention to the girl.

Delaying tactics of one kind or another are characteristic behavior of the Japanese when they are faced with an undesirable or unpleasant situation, or when they are not fully prepared to take action in a situation. Rather than come out forthrightly and end uncertainty with a confrontation, they typically use delaying tactics that, where foreigners are concerned, often compound rather than ease a situation.

Foreign visitors most often subjected to this usually subtle treatment are diplomats and businesspeople who go to Japan with propositions or requests that are not acceptable to the Japanese for any number of reasons. Unfortunately for both sides in these encounters, the Japanese are prevented from frankly rejecting the foreign approach because of a strict etiquette that prohibits blunt refusals and frank explanations. This etiquette leads to the development of numerous subterfuges for diplomatically delaying and eventually ending situations they do not want or for which they are not prepared.

One of the frequently used put-off ploys is subsumed in the word *ashirau* (ah-she-rah-oh), which means "to entertain," "to treat in a highly courteous manner," "to decorate," or "to garnish," and refers to the use of such tactics to soften up and distract people to the point where they can be manipulated.

The term *ashirau* reminds me of *ashi arau* (ah-she ah-rah-oh), which means "to wash one's feet." Anyone who has had his or her feet washed by someone else knows that it is a very pleasant experience. Of course, the aim of the Japanese in applying the *ashirau* tactic is to make the experience so enjoyable that the individuals receiving the treatment will feel indebted and grateful, and much less aggressive in attempting to achieve their original goals. The Japanese are naturally sensitized to the *ashirau* ploy, and almost always recognize immediately when they are being "washed off." Foreigners, on the other hand, are usually not aware of this aspect of Japanese culture, and fail to recognize a "foot-job" when they get one.

Uninitiated foreigners also routinely victimize themselves by failing to recognize or understand when the Japanese are expressing rejection. Probably the most commonly used code word to clearly indicate a lack of interest in a proposal is *muzukashii* (muu-zoo-kah-shee). Instead of a straightforward rejection, the Japanese, after listening carefully to a proposal—sometimes over a period of several meetings—will often put on a face indicating disappointment and respond with *Muzukashi desu*, "It is difficult."

Other more subtle "wash-off" terms include *kento shimasu* (ken-toe she-mahss), meaning "I will look into it," and *zensho shimasu* (zen-show she-mahss), apparently meaning "I will do my best," but actually meaning "I will do my best, but what you are asking for is impossible."

Not surprisingly, it normally takes non-Japanese a fair amount of in-depth exposure to both the Japanese language and Japanese etiquette before they learn these code words and how to interpret them. For the newcomer and short-term visitor, the most diplomatic recourse to this problem is to get help from someone who has already been baptized in Japanese culture and recognizes the verbal and nonverbal signals that mean "no way."

If a newcomer or novice is aware of this particular Japanese custom, and happens to be dealing with a Japanese who has had fairly extensive cross-cultural experience with Westerners, the simplest and fastest way may be for the foreigner to apologize for being direct and breaking with Japanese custom, and then ask the Japanese concerned to be totally frank so that time will not continue to be wasted if there is no genuine interest in a particular proposition.

For persons not up to this kind of cultural interplay, or if the situation is especially delicate for any reason, a better and safer approach is to have a Japanese friend or contact call or visit the company concerned, and inquire about the status of a proposal and whether it is being given or is going to be given serious consideration.

Etiquette restraints that apply between you and the Japanese contact do not apply to a third person. Furthermore, Japanese etiquette allows the Japanese to be more frank and forthcoming with other Japanese than it does with foreigners. It becomes a *Nihonjin-doshi* (Nee-hoan-jeen-doe-she) or "Japanese-to-Japanese" thing.

当たり前
Atarimae
(Ah-tah-ree-my)

It Goes Without Saying

In a culture as homogenous, as structured, and as old as Japan's, there are naturally a great many things that are taken for granted—things that are a part of the common experiences and beliefs of the whole country. These features of the culture have become what the Japanese call *atarimae* (ah-tah-ree-my), or "normal and natural" or "to be expected."

This huge body of common knowledge, behavior, standards and expectations provides extraordinary cohesion to Japanese society, and makes the average Japanese a lot more predictable than their foreign counterparts. But this does not mean that the Japanese are easier for outsiders to understand and to get along with.

On the contrary, because of these cultural circumstances, a great deal of the personal as well as business communication in Japan is indirect, abbreviated, or not spoken at all, because intentions and feelings can often be expressed and understood without verbalizing them.

To understand the Japanese—even in part—requires that an outsider have considerable knowledge of the "invisible" aspects of Japanese culture; and to get along with the Japanese in the sense of achieving business and political goals requires an enormous amount of in-culture experience. In fact, an awareness of the *atarimae* characteristic of the Japanese is more likely to be frustrating to the outsider than informative and helpful, because a great deal of what is *atarimae* is based on emotional factors rather than on practical and objective reasoning.

Because *atarimae* is such an integral part of Japanese culture, there are no written definitions or rules regarding its use; the ability to understand what is *atarimae* is passed on from generation to generation by observation and by imitation.

This silent absorption process is also the key factor in the traditional master–apprentice method of teaching and learning in Japan's arts, crafts and business in general; it is a learning process that takes place over a period of many years, and which sorely frustrates Westerners who cannot see or feel any progress being made. New Japanese employees are expected to learn what they need to know without being told. Westerners are always asking why and how. The Japanese typically remain quiet because asking why is considered rude, and asking how is an admission of ignorance, and they do not like to appear ignorant under any circumstances.

Generally speaking, business and political matters that fall into the *atarimae* category in Japan are not likely to be changed to accommodate the logic, rationality or convenience of outsiders. Exceptions to this invariably entail bringing extraordinary pressure on the Japanese to force them to break with their *shikitari* (she-kee-tah-ree), or "way of doing things."

One way to combat Japan's *atarimae* syndrome is to patiently and diplomatically explain that *atarimae* and *shikitari* are also features of other cultures, and that all cultures should demonstrate some flexibility so that *atarimae* does not become an excuse for failure.

Dealing with the *atarimae* factor in Japan is a subtle and difficult challenge. Just as Westerners tend to automatically assume that logic, fairness and mutual benefit will carry the day, the Japanese automatically tend to take the position that any foreign refusal to accept their terms results from the fact that the foreign side does not understand the Japanese way of doing things. In other words, the Japanese do not necessarily question the rightness or wrongness of either side; their tendency is simply to take the position that the Japanese way is the only way because it is the Japanese way.

As far as the Japanese are concerned, virtually every conflict that occurs between them and outsiders, whether in business, or in a political or personal situation, results from the fact that outsiders do not understand the *shikitari* or the *atarimae* of Japan.

後味
Ato Aji
(Ah-toe Ah-jee)

A Foreign Aftertaste

When the first Westerners showed up in Japan in the 1540s, the Japanese found it very difficult to be in close proximity to them, especially in enclosed areas, because the Westerners did not bathe or change their clothing regularly, and they gave off a strong stench. Most of the Westerners who took up residence in Japan at that time eventually discovered that bathing regularly would not harm their health, and they learned it had one direct benefit that they had no trouble at all appreciating. It dramatically improved their social lives with Japanese women.

Most of the Westerners living in Japan then, however, continued to eat a diet of meat and butter, and no amount of bathing would eliminate the body odor such a diet causes. Unfortunately, the smell of butter turned out to be especially nauseous to the Japanese, giving rise to the saying, *bata kusai* (bah-tah kuu-sie), or "smelling of butter," which was gradually used as an uncomplimentary way of referring to Western attitudes and behavior.

In the 1630s, because of real and imagined problems with Westerners, the Japanese government expelled all foreigners from the country, with the exception of a handful of Dutch traders who were isolated on a tiny man-made island in Nagasaki Bay. Japan was not opened to foreigners again until the 1850s.

The downfall of the shogun in 1868 resulted in a flood of Western ways and habits into Japan, but it was not until after World War II that the Japanese began gradually to add meat and butter to their traditional diet of vegetables and seafood.

Numerous Japanese friends and acquaintances who made business trips to the United States in the late 1950s and 1960s told me they became seriously ill after four or five days a meat-based diet. Some had to cut their trips short and return to Japan.

It was well into the 1970s and the appearance of McDonald's hamburger restaurants—and numerous imitators—before meat and butter became a regular staple in the diet of most young urban Japanese. This abrupt change not only eliminated most of their sensitivity to the smell of these previously taboo foods, but also resulted in a dramatic increase in their size. Older Japanese were much slower in adapting to a partial Western diet.

The Japanese, though overcoming their revulsion to the smell of butter, did not eliminate their sensitivity to Western attitudes and behavior. Japanese culture is so strong and so pervasive that the Japanese, including those who have been heavily exposed to Western influences, still automatically distinguish between Japanese and Western ways, and automatically make comparisons between the two. Most Japanese seem to be more susceptible to culture shock than their Western counterparts when they are stationed abroad for extended periods and are forced to associate with foreigners on a daily basis.

The reaction of the Japanese to Western attitudes and behavior is intellectual, emotional and spiritual. Some complain that interacting with Westerners for as short as a few hours is tiring and leaves an *ato aji* (ah-toe ah-jee), or "after-taste," that by its nature is unpleasant.

Westerners doing business with the Japanese should be aware of this cultural sensitivity and do what they can to leave as little *ato aji* as possible. This, of course, requires a great deal of sensitivity, plus expertise that comes only with familiarity with the culture.

See *Gaijin Kusai.*

阿吽の呼吸
Aun no Kokyu
(Ah-uhn no Koe-que)

The Japanese Sixth Sense

One of the most remarkable and intriguing aspects of Japanese culture is the prevalence and importance of nonverbal communication. By the end of the Heian Period in Japanese history (794–1192), when the shogunate government was founded, the prevailing life-style and etiquette among the upper class had become so homogenized that it was possible for people to practically read each others' minds.

By the time of the opening of Japan's doors to the West in the 1850s, the life-style and etiquette that had originated in the courts of the emperors and shoguns and in Buddhist temples over a period of more than a thousand years had seeped downward to encompass all levels of Japanese society. When foreigners began pouring into Japan in the 1850s, they were astounded by the uniformity of Japanese behavior. It seemed to them that the Japanese had been so programmed in their thinking and behavior that they were incapable of doing anything in a spontaneous, individualistic manner.

The feudalistic relationships that had been both the result and the medium of the cultural programming of the Japanese for more than a thousand years did not actually end until 1945, when the United States introduced democracy into Japan. Cultural programming that had persisted for more than a millennium could not be erased in a few years or even over a generation. All of the patterns of thought and behavior that distinguished the Japanese during those long centuries are still visible today, and they still have a dramatic impact on all personal as well as business relationships.

One of the old and still entrenched cultural factors that frequently confuses and dismays Westerners in Japan is described or referred to in the phrase *aun no kokyu* (ah-uhn no koe-que), which might be translated as "the knack of breathing or thinking or feeling in unison with others." In other words, the ability to think and behave as one and therefore anticipate what other people are going to say or do, and to agree with them—to breathe or to be as one.

While the phrase itself is not commonly used in ordinary conversation, what it refers to is so much a part of Japanese life that it cannot be avoided or ignored. In simple terms, it is a cultural "sense" that all Japanese have—"a sixth sense" that tells them when an attitude or behavior is "Japanese" and when it is not, and how to think and behave like a "Japanese."

In the day-to-day activities of the Japanese—at least among those who have not been de-Japanized—*aun no kokyu* is the cultural facility that tells them what to do or how to behave in a Japanese way in any given situation; this includes an awareness of who sits where in a living room or at a meeting, who begins eating first, how one bows or hands someone a name card, and the right way to negotiate business deals.

Aun no kokyu is the cultural facility that the Japanese are expected to use in order to conform to all of the attitudes and manners that make up the "the Japanese Way." Furthermore, "real" Japanese do not have to consciously think about engaging their *aun no kokyu* sense. It is always turned on, and works automatically. When new recruits enter Japanese companies, most of the attitudes and behavior they are expected to exhibit are not verbalized or given to them in the form of written instructions. They are expected to pick up these things through their *aun no kokyu*.

Foreigners who go to work for Japanese companies often feel isolated, misused, and abused because they are not familiar with the concept and practice of *aun no kokyu*, and they are not capable of "plugging into" the right cultural channel because they are not intimately familiar with Japanese culture in the first place. A great deal of the Japanese behavior that Westerners find contradictory, confusing, or simply irrational, is a result of the Japanese *aun no kokyu* sense in action.

There is no quick or easy way around this handicap, or in dealing with any situation anywhere that involves this cultural concept—which, of course, pretty much covers all things Japanese. The only answer to the challenge of coping with this Japanese sixth sense is to be aware of it, to appreciate its importance, and over a period of years, to gain experience in both accommodating oneself to it and helping Japanese contacts and counterparts think and behave in a non-Japanese way.

See *Atarimae.*

番記者
Ban Kisha
(Bahn Kee-shah)

The Way of the Japanese Press

Prior to the fall of Japan's shogunate government in 1868, the Japanese were not allowed to disseminate any kind of news, criticism or speculation. In fact, prior to modern times most Japanese were so conditioned to keep quiet and follow the official government line that it was generally unnecessary for the government to control public information with sanctions. Most individuals, as well as organizations, censored themselves—not out of fear of punishment, but because the Japanese had been brainwashed to believe that self-censorship was the right thing to do.

From the beginning of the 17th century to the fall of the shogunate government, the only news published in Japan for public consumption was in the form of handbills. One type of handbill was called *yomiuri* (yoe-me-uu-ree), or "read and sell"; these were printed only when significant events occurred, and were sold by street hawkers in the larger cities. The other one was known as *kawaraban* (kah-wah-rah-bahn), or "tile-block printing," which were text and drawings on sheets of paper for sale and for public posting.

The first regular newspaper in Japan, *The Nagasaki Shipping List & Advertiser*, was founded in 1861 in Nagasaki by an Englishman named A. W. Hansard, and was published only in English for the foreign community. The first Japanese-language newspapers, all of which were weeklies, were founded in Edo, Osaka, Kyoto and Nagasaki in 1868. The first daily Japanese newspaper, the *Yokohama Mainichi Shimbun*, was founded in 1871.

These first Japanese newspapers were generally referred to as "political forums," because they mostly contained political opinions and demands for the establishment of a parliamentary form of government. When the Imperial Court issued a decree announcing the formation of a parliament, or Diet, the new newspapers became little more than mouthpieces for the different political parties that sprang up.

From this period to the early 1930s, Japan's news media was a mixed bag that included responsible, conservative organs advocating political, economic and social reform; publications that continued to be totally controlled by the different political factions; and others containing local news, human interest stories and popular fiction. By the mid-1930s, the Japanese government had come under the control of militant expansionists who turned the country's major newspapers into propaganda organs, and used draconian measures to enforce severe censorship on publishing.

Government-imposed censorship of newspapers ended in 1945 with Japan's defeat in World War II and the reformation of the political system in Japan by American and allied forces that occupied the country until 1952. But this did not mean that Japanese newspapers suddenly became dedicated to free speech or became paragons of objectivity. Most of the major publications continued to shape the news to fit their views of what was suitable for the public and beneficial to the country. It was not until the 1980s and 1990s that the ranking newspapers in Japan began to flirt with unbiased reporting, and most still follow some practices that have been held over since the 1880s.

One of these practices is covered by the term *ban kisha* (bahn kee-shah), which literally means "guard or watch reporter," and refers to reporters exclusively assigned by their publications to cover prominent individual politicians.

It is the duty of the *ban kisha* to develop close personal relationships with their assigned "sources" so that they can obtain off-the-record information in exchange for exclusive information. Within this system the *ban kisha* and "their politicians" become dependent upon each other, bringing on a variety of abuses that invariably result from such incestuous relationships.

Ban kisha assigned to particular politicians have the front-row seats at all of their press conferences, and strictly control who gets to ask questions. They do not give the nod to anyone who is likely to ask embarrassing questions.

In the summer of 1993, the newly installed prime minister, Morihiro Hosokawa, a young, new-age, maverick politician who ended the decades-long rule of the Liberal Democratic Party, made a dramatic break with the *ban kisha* system by ignoring his assigned "watch-reporters" and selecting his questioners himself at press conferences—an action that made international news.

Hosokawa also broke other of Japan's semi-sacred political customs, and was very popular with the people of Japan. Among other things, he was the first Japanese prime minister to take questions from foreign journalists. Hosokawa was not popular with the old political guard, however, and his reform administration lasted for only eight months.

Despite the example set by Hosokawa, the *ban kisha* system survived, and it continues to play a significant role in life in Japan. The hope now is that as other younger generations of politicians appear, they will follow the example set by Hosokawa and refuse to link themselves with individual reporters.

バッティング
Batting
(Bah-teeng)

Driving Prices Down

I used to say that the United States did not discover Japan until the 1970s. That was the decade when the volume of Japanese TV sets, cars, cameras and other products pouring into the United States became a flood, and began drowning the American companies that had traditionally been in these fields. This inundation of Japanese products coming into the United States resulted in a few American companies finally realizing that they should be selling their products in Japan—something that was easier to talk about than accomplish.

These better-late-than-never pioneers in the Japanese marketplace soon discovered that doing business in Japan was fraught with barriers and challenges they had never dreamed of and could not comprehend. They found in many cases that it was absolutely impossible to break into the distribution channels for certain products. These channels, from manufacturer down to retailer, were so tightly knit that no outsider could penetrate them. The American inability to crack the market had nothing to do with the salability of their products, the prices they were offering, or the after-service they guaranteed. It had everything to do with the relationships that existed between Japanese manufacturers, wholesalers and retailers.

Some of these American pioneers eventually discovered that in Japan, large manufacturers such as Matsushita, Toshiba, Hitachi and others generally controlled the whole marketing process, from pricing to distribution and sales. These companies had their own wholesale subsidiaries, or they owned stock in, and had their own directors at the wholesalers they supplied, and were therefore able to control them. The companies also owned retail chains, and they had exclusive franchise-like arrangements with hundreds of other shops around the country. Another link in the bond between manufacturers and marketing channels was that the manufacturers typically acted as financiers for the wholesale and retail levels, providing goods on consignment for 180 days, paying large rebates, and extending full return privileges.

When foreign manufacturers began knocking on the doors of Japanese importers, wholesalers and retail chains, they found most of the doors closed and locked. Obviously, the Japanese system was designed by manufacturers to gain and control as much of the market share as possible, long before foreign companies began trying to get in. However, the system was more of a barrier to foreign makers than to potential Japanese competitors, because the foreigners were generally not even aware of the system, nor did they have the personal connections or relations to help them find backdoors, and they did not have or would not commit the financial resources necessary to hang in and do business the Japanese way.

A secondary aim of this system was to avoid the kind of competition that is the hallmark of the American and free market approach to economics—competition that the Japanese refer to as *batting* (bah-teeng), which is derived from the English word "bat," as the word is used in baseball.

In Japanese, *batting* refers to retailers and wholesalers competing with each other for the same product lines and for customers by offering special prices, special services, or other kinds of deals—all things that free-market advocates hold as sacred. The Japanese resistance to *batting* continued until the debacle brought on by the collapse of the "bubble economy" in 1990 and 1991. When the bottom fell out of the real estate and financial markets that had been growing out of control since the 1960s, maverick Japanese retailers began breaking the prices set by manufacturers and selling at discounts. They also began selling cheap imports from Korea, China and Southeast Asia.

By the mid-1990s even the strongest Japanese manufacturers had begun to feel the effects of widespread discounting of their own products and competition from cheap imports; but they had not abandoned their attempts to prevent *batting*. Till now foreign companies seeking to enter the Japanese market through established distribution channels are invariably asked to guarantee exclusivity in order to prevent *batting* in the marketplace.

募債パック
Bosai Pakku
(Boh-sigh Pahk-kuu)

Preparing for Survival

Standing in volcanic ash on the top of snow-capped Mt Fuji, Japan's highest mountain, it is still hard to accept the fact that the mountain is a huge volcanic cone. It is even more difficult to visualize the great cone spurting fiery ashes and red-hot lava, which it last did in 1707.

But in 1983, rumors were rampant in Japan that stately Mt Fuji was due to erupt anytime, and that a major earthquake would strike the country on September 1, the 60th anniversary of the Great Kanto Earthquake that leveled most of Tokyo and Yokohama. That year, both national and local governments conducted emergency evacuation and survival drills, and sent out hundreds of thousands of flyers urging people to stock emergency supplies of food and water in the event of a disaster. Many companies also stocked up on emergency-kits on behalf of their employees. The rumors, predictions and the government actions resulted in panic buying of canned foods, bottled mineral water, flashlights, medical supplies, scissors, can openers, rope ladders and charcoal for fuel.

Mt Fuji did not erupt, but there was, in fact, an earthquake in Tokyo in 1983 that caused substantial damage, and left 107 people dead. Two other earthquakes occurred the same year—one on Miyake in October, and one on Mt Shirane in November, neither of which caused appreciable damage. In the meantime, Japanese architects, engineers and others continued to assure people that their construction technology made new buildings and elevated highways virtually earthquake proof.

People became complacent again; they stopped buying emergency supplies, and many who had bought them earlier used them up or, over the years, threw them away. But on January 17, 1995, a little more than 12 years later than predicted, a great *jishin* (jee-sheen), "earthquake," did strike Japan, wiping out a huge portion of Kobe, one of the country's largest, most attractive, and most important port cities, and also wreaking havoc on the adjoining cities of Ashiya and Nishinomiya, sometimes called the "Beverly Hills of Japan" because of their upscale homes and scenic setting.

The Kobe quake killed more than 5,000 people, destroyed over 40,000 buildings, collapsed long sections of the city's main freeway arterial, and left more than 300,000 people homeless. In the aftermath of the earthquake, the government and the country's construction authorities were castigated for "misleading" the people.

As devastating and as deadly as it was, the Kobe quake had a very positive effect. It shocked the Japanese into realizing that their national wealth and economic superpower status did not make them immune to nature flexing its muscles. And once again *bosai pakku* (boh-sigh pahk-kuu), or "survival kit," became a popular term.

There are some 4,000 earthquakes a year in Japan that register on the Richter Scale, but the majority are so slight that they go unnoticed by the public. Every few years, however, there is a quake that is big enough to cause damage, and the best predictions are that the great Tokyo earthquake of 1923 must inevitably repeat itself.

Foreigners living in Tokyo and other crowded urban areas should make sure they have enough *bosai pakku* on hand to allow them to survive for an extended period—at least two weeks. There are also *bosai pakku* designed for travelers, and as much as travelers hate baggage, those who are traveling in Japan should consider the consequences of being caught in a destructive *jishin*—or in fires cause by something else. In any event, *bosai pakku* is a good term to remember.

仏教
Bukkyo
(Buuk-k'yoe)

The Wellspring of Japaneseness

Japan's traditional culture had three main roots—Shintoism, Buddhism and Confucianism. Each of these religions made fundamental contributions, but it has always seemed to me that the essence of Japanese character and Japaneseness was primarily influenced by *Bukkyo* (Buuk-k'yoe), or "Buddhism."

Bukkyo, founded in India in the 5th century B.C., was first made known to the emperor of Japan by a Korean mission in the year 552, though the official introduction of Buddhism into the country is generally given as 538. At that time, all Japanese were "Shintoists," in that Shintoism, the native religion, was the foundation of all public and private rituals of whatever kind.

In the decades following the arrival of Buddhism, there was considerable contention between Shintoism and Buddhism, but eventually Buddhism, which was a far more detailed and comprehensive approach to life, won out. Thereafter, Shintoism was to play a minor role until it was reinstated as the national religion at the beginning of Japan's modern history.

One of the key reasons for the power of Buddhism was that its whole philosophy was based on the search for a universal truth which applied to everybody and to everything at all times—instead of emphasizing specific beliefs, doctrines and dogma, as other religions did. Buddhism did not teach the existence of a god or a devil, holding instead that all confusion and suffering was caused by blind desire, and that the way to enlightenment was to renounce all lust and attachment.

Over the next 800 years, Buddhism was Japanized. Numerous sects, including Tendai, Shingon, Pure Land, Nichiren and Zen, evolved and grew into major branches. But all of the sects were similar, and developed characteristics that were strictly Japanese. Among the characteristics that have been identified with Japanese Buddhism are a practical morality, an emphasis on human relations, reverence for ancestors, worship of the individual sect founders, an emotional rather than a rational view of the world, and accepting things as they are.

In addition to its philosophical contributions to Japanese culture, *Bukkyo* also had a profound impact on Japan's arts and crafts, providing most of the impetus for virtually everything making up the Japanese life-style, from apparel and architecture to landscape gardening, the practice of martial arts, printing, literature, sculpture and more. Over the centuries the Japanese did not "practice" Buddhism as a religion, as they did with Shintoism or Confucianism. Buddhist tenets became so deeply impregnated in the culture that people simply lived them according to the customs of the day.

None of Japan's religions prohibited the pleasures of the flesh, and all gave precedence to human relations rather than hard, universal principles of conduct. As a result, the Japanese did not feel restricted in their daily affairs by any of their religions.

In present-day Japan, few people think of themselves as Buddhists or as religious in any sense of the word. But the cultural legacies of Buddhism are still discernible in the language, in the arts and crafts, and in the overall philosophical and aesthetic outlook of the Japanese. The various cult arts that have survived from the past—the tea ceremony, flower arranging, the martial arts, and most of the country's hundreds of annual festivals—are all rooted in Buddhist tenets.

To understand the deeper nuances of Japanese-style business management, and politics as well, it is necessary to know a great deal about the lingering influence of Buddhism, with its emphasis on aesthetics, on emotion, and on a "humanistic," rather than a logical or rational approach to interpersonal relationships.

Bunshu

(Boon-shuu)

The Country Divided

Until the 1980s, one of the biggest points of Japanese pride was the homogeneity of their culture and society. Most Japanese not only looked very much alike, it was also Japanese orthodoxy that most of them thought alike, acted alike, ate basically the same diet, and liked and disliked the same things. This homogeneity was seen as one of Japan's primary strengths, and as an asset that gave Japan an extraordinary social and economic advantage over most other countries. Generally speaking, this perception was accurate enough. People who lived on the northern edge of Hokkaido, the northernmost island, were very much like those who lived in southern Kyushu, even though the everyday language of the people of southern Kyushu was different enough to be called a dialect.

Prior to the 1980s, Japanese manufacturers and marketers typically bragged that they did not have to take consumer surveys to know what consumers wanted or would accept. They claimed that they did not have to test their advertisements or promotional material because all Japanese were on the same cultural wavelength, and that marketers knew intuitively what would work and what would not.

Again, all of this was basically true until the 1970s. Things had been changing in Japan since the 1950s, but these changes did not become that obvious in the marketplace for some two decades, and between 1970 and 1980, most Japanese businessmen blinded themselves to the rapidly evolving mindset and behavior of consumers, because they did not want to believe that fundamental changes were taking place.

By the mid-1980s, however, marketing surveys that had been started some ten years earlier began to reveal irrefutable changes in the attitudes and behavior of the younger generations of Japan, which by that time made up over half of the population. Much to the shock and chagrin of the older Japanese and most of the Japanese Establishment, there was no longer a single Japanese consciousness. Japanese society was splitting into groups that were characterized by age, by educational level, by social status, and even by regional differences.

Japan's business establishment was forced to recognize that there was no longer one huge market in which the whole population followed the same fashion and product fads, and bought whatever was put on the market. Manufacturers discovered that they could no longer drive the market at whatever speed and in whatever direction they wanted it to go. Regions and prefectures throughout Japan had begun to promote their own distinctive identities and markets. The standardization that had long been a key part of the national polity was being rejected. Individualism and independence had become the new code words. Japanese sociologists soon named this new phenomenon *bunshu* (boon-shuu), which can be translated as "divided masses."

Since that watershed decade, Japan's once homogenous population has continued to divide and to coalesce into increasingly smaller and more distinctive groups, creating a mishmash of markets that have replaced the former large mass market.

Other terms used by the media in reference to the smaller groups that have broken way from the central mass include *shoshu* (show-shuu), which means "small masses"; *kansei ningen* (kahn-say-e neen-gain), "people who determine their life-style on the basis of sentimentality"; and *hyogen zoku* (h'yoe-gain zoe-kuu), or "expressionist tribes"—people who attempt to express a certain individualism in their life-styles.

Another term that became popular during this period was *kurisutaru zoku* (kuu-rees-tah-rue zoe-kuu), or the "crystal tribe," from the title of a book, *Nantonaku Kurisutaru* (Nahn-toe-nah-kuu Kuu-rees-tah-rue), "Somewhat Crystal," by a Hitotsubashi University senior named Yasuo Tanaka. The book, which won the prestigious Kawade Shobo award in 1980, and was the literary bestseller of the year, depicted the attitudes and behavior of the generation of Japanese born around

1955—the first clearly identifiable generation to also be called *shinjinrui* (sheen-jeen-rue-ee), or "new kind of people."

The "crystal people," noted for a whimsical, intuitive approach to life, were primarily concerned about being trendy in the way they dressed, in where they dined, and in what they bought, all with the purpose of differentiating themselves from the largely bland and conservative mass of Japanese. Tanaka said he chose the word "crystal" to describe this generation because a crystal is neither transparent nor opaque, but rather bends light according to the angles of its surfaces.

The *bunshu* phenomenon caught Japanese manufacturers and marketers off-guard, providing new opportunities for American and European companies that were already in Japan, because they were experienced in dealing with segmented markets. Within the next decade, however, the Japanese performed another minor miracle by quickly accepting the new reality of the Japanese marketplace. Corporations small and large began designing and producing goods that were aimed at specific needs and specific groups of consumers.

Foreign companies entering and attempting to enter Japan in the 1970s and early 1980s were slow in picking up on the *bunshu* changes in the marketplace. Some foreign companies that do not have a presence in Japan today still tend to treat the market as a single entity, putting them at a serious disadvantage in their export efforts.

武士道
Bushido
(Buu-she-doh)

The Fighting Knight Way

The word *bushido* (buu-she-doe) was introduced to many non-Japanese people by a book with the title *Bushido: The Soul of Japan*. This book was written in 1899 by Dr. Inazo Nitobe. Many people familiar with the term are aware that it refers to the "code" of feudal Japan's samurai warriors. In his book, Dr. Nitobe defines *bushido* as "a code unuttered and unwritten, possessing the more powerful sanction of an actual deed."

Bushido literally means something like "military fighting way," but it is more commonly translated as "the way of the warrior." Developed over a number of centuries by the samurai class, which came into existence following the establishment of the shogunate form of government in 1185, and which thereafter ruled Japan as an elite military caste, *bushido* combines a moral and an ethical system with a highly stylized etiquette which came to be the defining character of the samurai; over the centuries the etiquette gradually influenced the rest of Japan's population as well.

The basic tenets of *bushido* are derived from Shintoism, Japan's indigenous religion, Buddhism and Confucianism, which were imported from China in the 6th century. Shinto's contribution to the way of the warrior was loyalty to the emperor, patriotism, filial piety, reverence for one's ancestors, and a godlike purity of soul.

From Buddhism came a belief and trust in fate, submission to the inevitable, an acceptance of death, a stoic composure in the face of calamity, and a sense of calm. Confucianism brought its five moral relationships to *bushido*, and thus became the foundation of the way of the warrior. These five moral tenets governed the hierarchical relationships between the ruler and the ruled, between fathers and sons, between husbands and wives, between older and younger brothers, and, last but not least, between friends.

Samurai youth were tutored in sword-fighting, spear fighting, archery, jujitsu, horsemanship, military tactics, ethics, literature, calligraphy and history. The youths were not instructed in mathematics or finance; even knowledge of the value of coins in use at that time was regarded as beneath the dignity and character of a samurai. Thrift was taught as a character-building trait—not for purposes of economy. Self-control, concealing one's thoughts, the repression of pain and sorrow, endurance and politeness were also instilled in samurai youth.

The bases of the moral foundation of *bushido* were a highly developed sense of justice; courage in the cause of righteousness; benevolence combined with love, affection and sympathy for others; politeness combined with gracefulness; veracity at all times and in all things; a highly developed sense of honor; and an absolute loyalty to the state and to one's lord.

Of course, these were the ideal moral standards of the samurai, and it is fair to say that few samurai ever fully lived up to all of them. But throughout Japan's feudal age, there were paragons of *bushido* who were role models, and who constantly reminded the people of the standards they were expected to maintain. Since life is never as simple as philosophy, there were constant contradictions in the lives of samurai that arose primarily from competition among their moral values. Loyalty to one's lord often took precedence over benevolence, justice, sympathy and veracity. Honor often came before any other consideration.

One of the greatest shocks to "the soul of Japan" was the introduction of Western-style commerce into the country beginning in 1870. As practiced at that time, and as it still often is today, commerce generally made a mockery of justice, loyalty, benevolence, veracity and all the other values that made up *bushido*. The culture shock experienced by Japan's samurai class as a result of the industrialization of the economy, which totally changed the samurai life-style, was made even more traumatic for them by the popular dismissal of all the philosophical values they had held sacred up to that time.

Events that occurred in Japan in the mid-1800s, when the country was opened to Western thought and commerce, resulted in the subversion of *bushido* to the interests of ambitious and unscrupulous military leaders who led Japan into a series of wars. Vestiges of *bushido*, however, have survived these wars and the traumatic events that have occurred since, and any understanding of the Japanese today must begin with some knowledge of the legacy left by more than six centuries of samurai rule.

Among the samurai-like characteristics that continue to be typical of most Japanese businesspeople are exceptional loyalty to their companies, a deep sense of honor and pride, a stylized etiquette, determination to succeed in the face of all odds, and a willingness to sacrifice their personal lives in the service of their employers.

Today, Japanese businessmen still believe in and try to practice the concept of *bushido no ichigon* (buu-shee-doh no ee-chee-gohn), or "the word of a samurai," which means that when they make a promise or commitment, they will keep it without any written contract or other formality.

Today the relationship between modern Japan and the age of the samurai is visible in the practices of aikido, judo, kendo and other martial arts in schools and halls throughout the country, and the rigorous training in etiquette that many companies give each year to new employees.

平等
Byodo
(Be-yoh-doe)

Japanese-Style Fairness

The concept of *byodo* (be-yoh-doe), or "equality," among people is a Western invention that apparently evolved from the Christian theological belief that all human beings are equal in God's eyes. Of course, there has never been a time in the history of any society when all people were treated as equals, but Americans and others have passed a body of law over the centuries that tries to enforce the concept.

There is no such historical legacy in Japan. Neither of Japan's two main religions, Buddhism and Confucianism, recognized or taught the principle of *byodo*. In fact, these two beliefs were based on exactly the opposite premise. Over the centuries the primary structure of Japanese society was based on inequality, that is, on the categorization of people in carefully delineated classes and ranks, with individual behavior determined and controlled by institutionalized and ritualized inequalities.

The American military forces had some success in introducing the idea of equality during their occupation of Japan from September 1945 to May 1952. The feudalistic structure of the family was outlawed, giving wives and children rights they had never had before. Political reforms gave people more rights as voters, and workers got the right to bargain collectively. Decrees alone were not enough to make the Japanese change their whole culture in a short period of time, however, and the concept of inequality continued to prevail in virtually every nook and cranny of the society.

By the 1960s, the first postwar generation of young Japanese had begun to demonstrate many characteristics of equality in their relationships among themselves, and the pace of the trend was to speed up from that time on. But demonstrations of equality among the young did not extend outside their own personal spheres. Inequality remained the prevailing principle in schools and in all economic and political organizations.

No matter how strongly individuals in the younger generations may have endorsed the concept of *byodo* in their private affairs, they were forced to conform to the prevailing concept of inequality the moment they began their education and joined the workforce. In today's Japan, people will generally claim that they are inherently equal to everyone else, but this is only "in principle." Despite the general acceptance of the principle of all people being created equal, their lives continue to be based on the concept of *fubyodo* (fuu-be-yoh-doe), or "inequality."

In practice, the Japanese continue to recognize that sex, age, education, schools attended and family background determine a person's rank in the overall hierarchy of every group or organization, and that rank establishes both guidelines and limits to what and how an individual can do things. It is therefore very important for foreigners dealing with the Japanese in professional organizations, companies and government agencies to be aware of the general lack of equality in Japan, and how this affects the individuals with whom they have direct contact.

The main factor where foreigners are concerned is that the behavior of the individual Japanese whom they deal with is controlled by the reality of their hierarchical rank within their organizations, and the behavior that is approved for that rank. With rare exceptions, even executives of the highest rank cannot act on their own initiative.

All Japanese are also extremely sensitive about the extent of the responsibilities and privileges that come with their place in the hierarchy, and they are very protective of their turf. If a person does not follow a precise protocol in dealing with people higher and lower in rank, considerable trouble can result for all persons involved.

Also, managers in Japanese companies sometimes keep things to themselves, either because they think an outsider's proposition has no merit or would not benefit them, or because they think it is a winner and they want to get as much credit as possible by keeping it to themselves for as long as they can.

Westerners often have difficulty understanding and accepting the limitations ranking puts on Japanese behavior, and often expect—and sometimes demand—responses from the Japanese that would seriously endanger their image and standing.

Generally, the only effective way to avoid problems associated with rank is to go through the individual designated as the *madoguchi* (mah-doe-guu-chee), or "window contact" in a Japanese organization, and to bring both the person's superiors and subordinates into the dialogue so that all appropriate persons are involved.

This approach should, of course, be done with the approval and cooperation of the *madoguchi*. But it is something that very often will not happen unless you—the outsider—diplomatically take steps to make it happen.

忠誠心
Chusei Shin
(Chuu-say-e Sheen)

Loyal to the Last

The Japanese are on the horns of a great dilemma. In all of their dealings in foreign affairs and in international trade, they face the problem of fundamental conflicts between their traditional way of thinking and doing things, and the demands made upon them to think and behave in ways that are acceptable to outsiders.

Many of the key cultural traits that make up the distinctive Japanese character and behavior, particularly when it comes to business and political relationships, are different enough that they almost always lead to misunderstandings when non-Japanese are involved. These misunderstandings, which come from subtle difference in values and expectations, invariably lead to friction, and often to conflicts of one kind or another.

There is, perhaps, no more significant example of these cultural differences than the concept and practice of *chusei shin* (chuu-say-e sheen), which might be translated as "ultimate loyalty." The cultural demands on the Japanese to demonstrate *chu-sei shin* to classmates and to teammates at work and at play are enormous, often transcending what Westerners regard as rational behavior.

This constant need for proof of loyalty also has a strongly ethnic and nationalistic element, and all Japanese are expected to "act" like Japanese, in a minutely prescribed sense, at all times. The Japanese who spend enough time abroad as students or employee expatriates to lose some of their Japaneseness may be regarded, upon their return home with suspicion and disdain. Even the slightest deviations from standard behavior can have serious consequences, ranging from overt physical and mental mistreatment of students by their schoolmates, to job discrimination.

In virtually every group situation in Japan, from elementary schools to the largest multinational corporations, people who have returned from abroad are often not treated as "real" Japanese, which means they are not trusted. Those who work for Japanese companies seldom reach the apex of power in such organizations. Corporate exceptions to this institutionalized practice of discriminating against anyone who is even vaguely perceived as having been de-Japanized are still rare enough that they are considered newsworthy.

There is a significant and growing effort in Japan, at a governmental level as well as privately, to "internationalize" the Japanese, but these efforts have had only minimal results. Once again it is a case of Japanese culture being so powerful and pervasive that it continues to be the standard by which everyone is measured, and, in larger, well-established institutions, it is used to suppress—or destroy—anyone who tries to behave differently.

Japan's amazing economic success between 1951 and the latter part of the 1980s made Japanese businessmen and bureaucrats proud and hard to get along with. From the mid-1960s to the early 1990s, foreigners wanting to do business with larger Japanese corporations and agencies of the government had to pass a variety of *chu-sei shin* tests that were usually spread out over a period of months or years, and often did not make sense to outsiders.

Things changed dramatically after 1990, when Japan's so-called "bubble economy" ruptured and brought everyone back down to earth. Japanese banks lost billions of dollars in asset values, and such famous names as Matsushita, Toshiba, Hitachi and Sony either lost money for the first time in their history, or saw their profits plunge to levels they had never before experienced.

Foreigners wanting to do business with Japan must still pass muster, but the tests are now a lot more transparent and they are easier than they were before the shock of the ruptured "bubble economy."

Daikan
(Die-kahn)

Mind Over Matter

When I was an employee of the Japan Travel Bureau in Tokyo in 1953, the ancient building which served as headquarters was neither cooled in summer nor heated in winter. In the frigid months of January and February, it was as cold inside the building as it was outside.

One morning when it was especially cold, I was astounded when a male customer in his late fifties or sixties came in wearing only shoes and a pair of shorts. He was a heavyset man who talked loudly and moved aggressively, obviously expending energy as a means of heating his body.

The experience was a dramatic reminder of the ancient Shinto concept that enduring the cold of winter was one of the fastest and most efficient ways to develop extraordinary mental control and intellectual and spiritual awareness—all of which were essential to mastering martial arts and other skills.

In early Japan it was the custom for samurai warriors, geisha and others to perform their exercises outside during the winter months and dressed only in the lightest clothing—a custom that was especially common during *daikan* (die-kahn), or "the great cold," which runs roughly from January 20 to around February 20. Following their exercises, students of martial arts would then drench themselves with icy water. Shinto priests and religious devotees have traditionally stood under waterfalls in the dead of winter to purify their spirits and build their character.

Until the 1960s, no attempt was made to heat Japan's school rooms, and hundreds of thousands of students, from kindergarten onward, were expected to endure the cold temperatures of the bitter winter seasons as part of their education and physical training.

In the 1980s an elementary school in central Japan received international attention because it required its students, girls as well as boys, to attend classes wearing only shoes and shorts throughout the winter. The children, shown on national television at study and at play, looked happy and robust, their faces bright and shining. None of them were shivering or huddling in attempt to share body heat. School doctors who were interviewed said the children gave no indication that they were suffering; nor were colds or other illnesses any more common among the children than among those who dressed warmly.

Japan's traditional attitude toward cold goes a long way toward explaining the characteristic dedication and diligence of the Japanese in all of the enterprises they undertake. Till this day, many corporate recruits are required to expose themselves to cold temperatures while wearing only loincloths, and take cold water showers as part of their training and orientation.

Many older employees voluntarily subject themselves to the same rigorous experience to sharpen their minds and build up their stamina. Such Japanese customs are a part of the old belief that the mind can prevail over matter if it is sufficiently trained, and this kind of training played a key role in the extraordinary skill developed by the Japanese in all of their arts and crafts, from carpentry and pottery to sword-fighting.

In present-day Japan, very few people are instilled with the mind-over-matter concept while they are young, or required to toughen their minds and bodies by exposure to *daikan* after they reach adulthood. But the concept itself remains very much alive in Japan, and it still influences the attitudes and behavior of most Japanese, especially those in the corporate world.

The long hours and the intensity with which many Japanese work are no different from the samurai warrior of old who practiced several hours a day for 20 years or more in order to master his art. Foreigners may view such practices as masochistic rather than spiritually and intellectually uplifting, but it cannot be denied that they played a role in Japan's rise to economic superpower status.

See *Kangeiko*.

談合
Dango
(Dahn-go)

Dividing up the Spoils

Living in or visiting Japan does not leave one with the feeling that the country is small. The archipelago stretches for some 1,800 miles from north to southwest, and over 80 percent of the landmass is made up of uninhabited mountains, making it possible to travel long distances, often without meeting any people.

Japan's population and industry, however, are mostly concentrated on relatively small coastal plains and in modest- to miniature-size valleys, and this concentration of people and industry has had a fundamental effect on the way the Japanese think and do business. Another key factor in Japanese psychology and business behavior is that when the feudal shogunate government fell in 1868, the new government took the lead in transforming the economy from one based on cottage industries to large-scale manufacturing and exporting.

This direct government support resulted in all of the primary areas of industry being dominated by a few huge, vertically integrated companies that worked closely with the various government ministries, and which eventually came to control some 60 percent of the country's gross national product.

Within this environment, these giant companies and relevant government ministries also collaborated to prevent competition that would disturb the system. Companies were regularly forced by the government to merge as part of the overall system of control. This concentration of business into carefully delineated categories in which there were only a few players and almost no open competition led companies, with the knowledge and approval of the government, to fix prices and divide government contracts up among themselves.

One of the key facets of this sharing of the industrial pie is described by the word *dango* (dahn-go), which foreigners have learned to translate as "bid-rigging."

In Japanese dictionary references to *dango*, the word's meaning is given as *sodan* (so-dahn), which means "consultation," "conference," or "talk." In any event, *dango* refers to companies in the same line of business getting together and agreeing in advance on who is going to get what part of the public contracts let out in Japan.

It was not until an international controversy arose over the contracts awarded for the construction of the Kansai International Airport in the 1980s that a few people in the foreign business community began to pick up on the word, and it eventually made its way into the international press. The international community immediately labeled *dango* one of the worst structural barriers facing foreign companies wanting to do business in Japan, and accused the companies involved in the bid-rigging and the Japanese government of using unfair, immoral and illegal business tactics.

These accusations caught the Japanese unprepared. *Dango* had been practiced in the country for generations and was an accepted way of doing business. To the Japanese, it not only spread business around, it also prevented the kind of competition that was common in the United States and elsewhere—competition that the Japanese had traditionally regarded as causing chaos and confusion in the marketplace. The international squabble over the use of *dango* in bidding for government and commercial contracts resulted in the Japanese government pledging to change the system to be more in line with Western practices.

Eventually, some legislative steps were taken in that direction. The powers of the Fair Trade Commission were increased and a token number of contracts began going to foreign firms. But getting a piece of the action in Japan and being able to perform in concert with Japanese contractors are very different things. Fewer foreign companies than expected went after Japanese contracts, and some of those who got them later gave them up and walked away.

As soon as the foreign hullabaloo subsided, the Japanese went back to doing business the way they had always done it, *dango* and all.

弾力的運営
Danryokuteki Un'ei
(Dahn-rio-kuu-tay-kee Uhn-eh-ee)

Run it up the Pole

During Japan's long feudal era, the shoguns and clan lords were acutely aware that if they wanted to stay in power, they had to make sure that people obeyed their laws, and the shortest and swiftest route to achieving this goal was through punishment and fear—punishing lawbreakers immediately and severely, and keeping the rest of the population in a state of fear.

After the end of the feudal period and the introduction of more democratic and liberal principles into Japan, the government could not so readily control lawbreakers or count on fear to keep others in line. Realizing that nothing undermines a government like issuing laws or edicts that it cannot enforce, Japan's political leaders and government bureaucrats had to come up with a different philosophy that would allow them to enforce new laws without having to pay a price if people ignored them.

Borrowing from their Chinese cousins, who have some 3,000 more years of experience in controlling people, the Japanese began using a technique known as *danryokuteki un'ei* (dahn-rio-kuu-tay-kee uhn-eh-ee), which means "flexible enforcement." By announcing that new policies or programs come under the umbrella of *danryokuteki un'ei*, Japanese government agencies are able to defuse much of any opposition, and then work behind the scenes to gradually get what they want. Variations of this technique are routinely used by both the Japanese government and Japanese corporations in their negotiations with both foreign companies and organizations.

Flexible enforcement has proven especially effective in joint-venture arrangements in which the Japanese side deliberately downplays the extent of its goals and expectations, with the idea that it will get what it wants later by taking a non-confrontational, incremental approach. This often works so well that the foreign companies do not realize, for as long as the first several years, that the relationship has changed dramatically.

Another area in which corporations make use of the *danryokuteki un'ei* concept is when buying or "leasing" technology. Rather than trying to get all rights to the technology up front, corporations will readily agree to limit their use of the technology. This way the Japanese side not only saves money, but also time and energy hassling over contract points—though planning all the while to eventually get all of the technology without any further payment or commitment, or to compromise the technology with their own research.

The Japanese government also routinely makes *danryokuteki un'ei* commitments to other countries, often as stopgap measures to eliminate or reduce foreign pressure for change—change which the Japanese government may, in fact, consider desirable. *Danryokuteki un'ei* may also be used by politicians as a stonewalling technique.

Outsiders dealing with the Japanese at any level should keep in mind that virtually every commitment the Japanese make has a significant element of *danryokuteki un'ei* in it, and that they naturally use this technique in ways and in areas that are calculated to provide them with the most benefit. From a Japanese cultural viewpoint, this kind of behavior is not seen as unethical or immoral, since they do not measure it by Western standards, and they are often genuinely surprised at the uproar foreigners sometimes make when they realize what is going on.

Obviously, the only defense against this kind of polite manipulation is to bring out, up front, any and all things considered undesirable, to put them in writing, and try to build safeguards into agreements.

See *Shido*.

男尊女卑
Danson Johi
(Dahn-sohn Joe-he)

Men Over Women

Many early societies around the world recognized the vital role that women have traditionally played in the survival and in the civilizing of humankind, often making them equal and sometimes superior to men in the managing of family, community, and tribal or national affairs; and such was the case in early Japan. Prior to the development of clan militarism from about the 10th century on, women in Japan routinely played prominent roles in government, and exercised many of the prerogatives now more generally associated with men. Among the upper classes, these prerogatives included the right to have sexual liaisons with more than one man, and in some instances to have multiple husbands.

With the rise of clan warlords and militarism, women were soon relegated to the status of chattel to be used by men for both economic and political advantages. This new philosophy, subsumed in the phrase *danson johi* (dahn-sohn joe-he), which literally means "men predominate over women," grew out of the adoption of Confucianism, which was introduced into Japan through Korea in the 5th century, and which gradually permeated Japanese culture over the next several centuries.

Japanese women were held in legal bondage by their fathers, husbands and employers until 1946, following Japan's defeat in World War II, and when the American government ordered the feudal family system abolished.

Legal freedom did not mean that Japanese women were able to remove the yoke of *danson johi*, however. By that time, the inferior status of women and the superior status of men was so deeply ingrained in the culture that it was virtually impervious to government edicts.

The first Japanese females to make a great and conspicuous break with the past were teenage girls and single women in their twenties. Within months after the end of World War II, hundreds of thousand of girls and young women were fraternizing with the even larger numbers of American and allied soldiers and foreign civilian personnel occupying Japan. Japanese women had always been interested in foreign men, but in this case the attraction was as much economic as social. For these hundreds of thousands of Japanese women, the foreign GIs and civilian employees of the occupation forces were virtually an inexhaustible source of money, food, clothing and almost every other item carried in the military post exchanges and commissaries.

In other areas of Japanese life, the results of the legal emancipation of Japanese women did not begin to show until the mid-1950s, by which time most of the ravages of the war had disappeared, and Japan had entered the first stages of an affluent consumer society.

During the last half of the 1950s, hundreds of thousands of Japanese girls began flocking to universities, young Japanese men and women began dating, the number of arranged marriages began dropping dramatically, and equally large numbers of young women began working in the new companies that continued to mushroom, creating a new class of independent and affluent Japanese.

Over the next three decades, *danson johi* practically disappeared within Japanese families. But generally speaking, wives and mothers went their own way; husbands and fathers went theirs; and there was very little communication between them. There was a woman's world and a man's world, with a minimum of overlapping. Men ran the business world and government and enjoyed themselves in the entertainment trades. Married women ran the household, raised the children, and spent their leisure time shopping, gossiping, watching television and engaged in cultural pursuits. Single women worked, shopped, traveled and carried on desultory affairs with men.

Instead of coming together in the wake of female emancipation, the two sexes created separate worlds of their own, and it was not until around the beginning of the 1990s, by which time the gap between husbands and wives and fathers and children had become a national crisis, that social and mental health authorities began to initiate programs to help men and women overcome their alienation.

The *danson johi* mentality is still normal among the vast majority of Japanese men, and it is reflected in every aspect of Japanese life, from the language that is used, to social manners, employment, compensation and privileges. But overall, Japanese women are not mistreated to the point that they are seriously frustrated and agitating for change. Feminism is not yet a force to be reckoned with in Japan, and probably will not be for at least several generations, because, generally speaking, Japanese women like the idea of having their own world.

断定
Dantai
(Dahn-tie)

The Three Musketeers Syndrome

This custom of forming exclusive groups became so deeply embedded in Japanese culture that it continues today to be one of the primary characteristics of Japanese society, at every level and in every area of endeavor. Today, as in the past, the *dantai* (dahn-tie), or groups that people belong to, including corporations, professional organizations, and the like, basically control the loyalty as well as the activities of their members.

Like many societies around the world, Japan was traditionally divided into precise social classes and groupings that included clans, towns, villages, associations, work teams and other special purpose groups. What gives this common kind of grouping special importance in the case of Japan was that each of the groups, at whatever level and of whatever size, was generally exclusive and antagonistic toward all others, particularly so toward groups with the same interests. Inter-group antagonism also prevailed among subdivisions in an organization, making it difficult for them to communicate and cooperate with each other.

As is so often the case with Japanese institutions and customs, there is a good and a bad side to the *dantai*. On the one hand, they enhance the effectiveness of the members of the groups, because the members support each other and work together as a team. On the other hand, *dantai* are a serious detriment to cooperating with other groups, and tend to stifle the kind of flexibility that is essential for making fast decisions and reacting in a timely fashion to outside influences. It is this *dantai* mentality and behavior that make Japanese corporations something like closed clubs, and therefore exceedingly difficult for outsiders to work with.

The *dantai* factor is also one of the primary causes of the faction-oriented character of Japanese politics that prevents the development of a system that truly represents the public, and leaves most power in the hands of the entrenched bureaucracy.

While the hundreds of thousands of *dantai* that make up Japanese society are ingrown, narrow-minded and territorially oriented, there is a plus side; group goals are coordinated sufficiently in Japan so that as a whole the groups move forward as a giant army that has extraordinary momentum and strength, giving rise to the image of Japan as a single, giant corporation.

A recent incident in Japan dramatically illustrated one of the advantages of the *dantai* conditioning at a national level. An elderly woman exiting from a commuter train in Tokyo caught her hand in the viselike grip of the automatic doors of the train as they closed. The woman was subsequently dragged for several hundred yards and killed. Within 48 hours, conductors on commuter trains throughout the country were using the public address system on each train to warn passengers of the danger of closing doors prior to every stop. Within a week after the accident, these warnings had been automated and had become an institutionalized part of the standard announcements on Japan's commuter train system.

Virtually all public and professional activities in Japan, from education, medicine, arts and crafts, to scientific research, personnel management and behavior on the factory floor, are characterized and controlled by *dantai*. This means that people, Japanese and foreigners alike, wanting to become involved with Japanese organizations, for whatever purpose, must keep in mind that they are not dealing with individuals but with exclusive groups, and that they must quickly adapt and fashion their behavior accordingly.

Japan's *dantai* therefore constitute one of the so-called invisible barriers that make it especially time-consuming and difficult, for both Japanese and foreigners, to establish good, productive relationships. Outsiders must bear in mind that they not only need to satisfy the requirements of individual subgroups in Japanese organizations, they must also satisfy anywhere from two or three to a dozen or more other groups in the same organizations, all of which have responsibilities and agendas that differ to some degree.

丼勘定
Donburi Kanjo
(Doan-buu-ree Kahn-joe)

Calculations in a Bucket

Japanese sociologists and other professionals often explain Japanese attitudes and behavior in terms of the country's rice culture and clan or tribal history. Among other things, they say the Japanese owe their proclivity for group behavior and cooperation to their traditional practice of growing rice in flooded paddies, which required a sophisticated irrigation system encompassing whole villages. They point to the clan system, which survived in Japan as a key social and political unit until the fall of the shogunate in 1868, as the source of Japanese loyalty to their families and employers and of the extraordinary spirit of competition the Japanese exhibit toward groups outside their circle.

Another historical factor that played a key role in shaping Japanese character was the existence of large numbers of tiny wholesale and retail businesses, most of which were founded and operated as family enterprises. The influence of these minuscule family-run businesses was so powerful that it permeated the culture, and today it still plays a significant role in all levels of business in Japan, from the surviving shops themselves to the largest corporate conglomerates.

I first ran into the "shopkeeper" mentality of the Japanese in the 1960s when I was serving as a consultant to a Japanese publishing company. I kept hearing the words *donburi kanjo* (dohn-buu-ree kahn-joe) in relation to some of the problems the publishing company was having. I knew the meaning of the individual words, but I did not know what they meant when they were used together. A *donburi* is a deep bowl of the kind often used for storing food, and *kanjo* means "bill," as in "restaurant bill," or "calculation."

It finally became clear to me that several of the section and department heads in the company were being accused of running their areas as if they were small, independent shops that had nothing to do with each other or with the overall goals of the company. In this case, the specific reference was to the accounting procedures. Instead of keeping detailed records, the accounting department had lumped everything together in one "bowl," with the result that no one could figure out why the company was not making a profit. When used in this sense, *donburi kanjo* might be translated as "calculation in a bowl."

Donburi kanjo is also used to refer to the practice, in large businesses, of offering a variety of products and services to a major customer without any attempt to track which section or department gets credit for the sale of which product or service. One aspect of this practice that often upsets foreign companies dealing with the Japanese is that there is generally no separate billing for the service portion of the sale or contract. The Japanese typically subsume the whole cost in one price.

When this subject is brought up, it is common for the Japanese to say either that the cost of after service is included in the price of the product concerned, or that the service is, or should be, free. The Japanese view is that after service is a given because the product is supposed to work, and to charge extra for such service is un-businesslike.

It is this aspect of "calculations in a bowl" that confuses, mystifies, and sometimes irritates foreigners doing business with the Japanese.

縁、情
En / Jyo
(Enn / Joe)

A Wet Japanese Thing

Among the many fascinating aspects of Japanese culture is the strong belief that a male and female may be preordained as "soul mates" from previous lives, and that they are destined to be rejoined time and again; this is a belief that is fairly common in other cultures as well.

In my own case (admittedly at a much younger age), I have met a number of Japanese women whom I felt I had known forever, and with whom I had an instant rapport that went well beyond normal attraction.

I also discovered that the Japanese put great stock in a concept known as *en* (enn), which refers to a kind of natural attraction between two people who meet often, but coincidentally, and who find that they have a natural attraction, and that their meetings bring them good luck.

People who are fortunate enough to have this kind of chance encounter say there is *en* between them, or that they are somehow connected by *en*. By the same token, when *en* does not exist between two people, there is likely to be friction between them, and every time they meet, it seems that something goes wrong. They just do not "hit it off," an experience that is familiar to everyone.

Because the Japanese are very sensitive to all personal relationships and always have their antennae up, they are always on the lookout for *en* when they meet new people. When the Japanese do meet new people, foreigners included, and do not get an immediate *en* reading on their cultural radar, they are inclined to be cautious about getting involved with them. This is an especially important issue where foreigners are concerned, because they are broadcasting on a different cultural frequency, and the Japanese cannot always pick up on the positive signals. More likely than not, the Japanese get only negative readings.

There is another word and concept that is closely associated with personal relationships in Japan. This word is *jyo* (joe), which is probably best, but not perfectly, translated as "warm empathy."

Some people have no *jyo* at all; but most people have some, and some have a lot. The Japanese, like most other people, instantly begin scanning everyone they meet in an effort to measure their *jyo*. Whether or not they choose to develop a warm, personal relationship with the new individual is determined by their *jyo* readings.

In the late 1950s and early 1960s, it became vogue in Japan to refer to people with *jyo* as "wet," and those without *jyo* as "dry." As usual, the pronunciation of the English words was Japanized; "wet" became *wetto* (wet-toe) in Japanese, and "dry" became *dorai* (doe-rye).

At first these terms were primarily used in reference to the romantic appeal of a particular person, with most Japanese men earning the label *dorai*, because at that time they had had very little if any experience in treating women in a *wetto* manner. The reason for this was that young Japanese did not begin to date in the Western fashion until the mid-1950s, and it was well into the 1960s before such courting became common.

In contrast to the Japanese, who tended to take women for granted and treat them cavalierly, Western men in Japan generally catered to the preferences of the Japanese women they met and dated, treating them in a romantic manner that most Japanese women had only read about or seen in foreign movies. As a result of this contrast in behavior, most foreign men in Japan got high *wetto* marks from Japanese women.

On the business side, *wetto* and *dorai* were not commonly used to describe the character and personality of businesspeople, but the concepts themselves played an equally important role. Foreign businesspeople who did not meet the *jyo* expectations of their Japanese counterparts were generally described as cold, insincere, arrogant, and so on.

In Japanese culture, both *en* and *jyo* have traditionally been essential qualities in business relationships, because the human elements involved made such relationships enjoyable; also, because detailed business contracts did not exist, business relationships depended entirely on personal ties. Although written contracts, particularly between Japanese and foreign companies, are the rule today, both *en* and *jyo* remain very important ingredients in all business relationships. Generally speaking, both must exist before such relationships officially begin, and if they are not constantly nurtured, they invariable degenerate and the relationship is likely to fail.

Japanese companies typically give *en* and *jyo* precedence in resolving issues involving pricing, delivery, claims and other sticky points that routinely develop between companies—a custom that foreigners often find "not good business" and therefore upsetting.

円高ドル安

Endaka-Doruyasu

(Enn-dah-kah-Doe-rue-yah-sue)

High Yen, Low Dollar

In 1871, three years after the fall of the Tokugawa Shogun and the return of Japan's emperor to power, the new Meiji government established the *en*, "yen," as the country's new currency. *En* means "round," and the newly minted coins were given this name because the coins used during the Tokugawa Period had been oval or oblong in shape.

The new currency was pegged to a parity of 1.5 grams of gold, which was the equivalent of one Mexican dollar, the standard unit for East Asian trade at that time. In actual practice, however, the value of the *en* was based on silver, and as the supply of silver increased, the value of the yen went down. When several Western nations adopted the gold standard, Japan did the same, setting the value of the yen at 0.75 grams, which was the equivalent of US$0.50.

Japan followed the United States' lead in 1917 and dropped the gold standard. When the United States returned to the gold standard after World War I, Japan was in such economic turmoil that it could not make the switch until 1930, which only aggravated the depression and forced Japan to once again abandon the gold standard. In April 1949, four years after the end of World War II, the Bank of Japan adopted a unified exchange rate of 360 yen to one US dollar, where it was to remain until the end of 1970.

In 1971, the exchange rate was set at 308 yen to one dollar, a rate that endured for only two years. When the United States devalued the dollar against gold in February 1973, Japan and most other industrialized countries moved to a floating exchange rate system.

For the next decade, the yen moved up and down between 296 to 210 yen per dollar, making the term *endaka* (enn-dah-kah), or "high yen," one of the most frequently occurring words in the Japanese mass media, and setting off an investment spree abroad, where the *doruyasu* (doe-rue-yah-sue), or "low dollar," made things unbelievable bargains for the Japanese.

But the real era of *endaka* did not begin until 1990, when the yen rose to 144 to the dollar, and then continued to rise to 134 in 1991, to 126 in 1992, to 111 in 1993, and to 102 yen to the dollar in the spring of 1994. By the fall of 1994, the yen–dollar exchange rate had exceeded the previously unimaginable rate of 100 to one, hovering between 98 and 96 yen to one dollar.

By this time, Japanese corporations and owners of successful companies had engaged in a frenzy of overseas investment, buying up manufacturing companies, entertainment companies, office buildings, hotels, golf resorts, and, in the case of Hawaii, whole blocks of residential homes.

But *endaka* was to be Japan's Achilles' heel. With the emergence of South Korea, Taiwan, Singapore and China as major export competitors, with the end of the Cold War, and with the general globalization of products and markets outside of Japan, the value of Japan's assets overseas collapsed, leaving its banks holding billions of dollars in bad loans.

Most authorities around the world say the value of the yen will remain high as long as Japan has a huge current account surplus and the United States has a huge account deficit, and that the only solution is for Japan to deregulate its market and allow its trade with the United States and the rest of the world to find a natural balance.

But in my view, a significant percentage of Japan's politicians, government bureaucrats, economists, media barons and others see *endaka* and Japan's enormous current account surplus as evidence of the superiority of Japanese culture and work ethic, and as something that is not only natural but desirable. These are the people who are going to fight deregulation and delay it for as long as possible, because they know that Japan cannot maintain its huge trade imbalance if it is forced to level the playing field.

The other side of this coin is the Japanese view that the combination of *endaka* and a huge current account surplus, along with domestic prices anywhere from 50 to 500 percent higher than those abroad, will ultimately be a fatal combination, and that Japan must deregulate and reform its economy if it is to survive. Some members of this group predict that eventually the yen–dollar relationship will reverse itself to a *enyasu* (enn-yah-sue) "low yen," *dorudaka*, "high dollar," situation.

Whether it is *endaka* and *doruyasu*, or *dorudaka* and *enyasu*, these terms have come to symbolize issues in Japan's trade and diplomatic relations with the United States and the rest of the world.

煙幕を張る
En Maku wo Haru
(Enn Mah-kuu oh Hah-rue)

Laying Smoke Screens

Until the end of Japan's Shogunate Period in 1868, businesspeople were considered the lowest of the main social classes. (There were no lawyers in Japan at that time.) Businesspeople were lumped into this lower class status because of the influence of Buddhism, which taught that deliberately making a profit from the labor of others was an immoral practice.

For most of the long Tokugawa Shogunate (1603–1868), Japan's samurai class was prohibited from engaging in any kind of commerce. The warriors and their families, which comprised about ten percent of the population, were supported by rice allotments from the government. The samurai sold the rice to the merchants, whom they despised, to obtain cash.

During this long period, a number of samurai families renounced their exalted status in order to go into business and prosper. Others married their daughters and sons into successful merchant families in order to improve their own life-styles. However, most of the warrior class adhered religiously to the philosophy that engaging in commerce and dealing with money was a contemptible enterprise, and the poverty and dissatisfaction of the samurai was one of the elements that contributed to the collapse of the shogunate system in the 1860s.

The rapid transformation of Japan into an industrialized country following the fall of the Tokugawa Shogunate was therefore a traumatic experience for the samurai, who had enjoyed the status of an elite for so long, and it is to their credit that they were able to switch from being anti-business and anti-money to being masters of commercial enterprise in less than 20 years.

One of the assets that the former samurai brought to Japan's new industrial economy was their knowledge of military tactics, including their skills in ferreting out intelligence about their adversaries and using the intelligence to their advantage.

Another of their traditional military-based skills was *en maku wo haru* (enn mah-kuu oh hah-rue), literally, "laying smoke screens," or the ability to conceal activities and true intentions from enemies in order to mislead them and seduce them into letting their guard down.

The ability to "lay smoke screens" had long been a vital factor in survival in Japan, because the country's traditional system of clans and fiefs was adversarial, resulting not only in the appearance of a professional warrior class, but also in the deeply entrenched customs of spying, of using professional assassins and saboteurs, the ninja, and otherwise trying to keep one's enemies off guard. Japan's new class of industrialists and run-of-the-mill businessmen, both former samurai and commoners, did not give up the age-old practice of *en maku wo haru* in their business dealings with each other and with outsiders. By this late date in their history, it was a perfectly normal part of their behavior.

Until the end of World War II, the Japanese government and larger Japanese corporations operated more-or-less as secret enterprises, with both engaging in a variety of clandestine activities that were similar to or the same as the activities that the shogunate and fief lords had engaged in until 1868. It was not until the 1960s and later that the Japanese government and corporations in general began to accept the idea that the public had a right to know something about government operations, and began to make such information available. This change in attitude and behavior did not end the practice of *en maku wo haru*, however, particularly among larger companies, where the custom had long since been incorporated into their overall management philosophy and their style of negotiating.

In today's Japan "laying smoke screens" is still an important aspect of the culture. It is done at a low and informal level by virtually everyone as part of an effort to present a certain image and to avoid exposing one's "real" self to the outside world. An example of *en maku wo haru* is the *tatemae* (tah-tay-my), "facade" or "public position," characteristic of Japanese behavior, which is nothing other than a smoke screen designed to conceal *honne* (hohn-nay), "real thoughts" or "real intentions."

The purpose of the *en maku wo haru* has not changed. It is to keep competitors in the dark as much as possible, and to conceal one's true objectives up to the last moment. Foreign businesspeople and politicians dealing with Japan almost always have to work their way though a "cloud of smoke" to get down to the heart of any matter.

円満
Enman
(Inn-mahn)

The Perils of Harmony

The original name for Japan was *Yamato* (Yah-mah-toe), meaning "Great Peace" or "Great Harmony," and the Japanese like to point out the importance of *wa* (wah), or "harmony," in their society. Japan, however, has never truly been a peaceful nation, and probably will not be for a long time to come.

In the past, the highly refined etiquette and the precisely structured form of Japanese society gave Japan the appearance of harmony; but that appearance was an illusion. Beneath the refined manners and behind the peaceful countenance epitomized by smiling Noh and kabuki masks, there was a violent id that was kept under control only by the most strenuous efforts and severe sanctions. It was, in fact, the Japanese' attempts to enforce group harmony on themselves that resulted in their psyche developing a Jekyll-and-Hyde nature. In their efforts to ensure absolute conformity, which is essential for perfect group harmony, the Japanese had to repress most of the natural feelings and impulses that are inherent in everyone.

Since repressing one's feelings is an extraordinarily difficult thing to do, equally extraordinary pressure was required to force people to do it. This pressure took the form of bullying, or *ijime* (e-jee-may), in subtle psychological ways, as well as physical pressure and punishment of some kind. *Ijime* became the tool that was used in an attempt to force everybody within a particular group to look alike, think alike, and act alike. The greater the degree of group harmony desired, the more pressure was necessary to achieve it.

Although people may repress their natural feelings, no one can ignore their emotions completely.

As a result, the Japanese developed a "Mr Hyde" side that was filled with repressed frustration and anger. While self-repression made individual Japanese passive most of the time, another set of dynamics took over when they were behaving as a group, and there was a natural tendency for the group to show extreme hostility toward any member or any outsider who did not conform precisely to their group image.

Traditionally, the Japanese establishment justified the force necessary to make people sacrifice their individuality by claiming that the sacrifice required strengthened their spirit and will, and made them superior people. Because of this conditioning over the centuries, the Japanese literally became incapable of identifying with and accepting people who were different from them. The natural Japanese reaction to any difference was hostility or, often, violence of some kind.

Required by their culture to become masochists, the Japanese naturally developed the sadistic impulses that are a corollary of the masochistic character. These impulses were expressed in the form of envy of anyone who was superior to the norms of the group—insiders as well as outsiders—and by bullying to punish nonconformists or to bring them down.

The ideal for all interpersonal relationships in Japanese society is described by the term *enman* (inn-mahn), which means "perfection," "harmony," "smoothness," and "peace"—a concept that applies more precisely to human behavior than the more popular word *wa*, or "harmony."

Thus it came about that while the Japanese were being programmed to live in *enman*, they were also being programmed to behave violently and sadistically toward anyone who did not dress, think and act as they did. From the 1850s when the country opened its doors to the outside world, to the end of World War II, Japan's history was filled with shocking incidents of sadistic behavior toward wartime enemies, and among themselves.

In present-day Japan the most common example of sadistic behavior, set off by envy and taking the form of bullying, occurs among students, and the problem is so serious that it is considered a national threat to the society. The *ijime* that is endemic in Japanese schools is not just a matter of the kind of minor teasing and physical abuse that is common among young people in most societies. Ignored by teachers and parents alike, many victims of the most severe forms of bullying attempt suicide.

Japanese social psychologists and other social critics readily acknowledge that the traditional image of Japanese society as *enman* or harmonious was an illusion, and that unless the Japanese quickly learn how to accept and live with diversity, their society will become more and more violent.

褌を締める
Fundoshi wo Shimeru
(Foon-doe-she oh She-may-rue)

Tightening Your Loincloth

There are many wonderfully graphic records of how people dressed, ate, worked and went about their daily lives in pre-industrial Japan, because there were so many artists who left detailed drawings and paintings to posterity.

The reason why artists were common in early Japan was due in large part to the writing system and to the apprenticeship system that prevailed in the handicraft industries. Learning how to draw the multi-stroke ideograms making up the writing system resulted in all educated Japanese becoming artists to some extent. Becoming a recognized tradesman in any of the dozens of handicraft arts, from carpentry and pottery to silk and papermaking, required years of on-the-job training under recognized masters, and resulted in a significant percentage of the population acquiring extraordinary mechanical and aesthetic skills.

These combined influences, along with such aesthetically oriented pursuits as calligraphy and poetry, inspired an artistic impulse in the Japanese that permeated the entire culture, including a long line of woodblock print artists who chronicled their times in full, fascinating color. Most of these artists specialized in scenes depicting ordinary people going about their regular routines, and it is to the *hanga* (hahn-gah), or "woodblock prints," they left behind that we owe so much of our knowledge of days gone by.

Among the images of life in early Japan that stand out strongly in my mind are porters who worked along the great roads crisscrossing Japan, along with carpenters and laborers, whose summer attire often consisted only of a loincloth called *fundoshi* (foon-doe-she), a band of cloth that was passed between the legs, drawn up snugly at the crotch, and tied around the waist.

As time went by, the saying, *fundoshi wo shimeru* (foon-doe-she oh she-may-rue), "drawing up or closing the *fundoshi*" became equated with getting ready to go to work, and, later, preparing to put extra effort into some task—the equivalent of "rolling up one's sleeves" in English.

The phrase *fundoshi wo shimeru* is seldom used in business settings anymore, no doubt because the *fundoshi* itself is now worn only by participants in some traditional festivals and on other special occasions; however, the concept is still very much alive and important. Most large Japanese companies have one or more regular programs for motivating their employees to "roll up their sleeves." These range from early morning exercise sessions and pep talks to singing the company song. Mass meetings in large public halls and smaller group meetings in restaurants or inns are also regularly used to inspire an aggressive team spirit.

Foreign businessmen operating in Japan are well advised to utilize the same or similar approaches to creating and maintaining high morale among their Japanese employees. In informal settings, they could also gain some mileage with humorous references to "tightening up the *fundoshi*."

フリーター

Furita
(Fuu-ree-tah)

The Day of the Oddballs

Traditionally in Japan, people who did not belong to an approved group of some kind were outcasts, or "non-persons," and were looked down on, and sometimes feared, because they represented a threat to the established system. This prejudicial attitude toward persons outside one's group survived the transformation of feudal and agrarian Japan to a modern industrialized nation, and did not begin to weaken significantly until the 1970s and 1980s when individual effort became an important factor in the computer and computer software fields.

Prior to this, artists and writers were among the few people who were accepted in Japanese society for their individual efforts, and even they had to have ties with the Establishment to survive. In addition, many of them were not recognized in Japan until they had achieved considerable success abroad.

By the mid-1980s, the few Japanese for whom individualism had been important in their success were the new heroes and heroines, and they were featured endlessly in magazines and on television as role models. Establishment figures in virtually every important field came out as enthusiastic advocates of personal independence and individual creativity. These newly enlightened advocates of individualism began predicting that Japan could not continue to prosper in the 21st century if its young people did not develop a spirit of individuality, nurture their natural curiosity, and become creative thinkers and doers. All this sounded marvelous to young Japanese, for they had already begun to spread their wings, and—outside of school—were experimenting and exploring as the youth of Japan had never done before.

But the brave new world of individuality and creativity called for by these newly converted Cassandras has not yet come to pass. Japan's educational, economic and political systems, and its scientific and professional communities are still bedrocks of groupism, where individualism and self-expression are generally not tolerated. Whether the forecasters are right or wrong, this situation is not likely to change dramatically for at least one or two generations, because the traditional ways and vested interests are simply too strong and too deeply embedded in the system and in the psyche of the Japanese.

In the meantime, the very small percentage of the Japanese who are making it, or trying to make it, on their own have at least been given a name that the Establishment is recognizing slowly. This new name is *furita* (fuu-ree-tah), which comes from the English expression "freelance writer," but *furita* is also used to refer to freelancers in general.

When I first heard myself described as a *furita*, I had no idea what I was being called, because I was not in Japan when the word became vogue in the news media, and was not aware the word had been adopted into the language. However, I was delighted to learn that "freelancer" had been Japanized, because not having a precise word for the concept made it difficult to explain, and adoption of the term was essential before the idea could be accepted as a legitimate professional category.

Most Japanese who understand the term are envious of *furita* or freelancers, because of the independence and freedom the concept suggests. And the goal of more and more Japanese is to establish themselves as freelancers, thereby avoiding most of the burdens involved in maintaining the personal relations required in the traditional group system, and benefiting directly from their own ideas and efforts.

This all would no doubt be helped along if the *furita* of Japan would form a group: maybe something like "The Oddball Association of Japan."

故郷
Furusato
(Fuu-rue-sah-toe)

Longing for a Spiritual Home

Despite a history that stretches back several thousand years, and a deeply ingrained belief in their uniqueness and cultural superiority, the Japanese typically suffer from the lack of a spiritual center, which causes them to feel out of place and alone in the world. Although tribal and territorial instinct remains strong in Japan, and is often expressed in the term *furusato* (fuu-rue-sah-toe), which is translated as "birthplace," "home village," "hometown," or "place of origin," it is not enough to quell the Japanese thirst for a spiritual home.

Furusato is commonly used in product descriptions, travel promotions, and so on to evoke strong spiritual feelings, and to remind the Japanese of their history. But these historical memories stop short of satisfying the Japanese psyche. There is inevitably something missing that leaves the Japanese a lonely people.

It would seem that the only explanation for this spiritual disquiet is the fact that virtually all of Japan's early culture was imported from China, first through Korea and then directly from the Central Kingdom itself. Despite long periods of virtual isolation from China, the Japanese have never been able to purge themselves of innermost feelings that they were little more than imitation Chinese.

Since the middle of the 19th century, the primary influence on Japan has been America and Europe, once again imposing a layer of foreign concepts and customs onto the Japanese psyche and continuing the cultural disharmony.

The Japanese are still struggling to come to terms with their identity and to find a place for themselves in the world. They are still searching for their *furusato*, and in moments of special candor and yearning, many Japanese say that China is their spiritual homeland.

There is one conflict with this yearning, however; the Chinese and Japanese do not like each other, and relations between them have never been good. Despite having imported well over 90 percent of their traditional culture from China, the Japanese retained enough of their indigenous character and personality that they are very different from the Chinese in their attitudes and behavior, and they naturally clash.

Historically, the Chinese have always looked down on everybody, including the Japanese, and they now have a long list of grievances against the Japanese that influence their behavior toward them in both overt and covert ways.

The Chinese now use the *furusato* longings of the Japanese as a lever to extract unequal economic advantages from them. In virtually every Chinese–Japanese business relationship, the Chinese use this cultural leverage as well as the guilt feelings of the Japanese to get the better part of the deal—something that puts the Japanese in a double bind.

In the short-term, the Japanese see China as a market that they cannot ignore, because if they do, they will lose out to the United States and other competitors. They therefore accept the often rude and arrogant behavior of Chinese officials, bureaucrats and businesspeople, because they feel they have no choice. At the same time, in the long-term view, the Japanese see China as replacing them as the superpower of Asia, economically as well as militarily, and they feel that they must play on the *furusato* relationship to create and sustain beneficial ties with China.

Among the characteristics that differentiate the Chinese from the Japanese are the following: individual Chinese are very strong intellectually and emotionally, and they are natural entrepreneurs; the Chinese think in rational, logical terms and are superior scientists; they are masters at diplomacy and politics as well as business; and the Chinese are not intimidated by anything or anybody.

The only way Japanese businesspeople and politicians can put up with the treatment they receive from the Chinese is to fall back on the qualities of the samurai, steeling themselves to accept any abuse, and to sacrifice themselves for their corporate lords and their country. The view that the Japanese and Chinese share a common *furusato* makes these burdens heavier, not lighter.

外人くさい
Gaijin Kusai
(Guy-jeen Kuu-sigh)

Smelling like a Foreigner

The Japanese have long been notorious for their racial, ethnic and social discrimination. They have traditionally been incapable of accepting other races and ethnic groups into their inner circle and treating them the way they treat other Japanese; even the Japanese who look or act a little different are not accepted.

As long as an outsider is a guest, whether in a home, a hotel, a place of business, or anywhere else in the country, the Japanese are so friendly and hospitable that it often becomes intrusive to foreigners who are not conditioned to such treatment. But once an outsider becomes anything other than a guest, the attitude of the Japanese changes dramatically, becoming anything from distant to cautious, insensitive, uncooperative and antagonistic.

This automatic discriminatory reaction of the Japanese no doubt derives in part from their historical isolation from other people. But most of it, I believe, derives from the traditional image they have had of themselves as being absolutely unique in the world, and also of being absolutely homogeneous. In other words, anyone who was not born and raised as "pure" Japanese, and who did not look or act "pure" Japanese, could not possibly be fully Japanese, socially or legally. Several hundred thousand people of Korean ancestry who were born and raised in Japan, look exactly like the Japanese, speak Japanese fluently, and act exactly like the Japanese, are still regarded as foreigners in a racial, ethnic, social and legal sense. A fairly comparable situation in the United States would be to ostracize the descendants of the English, the Irish or the Germans who immigrated to the United States within the last 100 years.

Till this day, any Japanese who associates with foreigners in Japan over a length of time, or who stays abroad long enough to pick up non-Japanese attitudes and mannerisms, is likely to be labeled as *gaijin kusai* (guy-jeen kuu-sigh), or "bad-smelling like a foreigner," and thereafter be discriminated against in some way.

The origin of the expression *gaijin kusai* is interesting. When butter- and meat-eating foreigners first arrived in Japan in the mid-1500s, their body odor was so powerful and so unpleasant to the Japanese that prolonged exposure to it made them ill. Thus from the beginning, foreigners in Japan were known by their distinctive smell. Soon thereafter, anything that the Japanese recognized as foreign, including attitudes, manners and products, was labeled *bata kusai* (bah-tah kuu-sigh), "smelling of butter," or *gaijin kusai*.

This built-in discriminatory faculty of the Japanese was heightened to a fanatical degree by the military during the 1930s when the use of English was prohibited. Words that had been derived from English were purged from the language, and the well-established Hepburn system of romanizing Japanese was shelved in favor of a Japanese system, the *Nihon shiki* (Nee-hoan she-kee), which often made no sense at all to foreigners. All foreigners in Japan were treated with paranoiac suspicion, as were the Japanese unfortunate enough to have anything other than pure black hair.

Japan's subsequent defeat in World War II, the military occupation of the country by several hundred thousand American and allied troops and civilian personnel, the influx of thousands of foreign commercial and diplomatic residents and from 1964 on, the mass exodus annually of millions of Japanese tourists abroad, the large numbers of Japanese businessmen and their families posted overseas, and the equally large numbers of Japanese students studying abroad, has not yet been enough to overcome the *gaijin kusai* mentality of the Japanese.

Till this day, one of the most serious social problems in Japan is the mental and physical abuse inflicted upon children who have lived and studied abroad, by their own schoolmates and often by their teachers as well. Like racial and religious prejudices throughout the world, Japan's anti-foreign feelings are so deeply embedded in the psyche of the people that it will, unfortunately, surely be several more generations before they will finally be diluted down to the point that anti-foreign feelings will no longer be a problem.

In the meantime, there are hundreds of thousands of individual Japanese who have been raised without anti-foreign prejudices, or who have essentially overcome whatever prejudices they inherited, and their numbers are growing.

See *Ato Aji.*

外柔内剛
Gai Ju Nai Go
(Guy Juu Nigh Go)

Soft Outside, Hard Inside

Pat McMahon, an actor and radio talk show host in Phoenix, Arizona, once posed a question to me that I remember well to this day because it got down to the crux of why the Japanese are often difficult for Westerners to understand and deal with on common grounds.

McMahon's two-part question, paraphrased, was, "Why are there so many contradictions in Japanese attitudes and behavior?" and "Why is it that the Japanese can be so cultured, knowledgeable, polite, gentle and generous on the one hand, and just the opposite on so many other occasions?"

The answer to McMahon's question appears very simple on the surface, but in reality it is quite complex. Japanese attitudes and behavior have traditionally been based on personal relationships and circumstances, rather than the logic, principles and the Christian concepts that have influenced most of the Western world.

In the traditional Japanese context of things, there is no absolute right or wrong. Everything depends upon the immediate circumstances; furthermore, many of the Japanese beliefs and customs that evolved from Shintoism, Buddhism and Confucianism are in direct opposition to Christian concepts. Japanese behavior, based on these traditional values, often contradicts Western concepts of rationality, human rights and common sense—and even decency.

Some of the more conspicuous attitudes and behavior of the Japanese that generally strike Westerners as contradictory involve the public consumption of pornography by men, and fertility festivals during which huge replicas of male and female sexual organs are paraded through the streets. The Japanese characteristic referred to by Pat McMahon, which is the one that most frequently misleads and mystifies

Westerners, primarily revolves around the differences between their individual behavior and their group behavior.

Individually the Japanese are indeed among the most polite, the kindest and the most generous people in the world, but in a group context, their values and motives are virtually the reverse. Their first priority is to protect and strengthen the group. To do this they automatically regard all other groups as competitors at best and as enemies at worst, and behave accordingly. While the Japanese group does its best to maintain a facade of internal and external harmony, its actions tend to be one-sided and as callous and ruthless as necessary to achieve its goals.

Another aspect of the character of the individual Japanese is described by the term *gai ju, nai go* (guy juu, nigh go), which means "soft on the outside, hard on the inside." This refers to the fact that Japanese culture conditions them to appear, in peaceful situations, soft and gentle, when inwardly they are tough, resilient and persistent in achieving whatever they set out to do.

Westerners, who are accustomed to dealing with what-you-see-is-what-you-get kind of people, are generally at a disadvantage when they come up against the Japanese. Too often the soft face of the Japanese results in Westerners suspending their critical faculties, and compromising their position and their goals.

The recommended response to the *gai ju, nai go* characteristic of the Japanese is to assume a similar mode of extraordinary politeness in an atmosphere that is totally devoid of any pressure or threat and persevere until you get what you want or what is really acceptable.

外来語
Gairaigo
(Guy-rye-go)

Words from the Outside

The Japanese language is a thing unto itself. There are a few ostensible similarities between Japanese, Chinese and Korean, but these similar characteristics are not among the original features of the language. They are things that have been added over the centuries.

When the Japanese adopted the Chinese system of ideographic writing between the 4th and 7th centuries, they maintained or only slightly changed the pronunciation of many of the ideograms. For example, the Chinese word for mountain is *shan* (shahn). The Japanese use the term *san* (sahn), as well as their own word, *yama* (yah-mah), for mountain.

When Portuguese, Dutch and English traders and missionaries began showing up in Japan in the 16th century, the Japanese very soon adopted a number of European words for things that were unfamiliar to them. For example, the Portuguese word for "bread" is *pan* (pahn), and until this day, *pan* is still the word for "bread" in the Japanese language.

Over the next several centuries, hundreds of additional foreign words were adopted into the Japanese language by the simple process of breaking them up into Japanese syllables and pronouncing them "in Japanese." The English word "bread," or *buredo* (buu-ray-doe), is also used in Japanese, for example, and "milk," or *miruku* (mee-rue-kuu), is used in addition to the Japanese word for milk.

During the nationalistic fever that developed during the war years from the late 1930s to 1945, the use of foreign words was forbidden by the Japanese government, resulting in a great deal of inconvenience for many people, particularly those involved in work or research using foreign technology. But when World War II ended, bringing on the "American period" in Japan, the Japanese penchant for importing and adopting foreign words really came into its own.

With some million or more American and allied military and civilian personnel thronging the Japanese islands, and with the proliferation of American films, English publications, and the introduction of thousands of concepts and things for which there were no native Japanese words, the Japanese began a wholesale process of simply turning foreign words into "Japanese" by the process described above.

The economic boom that began in Japan in the 1950s and lasted for over 30 years was a special catalyst, resulting in the importation of thousands of technical terms that were "Japanized" and added to the Japanese vocabulary.

Today, more than ten percent of all the words making up the day-to-day vocabulary of the Japanese consist of imported words, mostly English, that are known as *gairaigo* (guy-rye-go), which literally means "foreign language" or "imported words."

It is practically impossible for a Japanese to talk for more than a few minutes about almost anything without using one or more of these imported and Japanized terms. In all business categories, but especially in high-tech areas, the Japanese could hardly communicate without *gairaigo*.

But even though Japanese is peppered with English words, it does not mean that English speakers automatically know ten percent of the Japanese language. Without substantial experience and effort, the foreign words that have been Japanized are totally meaningless to foreign ears. Who would know, or even guess, for example, that the abbreviated *risutora* (ree-suu-toe-rah), a very popular term, means "restructuring," that *purei boru* (puu-ray boe-ruu) means "play ball," or that *rienjiniaringu* (ree-in-jee-nee-ah-reen-guh), usually shortened to *rienji* (ree-in-jee), means "reengineering"? Many of Japan's popular magazines have foreign-language titles and *gairaigo* in almost every sentence. *Gairaigo* is the mainstay of much of the electronic and print advertising in Japan.

One of my friends, who had no ability at all in "genuine" Japanese, could speak *gairaigo* or say English words as they are pronounced in Japanese with such expertise that he could communicate to a surprising degree.

Since there are no full ideographic characters for many of the foreign words, they are normally written in a script called *katakana* (kah-tah-kah-nah), making them instantly recognizable in Japanese-language texts. Japanese advertisers often use foreign words written in this script to give their advertisements an exotic nuance.

我慢比べ
Gaman Kurabe
(Gah-mahn Kuu-rah-bey)

A Test of Wills

Japan's samurai class, which administered the country from 1185 to 1868, were trained in endurance and stoicism since the early years of childhood. This training included following very precise and demanding rules in practicing swordsmanship and other martial arts several hours a day for many years, and in conforming to an exquisitely refined personal behavior, which included eating sparingly, and enduring cold and other hardships.

The ultimate demonstration of endurance and stoicism for the samurai was committing ritual suicide, *seppuku* (sape-puu-kuu), or in more colloquial terms, *hara-kiri* (hah-rah-kee-ree). *Hara* means "stomach," and *kiri* means "cutting," and that is an exact description of how thousands of samurai dispatched themselves during Japan's long feudal age. *Hara-kiri* was common during this age because there were so many occasions when death was chosen by samurai as a way out of a difficult situation, or when death was demanded by the shogunate or one's own lord for both real and imagined transgressions.

In fact, ritual suicide by this method became so common during the Tokugawa Shogunate (1603–1868), that the government issued one edict after another prohibiting the practice. But the custom was so deeply integrated into the psyche of the samurai that they continued to practice it as one of their special rights.

The process of *hara-kiri* was simple but exceedingly painful and difficult to accomplish, because the ritual had precise rules—one of which was not to disgrace oneself by showing any sign of pain as the stomach was slowly and methodically sliced open. Official and formal suicides were always viewed by a panel of witnesses, and detailed reports were filed on the each of the ceremonial events.

The stoicism that was a primary characteristic of samurai warriors and their families was not unique to the samurai, however; the ordinary Japanese had traditionally lived simple, hard lives, and only the tough survived.

In more recent times, the traditional toughness and perseverance of the Japanese was demonstrated time and again by earthquakes, fires and wars. During World War II, American and allied forces were routinely astounded by the ability of young Japanese soldiers to survive on small amounts of rice and pickled vegetables for months on end, and then to fight to the death rather than surrender.

This tradition of endurance and perseverance is still very much alive in Japan today, particularly among bureaucrats and businessmen who see themselves as the Japan's last bulwark of defense against the outside world. However, virtually all Japanese are imbued with a competitive spirit that is expressed by the phrase *gaman kurabe* (gah-mahn kuu-rah-bey), which means "perseverance test" or "endurance match" between individuals or groups.

The Japanese will often go into a *gaman kurabe* mode at the slightest hint of any kind of personal challenge, whether it is in eating, drinking, playing a game of baseball, or whatever. the Japanese simply do not like to be outdone or lose at anything, and generally they will go to extremes to prevent that from happening.

Young university students often engage in drinking contests and do not stop until they are senseless.

Businessmen out on the town at night with coworkers, clients or potential customers demonstrate their strength, spirit, endurance and perseverance by how much they drink. On numerous occasions I have advised newly arrived American businessmen to pace themselves when they go out at night with their Japanese contacts and hosts, and to not get caught up in the endless *gaman kurabe* exhibitions, only to see their innate machismo take charge, making them drink themselves sick.

Japanese businessmen, diplomats and politicians engaged in negotiations see the negotiating challenge as a *gaman kurabe,* and like their samurai and soldier ancestors, they commit themselves to endure and to persevere in the face of all odds. Such matches often come down to who can drink more tea or coffee, sit longer, and say the least.

Interestingly, the Japanese do not necessarily like to engage in *gaman kurabe.* They do it because it is "the Japanese way," and because they expect it of each other, and generally no one is willing to break ranks and dispense with the custom.

In fact, foreigners going into negotiating sessions with the Japanese can often win points by announcing up front that while they respect Japanese culture, they prefer not to engage in a *gaman kurabe* and respectfully recommend that everyone forego the custom.

我慢強い
Gamanzuyoi
(Gah-mahn-zuu-yoe-ee)

Suffering the Unbearable

When Japan's Emperor Hirohito (1901–1989) called upon his people to accept unconditional surrender to the United States and its allies at the end of World War II, he asked them to "bear the unbearable."

For a people who had been fiercely independent throughout their long history as a nation, and had never lost a war, the defeat and near-total destruction that Japan suffered in World War II had to be a traumatic experience of indescribable proportions. And yet the people of Japan not only endured, they came back stronger than ever, and within 20 incredible years had not only recovered, but had surpassed all of their prewar achievements.

In the next decade, the Japanese went on to become the second largest economy in the world, an accomplishment that was unprecedented, and which astounded even the Japanese, who, despite the shock of their defeat, still had a rather high opinion of themselves. There were many factors involved in Japan's phoenix-like rise from the ashes of World War II, not the least of which were massive infusions of technology and money from the United States and elsewhere. But most of the credit belongs to the character of the Japanese themselves, and particularly to their ability to endure when faced with seemingly overwhelming obstacles.

Emperor Hirohito's request that the Japanese bear the unbearable may strike Westerners as remarkable—as a singular moment in the history of Japan, and as something that went far beyond normal human experience. But that was not the case at all. Bearing the unbearable, or coming very close to it, had, in fact, been commonplace in Japan for centuries, and had become institutionalized under the broad term *gamanzuyoi* (gah-mahn-zuu-yoe-ee), which includes the notions of "strong forbearance," "strong perseverance," and "strong patience."

Japan's traditional political and social systems, in which the rights of the government to stay in power and maintain peace took precedence over all human rights, made it imperative that the Japanese be extraordinarily patient, develop the ability to persevere against all odds, and suffer stoically in the process.

Gamanzuyoi could be called the glue of Japan's traditional culture, for it was what held Japanese society together, what made it work, and what was responsible for its greatest efforts, whether they succeeded or failed.

All of Japan's most famous arts, crafts and aesthetic practices, as well as its ideographic system of writing, required enormous amounts of *gamanzuyoi*. The accomplishments of Japan's samurai warriors and those of its soldiers were founded in *gamanzuyoi*.

In modern-day Japan, both the educational and the business management systems would disintegrate were it not for the continuing willingness and ability of the Japanese to *gamanzuyoi*. And till this day, when the Japanese are asked to make a list of their most distinctive, admirable and important character traits, *gamanzuyoi* is invariably somewhere near the top of the list.

But little by little, the Japanese are becoming fed up with enduring the unendurable, and a growing number of voices can be heard saying they are not going to put up with it any more. As with so many of the other cultural traits of the Japanese, however, *gamanzuyoi* will remain a distinguishing characteristic for a long time, and will continue to be a factor in all of their international relationships.

Foreign businesspeople and politicians alike should be forewarned that any success they may have in dealing with the Japanese can only come about after taking their long tradition of *gamanzuyoi* into account, and they must be prepared to come up with equalizing strategies.

元号
Gengo
(Gane-go)

Keeping Track of the Years

Keeping track of the years in Japanese history can be confusing because several systems have been used simultaneously, including systems based on era names, the reigns of individual emperors, and during the Edo Period, the names of reigning Tokugawa shoguns. The most important era names in early Japanese history are the Asuka Period, which is generally said to have begun in 660 B.C. and to end in A.D. 710; the Nara Period, 710–794; the Heian Period, 794–1185; the Kamakura Period (which marks the beginning of the Shogunate Period), 1185–1333; the Muromachi Period, 1333–1568; the Azuchi-Momoyama Period, 1568–1600; and the Edo Period, 1600–1868. During the Edo, or Tokugawa Shogunate Period, there were 15 shoguns.

The last one, Yoshinobu Tokugawa, reigned some months in 1867 before the shogunate system fell.

Japan's modern history begins with the restoration of Emperor Mutsuhito as the symbolic ruler of the country on October 23, 1868, which according to the old Japanese calendar was the eighth year of Keio. Up until this time, the reign of each emperor had been marked by as many as five or six different *gengo* (gane-go), or "era names," that were adopted in succession, meaning that calendars had to be changed each time the era name changed, because each one started over at year one. There have been 231 *gengo* since the year 645.

Shortly after Emperor Mutsuhito was moved, at the age of 15, from Kyoto to Edo, the new government decreed that only one *gengo* would be assigned to each imperial reign. When presented with a choice of names the new young Emperor Mutsuhito chose Meiji (May-e-jee), which means "Enlightened Rule." During this period, all years were given in terms of Meiji, beginning with Meiji 1.

When Emperor Mutsuhito died in 1912, he was succeeded by his son, whose era was named Taisho (Tie-show), "Great Lawfulness." Next came Emperor Hirohito, whose reign was designated as Showa (Show-wah), "Enlightened Peace," which turned out to be the longest imperial reign in the history of the country. His son, Emperor Akihito, was crowned on January 7, 1989. His reign was named Heisei (Hay-e-say-e), which means "Peace and Prosperity."

Soon after the Meiji Restoration in 1868, the Japanese who were involved in international affairs began using the Western calendar for designating years, but the *gengo* system continued to be required under the terms of the old Imperial Household Law. When the Imperial Household Law was revised following the end of World War II, no mention was made of either the *gengo* or the Western system of counting years, and since that time both systems have been used.

As early as 1946, various groups in Japan began advocating that the *gengo* system be legalized. But the American-dominated occupation authorities objected to the idea because of its association with the emperor system. In the 1980s, new legislation was submitted to the Diet to once again give the *gengo* system legal standing. This legislation included the proviso that only public agencies would be expected to formally adopt the *gengo* system, while ordinary citizens could use whichever system.

The two groups that are the most vehement in their opposition to the *gengo* system are communists and socialists. They say that officially recognizing the system would be tantamount to restoring divine status to the emperor.

In present-day Japan some people use both systems, depending on whether the reference is to a date associated with a personal matter or a public matter. Most official documents are dated with the *gengo* system, and publishers of the Japanese language magazines and books usually use the *gengo* system. This means that foreigners who are involved with Japan must generally be familiar with both the Showa and Heisei Eras in order to function smoothly. The vast majority of the older Japanese who do not have anything directly to do with international matters are more likely to use only the *gengo* system in their references to years.

The *gengo* eras since the fall of the Tokugawa Shogunate are the Meiji Era, 1868–1912; the Taisho Era, 1912–1926; the Showa Era, 1926–1989; and the Heisei Era, 1989 to present.

議事録
Gijiroku
(Ghee-jee-roe-kuu)

Keeping Things Flexible

In old Japan, anyone accused of a crime was generally considered guilty until proven innocent, and justice naturally favored those in power. In any altercation, all parties involved were subject to punishment, regardless of the innocence of any of them; all were considered guilty of disturbing the peace and making problems for the authorities.

Decisions by city magistrates and others with the power to judge people and order punishment were generally not defined by laws, but by precedent, prevailing circumstances, and the character and motives of those passing judgment. In this environment, bringing disputes of any kind to the authorities at any level was a last resort that most people went out of their way to avoid.

Businesspeople in particular were sensitive about making themselves conspicuous to the ruling powers because there was no significant body of law to protect them. Both regional and national authorities could handicap or confiscate private businesses on any number of pretexts.

Furthermore, behavior in Japanese society in general was based on situational ethics, rather than unchanging principles, with the result that all relationships, personal as well as business, depended on arbitrary factors that changed with fortunes and circumstances.

Japanese society is now based on laws of principle, but these laws continue to reflect traditional values and are normally interpreted with far more flexibility than similar laws in the West. The Japanese still believe that absolute laws pertaining to human relations—which includes business, of course—are irrational and often inhuman as well, and they continue to do their best to avoid legally binding obligations.

While legal disputes are becoming more and more common in Japan, they are still looked upon as representing a failure in both morality and common sense, and generally involve considerable loss of face. Among other things, when two companies go to court, it invariably means that both sides have to reveal a great deal of information about their internal affairs, and in cases that attract the attention of the press, media reports often add to the volume and kind of information that is made public—both of which continue to be anathema to most Japanese companies.

One of the ways Japanese enterprises avoid lawsuits, and at the same time give themselves maximum flexibility in their relationships with other companies, is to refer, in disputes, to *gijiroku* (ghee-jee-roe-kuu), or "meeting minutes," rather than to binding contracts. *Gijiroku*, which are notes taken at meetings, are not binding under Japanese law, but they generally cover both the main points and the parameters of a business relationship, providing the direction in which the participants want to go.

This, say the Japanese, is enough to guarantee that both sides will do their best to live up to an understanding, and that detailed contracts are not only unnecessary, but are generally a hindrance, since any relationship should evolve with changing circumstances. This attitude is based on the assumption that both sides will live up to any verbal commitments—something that has a long and honorable history in Japan. But it also has a typically Japanese twist that tends to frighten outsiders.

In the Japanese context of things, a commitment is valid as long as it serves the needs of both parties. If a commitment ceases to serve the needs of either side, it can be arbitrarily changed or terminated by either side. This, say the Japanese, is just common sense.

The Japanese are acutely aware that most foreigners "live" by contracts, and cannot do business without them, and the Japanese routinely sign contracts with foreign firms. But negotiating these contracts is generally very time-consuming and frustrating for both sides, as each tries to include its own values and interests.

Non-Japanese should keep in mind that the Japanese do not regard contracts as carved in stone, regardless of how detailed it be, or how strongly it is worded. Furthermore, after a contract is signed, foreign businesspeople must be prepared to engage in continuous "negotiating" dialogue to keep the relationship balanced.

See *Atarimae*.

互助、互譲
Gohjo / Gojoh
(Gohh-joe / Go-johh)

Cooperating and Compromising

One of the Japanese negotiating techniques that foreigners generally have extreme difficulty dealing with is the strategy of waiting to the very last moment—or more likely than not, waiting until after a contract has been agreed to and signed—and then suddenly asking for one or more major concessions which they say they must have in order to honor the agreement.

These virtual demands for additional concessions are invariably couched in terms of an emotional description of how much the Japanese side would suffer if it abided by the terms of the contract—an institutionalized role-playing tactic that is commonly described as being a *naniwabushi* (nah-nee-wah-buu-she).

In its historical sense a *naniwabushi* is a sad, tear-jerking story often told in a song that touches the hearts and souls of the Japanese. In its modernized "business" sense, *naniwabushi* is a carefully planned and crafted ploy to win additional advantages after a deal has been cut, and when the other side is not likely to back out. From the Western viewpoint this tactic is deceitful and dishonorable, but it has been culturally sanctified in Japan for ages, and is generally accepted without undue malice—although those who are trapped by the ploy will likely reserve the right to take some advantage of their own sometime in the future.

A more basic concept in the Japanese art of negotiating and dealing with each other at all times is subsumed in the twin terms *gohjo* (gohh-joe) and *gojoh* (go-johh), which literally mean "cooperation" and "compromise," and which refer to compromising one's own desires or demands in order to cooperate in a mutually beneficial relationship.

Misunderstandings and friction frequently result between the Japanese and foreigners attempting to establish a professional relationship because of different cultural conceptions of the meaning of compromise. Westerners are, of course, familiar with the idea of compromising their positions in order to achieve part of their goals, using the justification that it is better to get part of what you want than nothing.

Gojoh has the same nuance in Japanese, but it also goes well beyond a trade-off that is controlled by a sense of fairness, equality, goodwill and mutual trust. *Gojoh* includes a strong personal element that revolves around mutual friends, mutual interests and common goals, and often results in a relationship being very lopsided, but mutually acceptable.

When evaluating a potential relationship, the Japanese generally look for the personal element first—for example, they are interested in whether they have former classmates in a company, or whether there are any family connections with the business. When the Japanese are able to use a personal approach in their attempts to establish business relationships, they are able to immediately take advantage of a much stronger likelihood that the other party will be more susceptible to both compromise and cooperation, and they can also call on these personal connections to keep a relationship going smoothly.

Internationally oriented businesspeople in Japan are gradually absorbing some of the Western concept of an objective approach to corporate relationships. But they cannot eliminate more than a token amount of the personal and emotional aspects of their culture without denying the culture altogether, and losing the ability to function effectively in their own country.

Foreigners dealing with non-Westernized Japanese businessmen have no viable choice but to adapt some of their attitudes and behavior to the Japanese culture in order to succeed in Japan's business environment. This simply means that the corporate relationship, to last and to go as smoothly as possible, must be based on relatively intimate personal contacts among several key individuals—contacts that are given the highest priority and continuously nurtured.

Such personal relationships are vital to the Japanese because they represent the most virtuous kind of behavior, and are the Western equivalent of being logical, fair, sympathetic and generous.

五十日
Gotobi
(Go-toh-bee)

Picking the Best Days

On several days each month in Japan's larger cities, the number of cars and trucks on the streets increases to the point that traffic noticeably slows down, often causing jams that last for hours. These days are not cultural or political holidays or special days, but these busy days have their origin in a business custom that goes back for thousands of years in Asia.

It has long been the custom for Asians to try to close all pending business before the end of the year, including paying and collecting bills, in order to start the new year with a clean slate. When commerce began to expand during the early decades of Japan's long, peaceful Edo Period (1603–1868), Edo merchants took this custom of year-end clearances several steps further, designating a number of days during the month for closing out accounts. These days, which came to be known as *gotobi* (go-toe-bee), or "fifth and tenth days," were the 5th, 10th, 15th, 20th, 25th and 30th of each month, days ending in "5" or "0."

There is no historical explanation for why the Edo merchants designated so many *gotobi* days in a month, but it is presumed that they did not want to extend credit for more than five days at a time in order to reduce the possibility of losses. Another factor that no doubt contributed to the development of the system was the old custom of selling goods on the basis of five-day *yakusoku tegata* (yah-kuu-soe-kuu tay-gah-tah) or "promissory notes"—Japan's earliest form of credit.

In any event, it became the custom for smaller businesses of all kinds to pay bills and salaries, deliver goods and collect bills on these days. Traffic increased substantially on these days, because it was customary for all such transactions to be carried out in person by the owners or representatives of the businesses concerned.

Following the end of the Edo Period in 1868, and with the introduction of industrialization to Japan, the large corporations that grew out of small commercial concerns continued the *gotobi* practice of paying and collecting bills. Among other things, the *gotobi* custom turned newly industrialized Japan into a paradise for accountants, makers of *soroban* (soh-roh-bahn) or "abacuses," small print shops that produced ready-made billing forms, and bill collectors.

As late as the mid-1980s, well over 95 percent of all the bills issued in Japan were still promissory notes, some of which did not mature for 180 days, and the *gotobi* system was still in effect; almost the only significant modern-day change in the *gotobi* custom is that larger companies now generally do their paying and collecting on the 25th and 30th, making these the busiest days of the month.

Foreign businesspeople who are new to Japan should keep the *gotobi* dates in mind, particularly the 25th and the 30th, because these are unusually busy days for Japanese businesspeople, and it is common for them to avoid making appointments or other commitments on these days. Foreigners in Japan can get some much needed cultural mileage out of letting their Japanese contacts know that they are aware of the *gotobi* custom, and that the Japanese may want to keep these days free.

逆輸入
Gyaku Yunyu
(G'yah-kuu Yune-yuu)

Reverse Importing

Soon after Japan began to emerge as an economic superpower, the government passed legislation authorizing individual Japanese to engage in *kojin yunyu* (koe-jeen yune-yuu), or "private importing," as a measure to help stifle criticism of the country's virtually closed consumer market. According to the law, individuals could import merchandise with up to a value of 35,000 dollars per shipment, as long as it was for the importer's private use.

When the law was passed, the government assumed that the total value of imports that might be brought into the country as *kojin yunyu* would not amount to more than a few million dollars a year, and would therefore be of no importance in the overall scheme of things.

What the government did not anticipate was the huge numbers of Japanese who would shortly thereafter begin traveling overseas as tourists, where they took advantage of the opportunity to buy well-designed and well-made items that could be bought overseas for as little as 20 percent of what they cost at home, if the product had gone through normal import and distribution channels in Japan. The Japanese marketplace at that time was so regulated that it was possible for a camera manufacturer to export cameras to a foreign country, then re-import them into Japan and sell them for a lower price than the same items could be sold if they had gone through regular domestic channels.

Another factor that the government did not foresee was the appearance of mail-order catalogs and catalog centers, and the growth of international parcel delivery systems, which made it possible for the ordinary Japanese to order items from overseas as easily as they shopped by mail-order in Japan.

By the late 1980s, *kojin yunyu* had become an important category of imports flowing into Japan from around the world, inspiring a number of entrepreneurs to begin importing directly and discounting their prices far below those maintained by domestic retailers, and helping to bring pressure on the Japanese government to further deregulate the market.

But there was one other type of import that was to have an even more important impact on the Japanese economy; this type of importing is known as *gyaku yunyu* (ghee-yah-kuu yuhn-yuu) or "reverse importing," also sometimes translated as "re-importing." *Gyaku yunyu* refers to products manufactured outside of Japan by Japanese companies, and imported into Japan.

In 1988, the Honda Motor Company became the first Japanese auto maker to import cars into Japan from its US plant in Ohio, an event that was major national news for days. Unknown to the general public, however, the *gyaku yunyu* volume entering Japan was already a vital factor in the overall economy. By the mid-1980s, a large percentage of virtually all the electrical and electronic products for which Japanese companies were famous, including radios, TV sets, tape recorders, electric fans, and radio cassette players, were being manufactured in Southeast Asia, and were exported to other countries as well as to Japan.

Matsushita Electric Industrial Company and other electrical appliance manufacturers were the first to begin manufacturing abroad and to engage in *gyaku yunyu* in order to take advantage of the strong yen and cheap labor in Malaysia and other Asian countries. With the bursting of Japan's "bubble economy" in 1990, the stream of Japanese manufacturers going overseas became more of a flood, resulting in an enormous expansion of the volume and importance of *gyaku yunyu* in the Japanese economy.

By the mid-1990s, Japanese manufacturers were being warned that *gyaku yunyu* could end up being one of the key factors that could eventually topple Japan from its enviable position as the only Asian superpower. These soothsayers warned Japanese manufacturers that by transferring technology to their foreign plants and training foreign managers and workers, they were creating competitors, while at the same time they were hollowing out Japan's industrial infrastructure.

In the meantime, the volume of *gyaku yunyu* going into Japan has continued to increase, and has developed a momentum of its own, following exactly the same pattern established earlier by American and European companies.

肌が合う
Hada ga Au
(Hah-dah gah Ah-oh)

Our Skins Meet

The Japanese and Westerners face an extraordinary challenge in dealing with each other because there is a fundamental difference in how they view and measure the world at large. Generally speaking, the Japanese view of reality is based on a sense of beauty, harmony and sentiment, while the Western view is based on more tangible things, such as a sense of the good and the bad, the desirable and the undesirable, the practical and the possible.

While the Japanese are gradually accommodating themselves to the rational, pragmatic, principle-based Western way, most of their attitudes and behavior are still colored by their traditional culture, which is different enough from the Western way to be the direct source of much of the friction and misunderstanding that occur between Japan and the rest of the world.

One of my encounters with the distinctive values and viewpoints of the Japanese occurred in Yokohama in the 1950s when I was interviewing a silk dealer. The dealer was not interested in my reaction to his merchandise. He wanted to know if I thought the creek-bed stones that made up a miniature garden in the lobby of his building imparted a warm, harmonious feeling.

Typically, the first Japanese reaction to any situation is sentimental or emotional. Whether or not it goes beyond this point depends on many factors, and if the right emotional buttons are not pushed in the correct order, a relationship generally will not develop very far. This is not to suggest that the Japanese are incapable of hard, pragmatic reasoning. They most certainly are, as it has been so dramatically demonstrated in history. But the process by which they plan and implement pragmatic projects is done within the context of personal feelings, and with objective principles coming second.

Among the key words that delineate and describe the emotional facet of Japanese culture, one of the most expressive is *hada* (hah-dah), or "skin," which is used in a literal sense as well as in reference to human relationships and behavior in general.

The Japanese have traditionally referred to a "meeting of the skins" rather than a meeting of the minds. In other words, meetings or agreements or relationships that satisfy human feelings come first, and ideologies or philosophies come second, if at all. In this cultural context, agreements are not necessarily rational or pragmatic from an objective Western viewpoint, because the primary Japanese goal is to satisfy the emotional needs of both parties.

Three of the most common "skin" expressions are *hada ga au* (hah-dah gah ah-oh), *hito hada nugu* (ssh-toe hah-dah nuu-guu), and *hada wo yurusu* (hah-dah oh yuu-rue-sue). *Hada ga au* literally means "the skins meet." In colloquial terms, it refers to a situation in which people get along well together; their skins are compatible, making it possible for them to work together as a team.

Hito hada nugu literally means "to take off one layer of skin," or to do everything possible to help someone. *Hada wo yurusu* means "to consent to or to allow someone to use your skin," or to trust someone to the point that you allow them to "wear" your skin.

The use of *hada* in this way is a result of the close, personal intimacy that is involved in Japanese relationships. Expressed in another way, the Japanese tend to be linked and bound together more by their feelings than by ideas—feelings come first in Japan. It is this Japanese need for physical contact that is at the heart of all the face-to-face meetings and business relationships, and it is why it is imperative for foreign businesspeople to make frequent visits to Japan if they want to keep their relationships with the Japanese in good working order.

The same need is also responsible for the custom of visiting offices of business contacts on numerous non-business occasions during the course of a year, and to congratulate people when they are promoted or get married, to express condolences when a family member dies, and at New Year's, to thank associates and friends for their business and to request the same for the new year.

Foreigners should keep in mind that "skin contact" in Japan does not refer to shaking hands or deliberately putting one's hands or arms on another person. But "skin" in this sense refers to feelings that are shared by coming together, eating together, drinking together, and discussing issues and achieving a consensus as a group.

励ます会
Hagemasu Kai
(Hah-gay-mahss Kigh)

Encouragement Parties

Few people have ever managed to get more out of the yin and yang of the universe than the Japanese. As has been stated so many times, Japan is a land of contradictions. People are either exquisitely polite or maddeningly rude; either abjectly humble or outrageously arrogant; either scrupulously honest or shockingly dishonest—all depending on the circumstances.

As a society that was conditioned by centuries of oppression under authoritarian regimes in which the people had no voice in government, and in which there was no body of human rights protected by law, the Japanese did not develop a universal morality based on unchanging principles. Their morality was based on political and social expediency, which could change with the context. And nowhere are the contradictions in Japanese culture more glaringly obvious than in the relationships between big business and politicians, though this is something the Japanese do not have a monopoly on.

From the beginning of Japan's modern era in 1868, the Japanese government and big business have been inseparably entwined—commercially, financially and socially. Until the last decades of the 20th century, the Japanese government virtually acted as the chairman of the board of large corporations, with various ministry bureaucrats exercising as much control over the companies as boards of directors. This incestuous relationship resulted in one scandal after the other, and was the impetus for the passage of a Political Funds Control Law in 1975, which was designed to prevent corporate executives from donating more than 1.5 million yen to the election fund of any politician or candidate for public office.

Not surprisingly, as a result of the law, donations went "under the table," and were disguised in various forms. The leading politicians went right on collecting millions of dollars every year in "contributions" that were invariably payoffs for government contracts.

There was one interesting side effect produced by the law, however. Incumbent politicians and candidates began holding fund-raising parties, called *hagemasu kai* (hah-gay-mahss kigh), at leading hotels. *Hagemasu kai* literally translates as "encouragement meeting" or "encouragement party," and the term is indicative of the Japanese penchant for using euphemisms and other code words for any affair or situation that is sensitive.

Since 1975, all national elections in Japan have been preceded by hundreds of *hagemasu kai*, during which the lobbies and banquet rooms of Tokyo's luxury hotels overflow with Diet members and their aides, candidates, lobbyists and corporate executives. For several weeks before the *hagemasu kai*, the secretaries and supporters of candidates sell tickets to the affairs. Well-to-do individuals and representatives from major corporations are expected buy tickets and to make large contributions.

By the early 1990s, some overseas companies in Japan had begun to work on developing close relationships with government officials, and foreign managers found that attending *hagemasu kai* offered their companies a special opportunity to publicly nurture such connections.

恥じらい
Hajirai
(Hah-jee-rye)

The Shyness Syndrome

It occurred to me a long time ago that the primary reason why so many Western men made the long and perilous trip to Japan in the 16th century, and again in the 19th and 20th centuries, was not because they were attracted to the arts or crafts of the country, or to the ability of the people to copy Western products and make improvements on them, or to the potential for converts to Christianity. The real reason was the subtle and seductive attraction of young Japanese women.

I came to this conclusion for three reasons. First, I myself was smitten by the magnetic attraction of young Japanese women almost from the day of my arrival in Japan, and I just as quickly discovered that virtually every other Western male who was in Japan at that time also succumbed to the unusual charms of the women. Second, it was obvious that Western men were not attracted to Japan by the personality, character, talents or accomplishments of Japanese males. And third, at least in the early years, the bureaucratic and authoritarian government made the official side of life in Japan anything from unpleasant to very precarious.

As time went by, I discovered that there were a number of elements involved in the attraction that young Japanese women had for foreign males, and one of the key ones was the peculiar kind of shyness of the women, combined with an apparent naivety and a very conspicuous naturalness when it came to their physical feelings.

Japan's traditional culture programmed girls to behave in a shy, *hazukashii* (hah-zuu-kah-she-e) or *hajirai* (hah-jee-rye), manner, to the point that shyness was equated with both morality and being Japanese. Any girl who did not behave in the prescribed manner was regarded as delinquent.

The shyness of young Japanese women, it turns out, is a powerful attraction for men; probably because it implies passivity, naivety, virginity and vulnerability—all characteristics that Confucian-oriented Japanese men traditionally regarded as the epitome of femininity in young, unmarried women and therefore shyness was required in their upbringing. What also interested foreign men was that while Japanese girls acted very shy on the one hand, they were at the same time regarded as sensual.

Young Japanese women are no longer deliberately programmed to behave in a shy manner; however, enough of the *hazukashii* legacy of the past still permeates the culture, and the women absorb sufficient quantities of it so that this characteristic distinguishes them from Western women.

Japan's *hazukashii* syndrome was not solely a female characteristic. In the past, Japanese men as well were conditioned to behave in a shy manner—to be reserved, modest, demure and quiet in the presence of others, especially their superiors. Both Japanese women and Japanese men typically describe themselves as shy when it comes to interacting with foreigners, particularly when they are called upon to speak English or other foreign language, or to participate in any kind of public dialogue or debate. The shyness element is, in fact, discernible throughout Japanese culture—from the everyday social behavior of people to advertising in the marketplace; there is a certain subtlety and modesty that is required in Japan.

But there is also a flipside to male shyness in Japan. In certain settings and in certain areas of Japanese life, Japanese men seem to forget their shyness and go to extremes in the opposite direction. They use sex-charged and abusive language and behavior toward young women, become aggressive and loud, and openly display and read pornographic magazines in the presence of women of all ages. In fact, in cabarets and other nighttime entertainment places, men break virtually every rule of traditional Japanese etiquette.

Being *hazukashii* is therefore a selective characteristic, and going from one extreme to the other is natural for the Japanese. But it can be a challenge for uninitiated foreigners, witnessing the exotic and fascinating on the one hand, and coarse and shocking behavior on the other hand.

鼻持ちならない
Hanamochi Naranai
(Hah-nah-moe-chee Nah-rah-nigh)

Looking Down on Foreigners

There has always been an elitist and arrogant element in Japanese culture. The Japanese myth of creation attributes the formation of the Japanese islands and the birth of the Japanese race to a pantheon of divine beings, and throughout most of Japanese history, people were taught the religious concept that they and the Japanese islands were special, that their gods looked after them and were their protectors and guiding lights.

This religious indoctrination, which, of course, is similar to that of Judaism, Christianity and Islam, did not end until 1945, and its legacy is still a discernible part of the psyche of the Japanese.

The Japanese belief in their divine origin and destiny came close to being shattered by their defeat in World War II. But their subsequent comeback in less than 30 years as the world's second largest economic superpower restored the traditional feeling among many Japanese that they are indeed a superior people.

Generally speaking, this feeling of superiority is primarily confined to specific elements in Japanese society, including certain members of government, certain successful businesspeople, selected educators and other professionals and hard-core nationalistic groups who support the emperor system.

Most ordinary lower- and middle-class Japanese have to work too hard, sacrifice too much, and put up with too much, to continue to believe that they are inherently superior to other people in any way. Furthermore, since Japan achieved superpower status in the 1980s, a sufficient number of setbacks have occurred to convince most people that their successes were as much a matter of happy circumstance as they were their own doing.

But elitist and arrogant behavior remains common enough on all levels of Japanese society that it is a significant factor in the lives of most Japanese, and this behavior also has a direct impact on Japan's international affairs.

Individual Japanese who demonstrate arrogant behavior toward other Japanese, as well as toward foreigners, are often referred to as *hanamochi naranai* (hah-nah-moe-chee nah-rah-nigh), which might be loosely translated as "someone who doesn't smell right"—in other words, a "stinker" who treats other people arrogantly.

The persistence of *hanamochi naranai* behavior in Japanese society became major news and the subject of a great deal of debate during the 1980s and 1990s as the number of foreigners in Japan—especially foreigners from Southeast Asia and the Middle East—spiraled upward. Prior to this, the most conspicuous foreigners living in Japan were Caucasians, who were not numerous enough to have a significant effect on society, and they were generally treated with courtesy if not respect. When large numbers of Iranians, Filipinos, Thais and others began flocking into the country, generally to work illegally, the etiquette and hospitality of the Japanese gave way to overt and arrogant discrimination.

The *hanamochi naranai* that is displayed toward Americans, Canadians, Europeans and other Westerners in Japan is generally subtle and covert, although it is fairly common for Westerners to be openly refused housing or entry into a club or massage parlor because they are foreign. In fact, it often seems that the *hanamochi naranai* syndrome lies latent in the stomach of virtually all Japanese who regularly come into contact with foreigners, because it can emerge unexpectedly and in unexpected ways from people who otherwise are the epitome of tolerance and goodwill. The reason for this is probably because the Japanese who have not become totally Westernized generally cannot feel comfortable when dealing with foreigners. There is almost always a certain amount of strain, uneasiness and suspicion that keeps the Japanese on edge, tires them and makes them susceptible to being critical.

Another factor that often seems to be at play is that when they are in groups, the Japanese—like other nationalities—often reaffirm their identity and brotherhood by ritualistically contributing derogatory comments about foreigners.

Where *hanamochi naranai* behavior toward other Japanese is concerned, it is mostly exhibited by people at a higher social level toward those below them, and by government officials and ranking members of professional organizations toward outsiders in general—all of which has been traditional in Japan from the earliest times.

花木
Hanamoku
(Hah-nah-moe-kuu)

Debauchery on Thursday Nights

During the 1960s and 1970s, the Japanese earned the seemingly well-deserved label of "workaholics"—an epithet that was primarily used in a negative sense because of the flood of exports from Japan that had begun to drown industries in other countries.

While the Japanese of that period did work ten to 14 hours a day, six and seven days a week, the "workaholic" label was not completely accurate, and was even misleading when used to describe the everyday behavior of the Japanese.

By the summer of 1953, only a year after independence had been returned to Japan by the allied occupation powers, there was a thriving nightlife in Japan's towns and cities. The more than 2,000 hot-spring spas and resort areas of the country were crowded with revelers nightly, and packed with people on weekends and holidays.

Throughout Japan, the hundreds of red-light districts and thousands of massage parlors were flourishing, and virtually every company in the country took its employees on two- or three-day recreational trips at least once a year. All of these activities and more had been traditional in Japan since ancient times, and especially since the peaceful and relatively affluent decades of the Tokugawa or Edo Period from 1603 to 1868.

Until around 1986, the busiest time for Japan's hundreds of thousands of bars, cabarets and night clubs was Friday evening, which had come to be known as *Hanakin* (Hah-nah-keen), "Flower Friday" or "Golden Friday." *Hana* means "flower," and *kin* is the "Fri" in "Friday."

On Friday evenings, huge numbers of Japan's several million salaried workers, particularly the men, who by then had gone on a five-day workweek, stayed out on the town eating and drinking until their favorite nightspots closed. Hundreds of thousands of salaried workers combined eating and drinking with mahjong, still one of the most popular pastimes in the country. The revelers would then use the weekends to recover from hangovers, lack of sleep and exhaustion.

But the growing practice for workers to reserve Saturdays as well as Sundays for both leisure and personal activities began to put a crimp in *Hanakin*, and by 1987 a new term, *Hanamoku* (Hah-nah-moe-kuu), came into popular use.

Moku is the "Thurs" in "Thursday," so *Hanamoku* is "Flower Thursday" or "Golden Thursday," and is used to denote the fact that large numbers of salaried workers were going out on the town on Thursday nights instead of Friday nights. As more and more Japanese joined the affluent middle-class, getting out of town on weekends became a national pastime, which made *Hanamoku* even more popular among those who did not want to give up their age-old custom of patronizing the country's colorful and exciting entertainment districts.

Another feature of weekend entertainment that had become significant by this time, the short trips were primarily to Guam, Taiwan, Hong Kong and South Korea. Most of these packaged tours started on a Friday evening, and lasted until late Sunday evening or early Monday morning. In the latter case, the weekend travelers went from the airport directly to work.

The addition of *Hanamoku* to the ritualized bar-hopping of low- and middle- ranking Japanese managers became another burden to some foreign businessmen who resided in Japan. Those who could not decline invitations to go out on Thursdays often ended up with hangovers on Fridays instead of on the more convenient Saturdays. But *Hanamoku* did not limit the opportunity for business visitors in Japan from experiencing the nightlife, because Japanese hosts do not feel nighttime entertainment should be reserved for a particular day of the week, in spite of the meaning of the term *Hanamoku*.

Today the largest and most popular entertainment districts in Tokyo, Nagoya, Kyoto and Osaka are generally filled with revelers virtually every evening except Sunday nights, when they are closed, and Monday nights, when they are less crowded than usual; for most people, however, the other nights of the week are just as good as *Hanakin* and *Hanamoku*.

Only two events seem to discourage large nighttime crowds at the entertainment areas of Japan: unusually heavy rain and holidays, such as the New Year period from December 30 to January 5, and Obon (Oh-bone) in July, when the Japanese traditionally visit shrines, temples and their ancestral homes.

反省
Hansei
(Hahn-say-ee)

I Won't Do It Again!

It is generally accepted that confession is good for the spirit and soul, and some people believe that Christianity has gone so far as to make the admission of sins a prerequisite for enjoying the blessings of the Church and the assurance of reservations in heaven.

Western justice, however, has never been as lenient as Japanese justice in its treatment of people who confess to wrongdoing. On the contrary, law enforcement agencies in the West put a great deal of effort into getting people to confess to crimes in order to justify punishing them. In Japan on the other hand, the treatment of people who confess to unlawful activity has been much more Christian. A confession and an expression of regret have traditionally been accepted in Japan as satisfying some of the demands of society for the punishment of miscreants.

This irony can probably be traced to the differences between Japanese gods and the God of Christianity. Japanese gods have traditionally been rather human in their behavior, suffering from many of the weaknesses of us mortals. No doubt as a result of their human characteristics, Japanese gods have been more generous and forgiving in their attitudes toward human transgressions. The primary requirement of Japanese gods is that people guilty of misbehavior or of failure to fulfill their obligations must demonstrate *hansei* (hahn-say-ee), or "self-reflection."

In Japanese philosophy, it is assumed that sincere *hansei* will result in the recognition of guilt and the resolve to do better in the future. This presumption suggests that the Japanese opinion of humanity is significantly higher than that which exists in most Western cultures.

Hansei has been institutionalized more-or-less across the board in Japanese society—in interpersonal relationships, in the justice system, and in the business community as well. If an individual in a company makes a mistake, he or she is generally not singled out for some kind of sanction. Instead, a group effort is made to find out why the mistake was made, and to institute changes in the system that will preclude such mistakes in the future.

Managers who continue to make mistakes are invariably called upon by their employees to *hansei*, and to thereby correct their thinking and their behavior. Groups of Japanese frequently come together in *hansei kai* (hahn-say-ee kie), or "self-reflection meetings," in an effort to find out what they are doing wrong, or to improve on their success by reflecting on their way of thinking and doing things.

Foreign businessmen, politicians, and diplomats who are dealing with Japan and want to bring about substantive changes in a relationship might do well to approach the challenge in the form of *hansei kai*—something that the Japanese fully understand and appreciate.

If a person is unfortunate enough to be accused of wrongdoing by the Japanese, the first and most important thing to do is to apologize, even if there is no guilt—in which case an apology for causing a flap is expected.

If a person is guilty, in any sense and to any degree, the person should announce that he or she will engage in some form of self-reflection in repentance, or *hansei shimasu* (hahn-say-ee she-mahss).

八方美人
Happo Bijin
(Hop-poe Bee-jeen)

Keeping Your Slate Clean

Success in the Japanese workplace has traditionally been defined as not drawing critical attention to oneself, not getting into any trouble, and incremental promotion slowly up the management ladder; and one of the key commandments for this kind of success is, "Never make a mistake." Obviously, the best way to avoid making mistakes is to do nothing or to do as little as possible on one's own, which is not as impractical as it sounds where Japanese companies are concerned, because acting individually has traditionally been taboo.

Much of the "company" character and behavior of individual Japanese—behavior which Westerners often find irritating—derives from the "never make a mistake" commandment. This behavior keeps employees from making proposals on their own; prevents them from making clear, decisive responses to proposals from anyone, whether from inside or outside the company; and generally precludes them from taking a strong, personal position on any subject.

There are a number of cultural reasons for this cautious behavior. One of these reasons is that the group orientation of the Japanese means that a mistake made by an individual member of the group reflects badly on the entire group. Another reason is that this same group orientation makes it "wrong" for individuals to take any action on their own, because individual action would usurp the rights and responsibilities of the others to act as a collective.

Until recent times, anyone in a Japanese organization, of any size, who acted on his or her own, was subject to serious punishment, ranging from being ostracized from the group to dismissal, or something more drastic.

Today the punishment for such behavior is likely to be more subtle, but equally damaging to an individual's career in the organization. What most often happens is that the other members of the group no longer trust and support an individual who has acted alone. Management takes note of the transgression. Advancement slows down or stops altogether. Assignments become less important or meaningless. This situation forces most Japanese employees to behave as *happo bijin* (hop-poe bee-jeen), which means "everybody's beauty," or "pretty to everyone."

The bursting of the "bubble economy" in Japan in 1990 and 1991 and the subsequent recession resulted in a movement away from the *happo bijin* syndrome. Leading Japanese businessmen, educators and others began publicly criticizing the passive conformity of ordinary employees and managers alike, calling on them to become individualistic and aggressive, and warning that Japan could no longer compete with the rest of the world unless people at every level were free to give full rein to their creativity and energy.

These calls were received positively by virtually everyone in Japan, giving the impression that the whole workplace was going to flip-flop and become a hotbed of individual creativity and entrepreneurial effort. But with some well-publicized exceptions, which involved companies owned and operated by noted mavericks of long-standing, the overall effect was minimal. Group orientation and collective responsibility are so deeply embedded in the culture of most Japanese corporations that there was no way significant changes could occur on a large scale in a short time.

It is therefore likely that the *happo bijin* syndrome will be a conspicuous feature of Japan's corporate culture for at least one or two more generations, and will continue acting as a brake on the kind of "foreign-style" freewheeling behavior that most Japanese admire intellectually, but are unable to emulate.

In the meantime, foreign companies doing business with and in Japan will continue having to learn how to deal with the Japanese who are *happo bijin*.

腹の虫
Hara no Mushi
(Hah-rah no Muu-she)

A Worm Told Me

In Japanese and other Asian cultures, the stomach or abdomen has traditionally been considered the center of one's being or life, and in that sense this area of the body is the equivalent of the mind or the heart in a Western context. In its Japanese context, the abdomen is the source of temper, courage, resolve, generosity, pride, and so on, as well as being the site of an instinctive or telepathy-like ability that makes it possible for some especially skilled people to read other people's minds. This mind-reading ability is known as *haragei* (hah-rah-gay-e) or "the art of the belly," and is one of the most important human relations skills in Japanese culture.

Hara no mushi (hah-rah no muu-she) literally means "stomach worms": *hara* means "stomach" and *mushi* means "worms." But figuratively it refers to a "sixth sense," or in more colloquial terms, "gut feelings," and is one of a number of colloquial expressions in Japanese that are based on this meaning of *mushi*.

The Japanese equivalent of "a little bird told me" is "a worm (or bug) told me," *mushi ga shirasemashita* (muu-she gah she-rah-say-mah-sshtah). The full expression would, of course, be *hara no mushi ga shirasemashita* or "a stomach bug told me."

Mushi ga shirasemashita is frequently used in reference to a premonition about the future—a job transfer, a promotion, or some other event.

One of the more peculiar uses of *mushi* is in the compound *mizu mushi* (me-zuu muu-she), which literally means "water bugs," but is the Japanese term for "athlete's foot."

Describing someone as *hara ga okii* (hah-rah gah oh-keee), literally "having a big stomach," actually means that the person is big-hearted, and the description is therefore complimentary. When *okii*, "big," is used with the other word for stomach, *onaka*, the combination may mean "to be pregnant" in certain contexts, and "to be fat" in others. There are many other Japanese expressions using the word *hara*, including the following common idioms.

Any time one is angry, discontented, disappointed, or when a person instinctively dislikes someone, the cause is often attributed to *hara no mushi*. A common expression used to explain why someone is disliked is *mushi ga sukanai* (muu-she gah sue-kuu-nie) or "my worm doesn't like that person." When someone is upset and cannot do anything about it, the feeling is described as *hara no mushi ga osamaranai* (hah-rah no muu-she gah oh-sah-mah-rah-nie), "my stomach worm will not or cannot calm down."

Being in a bad mood may also be attributed to one's "worm" being in the wrong place: *mushi no idokoro ga warui* (muu-she no ee-doe-koe-roe gah wah-rue-ee).

Knowing and using these terms as the Japanese use them can be an asset for a non-native in Japan, because it clearly demonstrates that a person is familiar with and interested in some of the more colloquial aspects of their culture and that the person wants to understand the Japanese. Because of the exclusivity of their culture, the Japanese have always automatically assumed that foreigners could neither understand nor appreciate Japanese food, Japanese thinking, or the Japanese way of doing things, and are invariably surprised and delighted when they do.

Given this circumstance, foreigners visiting Japan for the first time can assure themselves of winning some respect and approval by learning a few basic phrases such as those above.

臍を曲げる
Heso wo Mageru
(Hay-soe oh Mah-gay-rue)

Bending the Bellybutton

In the world of the Japanese, the stomach has traditionally played many of the roles that Westerners assigned to the heart. From ancient times, the Japanese believed that the stomach—not the heart—was the center of one's being. It was the stomach that the Japanese looked to in their efforts to understand other people—something that was referred to as *haragei* (hah-rah-gay-e), or "the art of the stomach."

Until recent times, most Japanese men wore a band of cloth called *haramaki* (hah-rah-mah-kee) wrapped around their stomachs in the wintertime keeps them especially warm. And, of course, when Japan's feudal-age samurai were called upon to commit ritual suicide, *hara-kiri* (hah-rah-kee-ree), it was the stomach they cut open.

Because of the importance of the stomach in Japanese life, there are numerous sayings and colloquial expressions that refer to this part of the body. For example, when people get angry, their stomachs are said to "stand up," or *hara wo tatsu* (hah-rah oh tot-sue).

One of the most meaningful, and somewhat humorous, of the common references to the stomach, is *heso wo mageru* (hay-soe oh mah-gay-rue), or, literally, "to bend the bellybutton." Because the stomach is seen as the site of human emotions, any tinkering with the *heso*, or "bellybutton," can have serious consequences. "Bending the bellybutton" refers to hurting someone's feelings, something to which the Japanese are extraordinarily susceptible; offended sensitivities are responsible for an enormous amount of suffering on the part of the Japanese, and on the part of victims of the Japanese at war.

One of the most famous incidents in Japanese history—the saga now known as "The Forty-seven *Ronin*"—is the story of a relatively minor provincial lord whose *heso* was bent by a high-placed official in the shogun's court. When the angry lord drew his sword and attempted to avenge the insult, he was taken into custody and ordered to commit suicide. Upon his death, the lord's fief was confiscated by the shogunate, and as a result of this, the lord's samurai retainers became *ronin* (roe-neen), or "masterless samurai," and vowed to take revenge against the official.

One year later the *ronin* raided the official's mansion in Edo, captured him, cut off his head, and took it to the grave of their lord. They then surrendered to the government, and killed themselves when ordered to do so.

Dealing with the Japanese, and especially managing them, is difficult because extreme care must be taken to avoid "bending" anybody's navel. The propensity of the Japanese to feel that their bellybuttons have been twisted is often a special problem for foreign businesspeople in Japan, because the Japanese who feel emotionally offended ordinarily do not speak up and openly complain about it.

In Japanese companies, Japanese managers are generally sensitive enough to the nonverbal signals sent out by people who have been emotionally hurt to recognize the situation and to do something about it. The most common method of getting the problem brought out in the open is for the manager directly concerned to take the emotionally offended person to a bar or cabaret if it is a man, and to a coffee shop or restaurant if it is a woman, and in this ritualized setting discuss the situation and come to a mutually acceptable solution.

Foreigners who are not fully tuned to the cultural wavelength of the Japanese generally miss the usually subtle signs of a *heso* out of shape, and they may not be aware that someone has been slighted. If these situations are not quickly and effectively addressed, the injured parties continue to grieve in silence, with their anger building up as time passes. Eventually, they will do something to resolve the situation themselves. In some cases they simply quit their job without any explanation. In other cases, they carry out some kind of revenge against the persons they hold responsible.

This revenge may be subtle criticism of the responsible persons in an attempt to tarnish their image. It may also be an attempt to attract enough support from others in the same section or department to boycott the individual and eventually get the person fired or transferred. There have been many cases in Japan in which Japanese employees of foreign-owned companies, who felt slighted by their foreign superiors, have managed to make their superiors look so bad that they were eventually recalled by their parent companies.

It is essential that foreign managers who cannot recognize the symptoms of *heso wo mageru* have good enough relations with Japanese employees so that one or more of them will keep them informed of any problems regarding *heso wo mageru*.

被害者意識
Higaisha Ishiki
(He-guy-shah Ee-she-kee)

The Victim Mentality

Researchers into the psychology of the Japanese have identified a syndrome that they call "conscious innocence," by which is meant that no matter what situation the Japanese become involved in, whether it is social, business or politics, there is a national compulsion for them to believe that their position is the correct one even when they are at fault by every criterion one could imagine. According to this research, the Japanese position is always the honorable one, which means they are "forced" by their honor to automatically transfer the blame for their own transgressions onto their victims.

Japanese psychiatrists have noted that when the Japanese encounter any kind of business or political challenge they immediately assume a *higaisha ishiki* (he-guy-shah ee-she-kee) or "victim mentality," describe themselves as weak and defenseless, and accuse the other party of taking some kind of unfair advantage.

It is also noted that the Japanese can be totally rational in their thinking and presentations as long as they encounter no opposition. This factor routinely results in foreigners misleading themselves in their business and political negotiations with the Japanese, because at the onset of their meetings, they are quickly convinced that they can "do business" with their Japanese counterparts.

However when the Japanese encounter opposition their tolerance soon gives way to irrational accusations and behavior, which are subconsciously designed to make it possible for them to justify whatever strategy or tactics that are necessary for them to achieve their goals. In addition, the Japanese have traditionally relied on subterfuges and other various kinds of deception to win their battles and wars, whether they are military or economic.

A look at the history of Japan reveals that Japanese society as a whole has always operated on the *higaisha ishiki* concept, in situations varying from ordinary social and domestic business relationships to their international trade and diplomatic affairs, including past wars of aggression.

The most common reaction of the Japanese to any kind of resistance or criticism is that the opposing party does not understand their philosophy or their policies, and that as soon as the other party does understand, opposition to the Japanese position will cease, and they will become willing partners, because the Japanese policies are correct and therefore should prevail.

One of the most common "victim" rationales the Japanese use to justify their own one-sided trade policies is that Japan is a small country with few natural resources, and it cannot compete with other countries on even terms, and it should not be expected to do so. Because of this prevailing national consciousness, the United States in particular is often seen as being unfair to Japan—the feeling is that America is sometimes trying to hold Japan down and prevent it from developing all of its economic potential.

There are a growing number of Japanese in both business and politics who have overcome the victim mentality that has historically been such an integral part of their culture. But their overall influence in their companies and government ministries and agencies is minor.

Another factor that Westerners invariably encounter in their dealings with English-speaking and rational Japanese is that they must revert back to traditional Japanese thinking and behavior when they are dealing with their own coworkers, or risk ostracism. In dealing with situations like these, foreigners are advised to use Japanese techniques in handling their Japanese counterparts.

These techniques include personally lobbying each member of the Japanese team in after-hours meetings over drinks, golf or other recreational activities; doing special favors for individual Japanese in the group; and prevailing upon influential third-party Japanese to lobby the members and their seniors on behalf of the foreign side.

Foreigners dealing with the Japanese should always be aware of the Japanese compulsion to amass enormous amounts of intelligence about everything and everybody that might somehow have importance in the future, and to reveal as little information about their own operations as possible.

Being able to prevent the Japanese from automatically adopting a *higaisha ishiki* mode is a rare ability, but it is one that foreigners must develop if they are going to establish and maintain mutually beneficial relationships with Japan.

品格
Hinkaku
(Heen-kah-kuu)

The Mark of a Gentleman

In the 1880s, only a few years after the fall of Japan's last feudal dynasty, a Japanese businessman went to London to study the English banking system. While there, a British banker treated him kindly and helped him accomplish his mission. During the course of the relationship, the banker was introduced to, and developed a keen interest in, the tea ceremony.

When the Japanese businessman returned to Tokyo, he made arrangements at his company's expense for a Japanese *daiku* (die-kuu), or "carpenter," to go to London and build a teahouse for his newfound British friend. When the *daiku* presented himself at the British banker's home, the Englishman did not believe that the man was a mere carpenter. The *daiku* behaved like a gentleman. His behavior and demeanor in general were so meticulous, so refined, that the banker mistook him for an affluent member of Japan's upper class.

More than 100 years later, when Hawaiian-American Chad Rowan, wrestling in Japan's semi-sacred sport of sumo as "Akebono," won his second tournament and achieved the rank of *Ozeki* (Oh-zay-kee), or "champion," talk of his being elevated to the exalted position of *Yokozuna* (Yoe-koe-zoo-nah), "Grand Champion," began almost immediately.

However, key members of the Sumo Association, which controls the sport with iron discipline, opposed Rowan's promotion to the sport's highest rank, claiming that he did not exhibit a satisfactory level of *hinkaku* (heen-kah-kuu), or "dignity," which is so valued in Japanese society.

The English word "dignity" does not do justice to the full cultural connotations of *hinkaku* in its Japanese context. Dignified behavior in American society—much more so than in Europe, to be sure—leaves one with a fairly broad range of acceptable conduct, and does not necessarily signify any particular cultural achievements. *Hinkaku*, on the other hand, incorporates a degree of character, spirit and cultural propriety that raises the individual well above the ordinary person.

In the Japanese context, *hinkaku* is directly equated with virtue and morality. A *takai hinkaku no hito* (tah-kie heen-kah-kuu no hi-toe), or "person with great dignity," is humble, totally honest, trustworthy and can be depended upon to always do the right thing—albeit, the right thing in the Japanese context of right and wrong.

The Japanese have been conditioned for centuries to be sensitive to *hinkaku*, and to expect it of people in responsible positions. The higher and more important the position, the stronger are the expectations for that person to exemplify *hinkaku*.

A significant reason why the Japanese have tended to look down on Westerners, particularly prominent businessmen and political leaders, was that they did not demonstrate the qualities of *hinkaku* that the Japanese had come to expect. Even today, the foreign businessman or politician who fails to behave with an acceptable level of *hinkaku* (except when in the institutionalized setting of drinking parties at geisha houses, night clubs and other private places), suffers a serious loss of face that reinforces the general Japanese belief that theirs is a superior culture.

Foreigners who want to be accepted by the Japanese as sincere, virtuous, dependable and worthy as friends, allies or partners, are advised to make sure they exude an ample degree of *hinkaku*.

To complete the Chad Rowan-Akebono story, the American sumo wrestler won the January 1993 sumo tournament and so impressed the Sumo Association judges with his behavior that shortly thereafter he was unanimously confirmed as Japan's first foreign sumo grand champion—an event as auspicious as the marriage of Emperor Akihito, then the Crown Prince, to a commoner, Michiko Shoda, in 1959.

昼行灯
Hiru Andon
(He-rue Ahn-dohn)

No Light in the Eyes

There are few things more revealing of a society than the humor of its people, and in Japan attitudes toward life and death, government power, religion, morality, lifestyle—all may be grist for the humor mill.

Fortunately for mankind, humor allows people to live with ordinary human frailties, life's problems and disappointments. Humor is often the only recourse that people have against the irrationality, stupidity and cruelty of governments and religions.

Japanese society, with its feudalistic structure, detailed and strictly enforced etiquette, high aesthetic principles, emphasis on the status quo, and callous attitude toward human life, gave rise to an enormous volume and variety of humor because people's lives were filled with such extremes. But despite the many negative aspects of Japan's traditional culture, much of the country's early humor was surprisingly benign. Typically, favorite subjects for humor included sex, toilets, inept public officials, leaders who behaved like fools, and people who were occupied with their own self-importance.

Hiru andon (he-rue ahn-dohn) is a somewhat humorous reference to people who are not bright enough or capable enough to stand out, and are more-or-less invisible. The term is a play on *andon*, the Japanese word for "lantern" or "lamp," and on *hiru*, the word for "daytime".

Japan's traditional *andon* were made out of rice paper stretched over bamboo ribs. *Andon* with very thin paper were used indoors; those used outdoors were made of much thicker, sturdier paper. The light given off by an *andon* was fueled by burning rapeseed oil and was relatively dim at best; the light from a lamp inadvertently left on during the day could hardly be seen at all.

Thus the term *hiru andon*, or "daytime lamp," came to be applied to people who seemed to perform no useful function, and there was no way of telling if they had any skill or if they were important. A person labeled *hiru andon* is not necessarily a slow person; *keikoto* (kay-e-koe-toe) is the term reserved for someone with that characteristic. *Keikoto* is a florescent lamp, which takes longer to light up than a light bulb.

Not surprisingly, *hiru andon* people were most common in government offices because these offices were inevitably over-staffed and included a larger-than-usual number of incompetent people who had obtained their jobs through connections. The term *hiru andon* has survived the passage of time, and is now applied to people in business as well as in government.

Accurately identifying a *hiru andon* is not as easy as an outsider might expect. Foreigners visiting Japanese companies have been known to mistake the department manager for a "daytime lamp" because he seemed to do nothing except shuffle papers and drink tea. Exceptionally talented people who are more aggressive than Japanese cultural approves of, or who are regarded as misfits because they have spent too many years overseas, may be deliberately given so little work—or none at all—that they appear to be *hiru andon*. Also, when someone is likable and earnest, but simply incapable of doing demanding tasks, they are often tolerated and allowed to do piddling things, in effect becoming "daytime lamps."

The personality and behavior of typical Japanese are such that foreigners generally cannot judge their ability until they have been directly involved with them for some time. In the first place, there is almost always a mutual inability to communicate fluently in one another's language. And in the second place, the Japanese will not normally describe their qualifications in any kind of introductory scenario.

Furthermore, because they are required to work as team members and to refrain from speaking out aggressively as individuals, the competency or incompetency of a person is only gradually revealed over a period of time. As it happens, the cultural characteristics of the Japanese often result in foreigners misjudging their abilities and relegating the most competent and productive Japanese to the *hiru andon* status.

Another factor which contributes to the Western inability to judge a good manager in Japan is the fact that in the Japanese context of things, managers who do not stand out as especially able or aggressive have traditionally been regarded as the ideal because they more likely to be good team players.

ほめ殺し
Homegoroshi
(Hoe-may-go-roe-she)

Praising to Death

Prior to elections in Japan, the streets and byways of the country are filled with buses, trucks and vans equipped with loudspeakers which belt out the slogans and speeches of the candidates. Candidates themselves spend time in the vehicles, personally bringing their messages to voters via loudspeakers. On other occasions aides, young women, often those with high-pitched voices, supplement recorded messages with live appeals.

In major cities like Tokyo, the raucous noise from these portable "bully boxes" can be so intrusive that they are a major nuisance from early morning to late at night, and result in numerous complaints from the public.

The loudest and most intrusive of these political loudspeaker trucks and buses are those operated by rightist groups. Their vehicles are invariably the biggest and their speakers the loudest. When they are not shouting out messages, they play ear-shattering martial music.

Rightist loudspeaker buses regularly target government offices and the homes of political opponents, parking as close to them as the law will allow, and blaring their messages from morning to night. The police do not bother the rightists as long as they keep their trucks and buses at the required distance from their targets. Ordinary citizens complain indirectly about the presence of the rightists, but take no action against them because the typical rightist is a hard case who does not take any kind of interference lightly.

I have often been rudely awakened early in the morning by rightist loudspeaker buses cruising up and down my neighborhood, because some political bigwig lived nearby. Part of their strategy is to make everybody in the neighborhood dislike the politician because he is attracting the noisy rightists to the neighborhood.

Japan's rightists are also known for using a tactic called *homegoroshi* (hoe-may-go-roe-she) against political opponents. *Home* is from the word *homeru* meaning "to praise." *Goroshi* means "kill" or "killing," and *homegoroshi* means "to kill with praise"—to destroy a person's reputation by using half-truths, exaggeration, innuendoes and other subtle techniques.

A *homegoroshi* smear campaign against someone is especially conspicuous in Japan because, in addition to the annoying loudspeaker vehicles—as many as 20 vehicles may be assigned to "attack" one individual—the kind of behavior involved in the strategy is so "un-Japanese" that it further upsets the public. According to the news media and police reports, *homegoroshi* campaigns invariably involve one of the country's large organized criminal gangs, yakuza, who typically finance such activities and sometimes provide manpower as well.

In some cases, Japan's politicians are blamed for bringing such attacks on themselves because it has traditionally been common for them to have relations with one or more of the larger yakuza gangs, particularly the Yamaguchi Gumi, which is the largest, the Sumiyoshi Rengo and the Inagawa Kai groups, which have interests in so many businesses that it is almost impossible to avoid them.

Given the changes occurring throughout Japanese culture, politicians themselves will be using sarcasm and other forms of *homegoroshi* to put their opponents down in the near future.

保証
Hosho
(Hoe-show)

Who is Your Guarantor?

As already mentioned, I am a great fan of Japan's *chambara* (chahm-bah-rah) movies, the period films with much sword-fighting and ninja heroics. One *chambara* TV series popular for years featured a high city official with a large floral tattoo on his upper right arm and shoulder, and who had a secret life as a playboy/crime-fighting hero.

The storyline of each segment in the series was always the same. Encountering a murderous gang when in his playboy guise, the hero would best the lot in a grand sword-clanging finale—always after displaying his huge tattoo early in the fight. After soundly thrashing the gang by knocking them out or rendering them helpless with the back of his sword (he was not authorized to kill them), the hero would disappear from the fight scene just before the local samurai police arrived, and then reappear in the next scene in his real identity as the local magistrate, sitting in judgment over the assembled gang.

During the hearing, witnesses would be called in to testify against the bad guys, but it always came down to the word of the witnesses against the baddies, who would boldly begin to shout, "*Shoko! Shoko! Shoko wa doko?*" (Show-koe! Show-koe! Show-koe wah doe-koe?) "Proof! Proof! Where is your proof?"

Just when the gang appeared to be getting the upper hand with their shouts, the kimono-attired, very formal and correct hero would suddenly begin to shout back at them in the guttural vernacular of the streets. Then with a great swish of his elaborate kimono, the hero would bring his right arm and shoulder out of his beautiful costume in an equally grand flourish, revealing his tattoo in all of its glory, and yelling something like, "You cretins remember this, don't you!" The shocked gang members would suddenly realize that the magistrate and the notorious playboy who had defeated them were one and the same person. Their shocked expressions would then dissolve into resignation, and they would kowtow in complete submission.

New enterprises in Japan, whether Japanese or foreign, must also present proof of their credibility and reliability in the form of a *hosho* (hoe-show), which means, "security, guarantee or a warrant."

The foundation for all business relationships in Japan is the kind and degree of trust that creates "peace of mind," or *anshinkan* (ahn-sheen-kahn), one of the most powerful code words in Japanese culture. The only way newcomers or outsiders can establish an *anshinkan* relationship with a Japanese enterprise is by presenting an acceptable *hosho*, which includes evidence of financial stability, as well as good character and personal responsibility.

To further complicate matters, the Japanese have great difficulty accepting and working with individuals who are not members of recognized or readily identifiable organizations; and they have the same problem working with companies they do not know. This puts the lone entrepreneur and the representative of an unknown company in the same boat; that is, having to provide sufficient *hosho* to prove they are trustworthy, and can be relied upon to do all of the things that are necessary to avoid failure and not embarrass anyone.

One of the ways for the entrepreneur and newcomer to penetrate this *hosho* barrier is to first develop a network of contacts in banks and other businesses to give themselves substance, because in the beginning they are like the invisible man; people look right through them.

Major foreign firms coming into Japan naturally have an advantage, but their representatives must go through a similar qualifying, *hosho*-providing process. The foreign success of their companies is not automatically accepted as evidence that they can be trusted and will not fail in Japan. In fact, famous and successful foreign companies in Japan have probably failed as often as medium-sized and smaller firms, mostly because the larger firms did not do the things that are essential for building trust and peace of mind.

Like the gang on trial, the Japanese want to see sufficient proof. And regardless of who you are or who you represent, the first hurdle that you must cross in Japan is to prove that you, as an individual, are of sufficiently good character to deserve trust. Not surprisingly, establishing personal trust and corporate reliability in Japan takes money and time—from many months to several years. Generally, the larger the project and the more entities that are involved, the longer this process takes.

一見の客
Ichigen no Kyaku
(Ee-chee-gain no K'yah-kuu)

Turning a Blind Eye

Until 1868, Japan was divided into some 270 provincial fiefs, each of which was presided over by a *daimyo* (dime-yoe), or "big name," who ruled as a warlord. The larger, the more powerful, and the more distant the fiefs were from the shogunate capital of Edo, the more autonomy the warlords exercised, and the more they behaved like independent sovereigns.

Many of these fiefs were, in fact, successors of independent clan-centered kingdoms that existed prior to the ascendancy of the Yamato clan, which established the imperial system around the year 300, and which gradually extended its hegemony over much of the rest of the country.

In addition to their long histories as independent or semi-independent kingdoms, the fiefs of Japan were separated by distance, by bodies of water, by high and rugged mountains, and by a number of dialects—all of which hindered direct communication. Furthermore, the Japanese warlords were a jealous, antagonistic lot who guarded their borders viciously and controlled the movement of their own people as well as that of visitors.

With the establishment of Japan's last and most powerful shogunate dynasty in 1603, the divisions between fiefs and the control of travel became more exacting. The new shogunate sought to perpetuate its rule by further limiting the categories of people who could travel, by requiring that all travelers have official travel documents, by employing ninja agents and others to spy on the fiefs, and by taking numerous other measures to keep the fiefs divided and too weak to mount an attack on the shogun's castle headquarters in Edo.

All of these factors combined resulted in the Japanese becoming extraordinarily insular and group oriented, exceptionally wary of anyone outside of their own group, and overly sensitive to any difference in appearance, behavior and language.

The influence of these geographic, political and cultural elements remains visible in Japanese attitudes and behavior today, affecting not only personal relations, but domestic and international business and political affairs as well.

One area of this influence is expressed in the term *ichigen no kyaku* (ee-chee-gain no k'yah-kuu), which can be translated as "an unknown customer," and refers to the propensity of the Japanese to ignore or to give bad service to strangers.

Until as late as the 1980s, it was very common for Japanese companies to refuse to accept orders from customers, or to buy from suppliers, with whom they had not previously established an acceptable personal relationship involving introductions and a variety of social rituals designed to bind the two groups together. The syndrome still exists today, and is of particular importance when the outside contact is a foreign firm. The Japanese are naturally more wary of foreign companies, and generally require far more trust-building interaction before they commit themselves to a business relationship.

Developing an acceptable relationship with a foreign company is more complicated for the Japanese than most Westerners presume. Because the Japanese experience, standards and expectations are different, they cannot quickly or easily judge the sincerity, honesty, trustworthiness, or the skills of individual foreigners. Because their communication skills are also usually limited—and the Japanese are generally required to speak the language of the foreigners in order to communicate with them—they are doubly handicapped in dealing with the non-Japanese.

Obviously, foreigners wanting to work for or do business with the Japanese should take these factors into consideration, and not expect too much too soon.

意表を衝く
Ihyo wo Tsuku
(Ee'h'yoe oh T'sue-kuu)

Springing Surprises

The Japanese, especially businesspeople and government officials, do not like unanticipated events or developments, and they are generally at a loss when the unexpected occurs because they have been so conditioned to plan and control every facet of their existence that it is difficult or impossible for them to react quickly to unanticipated situations.

Conversely, the Japanese also find it very difficult to stop a project after it is started, because doing so generally involves reaching a consensus among the many people involved, all of whom may have different opinions. This consensus-seeking necessity in Japan played a key role in prolonging World War II for more than a year after it was obvious that Japan was going to be defeated.

But as usual, there is a contradictory pattern of behavior that is also characteristic of the Japanese. While they do not like surprises themselves, *ihyo wo tsuku* (ee'h'yoe oh t'sue-kuu), or "surprising," others is one of their favorite strategies.

Knowing full well their own weaknesses in responding too quickly to unexpected developments, the Japanese routinely take advantage of the same weakness in others to gain some kind of benefit or profit for themselves.

Foreigners who have not dealt with the Japanese before are especially vulnerable to *ihyo* because it seems so out of character for the Japanese. The foreign side goes into meetings expecting the Japanese to be quiet, polite, formal and very business-like—which they always are to begin with. But the *ihyo wo tsuku* tactic is one of the oldest tricks in the Japanese art of negotiating, and they are very skilled at using it. Not surprisingly, it is generally used by the side that is in the strongest position.

There are a number of common *ihyo wo tsuku* gambits that Japanese business-people, diplomats, bureaucrats and others commonly use to throw their counterparts off-balance, and give themselves some kind of edge. These gambits include a sudden and unexplained announcement that they are withdrawing from the negotiations; bringing in a new and totally different proposal just when it seems that the parties have reached an agreement on the original agenda; suddenly accusing the other side of bad faith and unacceptable practices; announcing that they have found the same technology, product or service somewhere else at half the price.

Other negotiating ploys include the sudden necessity to get the approval of some government agency, although no indication of this requirement had been previously brought up; introducing a newcomer into the negotiating group and asking the other side to redo its entire presentation—a maneuver that can happen two, three or more times, and which almost always results in position "adjustments."

When both of the negotiating parties are Japanese, they are naturally aware of the possibility of a *ihyo* being sprung on them. If that should happen, the Japanese recognize that the other side is angling for a major concession of some kind, and that it is up to them to shift into a damage-control mode to avoid having to give up too much in order to put the negotiations back on track. The "surprised" party almost always has an automatic, standard response. They show great shock and dismay, and then go into a song-and-dance that if the negotiations do not proceed according to the original agenda, their company will suffer severe damage.

The smaller and the weaker the "surprised" company is, the more likely its negotiators are to claim that its existence will be put in jeopardy if they give up too much at the negotiating table.

These protestations and claims are invariably voiced in a controlled, but very dramatic manner; on many occasions the weaker group of negotiators humble themselves and literally beg the other side not to "kill" them. This institutionalized drama continues for some time, then generally both sides alter their positions to the point that the dialogue can be resumed and quickly concluded.

Foreigners going into negotiating sessions with the Japanese, especially representatives of large corporations, should, of course, always be prepared for the possibility of a *ihyo*.

One strategy that has worked when the "surprise" is obviously calculated to win a concession is to have something in reserve that can be offered in exchange for something from the Japanese side. It is always better to ask for something in return in order to keep the illusion of reciprocal balance in the relationship, even if what is requested is of little substantial interest or benefit.

いいとこ取り
Ii Toko Tori
(Ee Toe-koe Toe-ree)

Taking Only the Good

When the Japanese are asked to explain why and how a small country like Japan was able to become a world-class economic power in less than 30 years, they have a long list of ready answers. Most of these answers have to do with cultural attitudes and habits that have traditionally distinguished them from other people; their virtual obsession with form, order and etiquette; their group orientation and group loyalty; and their extraordinary diligence in their work, among other things.

The Japanese attribute these traits to a subtle mix of Shintoism, Confucianism, Zen Buddhism, and to a variety of other ingredients for which there is no known source.

One Japanese attribute for which there is no identifiable origin has been their willingness—almost obsession, in fact—to adopt both customs and technology from foreign countries, without any damage to their own culture.

Several times in the history of Japan, the latest being the 1950s, there have been determined efforts by Japanese leaders to replace much of Japan's traditional culture with foreign patterns of behavior.

This 1950s movement was especially pronounced in Japan's business world, but it failed dramatically. In fact, none of the movements ever succeeded to any significant degree, and in almost every case they eventually ended with the old ways being reaffirmed and strengthened.

I do not mean to imply that the Japanese have not changed since opening their doors to the outside world in the mid-1800s. There have indeed been dramatic changes in their life-styles as well as in their fundamental beliefs. But despite these changes, their inner core—their Japaneseness—remains intact, thanks in large part to a factor that they call *ii toko tori* (ee toe-koe toe-ree), which literally means, "take the good part."

The Japanese explain that they have traditionally had the ability to select only the best from foreign cultures and civilizations, and then to transform whatever they have borrowed, giving it a purely Japanese essence that makes it totally compatible with their traditional culture.

The Japanese tend to consider themselves skillful at borrowing only that which would not disrupt or challenge any aspect of Japanese culture; foreign values or ideologies, for example, are eschewed, and anything foreign that is adopted here quickly becomes Japanese. This, however, is not a skill at all. Having little or no knowledge of the foreign cultural values associated with the products, technology, concepts or practices they import, the imports naturally come in value-free, and therefore they can be easily Japanized.

This is why the Japanese play "American" baseball according to Japanese rules, and why the Japanese operation of a company as purely American as McDonald's gets called *Makudonarudo* (Mah-kuu-doe-nah-rue-doe), and young Japanese believe that both hamburgers and McDonald's were invented in Japan.

It is also the reason why outsiders generally find negotiating and doing business with the Japanese difficult and frustrating. The Japanese may be using Western technology and terminology, and using English or some other foreign language to communicate with their foreign counterparts, but for the most part they are still on their own cultural channel.

Visitors to Japan who cannot see beyond or behind the facade of Westernism automatically assume that what they see reflects the rationalism and value systems of the West. This invariably results in misjudging and misunderstanding the Japanese, and thereby giving the Japanese an advantage.

Interestingly, in the 1980s the United States and a number of European and Asian countries began turning the tables on the Japanese by adopting their practice of *ii toko tori*, importing and adapting Japanese management and manufacturing processes to fit their own needs.

This turnabout behavior caught the Japanese by surprise, even though they were preaching the superiority of their ways and saying that Americans and Europeans should learn from them. They just could not bring themselves to believe that it would happen.

一気飲み
Ikki-Nomi
(Eek-kee-No-me)

Playing to Your Peers

Prior to the end of World War II, Japanese society was still feudalistic, and individual freedom was practically nonexistent. Virtually every aspect of peoples' lives, including many details of personal behavior, was controlled by law and by custom.

In terms used by sociologist/author Michihiro Matsumoto, the Japanese were like ants, programmed to serve the interests of the colony, and with little or no allowance for anything that would undermine this primary responsibility. From birth, young people were molded to fit and to follow their preordained roles, and only the rarest of individuals had the courage and will to break away from the mass and follow a personal path.

The military occupation of Japan from 1945 to 1952 by the United States and its allies, and the elimination of feudalistic laws by the American occupation forces paved the way for fundamental changes in the way the Japanese thought and behaved. But it was the personal examples of individual freedom demonstrated by the Americans themselves that had the most immediate and profound effect on the Japanese—and in particular on the young and the women.

But the force of Japan's traditional culture was so pervasive that it continues today to shape and control the Japanese to an extraordinary degree, and is a significant obstacle to their being able to express themselves as individuals.

One of the ways many young Japanese today rebel against their still restrictive social system is to drink themselves into an alcoholic stupor in public displays known as *ikki-nomi* (eek-kee-no-me), which means something like "gulp-drinking." This practice is, of course, common in many societies—and particularly so among American university students—but it is especially conspicuous in Japan because it is such a departure from the formality and restraint exercised by the Japanese when they are not drinking. In *ikki-nomi* situations, the drinkers are spurred on by other members of the party shouting, "*Ikki! Ikki!*" in unison. The drinking invariably continues until the participants are helplessly drunk, and usually sick.

Another facet of drinking alcoholic beverages in Japan is the common practice of aggressively encouraging others to drink heavily at celebrations, parties, and at visits to bars and clubs. Foreign visitors frequently get caught up in this custom, and in an attempt to avoid slighting their hosts they drink to excess.

Fortunately, excusing yourself by saying that you are allergic to alcohol, or that you are under doctor's orders to refrain from drinking, is acceptable. Many people with this condition drink anyway, however, because not being able to drink is a serious handicap in the Japanese business world. Curiously, an unusually large number of Japanese are allergic to alcohol.

Regardless of what the excuse is for not drinking, some over-enthusiastic hosts do everything but physically force guests to drink—over any amount of protest. Visitors in Japan who are moderate drinkers or non-drinkers are almost always put to the test.

一匹狼
Ippiki Ookami
(Ee-pee-kee Ohh-kah-me)

Japan's Lone Wolves

Some years ago in Osaka, I was introduced to a young Japanese entrepreneur who had established a small chain of shops selling cowboy clothing and accessories imported from the American southwest. When we exchanged name cards, I was immensely amused to note that he had replaced his Japanese name with "Lone Wolf." I asked the young man if that was in fact his name, and he assured me it was, and that he not only used it in his business contacts, but that his friends also called him "Lone Wolf."

I didn't have to ask him why he had chosen this popular American term as his name. I knew that it was a total repudiation of all of the attitudes and customs making up the traditional Japanese way, and represented everything he wanted to be. Still, it was both amusing and fascinating that he had gone to what amounted to an extraordinary extreme to rid himself of his Japanese identity and to declare himself to be something that was, even at this late date, alien to the average Japanese.

I asked him how he got by with using such an odd name, and he gave me an answer that I should also have already known. He did all of his business with young people, who also wanted to be and were trying to be different in order to escape from the racial and cultural sameness of being Japanese.

There is more to the story and more behind the name the man gave himself. "Lone wolf" translates into Japanese as *ippiki ookami* (ee-pee-kee ohh-kah-me), and *ippiki ookami* is the prevailing jargon for a person, usually a man, who has totally opted out of the groupism and the consensus-building team approach that has been characteristic of Japanese life for centuries; or the person may be a company employee who exhibits strong go-it-alone tendencies and is famous—or infamous—for his un-Japanese-like behavior.

Ippiki ookami began to appear in small numbers in Japan as early as the 1970s, but it was the decade of the 1980s that saw their numbers grow into the thousands and begin to attract positive attention from the Establishment.

These new "lone wolves" invariably made their mark in areas where they did not have to work with anyone else to achieve results—mostly in computer programming, activities using computers, and other new businesses such as image-making and introducing innovative marketing techniques.

By the early 1990s, when Japan was still recovering from the bursting of the "bubble economy" of the 1980s, even the most traditional of Japan's corporations began to use the services of "lone wolf" experts, and to talk about the importance of individual initiative in the newly emerging economic world. Despite this public praise of individualism, however, the majority of Japanese corporations remained locked in the tight embrace of conformity and are generally incapable of tolerating "lone wolves."

A number of more courageous—and sometimes desperate—corporations have side-stepped the problems that would be caused if an *ippiki ookami* was actually turned loose within their own walls, by setting up small subsidiary companies for them and giving them free rein.

Some of the early marketing successes of foreign companies in Japan were the handiwork of Japanese "lone wolves" who broke virtually every rule in the Japanese book by creating new distribution lines and going around the barriers that normally kept foreign companies out. In fact, all Japanese managers who go to work for foreign companies must have some "lone wolf" in them in order to break away from the pack and depend only on their own talents and energy to survive.

For foreign corporations seeking to hire *ippiki ookami*, the challenge is to separate the losers who are out on their own because they failed to make it on the inside from the real "lone wolves" who chose to go it alone.

一歩間違うと
Ippo Machigau To
(Eep-poe Mah-chee-gow Toe)

One False Step and . . . the Sword!

During Japan's samurai-dominated feudal period, which began in the late 1100s and lasted until 1868, the various laws of the shogunate and the semi-independent clan fiefs, along with a wide range of unwritten codes and customs, were generally enforced with a harshness and finality that left no one in doubt about the dangers of behaving in an unapproved manner.

One of the government edicts passed shortly after the founding of the Tokugawa Shogunate, Japan's last great shogunate dynasty (1603–1868), made it legal for any shogunate samurai warrior to execute on the spot and without trial, any commoner found breaking a law or behaving in a disrespectful manner toward a samurai.

This regulation was known as *kirisute gomen* (kee-ree-sue-tay go-mane), which means something like "kill and toss in a 'sorry about that' comment and walk away." The samurai warriors of the some 270 clan fiefs that existed during the Tokugawa Period were quick to adopt the same practice.

Thereafter in the shogunate capital of Edo, which was then filled with warriors who no longer had any battles to fight, the killing of commoners by samurai became so common that the shogun was called upon to do something to stop the carnage. Some of the more arrogant samurai would get drunk and kill innocent passersby just to test new swords or show off their skill. Rather than repeal the law, however, the shogunate established a system of street corner *koban* (koe-bahn), or "police boxes," to help control the homicidal samurai.

Probably the most famous incident involving the practice of *kirisute gomen* occurred in 1862, when three members of the British Consulate stationed in Yokohama, two men and one woman, were out horseback riding one day and met the Lord of Kagoshima and his samurai retinue on the road.

The British diplomats failed to leave the road, dismount, and bow down, which was the custom when a provincial lord and his entourage were passing. The lord's samurai guards attacked the diplomats, immediately killing one man and wounding the other one. The wounded man and the woman managed to escape by spurring their horses away from the scene. Seven months later, in retaliation for the attack on the diplomats, a squadron of British gunships bombarded the clan's city of Kagoshima for three days, destroying large portions of it and killing an unknown number of people.

Long before this incident in Japan's history, behaving properly, which meant adhering to the very strict etiquette codes created by the samurai class, had become the established morality. In formal and official situations, the slightest deviation from the prescribed etiquette was treated as a very serious matter. More flagrant breaches of the system called for mandatory death sentences.

In addition to the importance of proper behavior in their personal manners, the Japanese for centuries had also been conditioned to strive for perfection in their work, and to avoid making any kind of mistake.

Since *ippo machigau to* (eep-poe mah-chee-gow toe), or "just one mistake," could be so devastating, it became characteristic of the Japanese to speak in vague terms, to emphasize flattery, to act only in concert with others, to avoid taking personal responsibility, and to copy and follow instead of lead.

Today, fear of making a mistake remains an important factor in the personal as well as professional lives of the Japanese, and most older people who have not been exposed to Western influences continue to exhibit, to a significant degree, all of the behavioral characteristics that were forged during the long feudalistic samurai age.

Westerners involved with Japan, particularly in business, invariably encounter this "fear of making a mistake" syndrome, along with all of its ramifications. Knowing something about its origins and influence may offer some solace to those having to deal with it.

色気
Iroke
(Ee-roe-kay)

The Sensuality of Japanese Women

It may have been silk, ceramics and other exotic Asian products that first attracted Westerners to China, Japan, Korea and other Asian countries, but once they reached these formerly distant and isolated nations, it was often the charms and availability of young women that kept them there. Virtually no story of Western men who spent time in Japan or other Asian nations during the first centuries of East–West contact would be complete without accounting for the influence that local women had on their lives.

This influence has not waned over the centuries. Shortly after the occupation of Japan officially ended in 1952, large numbers of importers from Europe and the United States began flocking to Japan to take advantage of cheap wages and the manufacturing talents of the Japanese. Even then, when these foreigners were in Japan as buyers and their Japanese suppliers did everything possible to cater to them, there were numerous problems, and in the earlier years many of the importers complained continuously about the lack of honesty, diligence and efficiency of their suppliers, often saying doing business with them just was not worth the hassle.

In my capacity as the editor of a trade publication covering Japan's export industries, I just as often asked these importers why they kept coming back if business in Japan was so much trouble. Practically all of them admitted it was because of the young Japanese women they had come to know.

Business and "public women"—those who work in the nighttime entertainment trades—have traditionally been intimately linked in Japan. The patronage of businessmen and politicians supported a huge infrastructure of red-light districts, assignation inns, hostess-staffed bars and cabarets and thousands of hot-spring resort spas.

Licensed red-light districts were outlawed in 1956. But their place was quickly filled by love hotels, bathhouses and other venues catering to the sex business, which reached its zenith in the 1960s and till this day is a major industry.

What was it about Japanese women that Western men found so attractive? The following, paraphrased, is what a psychologist friend (who took part in many of my bachelor adventures in Japan) has said on this topic:

"Great numbers of Japanese girls are the epitome of feminine cuteness and youth. They have a great deal of evident gaiety and playfulness. The undeniable attractiveness of this type for the Western man comes not from some sort of sensual appeal, but rather from a kind of subtle, innocence.

"The Japanese girl is brought up to react instinctively to the male with this air of innocence and admiration. She is extremely careful, even under the most trying circumstances, never to put a man's masculinity in doubt.

"To most Western men—and especially to the type who is unsure of himself sexually—this trusting innocence, this inviting naivety on the part of Japanese girls, has all of the direct and excitatory effects of an aphrodisiac.

"The trusting supposition of masculinity that this produces in men is its own proof. For both the Western man and the Japanese girl this can often be an unforgettable taste of honey."

Another and equally important aspect of the appeal that Japanese women have for Western men is that in Japan, sex has never been equated with sin or immorality. It has always been seen, and indulged in, as a normal activity that is essential for both mental and physical health. This attitude alone has a liberating affect on men raised in societies that view sex as forbidden fruit.

There are, in fact, a number of other attitudes as well as a number of physical attributes that combined to make many young Japanese women especially sensual. These include typically slender bodies with small hands and small feet, just enough color in their complexion to make them exotic, almond-shaped eyes that are exotic, and, often, long, loose hair, which is attractive to many men.

Iroke (ee-roe-kay) is one of the most interesting of the cultural code words relating to female charms. It refers to "pink," which is commonly used as a synonym for sensuality and sex, and often occurs in literary references to the first blooming of sensuality in young women.

The term may also be used in a business setting, in reference to a little *iroke*, or incentive to increase the appeal of a business offer or proposal.

一所懸命
Isshokenmei
(Ees-show-ken-may-ee)

Putting One's Life on the Line

Beneath the studied calm and deliberate movements that characterized Japan's traditional life-style for so many centuries, there was an enormous amount of tension which served to hold the society together on the one hand, but which also could be disruptive when the tension was suddenly released.

One of the sources of this tension was the constant threat of death under which most Japanese lived. Ordinary people were subject to being killed on the spot by rogue samurai, or by any warrior who was offended by them, or who thought they represented any kind of threat to their lord or to the shogun. Even the samurai themselves were not free from this fear. Samurai were obligated to give their lives—and often the lives of their family members as well—in defense of their lord and whenever it served their lord's purpose.

In addition to living with swords constantly poised over them, the Japanese were also required to live according to a system of etiquette that was so structured and formalized that it was like performing in a highly emotional drama at all times, with virtually no opportunities for them to leave the stage. And although the drama of Japanese life was extremely emotional, Japanese etiquette also made it necessary for people to suppress emotions and conduct themselves in the most serene and harmonious way, even when committing ritual suicide.

In a word, living the Japanese way was dangerous. People were required to stake their lives on their behavior, making such terms as *isshokenmei* (ees-show-ken-may-ee), or "to guard a place with one's life," very common and meaningful expressions.

Isshokenmei is still one of the most commonly heard expressions in Japan, but its meaning has changed somewhat. People who make a commitment to do something, or who are asked to do something, routinely emphasize their commitment by using the term in the sense of "I will do my best," or "I am doing my best": *Isshokenmei yarimasu!* (Ees-show-ken-may-ee yah-ree-mahss!)

Of course, the old connotation of staking one's life is still inherent in the use of *isshokenmei*, and the word remains characteristic of the Japanese attitude and approach to things. It is something like taking an oath, and in itself is another source of tension in Japanese society.

When the Japanese are on the receiving end of an *isshokenmei* commitment, their expectations are very high because it implies that the speaker will carry out the "do or die" implications of the word.

Foreign businesspeople interacting with their Japanese counterparts can judiciously use this word to emphasize their commitment to a relationship or project. But for it to be effective, it must be done within the context of *wa* (wah), or harmony.

One of the most important skills foreigners must develop in order to deal effectively with the Japanese, whether in business or politics, is learning how to function serenely in situations that are filled with tension. The "winner" in tense encounters is almost always the side that can maintain a harmonious mode and both outlast and outmaneuver the other side—strategies which are included in the term *isshokenmei*.

いただきます、ごちそうさま
Itadakimasu / Gochisoh Sama
(Ee-tah-dah-kee-mahss / Go-chee-sohh Sah-mah)

Thanks for the Hospitality

The Chinese treat eating as a celebration—a never-ending thanksgiving, and they approach the art of preparing, cooking and consuming food with unbounded gusto. The Japanese, on the other hand, have traditionally reacted to food and eating in a totally different way; generally speaking, there are four food traditions in Japan.

Japan's first food tradition is the original one developed by farmers and fishermen, and consists primarily of vegetables, rice and seafood prepared simply at home, and served without any special ceremony. Japan's second food tradition, developed by Buddhist monks, consists primarily of vegetarian dishes austerely prepared and served in small portions in keeping with the reserved nature of the religious order. Buddhist monks and temple guests are served this diet.

The third food tradition in Japan is known as *kaiseki* (kie-say-kee), and was developed by tea masters for guests before ceremonial tea. *Kaiseki* consists of miniature portions of vegetables and seafood, often boiled or dried. Nowadays, there are restaurants specializing in both Buddhist and *kaiseki* cuisine.

The most interesting of Japan's food traditions is the fourth one. This tradition is the one that was developed over the centuries for the hospitality industry; many of the dishes of this tradition originated in the kitchens of the early imperial and shogunate courts. This is the Japanese cuisine that is most familiar to the non-Japanese: sashimi, sushi, udon, soba, *yakitori* (yah-kee-toe-ree), *kushiage* (kuu-shee-ah-gay), *oden* (oh-dane), *unagi* (uu-nah-gee) and *oyako-domburi* (oh-yah-koe-dom-buu-ree), for example.

In contrast to the Chinese, who like a large variety of dishes, large portions, and a noisy, free-for-all atmosphere in restaurants, the essence of Japanese food is small portions, artistically shaped, and served on china and lacquer ware that is conspicuous for its beauty. Japanese table manners in fine restaurants—in contrast to banquet rooms or hot-spring spa dining halls—are as restrained and stylized as the food served. There is a precise etiquette for sitting, serving and being served, and eating.

The two "code words" *itadakimasu* (ee-tah-dah-kee-mahss) and *gochisoh sama* (go-chee-sohh sah-mah) are very important parts of the dining etiquette in Japan. *Itadakimasu*, said just before eating, literally means "to receive" or "to accept," but in this context it is an institutionalized term that has a ritual connotation, almost like a prayer. *Gochisoh sama*, which has the meaning of "thank you for the meal or drinks," is said after the completion of a meal, when leaving the table or shortly thereafter, to whomever has provided the meal, whether at a restaurant or at someone's home.

The use of *gochisoh sama* has also been sanctified over the generations and is expressed in a more-or-less ritualistic way, in tandem with *itadakimasu*. While both of these terms have been socially obligatory in formal situations for generations and are still universally used in Japan, they are also used in informal and casual situations, when they represent little more than thoughtful politeness. Whether the occasion is formal or informal, the words are very meaningful to the Japanese, and any failure to use them by a Japanese would be regarded as impolite or arrogant.

By the same token, the Japanese are pleased and appreciative when non-Japanese use these expressions, because using the two culturally important words is a very conspicuous indication that the foreigner has some knowledge of Japanese culture and is thoughtful enough to demonstrate it.

痛み分け
Itami Wake
(Ee-tah-me Wah-kay)

Sharing the Pain

One of the more traditional characteristics of American culture is that there are generally only two kinds of people. There are winners and there are losers, and little or nothing in between. This concept most probably came from the period of time when the European ancestors of Americans were hunters—when killing and taking all was the way of life.

In any event, it was the prevailing theme in American business as well as in politics from the time of the founding of the republic to the 1970s and 1980s, when Americans began to feel that the Japanese were ganging up on them, and it occurred to some that they could, in fact, learn something from the cooperative and sharing ways of the Japanese.

The Japanese, who credit their farm and village heritage for most of their cultural traits, naturally believe that their way of cooperating and sharing is the better way. The cooperative and sharing morality of the Japanese tends to be exclusive, however, and in practice, sharing and cooperation applies only to other Japanese. It is still not natural for the Japanese to equate other people with themselves.

This cultural feature—which is certainly not unique to the Japanese—has caused Japan a lot of trouble since the country began regular political and economic relations with other nations, and it is an ongoing factor in its present-day international affairs.

The flip side of the Japanese penchant for cooperating and sharing the good among themselves is a firm belief that when there is pain, everyone should share that as well. This concept is expressed in the popular business term *itami wake* (ee-tah-me wah-kay), which literally means "dividing the pain."

Itami wake is commonly used in reference to sharing losses and disadvantages, whatever they may be, including the disadvantages one party may have in negotiations; on such occasions, it is normal for the side that is being asked to give up the most to expect the other side to *itami wake*. Among the Japanese, the stronger side in negotiations will frequently agree to "share the pain," without being asked, as a conspicuous, but not unexpected, goodwill gesture.

In the Japanese view, the willingness of Japanese management to share the pain of economic hard times by not firing employees as readily as foreign companies do, their preference for rigging bids to make sure all the key Japanese players get a piece of the action, and their advocacy of industry-wide price fixing to guarantee market stability, are all positive aspects of their *itami wake* philosophy.

One of the reasons why the Japanese generally oppose the proliferation of foreign companies in Japan is a deep-seated fear that they will cause market disruptions and other problems, because foreign companies do not subscribe to the *itami wake* ethic. The Japanese tend to see the *itami wake* way as uniquely Japanese, or as so little developed in other countries that foreign businesspeople lack the necessary "sincerity" to follow the practice.

Foreign businesspeople can, of course, offset some of the traditional suspicions and fears of their Japanese counterparts by announcing at the beginning of any relationship that they are familiar with the *itami wake* custom and that they are prepared to follow it when there are rational, fair and legal reasons for doing so.

Letting your Japanese counterparts know you are aware of customs such as *itami wake* is a good way to earn credibility and to make them less likely to try to engage in unfair manipulations or other cultural ploys.

The Japanese tend to view their business relations with foreigners as combat, and to genuinely respect foreigners only if they prove themselves to be unbeatable, or if the relationship remains in a state of a draw.

違和感
Iwakan
(Ee-wah-kahn)

Allergic to Foreigners

The old saying, "birds of a feather flock together" is as true for humanity as it is for our feathered friends, but some humans have a need to flock more tightly than others. This describes the Japanese, and not surprisingly so—because of the close-knit, exclusive nature of their traditional culture. The proclivity of the Japanese to shun others for the company of their own countrymen goes well beyond what is normal for most people, including those from similar closed cultures.

There is, of course, the language barrier. Although most Japanese have studied English in school, their ability to use it in conversation ranges from very limited to nil. Those who can communicate in English fairly well, or even well, find it extraordinarily tiring. Some Japanese explain this by claiming that the Japanese language and thought processes are very different from those of English speakers, and that an entirely different part of the brain is used by the Japanese in thinking and speaking.

When they speak and think in English or in other foreign languages, they must use a part of their brain that they do not normally use for verbal communication. And that, these Japanese say, is why it is so tiring and so much of a burden for them to speak English and other foreign tongues.

Besides the language barrier, there are a variety of other cultural factors, both attitudes and customs, that separate the Japanese from non-Japanese and create obstacles to smooth and effective communication. In any event, a combination of these factors makes most Japanese businessmen and professionals feel so uneasy in the presence of foreigners that there is a special word to describe the feeling—*iwakan* (ee-wah-kahn), which means "a sense of incongruity" or "a sense of incompatibility."

In the full context of its meaning, *iwakan* incorporates both a sense of unease and suspicion, and, according to Japanese mental health authorities, is the source of a "foreign complex" that many Japanese, particularly men, suffer from.

Part of the *iwakan* foreign complex that afflicts many Japanese results from the Japanese feeling inferior to Westerners, especially Caucasian Americans and Europeans, because of physical differences in size and appearance and the historical perception that Westerners were more advanced technologically, and had a higher standard of living.

To help counter these feelings of inferiority, the Japanese long ago assumed a superior stance with regards to their family system, loyalty, diligence and spirituality; however, this does not eliminate the feelings of *iwakan* when they are actually confronted by Westerners.

Foreigners are also a significant part of this problem. The number of Westerners in Japan who can speak Japanese well enough to carry on a decent conversation is very small—unforgivably small, considering how many are directly involved with the Japanese on a daily basis. And generally speaking, foreigners make far less effort to accommodate themselves to the customs and idiosyncrasies of the Japanese than the Japanese do to cope with foreign expectations. Thus the failure of Westerners to meet the Japanese halfway in bridging the cultural gap contributes to the perpetuation of *iwakan* and the foreign complex.

Fortunately, the farther the Japanese are away from the metropolitan centers of Japan, and the less they have been exposed to foreigners, the less likely they are to suffer from either *iwakan* or a foreign complex. And not surprisingly, Japanese women, wherever they live, are far less likely than Japanese men to be victimized by either of these two complaints.

事情変更
Jijo Henko
(Jee-joe Hane-koe)

The Only Constant is Change

A long time ago, the Japanese accepted the idea that the world at large is in a constant state of flux and that, under the circumstances, the best philosophy of life is one based on flexibility—on being able to bend with the wind. Generally speaking, this age-old concept remains the bedrock of Japanese ethics and morality.

Westerners, on the other hand, have always tended to look upon the world as fixed in place, and at relationships and human activities as unchanging—at least in principle. This difference in Western and Japanese views is dramatically demonstrated in the penchant that Westerners have for detailed, iron-clad agreements and contracts. We take the view that the world would fall apart if contracts were not there to hold it in place.

Until contemporary times, detailed agreements or contracts were unknown in Japan. People formed alliances for both political and business purposes, but these alliances, like the cosmos, were open-ended, allowing for day-to-day adjustments that could be initiated by either side. Generally speaking, all agreements in Japan were based on the principle of *jijo henko* (jee-joe hane-koe), "changed circumstances" or "changing circumstances," meaning that the parties to an agreement understood that terms of a contract could never be absolute.

When the Western practice of written contracts was introduced into Japan, the Japanese looked upon them as evidence that Westerners were so unethical and immoral that they could not trust anyone to keep their word. The Japanese also regarded the idea of being forced to abide by a detailed contract as irrational and ridiculous, because there was no way that any situation could remain the same for either party over a period of time.

By the 1970s most Japanese companies had become resigned to the idea of signing contracts with foreign partners, but they did not give up on the concept of *jijo henko*, and generally they continued to interpret the contracts they signed as being only general guidelines, subject to revision as the circumstances warranted.

In the decades since, and during which time the Japanese have become much more heavily involved in business overseas, the Japanese have developed a new appreciation of Western-style contracts in their international affairs. At home, however, the Japanese still tend to regard the contracts they sign as being "adjustable."

The Japanese regularly "adjust" contracts and verbal agreements unilaterally, and occasionally abrogate them altogether, without any feeling of inappropriateness or unreasonableness. In their view, not adjusting the provisions of a contract when it is detrimental to their interests, is the irrational thing to do. Of course, the problem where Westerners are concerned is that Japanese often alter contractual agreements without consulting the other party to the agreement, though the other party is usually informed at some later date.

The Japanese see no contradiction in their casual treatment of contracts and their image of themselves as among the world's most honest, sincere, trustworthy and honorable people. They see these two things as belonging in totally different cultural spheres. Arbitrarily reinterpreting a contact to suit themselves comes under the sphere of personal matters where human feelings take precedence. When these circumstances occur, the other side is expected to understand and accept their actions even if it inconveniences them and costs them money.

It is understood in such situations that the side breaking the contract "owes" the other side a similar indulgence in the future, so that in the end everything will balance out—a very Buddhist concept.

Foreigners going into contractual arrangements with Japanese companies should be aware of the *jijo henko* factor in Japanese thinking and avoid unpleasant surprises by staying in constant contact with their Japanese partners, officially as well as unofficially. Unofficial contact refers to after-hours meetings in casual and recreational situations, because it is usually in these settings that Japanese reveal what is going on behind the scenes.

自己になる
Jiko ni Naru
(Jee-koe nee Nah-rue)

Trying to Feel Good

One of the primary policies of all of Japan's pre-democratic governments, from the feudal Shogunates to the authoritarian regimes of the 1930s and early 1940s, was to mold the Japanese into cultural clones of each other. Laws as well as social sanctions were designed to ensure conformity in child rearing, education and behavior in general. The Japanese were not only expected to think and behave alike, they were expected to look alike as well.

For the overwhelming majority of Japanese, individualism was strictly taboo. Any attempt to stand out from the crowd invariably resulted in some kind of punishment. But these restrictions and expectations did not squash the natural desire that the Japanese had for self-expression.

Despite living in an environment that was strictly controlled by a detailed and severely enforced etiquette and by government-encouraged taboos, the Japanese had a strong compulsion to *jiko ni naru* (jee-koe nee nah-rue), literally "to become one's own self," or to express one's own individuality and by extension, to personally look good, as opposed to looking like everyone else. For most Japanese over the centuries, virtually the only way in which individuality could be expressed was to excel at what everyone was forced to do.

Even during the most oppressive periods of the long Tokugawa Shogunate (1603–1868), there were people who went to extremes to express individual feelings and desires. One example of this was the surreptitious custom of well-to-do merchants and their families to get around laws requiring them to wear rough clothing made of cotton by lining their apparel with the richest fabrics they could buy. Other practices aimed at providing personal pleasure and ego gratification that were common in pre-democratic Japan—because they posed no threat and were therefore not forbidden by the government—included mastering some art or skill, like singing or dancing, which could be enjoyed without any fear of retribution.

In present-day Japan, there are still many restrictions on the freedom of the Japanese to *jiko ni naru*, particularly in business and in the various professions. The Japanese in every category of life, from common laborers to doctors, engineers, lawyers and business managers, still usually conform to the dress and behavior that is socially "prescribed" for their class and occupation. For them to do otherwise could be harmful—if not disastrous—to their careers.

Furthermore, it is still generally possible to identify people and their professions by their appearance and their behavior, just as one could during the feudal age when the kind of clothing people wore was determined by the government, and different groups of people had their own jargon and behavior. This does not mean that individuals in these groups do not engage in *jiko ni naru* behavior; however, it is often difficult for the person not familiar with the culture, such as the foreigner, to notice this behavior when it occurs.

Politicians in particular are known for constantly trying to look good in dress and behavior as well as attempting to take credit for as many good deeds as possible—all aspects of the modern-day interpretation of *jiko ni naru*. Attempts to *jiko ni naru* in business settings in Japan are especially fraught with danger because of competition and jealousy. Anyone who is especially talented and productive must be careful not to arouse the destructive envy of coworkers.

People who put on a show of being superior or who attempt to take personal credit for some successful product or project are likely to be ostracized. Coworkers can, and often do, destroy the careers of such people simply by passive resistance—by not cooperating with them.

Foreign businesspeople sometimes inadvertently contribute to the downfall of individual Japanese by singling them out as their favorite contacts, by making a big show of their personal contribution to a project, and by honoring them as individuals.

This situation is changing. In fact, since 1990 and 1991, when Japan's economy collapsed, a growing number of Japanese began preaching the benefits of self-expression and individual effort, especially in business and science. But it will be two or three generations before the taboos against *jiko ni naru* totally disappear—if they ever do.

自己流
Jikoryu
(Jee-koe-r'ee-yuu)

Doing it Your Way

Westerners have traditionally admired individualism, and most of the great scientific, social and philosophical advances in civilization have been made by individuals thinking and working alone, often in the face of opposition and derision.

In Japan, however, from the beginning, there have been few occasions when acting alone was culturally or socially approved. Individualism has virtually always been taboo, and expression of it has sometimes resulted in severe sanctions, including banishment and death. Throughout the centuries of Japan's feudal era (1185–1945) people were systematically conditioned by education and example to live and work in groups, to make decisions by consensus, and to conform to the will of the majority. Individualism was regarded with suspicion, as antisocial and as a threat to the government.

One of the rare and most conspicuous occasions when individual action was not only approved, but was highly praised, was when a warrior, with the approval of his commander, would challenge an enemy to meet him in individual combat before the main battle began.

The feudalistic laws that made individualism a dangerous sin in Japan were eliminated following the end of World War II, but the concept was so deeply rooted in the local culture that it continues today to be the prevailing force in Japanese attitudes and behavior.

By the mid-1980s, it was becoming increasingly evident to more and more Japanese that the traditional taboo against individualism was not only anti-human, it was also a major social and economic handicap that was holding Japan back. Since that time, criticism of the cultural taboos against individualism has grown in volume and vehemence, and a growing number of company executives are now urging their employees to think and behave like individuals.

But the old ways remain so strongly embedded in the culture that they are the norm at the majority of Japanese companies today. Computer software companies and various categories of service organizations seem to provide the only exceptions. And despite an intellectual recognition that individualism is essential for the creativity that is becoming increasingly important in international competition, people who behave in a manner called *jikoryu* (jee-koe-r'ee-yuu), which means "one's own style" or "personal style," in the workplace, especially if they work for large, older firms, are subject to severe criticism and may be kept from consideration for promotion.

Any kind of behavior that is not done in concert with one's section or department, as part of an overall group decision and group action, is regarded as disruptive at best and sabotage at worst. Anyone who aggressively promotes his or her own ideas or styles invariably encounters opposition, sometimes openly, but more often subtly. This opposition has a direct impact on the efficiency of the group, and regularly results in individualists being ostracized to the point that they voluntarily leave the group, or they are removed and assigned to a position that is totally unrelated to their former activities.

Japanese businesspeople are both fascinated and repelled by the characteristic *jikoryu* behavior of Americans. On the one hand, they envy Americans for the freedom they have to express themselves verbally, through what they wear, and even in what they eat. On the other hand, they are also frightened by the freedom that Americans have because it is opposed to virtually everything that is Japanese. As a result, the Japanese often look for the disadvantages of the *jikoryu* that they see that foreigners enjoy.

Foreigners involved with Japanese companies must keep in mind that the individual managers and executives they deal with are usually not individuals in the Western sense. They cannot act on their own. They can hold public discussions and do a lot of private arm-twisting. But they are generally not free to go around or over their group. Generally speaking, Western companies reward employees for initiative and taking calculated risks. In Japanese companies that kind of behavior is more likely to result in demerits—even when it benefits the company.

Even when the management of a company officially supports a *jikoryu* style of behavior, most of the employees shy away from it, resent anyone who behaves differently, and will usually try to isolate persons who attempt to express their individuality.

自由学園
Jiyu Gakuen
(Jee-yuu Gah-kuu-inn)

A New Kind of Freedom

Generally speaking the Japanese are frightened by the concept of cultural diversity. They look at the United States with its multiracial and multiethnic society, with all of its dissension and violence, and point proudly to their own homogeneity and far greater social order. The homogeneity and social order that Japan still enjoys, however, has come at a price that they increasingly believe is too high to pay, not only in human terms, but in political and economic terms as well.

Japan's monolithic culture was based on the suppression of virtually all individual, physical, intellectual, emotional and spiritual freedoms, to the extent that they were unable to develop a well-rounded sense of self.

Traditionally, individual Japanese owed total allegiance to whatever group or groups they belonged to, and could not make independent decisions on their own; Japanese society in general was designed to emphasize group rights at the expense of individual behavior. Independent thought and innovation were taboo. But things have changed. Most of the old customs and laws that had traditionally conditioned and controlled the personal behavior of the Japanese were officially abolished at the end of World War II.

The first postwar generation of Japanese grew up with more personal freedom than could have been imagined by their parents, and for the first time in the history of the country, juvenile delinquency and other types of disruptive social behavior became commonplace. The children of that generation were so unlike their parents that they came to be known as *shinjinrui* (sheen-jeen-rue-ee) or "new kind of people." By the end of the first two decades of that generation, most of the behavioral conditioning that in the past had produced homogenized Japanese in the traditional pattern had disappeared. Only the educational system remained.

Having been pressed too far in one direction, more and more Japanese in the 1980s and 1990s began calling for total *jiyu gakuen* (jee-yuu gah-kuu-inn), or "academic freedom," on the basis that the country could not survive in modern times without the creativity and initiative of personal freedom and a strong sense of individualism—a move that could represent an even greater threat to the country, particularly if it comes about in too short a period of time.

It has been amply demonstrated in the past in Japan, as well as in other repressed societies, that if social control is suddenly lifted or dramatically reduced, for whatever reason, even momentarily, violence almost always erupts.

The Japanese calling for *jiyu gakuen* naturally want the good without the bad; but the two cannot be separated. Personal violence is rising rapidly in Japan, most of it centered in schools, the last remaining bastion of the old, repressive society.

In the past, Japan represented a threat to its neighbors and to the rest of the world because of its homogenized society and militant behavior. With *jiyu gakuen* and the unprincipled individualism that goes with it, the Japanese are becoming an equally serious threat to themselves.

受験地獄
Juken Jigoku
(Juu-kane Jee-go-kuu)

Going Through Hell

Japan's indigenous theology does not hang the image of a Christian-type hell over people's heads as a way to frighten them into believing in and obeying religious tenets. This may be because the Japanese concepts of righteousness and sin are quite different from the Christian version. You might say that the Japanese view is a lot more human because it does not promise paradise in return for the repression of natural human desires or frailties.

Another major difference between Japanese and Christian theology is that in Japanese philosophy, there is no single all-powerful God with a monopoly on the souls and destinies of people. There were traditionally many Japanese gods, and because they had to compete for the faith and worship of adherents, they were not nearly as demanding or as unforgiving as the god of monotheistic religions.

Today, most Japanese are simply godless, but they do have to contend with a number of "hells" on earth that, like their long-forgotten gods, are man-made.

One of the most notorious of Japan's man-made hells is the *juken jigoku* (juu-kane jee-go-kuu), or "examination hell," which refers to the examinations students must take to get into universities, and the work involved in preparing for them. The *juken jigoku* were not deliberately created to torment the Japanese or to force them to behave in any particular way; but they might as well have been.

Throughout their history, the Japanese have been great ones for going to extremes to develop knowledge and skills and for continuously testing themselves. Among the samurai class in early centuries, these tests of skill included practice with genuine swords or, in later years, with sword-like wooden staves, which could result in death or serious injury. *Juken jigoku* grew out of this attitude toward learning and the propensity of the Japanese to rank everybody and everything in their world on an inferior/superior basis.

During Japan's long feudal period from 1185 to 1945, virtually every aspect of the culture and of the society was ranked. This custom of ranking both people and things did not end with the demise of the feudal area, however. It is still a primary feature of Japanese life, particularly in education and job opportunities. All of the better schools in Japan, for example, are ranked. The higher the rank the more prestige that accrues to the student, and the better the employment opportunities are for the graduate.

Competition for entry into the best universities begins at the kindergarten level and gets increasingly stronger as students go up the educational ladder. By the time they finish high school, the path to the ranking universities is extremely narrow, and crowded.

The difficulty of university entrance examinations increases as the rank of the university increases. Each year the hundreds of thousands of students who want to attend top-ranked universities must study from four to six hours a day, in addition to their regular high school studies, for one to several years in order to score well enough on the entrance tests to get into one of the top universities.

This regimen is so demanding, so debilitating, that it literally destroys the mental and physical health of thousands of students each year. A significant percentage of those who fail to get into the university of their choice each year continue their studies in commercial cram schools, and try again the following year.

Criticism of the *juken jigoku* system has been rampant in Japan since the 1970s, and reached a crescendo by the mid-1990s, but as of this writing the system persists. It is so deeply entrenched culturally and economically that there has been no political will to change it.

One of the more negative facets of the *juken jigoku* problem is that an overwhelming majority of the students who do succeed in entering a university are so burned out from the effort that they float through their four college years. Many make little effort to study or attend lectures, so their education basically ends with high school and preparation for the college entrance exams.

See *Juku / Yobiku*.

塾、予備校
Juku / Yobiko
(Juu-kuu / Yoh-bee-koe)

Knowledge-Cramming Schools

During the early decades of the Meiji Era (1868–1912), when Japan was being transformed into a modern industrial nation, very few Japanese had the opportunity to take advantage of the Western learning that had suddenly became available, but those who did have access to it applied themselves with extraordinary zeal.

One of the stories about the dedication and diligence of young Japanese students during this period involved a young man who set out to memorize every word in a large English-language dictionary. After getting to the point that he could recite all of the words on a page, he would tear the page out of the book and eat it in the hope that this would make all of the words on that page a permanent part of him.

This obsession with learning has continued to be characteristic of the Japanese since the Meiji Era, but it has resulted in a number of aberrations that have turned the whole process of education into a kind of hell for a great many young Japanese and their mothers. It is now often said that virtually all education in Japan stops with high school. The reason for this criticism is that high school students who want to go to college must study so hard in order to pass university entrance examinations that by the time they enter college, most are burned out and refuse to study any more.

Another factor in the negative reputation that Japanese schools have among students and their parents is that the primary method of learning is rote memory—committing huge amounts of information to memory in order to pass entrance examinations. Since the 1960s, these examinations became so competitive and so difficult that attending regular school classes was not enough for even those who were above-average students.

This situation spurred the rapid growth of *juku* (juu-kuu), or "private tutoring schools"—as commercial enterprises designed to augment the regular schools. Japan's first *juku* appeared during the Tokugawa Shogunate (1603–1868). These were small private schools founded by individual masters who taught different philosophical doctrines, and such specialized skills as martial arts. After the fall of the shogunate system of government in 1868, *juku* began offering classes in English, the abacus, piano and other such skills.

Present-day *juku*, some of which are huge in size with dozens of branches around the country and thousands of students, offer a wide range of subjects as well as preparation for specific entrance examinations.

By the 1970s, another form of *juku* had appeared that was geared solely to helping students pass school entrance examinations. These schools were the notorious *yobiko* (yoe-bee-koe), "cram schools," where rote memorization took on new meaning for millions of elementary- and middle-school students. By the mid-1970s, Japanese parents were spending in excess of a billion dollars annually to send their children to these special schools.

Surveys by Japan's Ministry of Education have revealed that around one-third of all elementary school students in Japan and close to one-half of all junior high school students attend either a *juku* or a *yobiko* after their regular school hours. Despite the cost factor and the hardship imposed on both parents and children, the number and importance of *juku* and *yobiko* continued to grow in Japan during the 1980s and 1990s. In fact, a number of *juku* have established overseas branches that cater to the families of Japanese businessmen stationed abroad.

It seems now that the only way these special cram schools could wither away would be for the Ministry of Education to greatly reform Japan's educational and entrance examination systems, changing their focus from memorizing facts to independent thinking and other skills.

See *Juken Jigoku*.

熟年
Juku Nen
(Juu-kuu Nane)

The Prime Years

During Japan's Tokugawa Period (1603–1868), the average life span for Japanese men was around 50 years. As a result, many shop owners and other independent people retired when they were 42 or 43 years old in order to ensure that they would have some leisure time before they died. By 1975, the life expectancy of Japanese males had risen to 71.7 years, and that for Japanese females to 76.9. Twenty years later the life expectancy in Japan was around 78 years for men and 83.5 years for women, and was still rising.

Up to this time, the government's social and economic policies had primarily emphasized children and juveniles, and virtually ignored those middle-aged and older. Men were still being forced to retire from their jobs at the age of 55, when they were still relatively young and often still had children in school. The vast majority could not find comparable jobs in industry because of the closed and hierarchical nature of the Japanese employment system.

But by the early 1980s, the aging of the population had begun to have a profound effect on Japanese society in general, forcing fundamental changes in virtually all areas of life. The whole way of looking at older people and the infrastructure that was necessary to account for them underwent a remarkable change. The idea that people, especially men, were worn out and useless by the time they were in their sixties was completely discarded.

A new term, *juku nen* (juu-kuu nane), was coined to refer to people between the ages of 40 and 80. *Juku* means "ripe" or "prime," and *nen* means "years"—in other words, "prime years." At first, the new term was applied only to men, but women were soon added to this new category of people.

Juku nen people quickly became targets for a whole new range of products and services. Schools and clubs for older people sprang up all over the country. The schools ranged from enterprises teaching traditional arts and crafts to modern-day work skills. The clubs included athletic gyms as well as clubs for traditional crafts, hobbies, group travel and other activities. Fashion magazines aimed at the *juku nen* generation proliferated.

Corporations came under pressure to raise their mandatory retirement ages, resulting in a variety of programs that would allow them to keep employees older than 55 or 58, but pay them less. These subterfuges included requiring employees to officially retire, whereupon they were rehired as temporary workers at lower wages.

Government ministries and agencies, which were prevented by law from having mandatory retirement ages, were caught in a bind as their employees continued working into their late sixties and seventies, and receiving virtually mandatory wage increases each year. Among other things, this situation contributed to the privatization of the Japanese National Railways. This company used to cost the government billions of yen in losses each year because of over-employment and high wages going to senior employees.

Japan's population is continuing to age rapidly. Its *juku nen* generations now account for over half of the population, a factor that is also continuing to alter the face and the infrastructure of the country. From the 1960s through the 1980s, it was conventional marketing wisdom in Japan that any product that appealed to children and teenagers was bound to be a success. By the mid-1990s catering to the *juku nen* market had become the new road to riches. Major contracting firms were vying to build retirement homes and retirement communities. New health facilities aimed at the elderly had become vogue. For the first time in the history of the country, there was a large *juku nen* population in their sixties and seventies who were still healthy and active, and had the leisure and money to enjoy themselves.

Another first in the history of the country that was especially meaningful to those who were familiar with earlier Japan was the common sight of *juku nen* husbands and wives, fashionably dressed and conspicuously urbane in their manners, strolling at shopping and entertainment districts in the evenings, on weekends, and on holidays. For this segment of Japan's *juku nen* generations, it is their season in the sun.

122

価格破壊
Kakaku Hakai
(Kah-kah-kuu Hah-kigh)

The Great Price Fall

One of the strategies used to rebuild Japan following World War II was to prohibit the import of most consumer goods, to focus on exports, and to allow domestic prices to rise higher and higher, completely divorced from open-market influences.

All during the 1960s and 1970s, real estate prices spiraled upward, achieving virtual orbital speed in the mid-1980s. Between 1985 and 1990, land prices in the central areas of Tokyo, Osaka and Kyoto increased by some 300 percent, pulling up the price of virtually everything else in the country. By 1985, the cost of consumer goods in Japan was anywhere from one to five or six times what it was in the United States and other countries—a situation that was both allowed and fueled by a complex web of government regulations imposed on imports and on distribution since the war years.

A glass of orange juice in a Tokyo hotel restaurant cost up to five times more than it cost in a similar establishment in New York. A cup of coffee was two or three times more expensive in Japan than anywhere else in the world. The Japanese press took a perverse pride in reporting that one square foot of land in the center of the Ginza, Tokyo's most prestigious shopping and entertainment district, was worth more than a hundred thousand dollars.

By 1990 Japan's "bubble economy" had reached its growth limits and began to collapse onto itself. Japanese banks, which had fueled the frenzy of buying trophy properties abroad at vastly inflated prices, were caught with billions of dollars in worthless loans. Finally, primarily as a result of pressure from the United States, the Japanese government began to eliminate or reduce some of the more onerous regulations it had maintained since the early 1940s. But both the government and Japan's top manufacturers continued to support outrageously high consumer prices in order to subsidize Japan's exports.

The end of the Cold War between the United States and the former Soviet Union, the growing economic power of Taiwan, South Korea, Hong Kong, Singapore and China and the rapid globalization of products and market prices brought more pressure against Japan's tightly regulated system, and brought on a phenomenon that came to be known as *kakaku hakai* (kah-kah-kuu hah-kigh), which literally means "price destruction," but is also interpreted as "price busting."

By the late 1980s, a few maverick discount shops and small retail chains, notably those specializing in men's wear, were already on the scene and making a name for themselves. Leading supermarket chains had also begun to lower prices on some items by importing directly and creating their own house brands. By 1992 *kakaku hakai* had become an "in" thing. With low-priced imports flooding into the country from Asia, price "deflation" turned into a revolution. Even the country's icon department stores were not immune to the discount fever that began sweeping the country.

By 1995 the Japanese government faced a profound, and to many a frightening, dilemma—either deregulate industry or see the economy self-destruct. For a government that had historically controlled virtually all economic activity in the country, this was a challenge that went to the very roots of the Japanese psyche. But the government was no longer in charge, and *kakaku hakai* had become a self-sustaining process. The government could slow it down, but it could not stop it. By the mid-1990s, there were four primary categories of "price busters" in the country—general discounters, specialty discounters, discount warehouses, and so-called flea markets.

The specialty discounters, often called "outlets," handle excess inventory, off-season merchandise, B-grade goods and store display items, with discounts ranging from 50 percent to 70 percent off the original manufacturers' retail prices. Specialty discounters that handle a complete line-up of goods in specific categories—such as Toys R Us, for example—are also known in Japan as "category killers." Most warehouse discounters in Japan are referred to as "wholesale clubs."

General merchandise discounters grouped together in one-stop shopping malls are known as "power centers"—one of the largest of which is the Joetsu Wing Market Center in Niigata Prefecture. Discounts of 50 to 70 percent are known in Japanese as *chogekiyasu* (choh-gay-kee-yah-sue), or "ultra-shocking cheap prices."

Given the staying power of Japan's government bureaucrats, and the enormous power and prestige they are being pressured to give up, it will no doubt be several decades before *kakaku hakai*, in concert with global market and political forces, can fully reform the Japanese economy.

隠し味
Kakushi Aji
(Kah-kuu-she Ah-jee)

A Secret Ingredient

The Japanese have always had difficulty exlaining themselves and their culture to Westerners. There are several reasons for this, including the fact that they cannot see themselves as others see them, and therefore cannot communicate on the same cultural channel. Part of the problem is also caused by the fact that some of the physical facets of Japanese culture are very subtle and often invisible to the eye, while some of the metaphysical elements in the culture are based on esoteric philosophies and values that are generally beyond the experience of Westerners.

Most Japanese are acutely aware that there is a fundamental difference in their traditional life-style that distinguishes it from all other life-styles, including the Korean and the Chinese. They often attempt to explain this difference by using the phrase *kakushi aji* (kah-kuu-she ah-jee), which means "hidden flavor" or "hidden touch."

There is a challenge in trying to identify the *kakushi aji* of a particular Japanese thing, custom, or belief—thus the use of the word *kakushi* or "hidden." The special touch that gives something a distinctive Japanese flavor is often as subtle and as elusive as a warm breeze. *Kakushi aji* can be a combination of muted colors; a single color highlighted by a touch of some contrasting color in the center or the corner of an object; or the use of natural materials like bamboo, stone and water to create a visual as well as an audible scene. It can also be a certain aroma, like that of fresh *tatami* reed floor mats or the sound of a flute or a distant temple bell, or the song of an insect—a spiritual and physical experience touching all senses.

Kakushi aji can be food and how it is prepared, or the tray it is served on—the bowls, the cups and other utensils—all of which have a distinctive Japanese character of their own that is both visible and invisible.

The *kanji* (kahn-jee) ideograms with which the Japanese language is written have a special metaphysical essence that goes far beyond their literal interpretation. Each of the characters is a miniature world of its own that resonates across the centuries, adding to the flavor of Japanese life.

Harmony, *wa* (wah), is also a key ingredient in Japan's *kakushi aji*. Whatever the parts making up the hidden flavor of anything Japanese, they must be compatible with each other and present a whole that is in perfect harmony.

Buddhism and Shintoism are no doubt the wellsprings of Japan's *kakushi aji*. Together they imbue the mind and spirit of the Japanese with an all-encompassing appreciation for the subtleties of life and its relationship with the cosmos.

All of Japan's artists and craftsmen of the past attempted, automatically and unconsciously, to imbue everything they did with *kakushi aji*. All present-day Japanese artists and craftsmen who work in traditional fields are still directed by the same aesthetic and spiritual values that motivated their predecessors. Japan's contemporary designers, engineers and fabricators as well are also influenced by the *kakushi aji* aspect of Japanese culture as well, and although it has been dramatically diluted by Western themes, it nevertheless remains strong enough to give them a special advantage over most of their foreign counterparts.

The fact that many traditional things have a *kakushi aji* is not, of course, unique to Japan. All traditional crafts in all cultures have their own unique style, but few people have gone as far as the Japanese in being consciously aware of it and in making it a key part of their everyday lives.

かませる
Kamaseru
(Kah-mah-say-rue)

Sharing the Spoils

How many Japanese does it take to change a light bulb? How many windows or counters do you have to go to in order to mail a letter in a Japanese post office? Traditionally, the answer to such questions was that it took whatever number that was necessary to give everyone something to do.

This concept, which is ancient in Japan, was based on the idea that everyone should have the opportunity—and obligation—to participate, and that work would be divided into as many pieces, parts, or steps that were needed to employ everyone. This facet of the Japanese way of doing things comes under the heading of *kamaseru* (kah-mah-say-rue), which means "to allow participation."

This approach to guaranteeing participation—full employment!—evolved within the family, and meant that food and other assets belonged to the whole family and were shared according to need, a philosophy that, of course, is common in most families. Unlike most other societies, however, the Japanese based their larger social and economic units on essentially the same principle, with far-reaching effects.

In keeping with their traditional beliefs of sharing and economic parity—but not with those outside their group—it was long the written and unwritten policy of the Japanese to give precedence to "full" employment regardless of whether it led to underemployment. This made sure that everyone got a piece of the action. One result of this system was that no matter how low a person's social and economic status, the family or the group they belonged to made sure they had enough of the basics to survive; and the gap between the life-styles of the rich and poor were not terribly extreme. In present-day Japan the disparity between the salaries of a company president and the lowest ranking employee in the firm is not nearly as extreme as it tends to be in American and European companies.

There is one aspect of this ancient Japanese penchant for economic homogeneity that continues to exist today, in weakened but still significant form, that directly affects foreign companies doing business, or wanting to do business, in Japan. Within the context of the *kamaseru* policy, there was always a tendency for the number of distribution levels between manufacturers and consumers to proliferate, with four or five levels becoming characteristic of most product categories.

The government also passed a number of laws to protect the *kamaseru* rights of small retailers. With each of these levels adding to the price of the product, this system resulted in the markup between the manufacturer's price and the retail price ranging from two to four times higher than it was in other countries. In addition to forcing retail prices up to outrageous levels, this system also brought enormous pressure against manufacturers to keep their costs down.

The inefficiencies of this system began to undermine Japan's whole economic house of cards in the 1980s, and by the 1990s, it had begun to slowly but surely self-destruct. Makers began bypassing one or more distribution levels, and sometimes went directly to consumers. Discount houses began appearing, undercutting the high prices of the retailers who were at the end of the system.

The decline of the *kamaseru* system continues today, pushed by a variety of things, including consumer demands for lower prices and pressure from imported products, particularly from China and Southeast Asia, where production costs are well below those in Japan. But enough of the old system survives that foreign firms operating in Japan must be aware of it, and must take it into consideration in their relationships with the distribution and retail levels of the market.

Most Japanese still tend to believe that the ideal marketplace is one in which the *kamaseru* principle is paramount. But they also tend to believe that this philosophy applies only to Japanese companies, and this position is reflected in many of the actions, and inaction, of the government.

看板
Kanban
(Kahn-bahn)

What's in a Name?

In the early 1980s, Western businessmen began to pay attention to intriguing stories they had been hearing about an "amazing" process that had allowed the Japanese to increase their productivity while lowering production costs, and thereby giving them enormous advantages over their foreign competitors.

This process management technique, known as *kanban* (kahn-bahn) in Japanese and "just-in-time parts delivery" in English, refers to getting parts onto factory floors just as they are needed, a concept I reported on in 1959 in my book *Japanese Etiquette & Ethics in Business*.

The *kanban* system was pioneered in the 1920s by Sakichi Toyoda, founder of Toyoda Automatic Loom Works, the predecessor of Toyota Motor Corporation, and perfected in the 1950s and 1960s by Taiichi Ono, manager and later vice president of Toyota Motor Company, now known as Toyota Motor Corporation.

Kanban literally means "sign," "signboard," or "name," and it came into use to describe the "just-in-time" parts delivery system because Ono had all of the parts needed each day listed on huge signs hanging over the factory assembly lines.

There is, however, another meaning of *kanban* in Japan that is vital in understanding the nature of Japanese companies and how they do business, and which is older than the use of it to refer to "just-in-time parts delivery." In its older use, *kanban* refers to the name of a company as well as to its product brands. "National" and "Panasonic," for example, are *kanban* of the huge Matsushita Electric Industrial Company, and Matsushita's primary *kanban* is the company name itself.

Japanese wholesalers and retailers put great stock in being able to display the *kanban*, or trade names, of the manufacturers whose products they handle. The logos of Matsushita, Hitachi, Toshiba, Canon, Sony, Fuji Film, and, more recently, IBM, Apple, Motorola and other foreign firms prominently displayed at retailers are a key part of the image and the success of the stores. While the same system exists in the United States and elsewhere, the display of trade names has far deeper psychological and emotional importance in Japan where the market is incredibly concentrated, competition is severe, and image is especially important. Display of the trade name, in fact, may take precedence over display of the products themselves.

The use and importance of *kanban* in Japan goes back to the early decades of the Tokugawa Shogunate (1603–1868), when shopkeepers, restaurants and other small businesses hung *noren* (no-rane) curtains in front of their doors to keep some of the dust out, to block the sun in summer, and to provide some privacy for patrons. Early in this era it also became the practice to put the shop's name or the family crest of the owner on the split curtains, a practice that was then followed generation after generation, eventually becoming a conspicuous and important part of the business and social culture.

The older the Japanese company the more its "face" is bound up in its *kanban*, and the more protective the company is of who uses it and how it is used. Foreign companies in Japan can hardly regard themselves as insiders, as having been accepted in the marketplace, until their *kanban* are instantly recognized by virtually all Japanese, and are sought after by wholesalers and retailers because of the prestige— and business they attract.

歓談会
Kandan Kai
(Kahn-dahn Kigh)

Let's Have a Little Chat

I remember with some amusement one of the "horror stories" told by an American businessman about his first encounters with the Japanese. Newly assigned to Tokyo as the representative director of a joint venture between a major American corporation and a large Japanese firm, this individual began attending the regularly scheduled meetings of the board of directors of the joint operation.

Since all of the meetings were conducted in Japanese, and his Japanese language ability was virtually nonexistent, he had to depend upon others to brief him on what took place at each meeting. As time went by he became increasingly frustrated. He had no idea if any of the comments he made at the meetings were accurately and fully translated, and he knew that everything the Japanese directors said was not being translated for his benefit. His only real communication with the Japanese side took place in the bar of the nearby Palace Hotel, when one or more of the directors invited him there for drinks after working hours.

The situation became increasingly intolerable because he was repeatedly asked to sign documents that were written in Japanese, without getting an explanation of their contents. Finally, he demanded that documents brought to him for his signature be accompanied by official translations, and after some resistance and foot-dragging on the part of the Japanese, it was agreed that he would be provided with translations.

Much to his chagrin, the American company director soon discovered that all of the after-hours drinking sessions he had been having with his Japanese counterparts were being treated as directors' meetings, with his comments duly recorded as the official position of the American side. What he had been experiencing was a kind of meeting that the Japanese refer to as *kandan kai* (kahn-dahn kigh), which can be translated more-or-less as "a casual meeting," or "a pleasant chat."

In their Japanese context, *kandan kai* are not insidious or covert. They are an institutionalized and sanctified way of getting together after working hours, when the etiquette of the office can be ignored, and employees can frankly sound each other out and come to a consensus about problems, projects, or other concerns.

Virtually all real negotiations and jockeying in decision making in Japan goes on behind the scenes, not in formal, open meetings, which are primarily to confirm agreements that have already been made. When foreigners are involved, the Japanese generally try to reach agreement by making use of both formal meetings and after-hours *kandan kai*. Discussions during formal meetings in the company boardroom are primarily an attempt to accommodate the foreign side because the Japanese know that is the way foreigners do it. But very few Japanese are able to wholeheartedly join in the give-and-take that characterizes foreign-style negotiating in formal meetings, and they often end up saying very little at such meetings, leaving the foreign side mystified and frustrated.

The only practical solution to this problem is for the foreign side to be aware of the existence and function of the *kandan kai*, and to take advantage of it. Generally speaking, the really sensitive and controversial points that the Japanese do not feel comfortable addressing in formal daytime meetings should be discussed in the evening over drinks and good food. Identifying these points is usually no problem. They are generally the ones the foreign side is the most anxious to get settled, and which the Japanese side has little or nothing to say about during formal meetings.

The foreign side should not leave arrangements for *kandan kai* up to the Japanese. And it is not proper protocol to come right out and say something like, "Since we can't settle that point here, let's do it tonight at a *kandan kai* over drinks." Just inviting the Japanese side out in the evening gives the right message loud and clear.

寒稽古
Kangeiko
(Kahn-gay-e-koe)

Discipline the Japanese Way

Many of the examples of extreme behavior that developed in Japan's traditional culture—like everywhere else in the world—were rooted in religious fanaticism.

Buddhism, *Bukkyo* (Buuk-k'yoe), one of the world's most benign and humane religions, was not above inspiring the Japanese—and other Asians—to acts that went well beyond the norm of rational behavior.

But unlike Christianity and Islam, Buddhism did not teach or condone aggressive, institutionalized brutality against other people. It taught that people should be harsh only with themselves as part of the discipline necessary to control their primitive emotions and capacity for cruelty, and to elevate their better selves.

Buddhist monks practiced asceticism as a means of releasing their souls from the bondage of their bodies and allowing them to merge with the godhead or cosmos. One of the ascetic practices originated by Buddhist monks was to deliberately expose themselves to the cold of winter as a kind of shock treatment to purify the mind and to steel the body to the rigors of the ascetic life.

Of course, the monks did not have to go to any special lengths to expose themselves to the cold of winter because their temples and dormitories, like all other structures in Japan, were not heated in the first place. But the monks institutionalized the practice of using cold as one of their key methods of discipline and training, calling it *kangeiko* (kahn-gay-e-koe), literally, "cold training" or "cold exercise." *Kan* means "cold," and *geiko* means "training" or "practice." The term can be translated as "cold season training."

On the coldest days of winter, usually in January, lightly dressed monks would often march through the streets of villages and towns, beating gongs and drums and chanting sutras to demonstrate their piety, and to set an example for laymen to follow. It was also customary for priests, as well as more dedicated samurai warriors, to stand under waterfalls on the coldest days in winter to strengthen their spirits and toughen themselves. While engaging in this *kangeiko*, the priests, and the more devout samurai, would also chant sutras in a loud voice.

Kangeiko gradually spread from the world of Buddhist priests and priestly warriors to other groups of professionals, from sumo wrestlers to singers and musicians. Singers came to believe that practicing outdoors during the coldest weather, until their voices cracked, would improve both the quality of their voices and their ability to perform. Musicians would engage in *kangeiko* until their fingers were so stiff they could not move them.

Sumo wrestlers, who always trained throughout the winter in unheated *beya* (bay-yah), "stables," while wearing only loincloths, staged special *kangeiko* exhibitions on the most frigid days as part of their normal routine. These practice sessions are sometimes called *kandori* (kahn-doe-ree), which might be translated as "cold sumo." Japanese singers and musicians no longer engage in *kangeiko*, but in sumodom the practice has survived, and is a popular annual event attended by crowds of fans.

But since sumoists train and perform throughout the winter in unheated venues, the *kangeiko* are no big deal for the wrestlers. Many baseball players, martial arts athletes and others also continue to engage in *kangeiko* during January and February as part of their spiritual and mental training. The annual judo *kangeiko* held at the Kodokan Judo Hall in Tokyo's Suidobashi district attracts hundreds of people.

From the 1970s on, some major Japanese corporations began requiring that their new white-collar employees undergo periods of *kangeiko* as part of their training. It also became common during this time for veteran corporate managers in their forties and fifties to voluntarily attend three- to ten-day sessions of *kangeiko* conducted by Buddhist priests at their temples.

The fact that kangeiko has survived into modern times is testimony to the importance that the Japanese attach to spiritual and mental training, and accounts for some of their tenacity in business and other endeavors.

See *Daikan*.

冠婚葬祭
Kankon Sosai
(Kahn-kone So-sie)

Doing Things with a Flourish

The romantic view of the history of Japan is a mighty saga of spectacular events, glorious battles, heroes and heroines dressed in flowing silk robes and communicating with each other in beautiful poetry, the rise and fall of great clans, the building of huge temples and castles, the pageantry of the imperial and shogunate courts, colorful processions of provincial lords and their retinues marching to and fro throughout the country, hundreds of annual picturesque festivals, religious observances, and more.

The scale of many of these events and undertakings was often enormous, involving tens of thousands of people and sometimes extending over long periods of time. But regardless of the scale or importance of their activities, the Japanese typically did things with an energy and imagination that not only seemed unbounded, but was also marked by an absorbing passion for precise form and ritual that sometimes took precedence over everything else.

During the first long centuries of Japan's history as a unified nation, religious and secular powers were combined in the person of the emperor, with the result that both religious and governmental affairs were administered in a ceremonial manner designed to please a myriad number of spirits, who presumably were impressed with ceremony and a show of great reverence toward their symbols and earthly representatives.

By the end of the 12th century, however, the Imperial Court had been stripped of its secular authority by upstart clan lords and their samurai warriors. Successive clan leaders were to rule the country as shoguns, or military dictators, until 1868. But this secular break with the Imperial Court did not end the rule of ceremony. The shoguns and the two-hundred-plus provincial fief lords fashioned their courts on the imperial pattern, perpetrating the ceremonial rituals that had evolved over the centuries.

As the rule of the shogunate and clan lords continued over the generations, their court rituals, combined with the various religious observances traditionally practiced by the general population, gradually influenced behavioral patterns on all levels of Japanese society and became the established etiquette.

Today, despite the extraordinary changes in Japan since the fall of the shogunate style of government in 1868, and a more pronounced break with the ancient feudal system in 1945, the Japanese still remain very much attached to *kankon sosai* (kahn-kone so-sie), or formalities and ritualistic ceremonies. The most common of the daily formalities engaged in by the Japanese encompass their custom of bowing as a way of acknowledging, meeting, thanking, petitioning, apologizing and taking leave.

There is also a precise verbal formality that makes up an essential part of Japanese etiquette, with special words and special word-endings that are used to distinguish inferior/superior relationships and the nature of an exchange. The vocabulary used in conversations between friends, casual acquaintances or strangers, for example, varies quite significantly, as does the delivery and tone of speech.

Meetings that are semi-formal and formal have their own *kankon sosai* that include seating people according to their rank and status, and institutionalized opening and closing remarks by whoever is in charge. Receptions, seminars and similar meetings are generally closed by drinking toasts. Congratulatory meetings often end with the host leading everyone in three shouts of *banzai!* (bahn-zigh), during which both arms are raised in the air.

Business meetings that are held at a public venue, such as an inn or a hall, for the purpose of forming or acknowledging some form of contractual relationship, are typically ended with all of the participants clapping their hands in an established rhythmic pattern for a total of 30 times—in three sets of three claps plus one.

The beginning of the construction of new homes or buildings is marked by Shinto rituals. The opening of new businesses is ceremonial, with the owners wearing formal attire, and with huge flower wreaths decorating the entrance areas. Some more traditional neighborhood businesses may also engage a *chindonya* (cheen-doan-yah) band to march around the area, playing a distinctive kind of music with drums, flute and cymbals and carrying banners announcing the opening.

Observance of these various rituals are a key part of fitting in and doing business successfully in Japan.

関西、関東
Kansai / Kanto
(Kahn-sigh / Kahn-toe)

East and West of the Barrier

Japan has a dozen or so area and geographical "code words" that one must know in order to follow day-to-day conversation as well as business discussions. The two most common of these terms are *kansai* (kahn-sigh), which means "west of the barrier," and *kanto* (kahn-toe), which means "east of the barrier."

Kansai, which is more cultural and historical in meaning than geographical, is loosely used in reference to the cities of Kobe, Kyoto and Osaka and the surrounding areas. *Kanto* refers to Tokyo and the surrounding area of the Kanto Plain.

The two terms came into use in the 10th century as a means of signifying eastern or western Japan, with the dividing line being a barrier station, or *sekisho* (say-kee-show), "military guard post," at the village of Osaka (not to be confused with the large city of Osaka) in what is now Shiga Prefecture, and which was more-or-less the geographical center of the main island of Honshu.

During the Kamakura Period (1185–1333), the dividing line between *Kansai* and *Kanto* was marked by three barrier stations. The first of these stations was at Suzuka, Mie Prefecture, the second at Fuwa, Gifu Prefecture, and the third at Arachi, Fukui Prefecture. Afterward, the dividing line was moved to Hakone, on the shores of Lake Ashino Ko, in what is now Kanagawa Prefecture, and where it was to remain until the end of the Tokugawa Shogunate in 1868.

Following the move of the emperor from Kyoto to Edo (Tokyo) in 1868, *Kansai* once again came to mean the Kyoto-Osaka-Kobe area in a cultural as well as in an industrial sense, and has since remained the same. *Kanto* is now associated only with the large Kanto Plain and all of the cities on it, including Tokyo, Yokohama, Kawasaki, Omiya and Yokosuka.

In present-day Japan, the two terms are also commonly used to distinguish between the dialects, attitudes and behavior of residents in the areas, as well as their food preferences and other distinguishing features. *Kansai* area people are said to be much more dedicated to business than *Kanto* people; *Kanto* people are said to be more fun and pleasure oriented; and Kyoto residents are said to most accurately represent the culture of old Japan.

These divisions are quite clear in the minds of the Japanese, and have a discernible influence in their political, economic and cultural beliefs. Tokyoites refer to *Kansai* in ordinary speech far more often than residents of that area use *Kanto* in their references to Tokyo and its satellite cities.

In addition to these two "cultural zones," Japan is also divided into four major industrial zones and four secondary industrial zones. The four primary industrial zones are Keihin: Metropolitan Tokyo and all of Kanagawa Prefecture; Chukyo: Aichi and Mie Prefectures; Hanshin: Metropolitan Osaka and all of Hyogo Prefecture; and Kita-Kyushu: Metropolitan Fukuoka. The secondary industrial zones are Keiyo: Chiba Prefecture, which adjoins Tokyo on the east; Tokai: Shizuoka Prefecture; Setouchi: Okayama, Hiroshima and Ehime Prefectures; and Hokuriku: Niigata, Toyama, Fukui and Ishikawa Prefectures.

The northern part of Honshu, the main island, is also often referred to as Tohoku (Toe-hoe-kuu), literally "Northeast," and includes the prefectures of Aomori, Iwate, Akita, Yamagata, Miyagi and Fukushima—the famous fiefs of Dewa and Mutsu during Japan's feudal age.

The classification of northern Honshu as Tohoku began in ancient times when it was the last stronghold of Japan's aboriginal people, known as Ainu (Aye-nuu), and was virtually another country. It was not until the Kamakura Period that the Ainu were defeated and the region came under the control of the Japanese government.

The Hakone Barrier, the last of the *sekisho* dividing *Kansai* and *Kanto*, was to become famous during the long Tokugawa Shogunate (1603–1868), because it was the only official gateway to Edo, the shogunate capital, from western and southern Japan, where most of the country's most powerful fiefs and feudal lords were located.

This mile-high gateway on the shores of Lake Hakone served not only as a military barrier, but also as a customs and immigration post. Everyone who passed through the barrier had to have official documents authorizing them to travel. Bypassing the barrier by taking some other route was punishable by death.

A replica of the famous Hakone barrier, on the opposite side of the road from where the original was, is one of Hakone's most famous tourist attractions.

官尊民卑
Kanson Minpi
(Kahn-sohn Meen-pee)

Bowing Before Officials

Kanson minpi (kahn-sohn meen-pee) is an old label dating from Japan's feudal days, but it refers to a concept and a practice that is still very much alive and often of critical importance in personal as well as business affairs in Japan. By itself, *kanson* means "a preponderance of official power." *Min* refers to "people" or "citizens," and *pi* to "respecting" or "giving preference to."

When these concepts are put together, the figurative reference is to the traditional Japanese habit of paying attention to and obeying government bureaucrats while ignoring the rights of ordinary citizens.

Obviously, *kanson minpi* goes way back in Japan. Throughout Japan's early history when emperors reigned, and during the following centuries when the country was ruled by shoguns, government bureaucrats had virtually absolute authority over the people. Their power could not be questioned, nor could their decrees be ignored. In this setting it became second nature for the Japanese to fear the power of the government, to look to it for guidance in virtually everything, and to conduct themselves in a quiet and passive manner.

The post-shogunate industrialization of Japan was carried out under the direction of the government, not by private entrepreneurs. In tandem with this development, government agencies were established to direct and control the behavior of businessmen. In essence, practically nothing had changed from Japan's earlier feudal era. Elite government bureaucrats still maintained virtually absolute control over lives and fortunes, including the inauguration and operation of new businesses.

During the American-led occupation of Japan following World War II, an effort was made to reduce the role of the government in business. Most of this effort involved an attempt to break up the huge *zaibatsu* (zigh-baht-sue) combines—including Mitsui, Mitsubishi, Sumitomo, Yasuda, Nissan, Asano, Furukawa, Okura, Nakajima and Nomura—that had controlled the bulk of Japan's GNP before the war.

But ultimately, the only thing the United States and its allies succeeded in doing was taking the *zaibatsu* out of the hands of the individual families that had originally owned them. Almost immediately after the occupation of Japan ended in 1952, the hundreds of companies making up the *zaibatsu* groups came back together as *keiretsu* (kay-ee-rate-sue) or "aligned" companies.

In the decades since the occupation years, the power of Japan's government bureaucrats has eroded considerably. But so much of the authority of the government has been institutionalized in laws, and the power of bureaucrats to go beyond enforcing these laws is so deeply entrenched in the culture, that *kanson minpi* remains a vital factor in virtually every area of Japanese life.

In fact, today it is not so much the intransigence of government bureaucrats and their hanging onto power that is handicapping Japan. It is the *kanson minpi* attitude that most people have in relation to doctors, lawyers, school authorities, professors, scientists, company executives and government officials that is holding things up.

On an individual basis, most Japanese are still afraid to complain, to disagree, to make suggestions on their own, to stand out as mavericks of any kind, because of fear that they will be ridiculed, shamed, ignored and possibly banished for daring to go against the system. Virtually the only exceptions to this rule are editorial writers, independent economists and old professors—all of whom are protected from retaliation by their positions and status, and whom everyone can also safely ignore.

Nationally, the *kanson minpi* attitude works against the spirit of independence and innovation that is critical to entrepreneurship and invention. It also imbues people who are in power with a tendency to be arrogant, autocratic and ruthless when they have the upper hand.

顔が広い
Kao ga Hiroi
(Kah-oh gah He-roe-ee)

Having a Wide Face

The old adage, "It isn't what you know, but who you know," has traditionally been one of the ten commandments of Japanese life. In fact, until the last two decades of the 20th century, being really brilliant in Japan was often more of a hindrance than a help, because standing out from the crowd in any way, especially in intelligence, was taboo. Rather than being fueled by innovations and inventions dreamed up by maverick individuals, Japanese society in general was programmed to function like a giant anthill—to use an analogy proposed by critic and author Michihiro Matsumoto—with everyone working in homogenized unity.

As late as the 1980s, exceptionally brilliant and talented Japanese musicians, scientists, designers and others were so restricted by what they could do in Japan that all of those who could went to the United States or Europe in order to take advantage of their knowledge and skills—sometimes returning to Japan after they had established themselves abroad.

The age-old "ant-like" mindset of the Japanese has been under increasing pressure since the 1950s, and there have been significant changes in every facet of Japanese life. But having a *kao ga hiroi* (kah-oh gah he-roe-ee), or "wide face," is still generally more important than having a high IQ, even when "brains" are combined with a good imagination, a practical bent and other positive attributes. Virtually all economic and political activity in Japan has traditionally been based on personal relations, on having and maintaining strong contacts in all of the pertinent areas of business and government, and the system continues to prevail.

In this environment, people with "wide faces"—meaning they know and are known by a large number of people—are among the most valuable assets a company or an organization can have. And it is generally a major compliment to be described as *kao ga hiroi.*

Yet another important version of this phrase is *kao ga kiku* (kah-oh gah kee-kuu), which literally means "the face pulls," "the face works," or "the face is effective"—meaning that the "face" or influence of the individual concerned is strong enough that he or she can get things done. It is the Japanese way of saying that a person has "clout."

Another version of *kao ga hiroi* is *kao ga ureteiru* (kah-oh gah uh-ray-tay-e-rue), which literally means "a person's face sells well." The figurative meaning is that the individual has a wide circle of friends and is popular among them. *Kao ga tsubureru* (kah-oh gah t'sue-buu-ray-rue) means "to lose face"; *kao wo tateru* (kah-oh oh tah-tay-rue) means "to save face or honor." *Kao wo kikasu* (kah-oh oh kee-kah-sue) means "to use one's influence." *Kao wo kashite kudasai* (kah-oh oh kah-ssh-tay kuu-dah-sigh) means "please lend me your face," or, more figuratively, "use your influence to help me."

Foreigners who show up in Japan without "face," that is, with no contacts or connections, are at a serious disadvantage. By the same token, individuals who have enormous "face," such as former presidents, ex-senators, ex-generals, former secretaries of state, and so on, can often achieve extraordinary things in Japan because of their *kao*—rather than any genuine skill or knowledge they may possess.

Foreign businesspeople who are approaching Japan for the first time and themselves do not have *kao* there, can "borrow" face from well-known individuals in their own countries, or from well-known Japanese.

People with clout in Japan include the obvious: politicians in office, bureaucrats, businessmen, professors, scientists and other prominent persons. The pool of people in Japan with "face" is larger than what it is in most other countries, because successful businesspeople, bureaucrats and professionals in Japan do not lose all of their clout after they retire or leave office.

Generally speaking, Japanese with "face" are more effective in dealing with other Japanese than foreigners would be in dealing with the same persons, even if the foreigners had an equal amount of "face." The reason for this is that the Japanese can communicate in the fullest cultural sense, and, very importantly, the Japanese can be held accountable by other Japanese. Because of the importance of *kao* in Japan, everyone spends a great deal of time and money to protect it and to "sell" it to their clients, customers and prospects.

顔を出す
Kao wo Dasu
(Kah-oh oh Dah-sue)

Showing Your True Face

The Japanese president of a very successful company, whom I have known as a close friend for several decades, attempted some time ago to open a corporate account in Phoenix, Arizona, with a branch of one of the largest banks in America.

The bank staff member in charge of opening new accounts had no idea how to open a foreign company account. However, because my friend persisted, the bank officer finally telephoned the branch manager, who was in his office a few yards away with his door closed, and asked for his help.

After the new accounts officer explained what my friend wanted to do, the bank manager gave the officer a list of requirements that had to be met before an account could be opened—all over the phone. But the procedure was still not clear.

After about half an hour, my friend gave up and left the bank, incensed that the bank manager had not been courteous enough or interested enough in his business to step out and personally take care of him. The following day he went to another bank, where the staff was courteous and helpful, and got his business.

In Japan, bank managers go to the offices of prospective clients. During the two major gift-giving seasons in Japan, in mid-July and just before the end of the year, many bank managers personally deliver gifts to the homes or offices of important clients. Japan's tradition of service is perhaps the most comprehensive and sophisticated in the world, and is personalized to a degree that goes well beyond what is regarded as "good service" in other countries.

A key factor in nurturing and maintaining personal and business relations in Japan is bound up in the concept of *kao wo dasu* (kah-oh oh dah-sue), which means "show one's face."

Given the personal nature of all relationships in Japan, it is practically unthinkable for the Japanese to conduct important business only by way of email, fax, phone or letter.

Although high-tech forms of communication and the other circumstances of international business have wrought significant changes in Japanese attitudes and behavior, face-to-face meetings still play a vital role in all Japanese affairs. Before clinching business deals, Japanese businessmen feel compelled to meet the other parties to read their faces and manners and to make visceral character judgments.

Foreign businessmen should be aware that meeting their Japanese counterparts regularly, in Japan as well as abroad, especially on sensitive and auspicious occasions, is a vital factor in getting inside the inner circle of Japan's business world. It is especially important for foreign businessmen in Japan to have regular face-to-face meetings with their customers, suppliers and other important contacts because expectations that they will abide by this fundamental etiquette are much higher.

Some of the occasions when *kao wo dasu* visits are expected are just before the end of the year, just after the New Year holidays, when important contracts are signed, and when a key contact is promoted or gets married.

Every foreign businessperson who hopes to succeed in Japan should, at the outset, go out of his or her way to create an annual schedule of courtesy calls, visits and gifts as part of their regular activities. This is not something that can be approached casually. It requires regular ongoing attention, and the keeping of records.

体で覚える
Karada de Oboeru
(Kah-rah-dah day Oh-boe-eh-rue)

Matter Over Mind

In feudal Japan, many of the more dedicated samurai warriors spent several hours a day for many years honing their sword-fighting skills. The most famous swordsman of all, Musashi Miyamoto (1584–1645), practiced the art of the sword daily for more than 30 years in an effort to achieve perfection. Miyamoto was successful enough that he killed some 60 opponents in death duels before retiring to the life of a painter, writer and teacher.

While the example set by Miyamoto is sensational, it was by no means rare. Prior to the introduction of industrialization into Japan in the 1870s, virtually all Japanese, in whatever art or craft, spent most of their lives trying to achieve perfection in their fields.

One of the more impressive images of the dedication of some present-day Japanese is the sight of people standing under waterfalls during the frigid weather of winter, their eyes closed and their hands clasped in a prayerful attitude. Another custom followed by many Japanese is sitting immobile in a meditation hall for hours at a time in an effort to gain spiritual enlightenment—a practice that is not as dramatic as being battered by cold water, but which can be even more painful to the novice.

Japanese athletes, particularly sumo wrestlers and baseball players, are required to train until they are literally exhausted, day-after-day, year-after-year, in a regime that Westerners find totally irrational. The purpose of all of this Japanese-style training is to transcend the normal physical limits of the body and achieve a level of skill that is on a metaphysical or spiritual plane.

The Japanese learned a long time ago that the human body is capable of incredible feats when the mindset that controls normal behavior is transcended, and this transcendent stage became the goal of many of their practices. The Japanese also learned that to function at a transcendent level for extended periods of time—as opposed to brief flashes of transcendence, which sometimes happen spontaneously to ordinary people—required that the body itself totally assimilate whatever skill was concerned, a process that they labeled *karada de oboeru* (kah-rah-dah day oh-boe-eh-rue), or "learning with the body."

In simple terms, *karada de oboeru* consisted of repeating physical actions at an increasingly difficult level until they became automatic—the same principle and the same skill that one sees in master musicians, jugglers, typists and others who perform flawlessly, seemingly without conscious effort.

Over the centuries, *karada de oboeru* became the underlying foundation for all of the arts and skills practiced in Japan, from such mundane things as weaving baskets and floor mats to writing. But it was in the martial arts and higher fine arts that *karada de oboeru* made its major contributions, allowing the more dedicated of these artists to achieve skills verging on the sublime.

Because of the overall role and importance of the *karada de oboeru* concept in Japanese life, it eventually permeated the thinking and behavior of people in business. Succeeding in business was seen as a matter of combining spirit and physical effort. In other words, work hard enough and long enough and with enough spirit, and anything can be accomplished.

The *karada de oboeru* concept is still visible today in the management philosophies and practices of most large Japanese companies. Dedication and spirit still rank higher than talent. Years of laboring away in on-the-job experience is still seen as the best way for developing the human relations-oriented managerial skills prized in Japanese companies.

The Japanese naturally believe that their particular *karada de oboeru* method of training is superior to all other methods, and they tend to look down on people who do not have the awareness, ambition or stamina to accept and follow their approach.

過当競争
Kato Kyoso
(Kah-toe-oh K'yoe-so)

Compete or Die

One of the ancient beliefs of the Japanese was that they were destined to spread their own unique brand of peace and harmony, *wa* (wah), to the rest of the world. This belief was also part of the thinking of many of the military men who were responsible for Japan's efforts during the 1930s and 1940s to turn Asia into a Japanese-run "co-prosperity sphere." Japan's subsequent defeat in World War II appeared to have smothered the embers of this ancient dream, but as early as the 1970s, it had came back to life, fanned by the country's astounding rise from the ashes of war to undreamed of economic power.

Japan's emergence as an economic superpower was just as surprising to most Japanese as it was to outsiders. Until it actually happened, any suggestion of the idea, to the Japanese or to foreigners, would have been met with scorn.

While economic success rekindled a great deal of the cultural confidence the Japanese traditionally had, it also presented them with problems that were previously unimaginable—problems of competing on a peaceful and equitable basis with foreign cultures and races. Prior to the opening of Japan to the West, there was no word in the Japanese language for Western-style competition. Yukichi Fukuzawa, a former samurai who founded the forerunner of Keio University and a major newspaper in the 1870s, coined the word *kyoso* (k'yoe-so), "fight each other," to approximate the meaning of the English word.

As Japan's economic juggernaut rolled around the world, complaints about the country's competitive tactics grew louder and more strident. The Japanese were accused of being too competitive by prominent foreign politicians who demanded that they work less, save less and spend more—a reaction that many Japanese felt was absolutely absurd, especially when it came from Americans whose motto, "may the best man win," had always been something they admired. Until it began to look like Japan would overrun the world economically, the fact that the Japanese worked like bees for low wages was all that most foreign businessmen involved with Japan cared about.

The general consensus seemed to be that a country that had traditionally suppressed individuality, ostracized mavericks, barred virtually every kind of innovative change, and regarded personal competition as immoral, would simply not be able to compete with freewheeling Americans and Europeans.

What outsiders failed to consider sufficiently was the power of Japan's group-oriented system when it was harnessed together on a national scale. Just as a well-drilled football squad can easily defeat an untrained opposing team with even double the number of players, the accumulative power of group-oriented Japanese companies was awesome.

Thus while personal competition in Japan was severely restrained—even in sports—and generally prohibited altogether within groups, competition between groups had traditionally been fierce, often to the point that individuals would sacrifice their welfare, their families, and even their lives for their groups, their companies and their country.

After the extraordinary competitive nature of the overall Japanese economic system became the subject of international condemnation, it was labeled *kato kyoso* (kah-toe k'yoe-so) or "excessive competition" by the Japanese who had begun to recognize that it had a serious downside for Japan as well as for the world at large. These critics recognized that Japanese-style competition had been carried to extremes at both the company and the national level, that it was destructive to the environment and to the needs and aspirations of the Japanese people, and that it was rapidly turning the rest of the industrial world against Japan.

But a business system that is based on attitudes and practices that permeate a culture as deeply as that of Japan's cannot be altered in a few years, or even a few decades. More importantly, most Japanese remain totally committed to their way of doing things, so there is minimal impetus to change a system that has propelled them to the forefront of world power.

Japan's so-called *kato kyoso* is not going to go away anytime soon. Other countries that want to compete more effectively with the Japanese must improve their own methods.

軽薄短小
Kei-Haku-Tan-Sho
(Kay-e-Hah-kuu-Tahn-Show)

Light, Slim, Short, Small

Current scientific efforts to discover, manipulate and otherwise use smaller and smaller atomic particles was "presaged" to some extent in Japan ages ago by many

Japanese craftsmen who focused on making their products as small as possible. These early Japanese craftsmen were under some kind of compulsion to reduce the size of every new product they invented or that came their way through Korea and China, to the absolute minimum that could be achieved and still remain practical to use.

The Japanese say this compulsion to refine and downsize things became a major element in their culture because they were acutely conscious from the earliest times of the smallness of Japan and the crowded conditions under which they lived.

Downsizing seems to me to be a concept that has a cultural origin. I believe that the Japanese penchant for miniaturizing things derives from an early space consciousness that had to do with their own self-image and an aesthetic impulse rather than the geographic size of the Japanese islands. There is ample evidence that Japanese craftsmen of old were motivated by a desire to refine and simplify things down to the point that they could be hand-held and hand-used, and that this refinement process included attempts to achieve the essence of beauty in form and finish— which is easier to achieve in small things than in large things.

Homes in Japan have traditionally been very small by Western standards, and most still are, making it mandatory that furnishings and home appliances be compact. The use of finely woven reed mats as the standard flooring in Japanese buildings also made it imperative that furnishings be lightweight.

Another factor in the "small" outlook of the Japanese was their own image of themselves as being small people. Like most people whose main diet was rice and vegetables, the Japanese were conspicuously small by world standards, and until the 1990s, they were constantly making a point of this to emphasize that foreign-made cars, appliances and other products were too large and were unsuitable for the Japanese market.

In any event, one of the primary goals of contemporary Japanese designers, engineers and manufacturers in creating new products or "Japanizing" existing ones is to apply to them the concepts of *kei* (kay-e), "light in weight"; *haku* (hah-kuu), "slim"; *tan* (tahn), "short"; and *sho* (show), "small." The success of virtually everything for which the Japanese are now famous, from electronic calculators and transistor radios to notebook computers, was based in large part on their small size, lightweight and refined design.

By the early 1980s, the Japanese had begun to emphasize that their traditional practice of miniaturizing things was a major asset in the international competition to make things smaller and more efficient, to save materials and energy, and to make products more practical to use.

Another point that Japanese manufacturers began emphasizing at the same time was that as electronic devices shrink in size they also generally become easier and cheaper to make, as a result of which Japan's traditional philosophy of *kei*, *haku*, *tan* and *sho* gives them a significant advantage over their foreign competitors.

The idea that "small is beautiful," which gained many adherents in the United States and Europe in the 1980s, was greatly influenced by the Japanese emphasis on *kei*, *haku*, *tan* and *sho*.

けじめ
Kejime
(Kay-jee-may)

Drawing a Line

Right and wrong are not absolutes in the Japanese context of things. Both depend on a wide range of circumstances that depend in turn on the individuals involved, their positions, timing and a host of other variables, including, of course, intent. In earlier times, right and wrong in Japan were based on the old universal concept of "might is right," and to some degree that is still the situation, but generally speaking, discerning between the two has become much more subtle.

Nowhere has the challenge of defining right and wrong been more dramatically illustrated than in Japan's ongoing saga of political scandals. Of course, it may be both unfair and a waste of time to discuss political leaders and their morality, but as the most prominent role models in the country, they are fair game.

Again generally speaking, politics in Japan has always been based on policies rather than principles, and the overriding policy of most politicians has traditionally been to get into office, stay in office, benefit financially, and take care of family, friends and supporters.

Conspicuously scandalous behavior by Japan's top politicians, from prime ministers on down, has given a new spin to an old word, *kejime* (kay-jee-may), which originally meant "difference" or "distinction," and was just a good, ordinary word. In its new cloak, *kejime* refers to an appearance of an impropriety that results in drawing a line in order to make a judgment about someone's behavior—and if they hold a prominent political or business position, demanding that they step down.

One of the most common ploys used by Japanese politicians to camouflage their nefarious financial dealings has been to conduct the deals in the names of their secretaries or mistresses and blame them if anything goes wrong.

What has changed in contemporary Japan that puts an entirely different slant on skullduggery committed by politicians is that the news media, at least since the 1960s, has assumed the role of *kejime* judge and jury. The news media, rather than the criminal justice system, has uncovered and exposed virtually all of the major scandals of the era, bringing down one cabinet minister and Diet member after another, and sent several prime ministers scuttling. The news media has presumed the right to apply a *kejime* judgment against anyone it thinks has crossed the line. It then applies enough public pressure against the politicians concerned to force them to resign. The fourth estate has assumed the role of morality watchdog.

Kejime is also an important factor in Japan's business world, particularly in relation to top management in major corporations and public organizations. But in the last several decades the word has not been used nearly as often in this arena as it has in the political world.

Presidents of corporations that are involved in major accidents or are found to be polluting the environment or engaged in any other kind of reprehensible behavior are subject to being targeted by the news media for a *kejime* judgment if they do not voluntarily resign on their own.

Although the term *kejime* may not be applied, there are regular occasions within companies when groups of employees decide that certain managers are not acceptable and mount sub rosa campaigns to oust them—a technique that has been used to get rid of any number of foreign expatriate managers who failed to hit it off with their Japanese employees.

嫌米
Kenbei
(Ken-bay)

Dislike of America

There is an old saying to the effect that "sticks and stones may break my bones, but words cannot hurt me." But that is true only in a very limited sense, because words are one of the most dangerous and deadliest of all human inventions. Since the age of speech began, words have angered, humiliated and wounded people, caused fights and murder without end, and brought on wars that have resulted in the deaths of untold millions.

Words are more important and more dangerous in some cultures than in others. Americans have traditionally been remarkably tolerant about words, but even today in a society that has become inured to the most vile and obscene language, there are still hundreds of words that result in emotional, irrational reactions that range from mild discomfort to wild rage.

The Japanese are far more sensitive to words than Americans, and the influence that words have on the Japanese is correspondingly both broader and deeper. The Japanese are so sensitive to words that they have separate vocabularies and grammatical structures for different occasions, according to the sex of the individuals involved, and according to their age and their social relationships.

Another characteristic of the Japanese is a strong penchant for coining new words, one of which, *kenbei* (ken-bay), created in 1991 by popular novelist Yasuo Tanaka, quickly resulted in what one Japanese magazine headlined as a case of "mass hysteria." Tanaka created *kenbei* by combining the first part of the word *kenasu* (ken-ah-suu), meaning to "despise" or "to speak ill of," and *bei* (bay), the first part of the word for America, *Beikoku* (bay-koe-kuu), which literally means "beautiful country."

To say that the introduction of *kenbei* resulted in mass hysteria is an exaggeration, but the response to the word nevertheless highlighted both the Japanese sensitivity to culturally pregnant terms and their compulsion to create new ones.

Kenbei was first used by Tanaka in an article entitled "Yukoku Hodan" (Yuu-koe-kuu Hoe-dahn), or "Foolish Talks on the Nation," published in a magazine called *Crea*. (The title is a Japanese abbreviation for the English word "creation.") Tanaka's article was a comparison of Japanese perceptions of the United States during the Vietnam War with those during the Persian Gulf War. He said that Japanese feelings toward the United States had changed from pro-United States and antiwar to both antiwar and a dislike of the United States.

There was virtually no public reaction to the new word or to Tanaka's theses. Indeed all was calm until shortly afterward when *Bungei Shunju*, one of Japan's best-known and most popular monthly magazines, published a piece written by Keio University Professor Jun Eto called "Shinbei to Hanbei no Aida-Nihonjin wa Naze Amerika ga Kirai ka?"—"Between Pro-America and Anti-America: Why Do Japanese Dislike the United States?"

Professor Eto, a nationally known and respected scholar, took the position that dislike of the United States in Japan had indeed become rampant, and like Tanaka, Eto said that instead of the Japanese being pro-United States and antiwar, they had become anti-United States and antiwar. Eto repeatedly used the word *kenbei* to describe the new feelings of the Japanese toward America.

Both Tanaka and Eto were guilty of making things up as they went, either for the sake of writing provocative articles—a time-honored custom in Japan among both popular writers and university scholars—or as a way of expressing anger at the United States for its attempts to pressure Japan into taking more meaningful steps to open its domestic market to imports.

Just as anyone could have easily predicted, Professor Eto's article caused a nationwide sensation. News media throughout the country picked up on the word *kenbei*, which has a very strong emotional ring to it, discussed it endlessly in print and on the air, and within a month it had become one of the hottest words in the Japanese language.

The furor caused by the new word prompted several of Japan's leading polltakers to survey the public on their attitude toward the United States. All of the polls reported that not only was the United States still the country most liked by the Japanese, the number of Japanese who liked the United States had risen substantially from the previous year.

The Japanese press reaction to *kenbei* was not a new phenomenon. Quite the contrary. Just like its counterparts abroad, the Japanese press is at its very best in making mountains out of molehills. Unlike many of the fad terms regularly introduced into Japan by the press, however, *kenbei* is not likely to disappear. Like Frankenstein's monster, it now has a life of its own.

研修
Kenshu
(Ken-shuu)

Having Fun at Company Expense

One of the most common sights in Japan is that of tour buses on the nation's roads taking loads of people to and from one or another of the country's thousands of hot-spring spas, mountain and beach recreational areas, and famous scenic spots.

All of Japan's several million elementary and junior high school students take annual group trips. Those who live in cities go to rural areas, and those who live in rural areas go to the cities. All go to famous scenic and recreational areas, to museums, and to other sites—adding to the number of people always on the move in Japan. It often seems as if the entire population of the country is having fun instead of working, which contradicts the image of the Japanese as workaholics. Another thing which detracts from the image of the Japanese as workaholics is the large number of company-owned *besso* (base-soh), or "villas," which are operated in popular recreational areas by companies for their employees, and which are always fully booked.

Among the most popular of all the group trips in Japan are the domestic and international *kenshu* (ken-shuu), or "study trips," which are taken by company employees. Shortly after Japan opened its doors to the outside world in the 1850s, the first *kenshu* group of Japanese headed for Europe and the United States, beginning a custom that was to grow into one of the most important activities in the country and which would play a vital role in its industrialization.

After the debacle of World War II, *kenshu* once again became a key in Japan's recovery, and in its emergence in the 1970s as an economic superpower. In the early stages of this recovery virtually all of the *kenshu* trips were overseas, and were aimed at bringing back product samples and technologies to feed the country's burgeoning export industries. But by the end of the 1950s, *kenshu* within Japan were so common that they had become a significant factor in the appearance and rapid growth of bus companies and railway lines, contributing at the same time to the hotel, *ryokan* (ree-oh-kahn) inn and restaurant industries.

From the first, there was an element of recreation in all of the *kenshu* trips, but especially in the domestic trips, because they represented the only chance that most company employees had to enjoy themselves at hotels, inns and restaurants during those years. As corporate affluence increased dramatically beginning in the late 1950s, the recreational aspect of *kenshu* took on a dimension of its own, contributing enormously to the growth of Japan's hospitality and entertainment industries.

During the 1960s, the concept of *kenshu* trips was expanded to include training programs that could last from days to months, resulting in an astounding growth in business travel by employees of major corporations.

Kenshu remain a major corporate activity in Japan, and are a distinctive feature of the Japanese business and nighttime entertainment scenes.

Ki

(Kee)

May the Force be with You!

The Chinese, the Japanese and other Asians have long believed that there is a special energy that flows through the human body from the outside, or from the cosmos, and that this energy is the provider of life and health. In fact, it seems that many if not most ancient cultures in the West as well had exactly the same belief; it may have been expressed in different terms, but it referred to the same thing. It was not until the advent of the scientific age, along with Christianity, that Westerners relegated this belief to the status of utter nonsense at best and a dangerous pagan superstition at worst.

When Christianity and Western science reached Asia, Asians accepted the science but rejected Christianity (they already had their own much older and more profound religions), but they did not renounce their belief in cosmic energy as the animator of all life. As far as they were concerned, the existence of cosmic energy was obvious. They also had proven more than 2,000 years earlier, in such practices as acupuncture and in a variety of health and martial arts, that some kind of special energy ran through the body. And the interest in this area has not waned in Asia; in the 1980s the Chinese government began a major research effort in an attempt to isolate and understand this power using scientific methods.

The Japanese call this special cosmic energy *ki* (kee), which is translated variously as "energy," "spirit," "mind," and "cosmic breath." *Ki* is one of the syllables in aikido, a popular form of martial arts, and in that word *ki* refers to using this special energy to stop or overcome an opponent. *Ki* also occurs in *kiai* (kee-aye), which means "shout," "yell," or "cry," and which is what Japanese kendo practitioners when they attack an opponent with their bamboo swords, and what Japanese athletes and businessmen do when they want to boost their energy, spirit and drive.

A *kiai* can be a slogan, a word, or a nonsensical sound. The point is that people can arouse themselves to achieve extraordinary feats of strength, speed and courage by shouting.

In the 1960s and 1970s, many Japanese corporations adopted the practice of *kiai* into their recruit training programs. Newly hired recruits sent to military-type training camps were required to spend time every day shouting as loud as they could—in some cases while standing in front of train stations where commuters were constantly coming and going. In later years, other companies began sponsoring programs that included a combination of meditation, *kiai* and dousing with cold water during frigid weather—for older managers who wanted to revitalize themselves.

Regardless of how such practices might sound to the rational and scientifically inclined Westerner, they do seem to work—anyone who has served in the marines has witnessed the effects of shouting. The reason these tactics have not been adopted wholesale by Western companies, as so many other Japanese management techniques have been, is apparently because Westerners look upon such behavior as beneath their dignity.

I will not make any predictions about Western companies integrating *kiai* into their training programs anytime soon, but the concept of *ki* and some of its more astounding uses are on their way to being accepted universally. Since the mid-1980s, a growing number of Japan's best-known and most influential business tycoons have been flocking to a *ki* master to learn how to make "the force" work for them. Also, Japan's prestigious Ministry of International Trade and Industry is working with the Tokyo University of Electro-Communications to try to find out what *ki* is and how to harness it, and the Sony Corporation also has a scientific team studying the phenomenon of *ki*.

According to the testimony of several top-level executives in internationally famous companies, including Sony and Sega Enterprises, *ki* has cured ailments, and it has made people more youthful and given them extraordinary energy and insight into managing their companies. With that kind of endorsement, and with the potential that *ki* offers mankind, no one will be able to afford to ignore it if it should prove to be real.

切っ掛け、攻め
Kikkake / Seme
(Kee-kock-kay / Say-may)

Putting on an Act

One of the most conspicuous and meaningful differences between Japanese and American behavior is the degree to which formality is employed and accepted. In general and across the board, the Japanese tend to be exceptionally formal, and Americans tend to be especially informal.

The studied formality of the Japanese is a legacy of their traditional system of etiquette, which was minutely detailed and rigidly enforced by all of the sanctions available to a warrior-dominated feudal government. Japan's traditional etiquette was role-playing carried to an extraordinary extreme, and required the kind and degree of mental and physical training that goes into making a great actor.

As mentioned earlier, until the middle of the 20th century, life in Japan was like living on a stage before a highly critical audience—a stage on which the curtain never went down. Failure to properly say one's lines or to precisely follow the physical movements prescribed for the role of each person was a serious transgression that could be fatal.

The exacting demands of this exquisitely refined and prescribed way of living have been described by some 20th century Japanese writers as similar to being bound in an invisible web, with no freedom of movement whatsoever. Every move that the Japanese made had meaning, and was therefore charged with some degree of emotion. All interpersonal relationships had a dramatic quality that put people on and kept them at an exaggerated emotional level.

One of the results of centuries of conditioning in precise, emotionally charged role-playing was that the Japanese became very clever at using dramatic behavior to achieve their ends, which was the only kind of behavior that was effective.

Japan's traditional etiquette has lost a great deal of its intensity since the 1950s, and the sanctions for failing to live up to the old standards are no longer life-threatening, but sanctions can be and regularly are threatening to one's livelihood and social standing.

Till this day the Japanese are extremely sensitive to any breach in etiquette, particularly in business and in other formal and semi-formal situations, and they must exercise extraordinary caution in their own behavior in order to maintain a facade of harmony.

The Japanese are also still masters at using emotionally charged, dramatic behavior to influence and control people, and they do it routinely. The most common use of a dramatic scenario designed to get something from someone begins with a *kikkake* (kee-kock-kay), a ploy in which Party A lays an emotional trap for Party B by emphasizing how diligent and faithful Party A has been in fulfilling obligations to Party B, and then by recounting the promises or commitments that Party B has failed to live up to.

The *kikkake* is then followed by a more direct attack, called *seme* (say-may), in which responsibility for the problem is placed directly on the shoulders of the other individual in a relatively loud, stern recitation of dissatisfaction with the issues at hand, detailing each facet that is unacceptable. Generally, a *kikkake* drama is climaxed by questioning the ethics and morality of the other party in order to shame them into righting whatever "wrongs" they are accused of committing.

The Japanese are unlikely to use the *kikkake/seme* strategy against a foreigner unless the person is in a power position, or unless the Japanese are confident that the foreigner is so committed to continuing the negotiations or relationship that he or she will accept the browbeating and give in to the Japanese demands, even if the person is not guilty of any misbehavior.

One of the reasons that a *kikkake/seme* drama is often effective when used against a foreigner is that the behavior involved contrasts so sharply with typical Japanese behavior that the foreigner is shocked and confused, and does not know how to quickly and diplomatically counter the accusations.

Denying the accusations, particularly in an angry, loud voice, does not work. If, in fact, the foreign party is not guilty of any transgressions and is sure there have been no misunderstandings, the best response is to call the other side's bluff. The best way to do that is to quietly but firmly make the point that you believe all of your actions have been honest, honorable and fair, suggest that maybe there is a misunderstanding on the Japanese side, and propose that they take whatever time they need to re-evaluate the situation, and end the meeting.

And, of course, foreigners can make use of the *kikkake/seme* strategy against the Japanese, but any such use should be based on real complaints—not an attempt to take unfair advantage, because that will backfire. Foreigners who are inexperienced in using this technique should get detailed advice from an expert before trying to use it.

帰国子女
Kikoku Shijo
(Kee-koe-kuu She-joe)

Strangers in a Strange Land

Returning to their homeland after a long absence is a joyous occasion for most people. After a lengthy residence overseas, people are not only welcomed back enthusiastically, they often also find that their foreign experience enhances their reputation and their personal and business prospects. Strangely, and sadly, such is generally not the case with the Japanese. For many Japanese, the experience of returning home after as little as three years abroad can range from unpleasant to tragic, even when the stay overseas had the approval of family, and was a company requirement.

Shortly after the arrival of the first European missionaries and traders in Japan in the mid-1500s, the Japanese government became obsessed with the desire to keep would-be conquerors and foreign influence out. In the late 1630s the newly established Tokugawa Shogunate expelled all Westerners from Japan and decreed that foreigners would no longer be allowed to visit the country, much less take up residence. The decree remained in force for more than 200 years, and it also prohibited all Japanese who happened to be abroad at that time from ever returning home.

There were only two exceptions to this law. A small number of Dutch traders were allowed to maintain a post on a tiny man-made islet in Nagasaki Bay and to receive one ship a year for the exchange of goods. Also, Chinese trading vessels were occasionally permitted to visit the port.

During the latter part of this period of isolation, sailing traffic around Japan increased. Ships were occasionally blown into Japanese waters by storms, and sometimes wrecked on its shores. Ships that survived the storms were forced to sail away. Survivors of shipwrecks were imprisoned, and it was not until near the end of this self-imposed isolation that survivors were allowed to leave Japan on other ships that came calling by accident or by design.

The Japanese government also refused to take back Japanese fishermen who had lost their ships at sea and had been rescued by passing foreign vessels, if the ships made port anywhere before arriving in Japanese waters. As pressure for Japan to open its doors to the outside world increased, a few of these stranded fishermen who had spent years abroad were finally allowed to return, but they were first imprisoned, and thereafter kept virtually under house-arrest for the rest of their lives. Japan began ending its exclusion policy in the 1850s, but it was the mid-1960s before all Japanese were free to come and go as they pleased.

Now at any one time there are hundreds of thousands of Japanese living and working abroad, and a steady stream of *kikokushijo* (kee-koe-kuu-she-joe), or "returnees from overseas," flowing back into Japan. But till this day, the *kikokushijo* face serious problems of discrimination. The children of returning families are routinely bullied by schoolmates, and made to feel like misfits by many teachers. This *ijime* (ee-jee-may), or "bullying," syndrome is so common and serious that it is recognized as a national problem.

Company employees recalled by the company that sent them abroad, find themselves resented by their coworkers, and often relegated to the sidelines by management in order to avoid causing serious internal friction. During the 1970s and 1980s, promising managerial candidates sent abroad by their companies to attend graduate schools were almost always assigned totally unrelated jobs on their return to Japan, because their coworkers would not accept their new ideas or foreign ways. It was not until the early 1990s, following the collapse of Japan's "bubble economy" and a sudden downturn in business, that most major Japanese companies began seriously trying to take advantage of managers who had spent time abroad.

But even then discrimination against *kikokushijo* continued, especially in middle management, finally resulting in a response that was typically roundabout, but will surely have long-range affects on the whole world of business in Japan. The directors of major companies, especially those in trouble, began bringing home the chief executive officers of their top subsidiaries abroad and appointed them presidents of the parent corporations, bypassing the problem of trying to reintegrate returned managers on lower levels.

Given the ongoing exclusivity of Japanese culture, however, the overall problems encountered by Japan's *kikokushijo* are unlikely to disappear for at least another generation or so.

気配り
Kikubari
(Kee-kuu-bah-ree)

Making Everybody Feel Good

Most of the early Western visitors to Japan in the 16th century, complained bitterly that the Japanese did not distinguish between the truth and the untruth. The Japanese were regularly accused of lying—even when the truth would seem to have served them better.

As time went by, Westerners in Japan elaborated on their criticisms of the Japanese, saying that they had no ethics at all, and that they were guided only by what was expedient at the moment. These early critics of the Japanese were right, but only from the viewpoint of their own standards. In the Japanese context of things, they were the ones who were right, and the Westerners were wrong.

This was one of the many cultural encounters between the Japanese and Westerners where both the subtlety and the rationale of the Japanese way was totally lost on the Westerners—a factor which, almost four centuries later, continues to plague Japanese–Western relations in politics as well as in economics.

There are dozens of cultural factors that define and control Japanese attitudes and behavior, and which distinguish them from the Western experience in a variety of ways; and certainly not all of these differences are negative features of Japanese culture. Many of the traditional cultural traits of the Japanese are, in fact, superior in every sense of the word, and are either downplayed or ignored altogether by many Western cultures.

One of these traits is subsumed in the word *kikubari* (kee-kuu-bah-ree), which means being extraordinarily sensitive to the feelings and needs of others.

In feudal Japan social attitudes and behavior were based more on personal relations, emotions and feelings than on cold, hard principles and impersonal laws—the latter being an invention of Western societies. The highest morality in Japan was fulfilling personal obligations and conforming to a precise etiquette that controlled every aspect of behavior.

In this kind of society, a person's morality was visible! It was manifested constantly through one's speech and whether or not one followed the precisely programmed etiquette in interacting with others. All Japanese were conditioned to conduct themselves in exactly the same manner for each situation, with the result that they all became acutely sensitive to any deviations from the established norm. Under the watchful eyes of the samurai warrior ruling class, the standards of etiquette became higher and higher, and the punishment for misbehavior became sure, swift and often fatal.

This combination of factors resulted in the Japanese becoming extremely demanding and emotional in their expectations from others, and made them equally sensitive to the feelings and needs of others.

One of the solutions to the problem of making this kind of society work was the development of the philosophy of *kikubari*, that is, paying special attention to the emotional as well as to the practical aspects of life. Because the Japanese were all programmed by virtually the same cultural software, they eventually got to the point that they did not have to verbalize their feelings or needs. They were all plugged into the same channel, and could automatically anticipate each other's expectations. One of these expectations was a level and degree of "service" that Westerners tend to regard as unnecessary if not irrational.

Konosuke Matsushita, founder of the giant Matsushita conglomerate, was one of the most famous believers in the virtue and value of *kikubari*. One of Matsushita's rules was that every need and expectation of a customer should be anticipated, and that any customer who was dissatisfied with a product for any reason should be treated with even more consideration and politeness than when he or she bought the product. *Kikubari* in its traditional state does not allow for halfway measures. As practiced and taught by the Japanese, it means that the seller or provider must go all the way to make sure that the customer is not only satisfied but feels good.

While the importance of *kikubari* is gradually decreasing in Japan because of cultural dilution and economic changes, enough of it remains to make it an essential ingredient in achieving success in Japan in any field.

気持ち
Kimochi
(Kee-moe-chee)

Doing Things for Feeling

Generally speaking, Westerners are conditioned to deal in hard facts. To Western businesspeople, that essentially means get the order, get the money, and get on with things. Americans, especially, were traditionally programmed to separate their feelings from their business, to keep their business dealings with other companies on a totally objective plane, and to keep their private lives out of the office or factory.

When American businesspeople began discovering the Japanese market in the 1970s, one of the cultural differences they encountered was the extent to which the personal or human element played a vital role in the Japanese economy—something they had been taught to virtually ignore. They learned that products and prices were practically meaningless until they had resolved all of the personal issues involved in getting into the Japanese market. They also learned that this was extremely difficult to do, sometimes requiring several years to accomplish, and was invariably costly.

One of the key factors in the personal element in Japanese business—and in how they conduct their private affairs—is expressed in the term *kimochi* (kee-moe-chee), which means "feelings." In short, *kimochi* or "feelings" must be satisfied first before a business relationship can begin with a Japanese company, and the good feelings must be sustained thereafter in order for the relationship to continue on a mutually acceptable basis.

The Japanese are not adverse to facts and figures. In fact, they typically go overboard in accumulating data. But their final decision in matters at hand is almost always based more on *kimochi* than on hard data—a circumstance that foreign businesspeople and politicians often find mystifying and frustrating.

Until recent years, it was the rule for Japanese companies to continue doing business at a loss for years rather than break old, established relationships out of respect for the feelings of the people involved—a circumstance that often prevented them from taking on new suppliers and product lines that could have been very profitable. Such un-businesslike behavior is still common in situations where companies have been doing business with each other for one or more generations, and it still acts as a barrier to the free flow of market forces in the country.

Foreign companies wanting to do business in Japan with certain wholesalers or retailers would be wise to first find out if they have any of these barrier relationships. Once that is done and there is an expression of interest from the Japanese side, the second challenge is to establish a network of personal connections based on levels of *kimochi* that satisfy the needs of the appropriate Japanese managers and executives.

Successfully negotiating a business relationship with a Japanese company does not end the need for investing *kimochi* in the relationship. In fact, it often becomes even more critical, because after the courtship and honeymoon are over, differences in perceptions, opinions, approaches and requirements invariably surface, requiring that the two sides remain in a constant state of adjusting the relationship. If the *kimochi* ties between all of the key individuals involved on both sides is not strong enough to withstand all of the pushing and pulling that normally occurs, the relationship will be an unpleasant one and may be shortlived.

On the private side of life in Japan, *kimochi* actions are not always quid pro quo. People routinely do favors for others as expressions of friendship and goodwill and without expecting anything in return. When people feel embarrassed or put in an awkward position by a gift or favor, all the giver has to do to put them at ease is to say, *Kimochi desu* (Kee-moe-chee dess), or "It's feeling."

勤勉性
Kinbensei
(Keen-ben-say-ee)

The Diligence Syndrome

During Japan's long Shogunate Period (1185–1868), the Japanese developed a work ethic that was in keeping with the times. There was no such thing as an established eight-hour workday, or a six- or seven-day workweek. Working hours and times were determined by the nature of the work, the hours of sunlight, the seasons, the climate, by festivals and other public events, and so on. The highly disciplined nature of the warrior-dominated society and the demands created by the clan and shogunate systems of government made it imperative that most Japanese work hard, long hours.

The labor of the common people totally supported the samurai class, which made up some ten percent of the population. The life-style of substantial numbers of clan and samurai families was highly refined, relatively affluent, and required large numbers of skilled, meticulous and attentive servants and craftsmen. Clan and government projects, from road and building maintenance to the construction of shrines and temples, were also never-ending obligations for which there were very high work standards. There were also budgets and deadlines that had to be kept.

Another historical factor that played a key role in the work habits of the Japanese was the regular incidence of urban fires. Japanese homes, made of wood, paper and straw, were built close together. In every home, open-fire pots used for cooking and heating made conflagrations endemic. During windy seasons in Edo, the shogunate capital from 1603 to 1868, fires that destroyed from dozens to hundreds of buildings were so common that they were referred to as "the flowers of Edo," and people would gather at night on hills in and around the city to watch the bright orange flames.

Because these fires most often occurred in winter, when it was often bitterly cold, workmen by the thousands were kept busy working around the clock replacing the homes and buildings and their furnishings.

The opening of Japan to the outside world in the 1850s was to add an even more important factor to the historical work ethic of the Japanese: an all-encompassing pride. By this time, the Japanese had become impregnated with the idea that they were socially and morally superior to any other people. When they discovered how far behind they were in virtually every technology except handicrafts and wooden buildings, they were both astounded and shocked. But rather than dishearten the Japanese, the shock of seeing the industrial and military power of the West galvanized them into a working frenzy to not only catch up with but to surpass the West.

This compulsion gave new meaning to the word *kinbensei*, (keen-ben-say-ee), or "diligence," which had already been long associated with the Japanese. From 1870, following the downfall of the shogunate in 1868, until the end of World War II, the Japanese labored as if they were possessed.

But defeat in World War II was an even greater shock to the Japanese than the opening of the country to the West, and within days after the fighting ended, the Japanese began to rebuild—this time with an even greater compulsion to regain their pride and to prove once again that they were a superior people. *Kinbensei* was taken to the extreme. Driven by unbounded pride founded on both race and culture, the Japanese made diligence into a kind of cult. Human weaknesses were ignored. The fabled *Yamato damashii* (Yah-mah-toe dah-mah-shee), or "Japanese spirit," took over.

For the next three decades the word *kinbensei* became virtually synonymous with *Nihonjin* (Nee-hoan-jeen), the word for a Japanese person—and the words were often used together in *kinbenna Nihonjin* (keen-ben-nah Nee-hoan-jeen), or "diligent Japanese." During that time the Japanese automatically attributed much of their phenomenal success to being far more diligent than other people.

By the 1980s, however, the situation had begun to change dramatically. Japan's postwar generations, especially those born after 1970, were no longer imbued with compulsive *kinbensei*. Raised without knowing hunger or fear and inundated with toys, clothing, entertainment devices and other distractions, this generation grew up in an entirely different world.

Younger Japanese are no longer blindly driven by a cultural superiority complex or by insatiable pride. Their loyalty and dedication to Japan are real enough, but they are no longer obsessive. This change in the character of younger Japanese is one of the most serious concerns facing the country today. In the government as well as in corporate Japan, older officials and executives are fighting a rearguard battle to preserve as much of the cultural *kinbensei* of the Japanese as possible.

禁煙権
Kin'en Ken
(Keen'inn Ken)

Nonsmokers' Rights

On August 25, 1543 a Chinese junk that had blown off course landed at the small Japanese island of Tanega (Tanegashima), some 233 miles south of Kyushu. Several Portuguese traders who were aboard the junk quickly introduced the islanders to guns, venereal disease and tobacco. Within a short time all of these new imports were introduced into the main islands of Japan.

Some years later, the Tokugawa Shogunate attempted to ban the habit of smoking, calling it dangerous to the health and a serious fire hazard, as Japanese buildings were constructed of wood, paper and straw, and burned like tinder. The ban was ignored. Over the following decades the order prohibiting smoking was repeated each time smoking was blamed for a major fire. But these bans were also ignored. The development of the *kiseru* (kee-say-rue), a long-stemmed pipe with a tiny bowl, greatly expanded smoking, and as a result, tobacco became an important industry.

In the 20th century, tobacco and cigarette production was a government monopoly in Japan, and well over 70 percent of the adult male population smoked, and the effort to ban smoking grew also. In 1978 a citizen's action group called the Japan Action for Nonsmokers' Rights was formed to lobby for nonsmokers' rights in public places. The group demanded that Japan National Railways, now called Japan Railways, designate half of its coaches nonsmoking cars. The railway system ignored the demand, and the group sued the company in 1980.

As a result of this legal action the government-run railways voluntarily designated one car per train on the high-speed Shinkansen (Shee-kahn-sane) (Bullet Train Line) as a nonsmoking coach. The car turned out to be so popular that people would stand in the aisles in the nonsmoking coach rather than subject themselves to the other coaches.

The movement to win *kin'en ken* (keen'inn-ken), or "nonsmokers' rights," grew rapidly during the rest of the 1980s. A "No-Smoking Week" was established in 1984, and in 1987 the sixth World Conference on Smoking and Health was held in Tokyo. Over the following years the partly privatized railways added additional nonsmoking cars to each of its trains, and by the end of the 1990s there were three or four nonsmoking coaches on every long-distance train. Smoking on local trains and subway systems was not allowed because the cars were so jammed with passengers during rush hours that lighting up and smoking would have been virtually impossible.

The *kin'en ken* movement has continued to grow in Japan, and by 1995 smoking was totally prohibited on some subway station platforms, and was restricted to certain times and certain areas on other subway and commuter train platforms. The government and the courts have been reluctant to get involved in the controversy, however, and most actions on behalf of nonsmokers have been voluntary.

The general attitude in Japan is that more than half of the population smokes because of stress; and the feeling is that the smoking problem will not be resolved until people are able to change the way they live and work. In the meantime, health authorities report that the number of teenage Japanese girls taking up the smoking habit began rising rapidly in the early 1990s, counteracting the number of adults who were breaking the habit because of health concerns.

綺麗ごと
Kirei Goto
(Kee-ray-ee Go-toe)

Making Pretty Talk

Ages ago, I used to go to a bar in the Oji district of Tokyo just to listen to the Japanese spoken by the woman who ran the place. She was a native of Kyoto, the imperial capital of Japan from 794 to 1868, and she spoke the feminine dialect for which that city is famous—a dialect that is warm, soft and so sensual that I found it irresistible.

I had learned earlier that there were many other Japanese dialects, as well as several levels of "standard Japanese" that played important roles in all social intercourse in Japan. I had also discovered that the language used was determined by the sex, age and social status of the speakers. One had to know how and when to use the proper level of Japanese in every given situation in order to stay out of trouble and to succeed in personal affairs as well as in business. During Japan's long samurai period making a mistake in the use of the language was an affront that could have extremely serious consequences, including a death sentence.

Because of the importance of using the right kind and level of speech in specific situations, the Japanese became hypersensitive to accents and to unusual speech habits, and critical of any deviation from a very narrow norm. The higher the social level and the more formal the situation, the more important it was to use the appropriate *keigo* (kay-ee-go), or "respect language." Despite all of the social and cultural changes that have taken place since 1945, the Japanese are still sensitive to the appropriateness of certain linguistic forms in speech, which are enforced by the risk of both social and economic sanctions.

While young Japanese have been influenced by the wholesale adoption of English words, the study of foreign languages, and the integration of rock music into their lives, and although they do mangle and mix their language to suit their moods during their private time and during informal conversation, they must speak "proper" Japanese in order to join the Establishment.

At the same time, older Japanese who have developed non-Japanese speech habits to any significant degree—by spending time abroad or by associating with Westerners in Japan—generally find that they are no longer regarded as "pure" Japanese, and may have endangered their careers.

Because of the importance of language in Japanese society, many Japanese, especially those who are better educated, develop extraordinary skill in using *kirei goto* (kee-ray-ee go-toe), figuratively "pretty words," in order to influence and otherwise manipulate people. *Kirei goto* is used as a show of respect toward others, to persuade others, or to make excuses. The "pretty words" may or may not be sincere, and *kirei goto* is almost always used with guests and anyone else the Japanese want to impress.

The challenge is to be able to tell the difference between *kirei goto* that is just a formality or a ploy, and comments that are truly from the heart. Oftentimes, the only way that one can circumvent "pretty words" in Japan is to invite the individual or individuals concerned to a nighttime drinking party and get them tipsy.

帰省ラッシュ
Kisei Rasshu
(Kee-say-ee Rah-shuu)

The Homeward Rush

Despite all of the modernity that one sees in Japan, from high-rise towers to high-speed bullet trains, most Japanese are only a step away from their past. The umbilical cord between them and age-old traditions remains in place.

For the Japanese, entering a traditionally styled inn or restaurant, donning a kimono or *yukata* (you-kah-tah), attending weddings, funerals, festivals and other ceremonies—even the sound of a Buddhist temple bell in the distance—are constant reminders of their link with the past.

When the Japanese are wearied by the stress of modern-day life, they are able to go back in time to a life-style that is calm and soothing, restore their spirit, and face the present with renewed energy.

The most common of these renewing rituals is a visit to a hot-spring spa where the way of life has not changed for hundreds of years. There the people are able to enter what amounts to time capsules—bathing in hot mineral water, eating traditional foods, sitting on *tatami* reed-mat floors, sleeping on futon, and strolling around in scenic isolated places, just as their ancestors did generations ago.

But the single largest "return to the past" event in Japan occurs each year in mid-August in conjunction with the ancient Obon (Oh-bone) festival, when the souls of the dead were traditionally believed to come back to visit the living. During this period, millions of Japanese leave the cities and return to the traditional homes of their ancestors, creating an outflow of people that is known as *kisei rasshu* (kee-say-ee rah-shuu), literally "homecoming rush"—or, when viewed from the cities, the "homeward rush." On this annual occasion, Japan's railway and bus companies put thousands of additional trains and coaches into service, and on peak days as many as 30 million people are on the move between the major metropolitan areas and outlying prefectures.

In addition to being a cultural and social event of extraordinary importance, the *kisei* custom is also a major economic event, resulting in the expenditure of billions of yen for transportation, food, drinks, accommodations and gifts. Because of the scale of the *kisei* custom, combined with other Obon events, it is one of the key periods during the year for retail businesses, rivaling Christmas in the United States.

Not all Japanese return to their ancestral homes during Obon, however. Millions of them join the exodus from the cities, but their destinations are the beaches, mountain resorts and the dozens of famous mountain-climbing areas in the country.

Foreign businesspeople contemplating trips to Japan during the Obon season, generally July 20 to August 20, should keep in mind that this is the primary vacation period in Japan, and that any meetings they expect to have during this period should be arranged well in advance.

Annual passenger statistics released by Japan's transportation systems show that during most of the *kisei* period passenger volume ranges from 100 to 200 percent over capacity. Anyone expecting to travel within Japan during this period, for pleasure or business, is therefore well advised to make both transportation arrangements and hotel reservations as early as possible.

気を許す
Ki wo Yurusu
(Kee oh Yuu-rue-sue)

Letting Your Guard Down

During the heyday of Japan's last great shogunate dynasty, which began in 1603 and ended in 1868, one of the strategies used by the powerful Tokugawa shoguns to keep the provincial fiefs in line was to employ scores of professional spies, assassins and saboteurs, or ninja, who, if they existed today, would make Ian Fleming's fictional James Bond look like a wimp.

The ninja, who practiced the art of ninjutsu, sometimes translated as "the art of invisibility," but which literally means "stealing in," were not government-trained secret agents. They belonged to small, independent family clans who lived in remote mountainous areas, and who specialized in ninjutsu as a family tradition; the ninja were for hire by both the shogunate and the anti-shogunate forces, much like present-day freelance spies and killers.

The training of ninja began in childhood. By the time they were adults, they were masters of disguise and of a variety of weapons and poisons, and they could run so fast, jump so high, and perform dozens of other feats that were so extraordinary that common people believed they were capable of magic. Because of their calling, captured ninja were shown no mercy and were invariably put to death in the most painful and gruesome ways imaginable. Obviously, ninja did everything possible to avoid capture, and suicide was among their options when escape became impossible.

One of the tricks used to get a person to reveal his or her identity as a ninja was to put the person in a position in which some spectacular ninja-like feat was necessary; if the person performed the action, such as leaping aside or jumping onto a high fence, he or she was obviously a ninja.

Ordinary Japanese have never had as much reason as ninja to be on the alert and keep their guard up, but the demands of Japan's traditional etiquette during most of the feudal age (1185–1868) were so high that the comparison is not that farfetched. In many formal situations in feudal Japan, the wrong facial expression, an unprescribed move or the wrong word, even the wrong tone of voice, could have serious consequences. In many situations that were common to those times, the consequences could be loss of position, banishment or death.

This system of behavior was so demanding that it required years of effort to learn and an extraordinary amount of energy and presence of mind to maintain. Virtually the only time the Japanese could *ki wo yurusu* (kee oh yuu-rue-sue), or "relax" or "forget etiquette," was when they were in a formally recognized drinking situation. The feudal system that made it possible to perpetuate such a minutely prescribed and strictly enforced standard of behavior officially ended in 1945, but its influence still permeates Japanese society and continues to set both the pattern and tone of adult Japanese behavior today. The grip of the system is still powerful enough that it keeps the Japanese under a stifling blanket of stress, making it difficult or impossible for them to let their guard down and "be themselves" in social and business interactions.

This culturally conditioned mentality and behavior naturally has a fundamental affect on how the Japanese react to foreigners, and how foreigners react to them. In informal, casual situations, foreigners tend to be impressed with the courteous, stylized behavior of the Japanese. But in business and political contexts, the influence of such "uptight" behavior is a serious handicap for both the Japanese as well as their foreign counterparts.

When the Japanese go abroad and are no longer under pressure to "act Japanese," it is something like being let out of a cage. If they associate mostly with Westerners for as little as two or three years, they lose most or all of their Japaneseness—and when they return home the pressure to conform is even more oppressive, and they end up feeling like misfits.

こじんまり
Kojinmari
(Koe-jeen-mah-ree)

As Snug as a Bug in a Rug

Back in the 16th century, Sen no Rikyu, who was probably Japan's most famous tea master, made each of his new teahouses smaller and smaller as he increasingly refined the ritual in an effort to get down to the essence of aesthetics, human relations and the cosmos.

Eventually he ended up with a teahouse, or tearoom, that was only large enough to comfortably seat the number of guests he wanted to have, which was usually three to five. In addition to reducing the size of the tearoom down to only what was essential, he also lowered the height of its door down to where guests had to literally crawl through it.

In the 1960s a very ordinary Japanese entrepreneur went Sen no Rikyu one better. He introduced what quickly came to be known as "capsule hotels" near major transportation terminals in Tokyo. These hotels featured "rooms" that were just big enough for a cot, a small TV set, and hooks to hang one's clothes on. Some of the more deluxe models had telephones connected to the front desk, a radio and a clock. In effect, they were very much like sleeping berths on trains. The capsule hotels got a lot of derisive and supposedly humorous comment from Westerners, but they were popular with Japanese and were a commercial success.

Till this day most Japanese apartments and homes are small by Western standards, and yet the Japanese do not feel deprived. (This writer once lived for a few weeks in a free-standing "house" in Tokyo's Naito-cho district that measured approximate 6 feet by 6 feet—a two-*jo* (joe), or two-mat guest "house.")

It turns out that the Japanese sense of space and being is quite different from the Western sense. Most Westerners have a compulsion to live in a large house, and the larger the house, the more impressive and desirable it is. The Japanese, on the other hand, are primarily motivated by feelings that are expressed in the word *kojinmari* (koe-jeen-mah-ree), which means "snug," "cozy," and "neat." They feel much more secure and spiritually comfortable in a small space, and regard large-size Western rooms and houses as not only unfriendly, but wasteful.

Some time during the Heian Period (794–1185), the size of a room was commonly determined by the amount of space a person occupied while sitting and sleeping, and by the person's social rank. A person of the first rank was allotted the largest space, which measured only 4 feet by 7 feet. An ordinary person, according to records of that time, was expected to make do with a space measuring 3 feet by 6 feet. Of course, rooms were built larger than this, but these standards were indicative of the Japanese attitude toward space. Early in Japanese history, a room 9 feet by 9 feet in size—the area of four-and-a-half *tatami* mats—became the standard size for most rooms in Japan.

The *kojinmari* concept remains important in contemporary Japan, not only because of its influence in the building industry, but also because it has an effect on virtually every area of Japanese life, from the number of passengers that can be crammed into a subway or railway car to the arrangement of desks in offices.

At the same time, the Japanese have been facing a serious crisis since the 1980s. By that decade, younger Japanese were growing conspicuously taller and bigger in all respects than their parents. By the end of the 1980s, this problem was becoming acute, because the young could no longer fit comfortably at school desks or in the seats of buses. Even the floor bedding, futon, on which the Japanese traditionally slept was not long enough for this new generation.

Having been conditioned by the *kojinmari* concept over the centuries, most Japanese still feel exposed and uncomfortable when they are out in the open and alone. More adventurous types among the younger generations now travel alone and do things their way, but most older Japanese still prefer to travel in groups and do things in unison.

Foreigners selling personal-use products in Japan need to be aware of the concept of *kojinmari*. If a product does not fit the Japanese concept—even when this concept is outdated—it may be rejected as not being suitable for the Japanese.

Most Japanese still think in terms of themselves as being smaller than Westerners, of Westerners eating more than Japanese, and so on—stereotypes that no longer have any basis in fact, but which are very real in the Japanese mindset. It is often necessary to go to some extreme to break the "small" fixation in which the Japanese have existed for so many centuries.

On a personal note regarding eating and physical size, I do not know a single Japanese, male or female, of any size or age, who eats less than I do. On the contrary, I am regularly amazed at how much the Japanese, who are generally smaller than I am, put away every meal. The Japanese are also getting taller. Until the 1970s, I could look over the heads of 90 to 95 percent of all the Japanese I met. By the mid-1980s I was nose-to-nose to 10 to 15 percent of the teenage boys I encountered. Now, somewhere around 30 percent of male Japanese under 30 are as tall or nearly as tall as I am (5 feet 9 inches), and I regularly encounter teens who are close to six feet tall.

心構え
Kokorogamae
(Koe-koe-roe-gah-my)

Attitude is Everything

Zen Buddhism teaches that if the body and mind have been totally integrated by a combination of meditation and the appropriate physical exercise, the doing of a thing is as easy as thinking it—and as far as the mind is concerned, the thinking and the doing are the same thing. This philosophy, expressed in the word *kamae* (kah-my), or "attitude," became solidly entrenched in Japan between 1141 and 1215, and was to have a profound influence on the development of Japanese culture thereafter.

Till this day, *kamae*, usually expressed in the form of *kokorogamae* (koe-koe-roe-gah-my), or "mental attitude," or literally, "heart attitude," remains a key element in all education, all training, and ideally in all work performed in Japan.

In Japanese culture, the first step in developing skill in any activity is learning, and thereafter keeping, the right attitude. Different skills require different attitudes, and one of the jobs of master teachers is to impart the correct attitude to students or novices.

Westerners who have become involved in such martial arts as aikido, judo or kendo know that form alone, no matter how perfect, is not enough to produce a winner. They learn that without the proper *kokorogamae*, they do not stand a chance when facing an opponent who has mastered both *kamae* and form. Attitude is the thing that gives extraordinary power to Noh and kabuki actors. With attitude alone, master kabuki and Noh actors can express virtually every human emotion known, and with one or two steps or a hand gesture, create an illusion of action that is so powerful the audience is swept up in the drama.

During Japan's long samurai period when skill with a sword was often a matter of life or death, the greatest masters of the sword were those who first learned the right attitude. It was said that a master swordsman could instantly judge the skill of an opponent by his attitude—before an opponent made the first move. The face of the master swordsman was said to have been like the apparently frozen expression of a Noh mask—saying nothing and yet saying everything at the same time—an expression that one still sees today in middle-aged and older Japanese men.

When Japanese corporations are interviewing job applicants, the first thing they measure and judge in the candidates is their *kokorogamae*. If they do not have the "right attitude," they will not be hired, regardless of how brilliant a candidate might be or how many skills they may have developed.

In promoting employees, Japanese companies rate attitude above virtually everything else. Their philosophy is that the higher people go up the managerial ladder, the more vital it is for them to have the right attitude. And in the Japanese context of things, the right attitude for a corporate employee includes such things as being a good listener, and being humble, polite, observant, cooperative, diligent and determined, but not openly aggressive.

Any analysis of Japanese character and behavior in planning and implementing projects, in interacting with coworkers, clients and customers, and in the way they work invariably begins and ends with an evaluation of their *kokorogamae*. Traditionally, the "right attitude" was programmed into all Japanese by the culture. It was something that the Japanese absorbed as they grew up, because the whole culture was based on precisely identified attitudes that had long since been their second nature whether in private or in public.

When Japanese businesspeople meet their foreign counterparts for the first time, the judgment they make about whether or not they want to pursue the relationship often hinges on what they read in the attitude of the foreigners. Western golfers, bowlers, tennis players and other professional sportspeople learn very quickly that if they do not have the right attitude, they cannot become champions.

But most Westerners do not knowingly and deliberately make use of this knowledge in their daily lives. This is one of the reasons why most foreigners are generally at a disadvantage when dealing with the Japanese—when the Japanese are in groups—because the attitude of the Japanese often gives them unassailable power.

国際化
Kokusaika
(Koke-sigh-kah)

Becoming Less Japanese

As early as 1960, a number of Japanese politicians, economists, sociologists, educators and others began calling for the "internationalization" of Japan. Some, including this writer went so far as to say that the Japanese would have to completely "de-Japanize" themselves if they wanted to survive and prosper in the coming global economy. These calls for *kokusaika* (koke-sigh-kah), or "internationalization," became louder and more common as the years passed, reaching a crescendo by the mid-1970s.

In response to these calls, thousands of promising young Japanese managers were sent abroad between 1960 and 1975 to study foreign languages and to gain foreign management experience. But once these ambitious young people returned home, virtually all of them were treated as "outsiders," and were shunted off into peripheral or dead-end jobs.

Despite a recognition among Japanese companies that they would benefit by internationalizing their operations, the exclusivity of Japan's corporate culture was so powerful that it could not accept people, even its own, who had been exposed to the outside world, and who had come back to Japan with attitudes and ideas that were un-Japanese. Thus, some of the most intelligent and experienced people in Japan fell victim to the *shimaguni konjo* (she-mah-guu-ne kohn-joe), or "island mentality," with which the Japanese had long been associated, and which they routinely used both as a weapon and as an excuse.

Then, over the next decade another remarkable movement took place. The cries for *kokusaika* became muted—almost completely drowned out by an equally large and even more vociferous number of Japanese voices saying that it was not the Japanese who should change. They said it was Americans and others whose economies were suffering and whose societies were roiled by growing social problems that should change. At the end of the 1980s, when it was becoming more and more obvious that the artificially inflated nature of Japan's economy had reached the outer limits of its "Big Bang," and that American manufacturers in particular were recovering their competitiveness, the pro-*kokusaika* voices came back, stronger than ever.

When Japan's "bubble economy" collapsed in 1990 and 1991, *kokusaika* became the official orthodoxy of the majority of politicians, economists and businesspeople. The biggest holdouts this time were government bureaucrats, but since it was they, and not the political leaders who ran the government, steps to legislate and implement internationalization measures were severely blunted.

By this time, however, most of Japan's famous companies, such as Sony and Matsushita, had developed large cadres of employees who had international experience. But this time they avoided most cultural clashes with their other employees by keeping the two groups as separate as possible, and in a growing number of cases by bringing top-level overseas executives back as directors, executive vice presidents, and presidents of the parent companies. Now a growing number of Japan's multinational companies conduct educational programs for their employees. These programs are designed to create a common management system for their domestic and international operations, programs that are based on merging the best of the Japanese and Western approaches.

This is not to suggest that any Japanese company now operates in a manner that would make it possible for a foreign employee to join the company, quickly feel at home, and begin working effectively and happily with his Japanese coworkers and superiors. *Kokusaika*, even in companies that have extensive retraining programs for their non-Japanese employees, has not yet reached that point, and is not likely to do so for some time to come.

In fact, the responsibility for change does not lie only on the shoulders of the Japanese. Foreign employees of Japanese companies should also be willing to change their thinking and their ways, when these changes would result in them becoming better employees regardless of whom they work for.

The internationalization of Japan, in the sense of making all Japanese more rational in their behavior, more open-minded and tolerant of other people and other ways, more willing to live with and cooperate with non-Japanese as well as the Japanese who act "un-Japanese," will not happen until this kind of thinking is built into the educational system from kindergarten on up.

That sea change will require a long, multigeneration time span because it can only happen little by little, in tiny, almost invisible increments.

小回りがきく
Komawari ga Kiku
(Koe-mah-wah-ree gah Kee-kuu)

Bypassing the Bureaucracy

During the heyday of Japan's rise to economic superpower status, one of the things that the Japanese invariably faulted American companies on was the service they provided to their customers. The Japanese attributed a great deal of their own extraordinary success in the American market, and the lack of success by American companies in penetrating the Japanese market, to a fundamental difference in the way the

Japanese and Americans view customer service. In supporting their case, the Japanese would list one example after another in which American companies took advantage of the inexperience and naivety of their customers—callously inconveniencing them, ignoring their complaints, and often blaming them for whatever problems occurred.

The Japanese owed their view of service and the priority that they gave it to historical factors that had conditioned them for centuries to go to extremes to satisfy customers with good service and to promptly redress any complaints that a customer might have.

This historical influence was a part of the highly refined life-style that began developing in the Heian Period (794–1185) and which became something of a cult by the Tokugawa Period (1603–1868). During this latter era, providing the very best products that human effort could produce, guaranteeing them unconditionally, and making an exquisitely detailed kind of service to superiors a paramount obligation, became virtually mandatory—and in some cases a matter of life and death. Everyone in power, from the emperor, shogun, ministers and provincial lords down to individual samurai warriors, demanded a standard of personal service from their servants, retainers and suppliers that was incredibly high.

During the 50 some years that Konosuke Matsushita ran the huge Matsushita complex of companies, he constantly preached that all Japanese businessmen should treat customer complaints like "the voice of God" and redress them immediately and in good spirits even if the customers were wrong.

While the quality of service that existed during Japan's feudal age and that which was advocated by Konosuke Matsushita have degenerated significantly in today's Japan, enough of the traditional service ethos remains to set the Japanese apart and to give them special advantages. It is still the policy of most Japanese manufacturers, wholesalers and retailers to educate their employees in the philosophy of *komawari ga kiku* (koe-mah-wah-ree gah kee-kuu).

By itself *komawari* means "small, sharp turns." *Kiku* means "to be effective, to work." When these two words are put together, it means that employees are expected to personally take immediate action if a customer complains to them, no matter what section or department they might be in, and to follow up and make sure the complaint is satisfactorily resolved. The phrase specifically incorporates the concept that the employee approached must not allow the complaint to get bogged down in the bureaucracy of the store or company, and end up being unsolved or delayed.

In practice the person who receives a complaint may not be in a position to resolve it personally, but *komawari ga kiku* demands that he or she stay involved to make sure that the problem is being handle by a responsible person and that customers do not feel like they are being given the runaround.

Despite the incredible degree of bureaucracy that is characteristic of Japanese organizations, when there are consumer complaints or other emergencies, the *komawari ga kiku* philosophy makes it possible for the Japanese to do things quickly and efficiently, as they are programmed to do so.

顧問
Komon
(Koe-moan)

The Indispensable Go-Betweens

During the Tokugawa Shogunate, Japan's last great shogunate dynasty (1603–1868), the city of Mito, northeast of Tokyo in present-day Ibaraki Prefecture, was the headquarters of one of the three main branches of the Tokugawa family; the others were the Kii and Owari branches.

The head of the Mito Tokugawas occupied the hereditary position of vice shogun, and was therefore barred from becoming shogun. But the vice shogun had great prestige and considerable power. The most famous of the long line of vice shoguns was Mitsukuni Mito, head of the Mito branch of the Tokugawa family, who was renowned for his wisdom and sense of justice and was a key advisor to the reigning shogun. After Mito retired, he became known by the name, Kohmon, and it seems that he traveled about the country doing good deeds.

In any event, in the 1970s an imaginative television producer came up with a weekly samurai drama called *Mito Kohmon* (Mee-toe Koh-moan), which was a fictionalized account of the retired vice shogun's travels. In the series, Mito Kohmon is depicted on an unending walking journey around the country, accompanied by three or four young companion-bodyguards, one of whom is usually a pretty girl.*

The former vice shogun and shogunate advisor, who is addressed as Go-Inkyo Sama (Go-Inn-k'yoe Sah-mah), or "Honorable Retired One," travels incognito, and in each show he and his companions come across some evildoers in one of the villages or towns they are passing through, and stop long enough to bring the criminals to justice. The highlight of each show is a rousing sword-fight with the bad guys, which always ends when the former vice shogun's bodyguards hold up the crest of the Tokugawa family and identify him. Finding that they are fighting a high personage from the mighty house of Tokugawa, the evildoers fall to their knees in abject submission. The series became one of the most popular and longest running shows in Japan's television history.

The word *komon* (koe-moan), with a short "koe" sound, is the Japanese word for "advisor" or "counselor," and there are thousands of them in Japan today, playing key roles in virtually every area of business, politics and professional affairs. *Komon* remain important in Japan because the closed, group-oriented nature of the culture affects Japanese organizations as well as foreign enterprises. The most powerful and effective *komon*, like their Tokugawa predecessors, are retired from important government ministries and agencies, or from major corporations that work closely with the government.

Komon are retained by private enterprises as well as various branches of the government because of their experience and knowledge, but are especially valued for their connections.

The Japanese, just like foreigners, need go-betweens to help them break the barriers that exist between all groups in Japan, to establish contact in the accepted manner, and to successfully develop the desired relationships. This process is naturally more difficult and time-consuming for foreign companies that do not already have well-established records and connections in Japan, because they have to start from scratch—beginning with the difficult task of finding a *komon* whose background meshes with their needs.

Since having an experienced and highly respected *komon* can mean the difference between success and failure in starting new enterprises in Japan, any company contemplating going into the Japanese market would be wise to bring in such an advisor at the beginning of the planning process.

In addition to knowing who in the industry to contact to make things happen, and how to contact them properly, a really good *komon* can advise newcomers on every nuance of the often mysterious and always delicate steps that must be taken to succeed in Japan. With rare exceptions, a Japanese *komon* is far more effective than a foreign consultant, even though the latter may have a long background in Japan and speak Japanese. Japanese culture is so exclusive that a non-Japanese is always an outsider and, regardless of his or her qualifications, is not given the same credibility and trust as a Japanese.

In the early years of the Mito Kohmon *series, the role of the pretty girl was played by Izumi Yamaguchi, who, when she was in her early teens, often baby-sat my eldest daughter.*

コミュニケーション・ギャップ
Komyunikeshon Gyappu
(Koe-m'yuu-nee-kay-shoan G'yahp-puu)

The Communication Gap

Many of the meetings between Westerners and Japanese that I have participated in during a period of some 50 years have had one thing in common: The attempts of the two sides to communicate with each other were marked by varying degrees of ambiguity, which in turn led to different interpretations of the meetings. In some cases, the ambiguity was caused by purely linguistic problems. Whoever was doing the interpreting simply did not do a good job. In most cases, however, the misconceptions resulted from different cultural values and customs.

The feelings of uneasiness that generally enveloped both the Japanese and foreign participants in the meetings I witnessed were often so subtle as to be invisible, and they frequently were of a nature that no amount of goodwill or cross-cultural insight could totally overcome. At other times, they were as conspicuous as the raising of a red flag, and were easily resolved.

One failing that both sides invariably exhibited was saying "yes" or nodding "yes" during presentations and exchanges when they really did not understand what was being said. Westerners generally gave the "yes" signal because they did not want to appear ignorant or uninformed, and because they hoped they would pick up on what was said as the dialogue continued. The Japanese nodded and did not asked questions because they had been culturally conditioned to say as little as possible, to not ask questions in a public forum, and to depend on informal discussions outside of meetings—and because nodding "yes" or saying *hai* (hi), "yes," while listening to a conversation was only an affirmation that they were listening and were signaling the speaker to continue.

The difficulty that Japan has communicating with the rest of the world is one of the biggest problems the country faces, and the phrase *komyunikeshon gyappu* (koe-m'yuu-nee-kay-shoan g'yahp-puu), "communication gap," is constantly in the news media and on the lips of businesspeople, politicians and public commentators.

As in the meetings referred to above, the communication problem begins with language. Probably no more than six or seven percent of all Japanese in responsible positions speak English or any other foreign language well enough to express themselves fluently.

The number of highly placed foreigners who speak Japanese is so small it is hardly worth mentioning; and practically all foreigners who are involved with Japan leave it up to the Japanese to speak the language of the visitors or to provide interpreters.

The second part of the communication gap that bedevils Japan is strictly cultural, and much of it is unbridgeable—a gap that simply cannot be closed. This virtually permanent gap is made up of beliefs and behavior that are unique to both sides, and are either not understandable or are not acceptable by the opposing sides. Also, both sides tend to naturally believe that all they have to do to get the other side to accept their position is to explain it, and all will be well.

This situation is especially frustrating to the Japanese, because they know it is up to them to explain themselves, yet they are handicapped by their poor ability to converse in foreign languages, by their inexperience in presenting frank, unambiguous arguments on their own behalf, and by their reluctance to be openly frank and aggressive in such matters. They also believe that there are many things about their culture that are self-explanatory, that are superior, and that should not be changed to accommodate anyone.

Another aspect of this communication gap is that until very recently the Japanese limited their "cultural exports" and cultural explanations to kabuki, Noh, sumo, some arts and crafts—such as origami—Japanese food, and karaoke singing in bars. Needless to say, these aspects of the culture do not contribute significantly to an understanding of Japan. In fact, by themselves, they obfuscate the culture, making the Japanese seem alien instead of just different.

There is presently a growing effort to export the Japanese language and Japanese literature, two of the traditional carriers of culture. (Other carriers like music and religion may come some time in the future.) A significant part of the communication gap, however, is also generational, so the gap is not going to go away anytime soon.

懇談会
Kondan Kai
(Koan-dahn Kigh)

Personalizing the Business Process

Some years ago one of my university classmates who worked for a major American corporation was sent to Japan, in the capacity of representative director, to liaison with the firm's Japanese joint-venture partner.

For several months after his arrival in Tokyo, my friend kept asking when the next directors' meeting was going to be held, but his Japanese colleagues kept putting him off. In the meantime, however, the same Japanese executives would invite my friend to the nearby Palace Hotel almost every week for drinks and dinner. Finally, exasperated at being put off so long, my classmate demanded that a directors' meeting be called. It was at this point that he was informed that the informal chats he had been having at the Palace Hotel were "directors' meetings," and the Japanese side had been getting all the input from him that it wanted.

This kind of insidious manipulation of foreign joint-venture partners is no longer common in Japan, but *kandan kai* (kahn-dahn kigh), "informal chats" or "informal meetings," retain prime importance in the Japanese way of doing business—and it is still common for the foreign side in such conversations to be totally unaware of their function and importance.

Generally speaking, top executives in larger Japanese companies do not make decisions and then pass them down for implementation. The few exceptions to this are invariably companies that are still run by the founders who are especially talented in some area and have very strong personalities. Top executives in Japanese companies are responsible for establishing the direction of their firms and providing philosophical guidelines, but it is up to middle management to initiate and implement concrete proposals for getting the company where it wants to go.

These proposals are not made arbitrarily or independently, however. They are first circulated to all middle managers in the company who would have any role in the project. The proposals are then discussed, endlessly it sometimes seems, in *kandan kai* among the middle managers after-hours in bars or restaurants following two, three, or four hours of drinking and eating. This decision-making process generally takes several months, and it may take a year or more if the project is a large one, and especially if it involves foreign participation.

If the project appears to have merit to most of the middle managers—and in the early stages it is rare for anyone to take a position—the concept is refined by input from different sections, departments and, sometimes, outside consultants or mentors and gradually moves up the management chain. If all of the concerned middle- and upper-level managers sign off on the project, it is then submitted to the directors, one or more of whom may have played a behind-the-scenes role in getting the proposal this far, and may already have had *kandan kai* with other directors about it.

Finally, if every possible question the directors might ask has been answered in the documentation accompanying the proposal, and if all of the key managers have put their stamp on it, it will almost always be accepted by the board of directors.

This process of qualifying new projects makes it extraordinarily difficult for a foreign company to work out a complex arrangement with a Japanese company. In order to be in the game, the foreign side must participate in many—sometimes dozens—of the *kondan kai*, either in Japan, in their home country, or both. This means, of course, that the foreign side must be able to communicate clearly and thoroughly to several—if not dozens—of members of the Japanese company, and to satisfy the seemingly infinite obsession for more and more information and documentation.

There are numerous cultural subtleties that are involved in this kind of negotiation, and several books have been written on the subject. It takes a special kind of personality, including extraordinary patience and perseverance, to do it successfully. Generally speaking, the best approach for the foreign side is to engage the services of a highly competent, highly respected Japanese consultant to lead and guide them through what amounts to a minefield of pitfalls and booby traps.

コネ
Kone
(Koe-nay)

The Importance of Connections

Until recent decades, the Japanese were often described as among the loneliest of all people—a situation that was rooted in their traditional culture in which people belonged to specific families, groups, villages, clans and other groups which were so exclusive that one did not readily make friends outside of one's own immediate circle.

This group exclusivity factor, which made all outsiders adversaries to varying degrees, affected every area of Japanese life, and was especially important in business and in professional activities of every kind. Because the Japanese were conditioned to be wary of outsiders and to keep everything possible "in-house," larger corporations made a special effort to be self-sufficient.

As part of the industrialization process between 1870 and 1895, major Japanese corporations in key industries established a pyramid of *kogaisha* (koe-guy-shah), or "subsidiaries," to act as parts suppliers, wholesalers, and for other purposes; the larger and more successful of these corporations became the notorious *zaibatsu* (zigh-baht-sue) of pre-World War II Japan.

When it was impractical for companies to establish their own *kogaisha*, they forged *keiretsu* (kay-ee-rate-sue), or "aligned relationships" with firms with which they usually had some kind of previous connection. By the 1940s, the ten largest of Japan's *zaibatsu* each had anywhere from 100 to 300 firms under their control, and altogether they were responsible for more than 60 percent of the country's gross national product.

Following Japan's defeat in World War II, the United States took the lead in trying to break up the *zaibatsu*, but as soon as Japan regained its sovereignty in 1952, the former *zaibatsu* members came together again as *keiretsu* companies.

In the decades following the occupation, all of Japan's prewar companies and all of the new ones that were established after the war did their best to follow exactly the same pattern as the old conglomerates, establishing subsidiaries and affiliations with varying degrees of success.

From the 1950s to near the end of the 1980s, these company groups operated more-or-less like exclusive clubs. Generally speaking, one group did not do business with another group, and there was almost no contact between them.

These group and exclusivity factors were so restrictive that departments within companies generally acted like exclusive preserves of their own, making communication between them difficult and sometimes impossible.

It was virtually mandatory that persons have *kone* (koe-nay), or "connections," inside a company or know someone who could provide a formal introduction, *shokai-*

jo (show-kigh-joe), to a member of the company, before it would be possible to approach a company about any kind of business relationship. *Kone*, which is short for the English word "connection," could be a relative, a schoolmate or a fellow alumni. Lacking these personal connections, a *kone* could be a banker or a staff member of some other company that had connections in the firm concerned.

There have been occasions when Japanese companies would receive and pay serious attention to foreigners who came to a company without *kone* or *shokaijo*, but these instances were relatively rare. More likely than not, visitors without introductions would be greeted and listened to politely, but nothing would evolve from the initial contact.

It was not until the latter part of the 1980s, after Japan's economy had become huge and complicated and both domestic and international competition had become severe, that companies began to cross group lines. It took the shock of a sudden "bursting" of the Japanese economy in 1990 and 1991 for the highest levels of Japanese management to recognize that their traditional exclusiveness designed to keep strangers out was a serious handicap, and that it should be dropped.

Thereafter, both business and general news media carried numerous interviews with leading corporate executives who called for companies to establish an infrastructure for handling personal approaches by individuals who had no *kone* or introductions. Since that time, many companies have taken this important step, but generally there is no way to identify them in advance. Only a few have been aggressive enough to list newly established "new business" offices in their advertisements.

As a general rule, it still pays to have a *kone* with a Japanese company before considering a business approach of any kind.

混乱
Konran
(Koan-rahn)

Keeping Things Under Control

One of the features of life in Japan that most impressed Western visitors following the opening of the country to the outside world in the mid-1800s was the precise form and order in Japanese manners, including the way people went about their work and took part in recreation.

Japanese behavior was programmed down to the smallest and seemingly most innocuous detail. Generally speaking, the whole society functioned as a well-practiced troupe of actors who were so versed in their lines and cues that behaving in any other manner was virtually unthinkable. The day-to-day conditioning that was necessary to achieve such carefully prescribed form and order was solidly based in the philosophical, religious and political systems that prevailed in Japan during its long feudal age.

It was not only morally right to behave in such a manner, it was demanded by the government, and rigid conformity was enforced by the ruling samurai class.

It was the aim of the government to control both the emotions and the actions of people to the point that they would always behave in the manner that was prescribed for their age, sex and station in life, and which would satisfy the goals of the government—a political policy that served the shogunate well for many generations. In this programmed society, individual thought and independent innovation were generally taboo. The watchword was not only *wa* (wah), or "harmony," it was a special kind of harmony that became synonymous with being Japanese.

Because of this pervasive conditioning in both the concept and practice of harmonious behavior, the Japanese became especially sensitive to disharmony, or *konran* (koan-rahn), which literally means "wild confusion." Any flouting of the standards set and enforced by the government was routinely met with serious sanctions, and in matters of etiquette involving the privileged samurai and government officials, these sanctions could be fatal.

As a result of lifelong conditioning to avoid *konran*, the Japanese developed a variety of habits and subterfuges for contending with what could be very dangerous situations in their day-to-day activities. One of the more common of these practices was to simply ignore things—to behave as if unpleasant situations did not exist. Another way of dealing with potential *konran* situations was to give a neutral or noncommittal response to questions or requests, or to respond without any consideration for the truth or for real intentions. The Japanese also became masters at using ritual to mask their true feelings and at manipulating people—not necessarily out of any inherent maliciousness, but as a means of self-preservation.

Konran is now quite common in Japan, with fairly frequent mass melees in the Diet being one of the more conspicuous examples of the changing times. But enough of the conditioning in harmony and avoidance of disharmony remains, to provide Japan with one of the most orderly and most efficient of contemporary societies.

Interestingly, there has been a movement since the 1980s to help the Japanese take a confrontational approach in business negotiations and in political dialogue, particularly in dealings with foreigners. When the first debate-type programs began appearing on television in the early 1990s, they were so unusual and out of character for the Japanese, that the programs attracted a large audience because people were fascinated by seeing and hearing prominent Japanese businesspeople and politicians actually argue in public.

However, the age-old taboo against *konran* is not likely to disappear from Japanese culture anytime soon; it is far too deeply entrenched in every aspect of the culture, and particularly in business.

コピー食品
Kopi Shokuhin
(Koe-pee Show-kuu-heen)

Imitation Food

Japan's "national menu" of foods is not as long as that of China, but the Japanese are just as proud of their traditional cuisine as the Chinese are of theirs. All of Japan's regions have their own special dishes that have been an important part of their attraction as tourist destinations. Also, as in China, the making of the various traditional ceramic and lacquer ware utensils in Japan has been a distinctive art since early times, adding a unique ambiance to the dining experience. Anyone who has spent time in Japan and dined in Japanese homes or traditional Japanese restaurants is aware of the importance of aesthetics in both the preparation and in the serving of Japanese food. Furthermore, the Japanese have always been especially proud of using only natural ingredients in their cuisine and preparing it in such a way that both natural appearance and taste are preserved.

It is therefore something of a surprise that Japan is a leader in the manufacture of *kopi shokuhin* (koe-pee show-kuu-heen), which literally means "copy food," but refers specifically to imitation crab, scallops and other seafood dishes primarily made from fish paste.

In the 1970s Japanese food processors developed a method of adding starch, flavorings, preservatives, dyes and other additives to fish paste, *surimi* (sue-ree-me), made from Alaska pollack and walleye pollack, to produce products that are virtually identical in shape, color, taste and smell to crab meat, scallop and squid fillet. Because *kopi shokuhin* products cost less than one-third of genuine crab, scallops and squid, they have been a tremendous success in both restaurants and homes, where they are used primarily in soups, tempura, sushi and *oden* (oh-dane), a kind of stew.

By the early 1980s, Japanese manufacturers were exporting *kopi shokuhin* to Australia, the United States and other countries around the world, and from the mid-1980s on, they began opening fish-paste factories in the United States and elsewhere.

With the success of imitation crab, scallops and squid, the Japanese manufacturers began producing imitation herring roe and salmon roe out of salad oil enclosed in a gelatinous membrane, which is produced from seaweed.

Aficionados of Japanese food should be aware that when they order any of the above dishes in Japan, in the United States, or elsewhere, more likely than not they are getting *kopi shokuhin*. They may look the same and taste the same as crab, scallops, or squid, but fish by any other name is still fish.

凝り性
Korisho
(Koe-ree-show)

Dealing with Perfection

Most of the arts and handicrafts for which the Japanese have traditionally been famous were introduced into the country from Korea and China between the 4th and 7th centuries. Along with these various arts and crafts came the apprenticeship system of on-the-job training, which had already been entrenched in Chinese society for more than 2,000 years.

Prior to this, skills and knowledge in Japan had, of course, naturally been passed on from older people to the young, but regular contact with the far more advance societies of Korea and China brought very ritualized and formalized structure to the transmission of technical skills. The Japanese made the apprenticeship method of teaching one of the primary pillars of their society, and it was to play a fundamental role, not only in the development of tangible Japanese culture, but also in molding Japanese character and personality.

As the centuries passed, the standards of master artists and craftsmen gradually rose as each generation built on the accomplishments of their forebears. Precise techniques for teaching and learning became formalized, and in some cases ritualized to the point that deviations from the established way were absolutely prohibited. By the end of the important Heian Period (794–1185), during which time cultural imports from Korea and China were Japanized and integrated into the indigenous culture, the Japanese were routinely producing ceramics, pottery, lacquer ware, paintings and other arts and handicrafts that later generations would regard as masterpieces.

Apprenticeships in Japan's many arts and crafts ranged from ten to as many as 40 years, imbuing the Japanese with patience and perseverance, and conditioning them to appreciate and expect products that were aesthetically pleasing and superior in quality. Because the apprenticeship system also conditioned people to follow exact forms and procedures, the Japanese became extraordinarily sensitive to the way things were done, and eventually deviating from the stipulated procedures came to be considered un-Japanese and a threat to society.

More importantly, however, the formalized apprenticeship system led to higher and higher aesthetic and quality standards. The desire to make things better and better became compulsive.

Japan's traditional culture therefore tended to produce people who were *korisho* (koe-ree-show), or "perfectionists." Anything less than perfect immediately caught their eye, and even if an imperfection was so slight it was barely noticeable, it would be conspicuous to the Japanese and they would reject the product. Westerners doing business with the Japanese invariably encounter the *korisho* syndrome. Although the penchant for perfection has weakened considerably in recent decades, it is still a significant factor in the Japanese reaction to everything—from how one holds and uses chopsticks to the stitching inside a piece of clothing.

Understanding the Japanese compulsion for form, order, quality and their aesthetic tastes is essential before the foreign business can establish a basis for communicating with its Japanese counterparts. Prospective deals with Japanese companies can evaporate if the foreign side presents an unstructured, disordered image, regardless of how attractive its products may be.

Persons interested in doing business in Japan must also be prepared to raise certain product standards to meet those of the Japanese, rather than expect the Japanese to lower their standards.

腰掛け
Koshikake
(Koe-she-kah-kay)

Watching Out for Chairs

One of the characteristics of Japanese companies that often frustrates foreigners is the difficulty in determining who among the employees is in a position of authority and responsibility. In most companies not managed by their founders or owners, no single individual, including the company president, can be—or, indeed, wants to be—responsible for substantive decisions.

Another feature that is common in larger Japanese companies, and which also causes problems for outsiders, is the existence of employees who have titles and occupy important-appearing desks, but who have few duties, little or no work to do, and who can initiate little if anything on their own. Some of these people have been sidelined because of some kind of problem with the company; they may have fallen from grace because they tried to do something on their own, or they may have an abrasive, aggressive personality that clashed with the corporate culture.

Others in this category are in positions that are known as *koshikake* (koe-she-kah-kay), which literally means "chair," but which refers to positions that are temporary, or are treated as temporary by the people in them. Company directors sometimes create *koshikake* for individuals to whom the company owes some kind of debt, or for individuals whom a director wants to be obligated to the company. A senior manager or a retired government bureaucrat, for example, may be given a *koshikake* post as a vice president.

Also, managers are frequently assigned to *koshikake* positions for a variety of reasons; returning to the head office after an assignment overseas might qualify one for such a position, for example. And most large Japanese corporations regard virtually all of the positions filled by young female university graduates as *koshikake*, because they expect the women to quit work as soon as they get married.

The *koshikake* system sometimes affects foreigners who are initiating contacts with Japanese companies. In some cases, foreigners who approach a company without introductions are deliberately steered to people in *koshikake* positions, both to politely "get rid" of the visitors and to give a person in the temporary positions something to do—especially if the person speaks some English.

However, all is not necessarily lost when foreigners are directed to *koshikake* staff members. These members may be among the most experienced and capable persons in the company, and even though their status is temporary, they may be in a position to see that the visitor gets a hearing with the right individual.

At the same time, there are *koshikake* positions that are totally dead ends. It therefore behooves the outsider trying to get inside a Japanese company to try to discover as early as possible if his or her contact is in some kind of transit status, if they are in a "doghouse," or if they are still plugged into the inner circle of management. Someone who has the title of *kacho* (kah-choe), "a section chief," or *bucho* (buu-choe), "a department head," but has no staff, is very likely in some kind of limbo, for example.

I have encountered people in *koshikake* positions who were brave and angry enough at their own companies to tell me outright that they had absolutely no authority and that no one listened to them.

In most cases, it is possible to determine the status of an individual by asking perfectly acceptable questions about how long they have been in their positions, how much longer they expect to be there, and how many people they have under them in their section or department.

Foreigners who have extensive experience in Japan, and who are really tuned into the atmosphere and behavior in Japanese companies, can sometimes recognize a person in a *koshikake* position by subtle signals that are sent out by those around the person and by the individual's own behavior.

交渉
Kosho
(Koe-show)

Coming Out Fighting

A professor of languages at Japan's prestigious Tokyo University once noted that the Japanese language is so imprecise that the Japanese themselves generally understand only about 70 percent of what they say to each other the first time around. The professor added that the Japanese either have to repeat themselves—sometimes going to the extreme of drawing an ideogram to clarify a point—or they must fill in what they believe the meaning to be from their own common store of cultural knowledge.

Since the Japanese face such a formidable obstacle in communicating among themselves in their own native tongue, it should not be surprising that the barriers facing the Japanese and foreigners trying to communicate with each other are even more challenging. This challenge is made still more complicated by the fact that a great many concepts in Japanese do not have exact English-language equivalents, just as there are many English words with no precise Japanese equivalents.

A perfect example of this problem is the English word "negotiation" and its nearest Japanese equivalent, *kosho* (koe-show). The cultural nuance of "negotiation" is relatively neutral. It simply means that two or more parties talk over a matter until they reach agreement. Verbal battles may be fought during negotiations, but the concept of negotiating does not require or imply such battles.

Generally speaking, Westerners see negotiating as a civilized way of reaching agreements that are fair and mutually beneficial. Businesspeople go into negotiating sessions armed with facts that they attempt to present in a rational, straightforward manner. "Negotiating," as such, is not an inflammatory word.

This is not the case with *kosho*, the closest Japanese equivalent to "negotiate." In its normal Japanese context, *kosho* conjures up images of conflict, of using all sorts of devious strategies, of fighting a battle in which there is a winner and a loser. This means that the Japanese prepare for *kosho* sessions in a different way from which Westerners prepare for negotiations; the Japanese come into "negotiating" sessions with a different attitude, and present their side in a different manner.

The Japanese tend to view negotiating with Westerners as a battle because they see a great deal of the typical behavior of foreigners as aggressive and predatory and designed specifically to take advantage of other people. And, of course, there are enough historical precedents to give credence to this Japanese belief, so it is important for the foreign side to avoid any signs of trying to verbally or physically overpower their counterparts.

At the same time, the foreign side must also be prepared to deal with both arrogance and aggression on the part of the Japanese—a mode they characteristically assume when they have the advantage. In their *kosho* "battles," the Japanese typically use a passive-aggressive-cooperative approach. They generally come into negotiating sessions in a passive, receptive mode; listening and asking questions to draw the other side out. This strategy often leads Westerners, particularly Americans, to believe that they are really making progress, with the result that they reveal their weaknesses as well as their strengths, and put themselves at a serious disadvantage.

173

Another strategy of Japanese negotiators is to be cooperative and good-natured right up to the point where it seems that an agreement has been reached, and then suddenly they become rude and critical, a ruse that almost always shocks the foreigners and throws them off-balance. By this time, the foreign negotiators have already started congratulating themselves; their defenses are down, and they are extremely vulnerable to accepting less than what they thought they had achieved in order to prevent the whole effort from being a failure.

Foreigners going into *kosho* meetings with the Japanese should be prepared for this strategy. The best advice is to react calmly when this occurs: gather up documents and notes, and say, "We see that you need more time to discuss this among yourselves, so let's take a break and reconvene at a later date." Then get up, smile broadly, shake everybody's hand, thank them, and then leave.

It is also common for Japanese negotiators to use the "good cop, bad cop" approach, with the bad cop—usually a low-ranking manager—asking all of the controversial questions and putting the other side on the spot.

Generally speaking, Westerners going into negotiations with the Japanese for the first time almost always underestimate them. By Western standards, Japanese negotiators may not look smart, act confident, or appear aggressively capable, but this characteristic cultural behavior is misleading. The nature of their culture makes it imperative that the Japanese become very clever at masking their feelings, their knowledge and their experience, and their skill in manipulating people to get what they want.

口コ ミ

Kuchi-Komi

(Kuu-chee-Koe-me)

By Word of Mouth

Foreign businesspeople in Japan are constantly being warned that the Japanese market is geographically so small and is so sensitive to everything that goes on in the business world that it is impossible to keep secrets.

Japanese businesspeople also appear to be proponents of the chaos theory—they seem to believe that every action, no matter how small or insignificant, eventually has an impact on the rest of the world; and this is one of the reasons why the Japanese have traditionally preferred to maintain control over as many aspects of their operations as possible, from the sourcing of raw materials and manufacturing down to retailing the finished products. These competitive factors in the Japanese marketplace are also used as justifications for seeking exclusive arrangements with foreign suppliers.

Long before television and other mass media existed in Japan, it was common for both news and confidential information to travel to the farthest reaches of the Japanese islands in a matter of days. Ordinary news was carried unofficially by people who were referred to as news hawkers as well as product peddlers who roamed the country, and officially by mounted messengers who were sent out by the shogunate government in Edo.

All of the major roads in the country had post-stations at regular intervals along the way where official messengers and other ranking government agents could exchange horses and rest overnight on the longer routes, a system which predates the pony express in the United States by several centuries. In addition to these official and public information avenues, the shogunate and all of the clan lords maintained secret agents to spy on each other, so there was a constant flow of information to and from Edo.

The shogunate had administrative officials and police, as well as undercover spies, in every part of the country, and within a matter of hours or days the government had reports on everything of any consequence that took place everywhere and anywhere in the country.

From the late 1630s to 1868, most of Japan's clan lords, some 270 in number, had to travel to Edo every other year with a large retinue of servants, retainers and samurai guards, and spend a year in the capital city in regular attendance at the shogun's court. All of this traveling to-and-fro by dozens of thousands of people, many of whom were on the road for weeks at a time, contributed to the flow of information about the country and helped make the Japanese among the great talkers and gossipers of the world.

Thus, from the mid-1600s on, Japan was "wired" by a word-of-mouth internet that blanketed the country—a process that is now referred to as *kuchi-komi* (kuu-chee-koe-me). *Kuchi* means "mouth," and *komi* is short for "communication"—a combination meaning "mouth communication," or in more colloquial terms, "word of mouth."

Japan's *kuchi-komi* network was one of the primary factors in the spread of culture from Kyoto and Edo to the outlying provinces, and for the general cultural, economic and political homogenization of the people. The network was also one of the assets that made it possible for the Japanese to deal with foreign powers more effectively than most Asian and other undeveloped countries when they were first approached by industrialized nations of the West.

Today, despite the telephone, the fax, computers and other high-tech means of communication, the Japanese are still heavily dependent upon face-to-face meetings and discussions in their daily private and business affairs. Generally speaking, the Japanese do not feel comfortable with long-distance communication, especially in important business affairs, and as a result, Japanese businesspeople have more face-to-face meetings than virtually any other people.

· Foreigners doing business in Japan soon discover that *kuchi-komi*, especially in the form of "free advertising," can be used to their advantage.

黒子
Kuroko

(Kuu-roe-koe)

The Men in Black

One has to have a vivid imagination in order to fully enjoy Japan's classical kabuki theater, because it is necessary to ignore much of what transpires on stage. Foreign visitors to Japan who are exposed to the kabuki experience without a preliminary orientation about what not to look at—and why—may come away with the opinion that there is less to Japanese culture than what they have heard. The fact is, however, that foreign kabuki viewers are being presented with an opportunity to learn something about the Japanese that is vital if they intend to get involved with them in business or other professional matters.

This lesson, in part, is that it is often what is ignored—or what one pretends not to see and does not talk about openly—that is important in Japan. In the case of kabuki, what is ostensibly unseen or ignored are the *kuroko* (kuu-roe-koe), or black-clad helpers on the stage who assist the actors in changing their costumes while they are still on stage in full view of the audience.

If a viewer focuses on the *kuroko* in kabuki, as most foreign visitors tend to do, it prevents one from getting into the spirit of the story and reduces the whole experience to an amateurish exhibit of illusions that does not fool anyone.

There are numerous historical instances in Japan where similar illusionary devices were used to deceive rather than entertain or instruct. One of these instances was the use of *kagemusha* (kah-gay-muu-sha), literally "shadow warriors," by military leaders who did not want to expose themselves to danger, and so they put others up to front for them. A more colloquial use of the term was "dummy generals."

Another common feature of life in old Japan were the so-called *kakure oyabun* (kah-kuu-ray oh-yah-boon), or "hidden bosses," referring to gang leaders and others who kept their identities a secret and operated through front men.

This propensity for key people in Japan to stay in the background continues today, and is a frequently used ploy in both business and politics. Ranking managers or executives who are members of teams engaging in negotiations with other firms will frequently play the role of *kuroko*, concealing their rank and position at the beginning of the discussions, and often waiting until near the end or until an impasse is reached before revealing their identities.

These business *kuroko* stay behind the scenes by passing out nondescript name cards (or no name cards at all, claiming that they just ran out), by sitting in inconspicuous places, and by remaining quiet. The Japanese are naturally familiar with this practice, but even they cannot always identify a *kuroko* in a typical discussion group of ten or more people. The challenge is naturally even more formidable for foreigners.

In some Japanese negotiating teams the ranking individual will not make any attempt to conceal his identity, but will remain silent, letting the lower-ranking members of the group do all of the talking. This latter practice is not meant to deceive anyone. The middle managers in such groups are the ones who have spent days or months preparing for the meeting and are expected to be knowledgeable about the topic, while the senior person may know very little about it. One of the obvious reasons why Japanese leaders generally prefer to remain in the background is that it allows them more time to think and plan, and more freedom to maneuver. It also allows them to avoid criticism and responsibility if their plans go awry.

玄人
Kuroto
(Kuu-roe-toh)

Professionalism in Japan

Westerners have a great deal of difficulty in keeping a balanced view of Japan because they encounter so many apparent contradictions in the behavior of the Japanese, particularly among those Japanese who are well educated, obviously intelligent, and in senior positions. These problems with cross-cultural perceptions are quite natural: the Japanese have one view of what constitutes intelligent, responsible behavior and Westerners have another view.

Probably the most fundamental difference between the typical Japanese and Western viewpoints is their focus; Westerners tend to focus on individuality, personal responsibility and personal accomplishment, while the Japanese have been conditioned to have a much more amorphous view of themselves and their responsibilities.

In the traditional Japanese context, people are members of groups first, and individual rights come second. Responsibility is team oriented rather than individual oriented. the Japanese do have a strong sense of individual responsibility, but it is primarily directed toward their group, not toward themselves. Individual Japanese in responsible positions often cannot act in what Westerners regard as a rational, pragmatic way, because generally Japanese must think and perform as just one spoke in a wheel. Of course, there are exceptions, but this is the situation for most Japanese.

The problem Westerners have with interacting effectively with the Japanese is compounded by the fact that on first meetings and during the early stages of any dialogue, the Japanese typically demonstrate a degree of humanity, sincerity, intelligence and goodwill that is impressive to say the least. But because of behind-the-scenes restraints on Japanese behavior, their subsequent actions often appear to Westerners as naive, indecisive, obstructive, insidious and untrustworthy.

Given this situation, Japanese standards for experts or skilled professionals, *kuroto* (kuu-roe-toh), are quite different from Western standards. Japanese *kuroto* in such areas as mahjong, music, advertising copywriting and engineering are judged by the same standards as their Western counterparts. But in the management of people, whether in politics or business, the standards for judging professionals and professionalism are quite different.

The first and foremost qualification for *kuroto* managers in Japan, at whatever level, is that they have a profound understanding of human (read "Japanese") nature; also, they must be especially adept at maintaining a positive, cooperative and harmonious atmosphere among their employees. *Kuroto* executives often do not have any technical expertise, and may not be that knowledgeable about their own industry or company. But they do have the human attributes that are so essential to Japanese-style management.

When a high-powered board chairman or president of a major Western corporation who dominates his company like a dictator meets his Japanese counterpart, the contrast is dramatic and the reaction from the Western side is often one of surprise and disappointment. Western executives are used to dealing with individuals, but to succeed in Japan they must learn how to deal with amorphous groups in which authority and power are diffused among large numbers of people. The best attitude to take in dealing with a large Japanese corporation is to think of the company officials like the leaders of some countries: the company president may have the power of a British king or queen, for example, and the directors and vice presidents might be similar to cabinet ministers. It is also important to keep in mind that a Japanese company is actually run by its bureaucrats, that is, its section, department, and division chiefs.

空気
Kuuki
(Kuu-kee)

The Japanese Atmosphere

Some scholar-consultants who advise foreigners on dealing with the Japanese maintain that the best approach is to emphasize the cross-cultural similarities and downplay the differences. When I hear this kind of advice, it always occurs to me that these advisors have never actually engaged in business in Japan, and are advancing a theory that sounds good, but which does not necessarily hold up in practice.

Of course, there must be common ground before any kind of positive relationship can be developed, but if differences are ignored and bridges are not built over them, solid ground will not be reached. More than a few foreign businesspeople accept this line of advice which advocates minimizing differences, however, because the alternative—identifying and dealing head-on with the differences that do exist—is often very intimidating, it may not appear to be a rational choice. Foreign businesspeople who buy into the concept that the Japanese "are just like us once you get behind the surface etiquette," have to wear blinders in order to maintain this approach for any length of time.

Differences between the Japanese way and the Western way are, in fact, so obvious that they are visible for all to see, as a visit to almost any Japanese company will evidence. The *kuuki* (kuu-kee), or "atmosphere," in a typical Japanese company looks different, feels different, and is different in blatant and subtle ways—and these ways are just surface indications of the profound differences that lie below.

Westerners who have never done business with the Japanese before, routinely come to Tokyo and begin serious negotiations the day following their arrival. Their primary motivation, of course, is to save money by limiting their stay in Japan to as few days as possible. But chances are they will end up having to spend many times more than they expected to spend because negotiations invariably require several meetings over weeks or months of time. While there are no guaranteed ways to shorten this period, the least that businesspeople should do is to come to Japan a minimum of one week, and preferably two or three weeks, before their meetings are scheduled to start, and absorb some of the cultural *kuuki* of the workplace.

Ideally during this period the newcomers would attend two or three orientations sponsored by their chambers of commerce in Japan, visit two or three factories and department stores, a similar number of shopping and entertainment districts, and as many head offices of medium- to large-size corporations. People who are not capable of arranging this kind of schedule before or after arriving in Japan, or who fail to take other steps to prepare themselves, almost always end up having to subject themselves to the mercy of their Japanese contacts.

The *kuuki* of a Japanese company goes well beyond outward appearances. It has to do with the attitude of the employees, how they behave and communicate with each other and with outsiders, how they gather and absorb information and direction, and how they make decisions. Japanese supervisors and managers do not manage by giving orders and supervising. Employees are expected to know what to do by staying in tune with their work groups, and managers keep informed about the company's projects and goals by attending frequent meetings.

The overall *kuuki* in the typical Japanese company is very much like that of a large organism that functions on the basis of collective behavior and intuition. In some companies this functioning is as exact as that of the workers in a beehive—but without the queen bee. Employees have their antennae up at all times. Managers who are the best at perceiving the collective thoughts of top executives and directors are the ones that rise to the top.

Outsiders wanting to do business in Japan should also be skilled in reading the *kuuki* of Japanese companies.

競争
Kyoso
(K'yoe-soh)

The Ultimate Competitors

Although there was no specific word for "competition" in the Japanese language until one was created in the 1880s in order to be able to refer to the Western way of doing business, individual and group competition have played a key role in Japanese society from the beginning.

In earlier times, competition at an individual level included combat: sumo champions fighting each other—sometimes to the death; sword duels which ended when one duelist was severely wounded or, preferably, fatally wounded, since losing and surviving resulted in loss of face; and regular contests between individuals in kendo schools, archery contests, and in other areas.

For decades after the founding of the Tokugawa Shogunate in 1603, drunken samurai in Edo were notorious for competing in demonstrations to prove their superior ability to cut through the bodies of innocent passersby with one slash of a sword. During the heyday of the Tokugawa Period (1700–1800), profligate sons of rich merchants would compete with each other to see who could spend the most money in restaurants, geisha houses and courtesan districts. In fact, virtually every aspect of Japanese life was an unending contest to live up to an excruciatingly exact etiquette and to compete with every other individual one encountered in play, work and socially—not only in manners, but in style, dedication, endurance and in other ways.

Competition in Japan has always had a special character that distinguishes it from competition in Western countries. In traditional Japanese thinking, the concept of equality does not exist. There is always something that differentiates people, setting them forever apart, and making one superior to another—an attitude that also applies to objects and products in Japan.

The Japanese have always recognized that all men and women are not created equal, and they did not develop institutions of any kind that attempted to treat people as equals. Furthermore, Japan's traditional culture did not include the concept of universal fairness—of everyone being inherently deserving of the same degree of fair treatment. Until 1945, the social, economic and political construct in Japan was a vertical arrangement, with ascending layers of people and institutions that began with the masses at the bottom and ended with the figure of the emperor at the top. Right and wrong was decreed by those in the upper layers of this pyramid-like social structure. Morality, along with governmental policies and practices, were based on circumstances instead of principles.

The success of this tightly controlled hierarchical society was dependent on the strict fulfillment by each layer of people of a precisely detailed set of obligations they owed to those in layers above them. People in higher layers did, in fact, have some obligations to those below them, to retainers, to employees, or to the public at large—but these obligations were subject to arbitrary change or elimination by those in power.

For this system to work well, the highest possible order of cooperation within and between the layers of people was essential. This was accomplished by extreme measures to encourage harmony and discourage personal, unstructured competition. *Wa* (wah), or "harmony," was the overriding consideration in all Japanese relationships; there was, on the other hand, simply no word for the concept of competition.

It was not until shortly after the beginning of Japan's modern age that a word was created to account for Western-style competitive behavior. This word, *kyoso* (k'yoe-soh), was coined in the 1880s by Yukichi Fukuzawa (1835–1901), a noted writer, publisher, educator and a leader in transforming Japan from a feudalistic shogun-dominated country to a modern nation.

Fukuzawa, who was one of the first Japanese to travel to the United States and Europe, was fascinated by the social, political and economic competition that he witnessed in the West; as founder of the predecessor of Keio University, he also helped spread knowledge about the West. Determined to teach the Japanese how to harness the energy and productivity created by competition, Fukuzawa came up with the word *kyoso*, which literally means "fight against each other."

The concept of competition went against the cultural grain of the Japanese, so Fukuzawa's new word was controversial from the start. But as long as *kyoso* was aimed at outsiders, and not other Japanese, it was not only accepted, it became a key element in the compulsive drive the Japanese had to match and surpass the West.

Kyoso is still the official term in Japanese for competition, but it is still looked upon as something that is unsuitable for the Japanese, and the word does not mean in Japanese what it does in English. In English, competition in a business context means that companies of any size are free to compete in any market they choose to enter, a Darwinian sense of survival of the fittest. In the Japanese context of things, this kind of competition invariable leads to disharmony and confusion.

To the Japanese, a small company cannot compete with a large company and should not be allowed to try, because this would upset rather than stabilize the market. The Japanese feel that competing companies should be of roughly equal size and strength; they should have a roughly equitable share of the market; and they should compete with each other in a "cooperative manner" in order to keep the market stable.

In other words, when a Western businessperson or politician says "competition," the Japanese hear "confusion," and this is disturbing to them. It is therefore essential that Westerners and Japanese come to a mutually acceptable definition of *kyoso* in any business dialogue.

競争と協調
Kyoso to Kyocho
(K'yoe-soh toe K'yoe-choe)

Doing Business with Enemies

From the mid-1950s to the mid-1980s, it often seemed to outsiders that Japan's leading manufacturers could do no wrong. In fewer than 30 years they had become multinational giants, overrunning foreign competitors in blitzkrieg fashion, and filling the stores and display rooms of the world with an avalanche of increasingly well-designed and well-made goods.

In their rush to capture world markets, large corporations of the New Japan, including appliance manufacturers such as Matsushita, Sony and Toshiba, and automobile manufacturers like Nissan and Toyota, ran roughshod over the formerly dominant *zaibatsu* (zigh-baht-sue) trading firms, pushing Mitsui, Mitsubishi, Itochu, and the other *sogo shosha* (soe-go show-shah) into the background and threatening their very existence.

Following a traditional, compulsive principle of *jimaeshugi* (jee-my-shuu-ghee), or "being self-sufficient," Japan's ranking manufacturers became vertically integrated giants, using dozens to hundreds of wholly-owned subsidiaries and totally controlled suppliers to make or supply everything they needed. Manufacturers also established their own sales and distribution networks, in Japan as well as overseas, in order to control the marketing as well as the manufacturing process.

This compulsive *jimaeshugi* behavior was a direct descendant of Japan's feudal clan system in which the country was divided into some 270 fiercely independent fiefs, each of which had an overpowering emotional and political urge to control every aspect of their existence in order to guarantee security and survival.

Until the 1980s, each of Japan's great company groups functioned very much like a clan surrounded by enemies. For the most part, they did not ordinarily do business with other "clan companies," and when forced to do so on a small scale for whatever reason, it was necessary that the companies involved first go through a complicated ritual of establishing "diplomatic relations" more-or-less like those among sovereign nations.

The reason for this go-it-alone approach to business was that the companies did not trust outside firms to provide quality parts on time; they did not want to share manufacturing know-how or patent secrets with outsiders; and finally, by keeping everything in-house, manufacturers could guarantee customer satisfaction. For these and a number of equally important cultural reasons, it was even more unthinkable for Japanese companies to go into a parts manufacturing arrangement with foreign firms.

Oddly enough, however, where technology was concerned, it was often easier for a Japanese company to go into business with a foreign company than with another Japanese firm, because the Japanese firm could keep the foreign relationship at arm's length, take advantage of the foreign company, and not expose itself.

But as Japan's economy grew and became more complicated, more market-driven, and more open to inroads by foreign companies and imported products, it became increasingly difficult for Japan's "clan companies" to function independently. Finally, by the early 1980s, Japan's huge conglomerate groups had begun to recognize that not being able to do business across "clan borders" was more of a handicap than an advantage. By the end of the 1980s, a new business-culture code phrase was in vogue: *kyoso to kyocho* (k'yoe-soh toe k'yoe-choe), or "competition and cooperation."

Throughout the decade of the 1980s, there was a frenzy of cross-company group tie-ups under the new *kyoso to kyocho* banner. Among the more conspicuous of these new relationships were those involving previously exclusive parts suppliers to Japan's two largest automobile manufacturers, Nissan and Toyota. For the first time in their histories, these suppliers began cutting deals with other automobile makers.

By the early 1990s the concept of *kyoso to kyocho* was well established in Japan, not only among domestic enterprises, but between Japanese and foreign companies as well. In fact, many such arrangements in Japan go considerably farther than similar ones in the United States and Europe, because Japan's antitrust laws are not as restrictive or as efficiently enforced, allowing for more leeway in price fixing and market segmentation.

While certainly not intended, adoption of the *kyoso to kyocho* philosophy by Japan's leading companies went a long way toward reducing the obstacles foreign firms faced in getting into the Japanese market.

Kyuyo

(Que-yoh)

Getting Away from it All

In olden Japan it was common for people in responsible and highly stressful positions to retire early to a peaceful and usually rustic existence which provided opportunities to relax, to commune with nature, to write poetry and essays, to tend gardens, and so on. Buddhist monks, especially, made a practice of isolating themselves in distant mountain huts where they would spend years contemplating the mysteries of life. Nevertheless following the industrialization of Japan between 1870 and 1895, opportunities for relaxation fell by the wayside, only to be reinstituted in the 1960s with a modern spin.

By the 1960s, the pace of business and life in general in Japan had intensified to the point that people were simply burning themselves out, causing a variety of emotional complaints and illnesses, and in extreme cases bringing on *karoshi* (kah-roe-she), or "death from overwork."

The diligence of Japanese managers from 1960 through the 1980s was such that most of them worked from ten to 14 hours a day, six to seven days a week, and most also refused to take their annual vacations. In some of the more competitive fields, companies and other organizations began resorting to enforced *kyuyo* (que-yoh), or "recreation retreats," for key employees, requiring them to take time off and get away from everything for weeks and sometimes months.

Sports are among the most competitive activities in Japan, and the use of *kyuyo* to keep the performance of players and managers at their peak is a common practice. Baseball club owners in particular make use of *kyuyo* to keep their managers and players on an emotional high. Every time a team hits a losing streak, its manager is in danger of being sent to the mountains for *kyuyo*, not so much for the manager to recharge his emotional batteries, but to shame the players into trying harder. Rather than fire managers whose teams are not performing, something that would bring shame to the managers as well as to the owners and players, baseball club owners often send them away on *kyuyo* that simply never end. As writer Robert Whiting chronicled in his entertaining and insightful book, *The Chrysanthemum and the Bat*, Japanese baseball team managers who want out for whatever reason also generally do not resign outright. They request permission to take a one-way *kyuyo*.

Foreign business executives in Japan might want to make use of the institution of *kyuyo* to actually reward Japanese managers who have performed exceptionally well, or to impress upon a particular manager's Japanese staff that their performance is not acceptable. Obviously in the latter case, it is necessary to let the staff know that the manager's *kyuyo* is to give him time to think about why the performance of his section or department is disappointing—with the hope that the staff too will reflect on their attitudes and behavior and make a commitment to do better.

The power of this kind of cultural strategy stems from the collective sense of shame that is built into the psyche of the Japanese. Every time a Japanese is singled out for censure, ridicule, or punishment, coworkers or other persons in the same group also feel shamed. The Japanese also feel shame when they are not doing well or when they see a compatriot do poorly in competition with foreigners. In some cases there are demands that the "guilty" Japanese be punished.

目利き
Mekiki
(May-kee-kee)

Made to Please the Eye

Foreign exporters trying to get their products into the Japanese market invariably encounter a Pandora's box of barriers that range from government regulations and resistance from local producers to outcries from "academics" who claim the products concerned are not suitable for Japan. In the past, some of these assertions about the suitableness of foreign products have been so ludicrous that they made the Japanese the laughingstock of the world. At one time, for example, it was claimed that snow in Japan was different from snow in the rest of the world, so foreign-made skis would not be suitable for Japan. On another occasion it was asserted that Japanese intestines were longer than the intestines of Westerners, and therefore certain foods were not appropriate for the Japanese market; another claim was that Japanese skin was different from foreign skin so foreign soap would not get the Japanese clean, and so on and so forth.

Despite the ludicrous nature of these claims, they succeeded in doing what the Japanese had intended for them to do—they kept certain foreign products out of the country permanently or until the Japanese were good and ready to accept them.

But there was a far more serious obstacle to getting foreign-made products into Japan, including those on which there were no government restrictions, no objections from Japanese industry, and no comical claims of unsuitability. This obstacle is a culturally induced reaction of the Japanese that is subsumed in the word, *mekiki* (may-kee-kee), which is made up of *me*, meaning "eye," and the noun form of *kiku* (kee-kuu), which means "to be effective," "to be good for."

When these two words are put together to form *mekiki*, the new compound is translated as "good for the eye," which refers to anything that is manufactured and finished with such care that it has absolutely no visible flaws.

I was once involved in an effort to export American-made sweatshirts and other apparel into Japan. The Japanese importer-distributors would go through every shipment, pulling out items that had loose threads hanging from seams, labels that were sewn on a little bit crooked, or any other thing that they considered a flaw—all things that American manufacturers and consumers routinely ignored. On some of the shipments there were so many of these "minor" flaws that the Japanese would either refuse them, or demand that the price be discounted because they could not be sold in first-class outlets.

This reaction to imperfection was a symptom of the *mekiki* syndrome that is deeply embedded in the Japanese psyche. They were so used to having everything made so finely and detailed so meticulously that any variation stood out like the proverbial neon sign.

Until around the end of the 1980s, every sample foreign product offered to Japanese importers and users got the kind of scrutiny that Americans and other Westerners might give to an outrageously expensive diamond before buying it—but not to a shirt, or to an apple, or to an automotive part that was to go under the hood of a car.

Over the decades, the *mekiki* syndrome alone has prevented hundreds of foreign-made products from getting into the Japanese market, and held up others for years while the manufacturers tried to meet the standards demanded by the Japanese.

Japanese *mekiki* standards do not apply only to a product alone; they also apply to product packaging. It can almost be taken for granted that American-made packaging will not be acceptable in Japan while some European-made packaging meets Japanese standards. When the item concerned is a consumer product made for the high end of the market, the Japanese frequently resort to doing the packaging themselves—sometimes after the foreign side has made several attempts to bring the packaging up to Japanese par.

In the late 1980s, by which time Japan's "bubble economy" was beginning to lose gas, maverick Japanese importer-distributors started bringing cheaply made and lower-priced products in from China and Southeast Asia. When the bubble economy burst in 1990 and 1991, Japanese consumers began looking for bargains rather than over-priced brand names, beginning a gradual erosion of the *mekiki* syndrome.

It is now possible to find all kinds of foreign-made consumer products in Japan that have all kinds of flaws, and they are obviously selling. But they represent a very small portion of the market. Generally speaking, American and European manufacturers who are exporting to Japan, or want to export to Japan, must still meet the traditional *mekiki* standards.

Products that meet the standards of the Japanese are often referred to as *hon mono* (hoan-moe-no), or "genuine things" or "authentic things." Another term *kuwashii hito* (kuu-wah-shee ssh-toe) is also often applied to people who are especially meticulous in their work or who have especially detailed knowledge about a place or thing.

女々しい
Memeshii
(May-may-she-e)

Who's a Wimp?

Prior to the beginning of World War II, it was common for Americans and other Westerners to disparage the Japanese by laughing at their small size and joking about how many of them wore glasses. Journalists, editorial writers, and even some politicians spread the word that the Japanese were not a serious military threat because they could not see well enough to shoot anybody. British forces in Singapore were so certain that the Japanese army could not get troops and armaments through the jungles of Malaysia that they ignored advice to establish a defense line along the border.

This underestimation of the Japanese by virtually everyone played a significant role in the subsequent Japanese conquest of most of China, virtually all of Southeast Asia, and much of the Southwestern Pacific.

During the war years, the Japanese were recognized as skilled and effective fighters, making up for their small size and other handicaps by a toughness and tenaciousness that most Westerners had never seen before. However, the Western image of the Japanese as inferior did not disappear as a result of Japanese successes in war, and once Japan was defeated the old image of the people came back in full force.

Japan's rapid comeback as an economic superpower following the end of World War II created a painful contradiction for most Westerners—especially Americans. They simply could not accept the evidence that their traditional image of the Japanese was wrong. All during the 1960s and 1970s, Americans in Japan used one rationale after another to explain how the Japanese could be so successful despite their perceived weaknesses, and in most cases these explanations were not complimentary.

Today many Americans, including businesspeople who have had substantial experience in Japan, still view the Japanese as both culturally and physically inferior. Much of this prejudiced perception derives from cultural differences, many of which are illustrated by the word *memeshii* (may-may-she-e), which means "effeminate" and "unmanly." *Memeshiimono* (may-may-she-e-moe-no) is the Japanese equivalent of "sissy" or "wimp."

Japanese culture is fundamentally feminine in the sense that it emphasizes passivity, smallness, neatness, nurturing, emotion, intuition, aesthetics and other things that Westerners have traditionally associated with women. Thus, in the conscious as well as in the subconscious eyes of Western men, a great deal of the behavior of Japanese men is effeminate. When this is combined with the generally smaller stature of Japanese men, the message that Western men get is quite powerful.

It goes without saying, of course, that the Japanese interpret manliness and femininity quite differently. In the Japanese context, "real" men do not talk very much; they never brag, and they demonstrate their strength and virtue by quietly persevering against all odds. Japanese men also demonstrate their manliness by upholding their honor, the honor of their families and companies, and by sacrificing themselves for their companies or for their country. There are other less elevated ways that Japanese men have traditionally demonstrated their masculinity, including drinking regularly and heavily, consorting freely with many women, and, in extreme cases such as war, being absolutely merciless.

Japan's most powerful men almost always exercise their power from behind the scenes, maneuvering quietly and using emotional appeal—like women are wont to do—to achieve their goals. When these men are seen as virtuous, not trying to accumulate power or wealth for their own personal use or glory, their subordinates and the public at large are culturally conditioned to voluntarily support them. They do not have to give direct orders or throw their weight around. All they have to do is hint at what they want done or what they would like to see happen.

The Japanese regularly point out that the man to respect—and to fear—is the one who is quiet and unobtrusive; the one who does not make himself conspicuous—which, of course, is generally the exact opposite in the United States and other Western countries. As a result of the tendency of Western men to regard a large percentage of all Japanese men as *memeshii*, they typically underestimate them. And, of course, this misreading of Japanese character negatively affects the Western businessperson's ability to select the best Japanese employees or business partners.

面目丸潰れ
Menmoku Maru Tsubure
(Mane-moe-koe-kuu Mah-rue T'sue-buu-ray)

Losing One's Face

During Japan's long shogunate age (1185–1868), the ruling samurai warrior class developed the painful and gory *hara-kiri* (hah-rah-kee-ree), or "belly-cutting," method of committing suicide. As is generally known, *hara-kiri* for men consisted of inserting the blade of a long knife into the abdomen on the left side, slicing through the bowels by pulling the still inserted blade to the right side, and then cutting upward for two or three inches to make sure that key organs were severed. Samurai women were allowed to cut their throats.

The *hara-kiri* method of self-immolation took extraordinary will power and physical strength, and subjected the individual to intense suffering, sometimes for as long as an hour or more, particularly if the victim was unable to complete the cut. Because so many people botched the belly-cutting it soon became the practice for an assistant to stand beside them with sword in hand and lop off their heads after the first cut.

Hara-kiri as both a method of execution and suicide was reserved for the samurai class as the ultimate affirmation of their superior standards. Even upper-class lawbreakers, as well as captured enemies and others condemned to commit hara-kiri because they failed to obey etiquette or failed in some task, could partially redeem themselves by bravely and efficiently performing the painful ritual.

The primary motivation that made it possible for the development of this extreme method of self-immolation was the importance to the samurai of avoiding *menmoku maru tsubure* (mane-moe-kuu mah-rue t'sue-buu-ray), or "loss of face." To chose to die by any other method was tantamount to denying their heritage and demonstrating to the world that they were cowards who were not worthy of the rank of samurai. The super pride of Japan's samurai class gradually seeped down into the general population, making all Japanese extraordinarily sensitive about *kaomake* (kah-oh-mah-kay), and instilling in them an equally strong motivation to protect not only their own face, but Japan's face as well.

Foreigners dealing with Japan today should be extra careful to avoid causing any Japanese to lose face, whether or not the cause is justified, because having lost face Japanese feel compelled to get revenge to wipe out the insult. This may range from becoming uncooperative, to some kind of sabotage or efforts to inflict some other kind of personal damage to a person's reputation or position.

Kaomake or "face loss" may occur when one does such things as ignoring the ranking system in a Japanese company or government agency, going over the head of an individual, publicly accusing someone of a mistake or undesirable action, and so on, all of which are common in the United States and other Western countries.

The point to keep in mind is that the Japanese are much more sensitive about losing face, and this sensitivity should be taken seriously by anyone wanting to maintain good relations with the Japanese. In situations where the foreign side simply cannot give in and let the Japanese have their way, it is far more effective to engage in behind-the-scenes maneuvers to bring about the desired result, thereby allowing the Japanese to avoid *kaomake*.

見込発注
Mikomi Hatchuu
(Me-koe-me Haht-chuu)

Anticipating Customer Needs

During Japan's feudal years, which historians date from the beginning of the shogunate form of government in 1185, the Japanese became homogenized to an extraordinary degree, despite regional differences in language and culture. This homogenization process began with the ruling samurai class, which made up the elite in every province and city of any size, and was spread by the samurai throughout the country during the 1st century of the Tokugawa Shogunate (1603–1868), when provincial lords were required to keep their families in Edo at all times, and the lords themselves had to spend every other year in Edo in attendance at the shogun's court.

The etiquette that developed among the samurai class in Japan during the long shogun era was patterned after the etiquette of the Imperial Court in Kyoto. Behavior was prescribed down to the slightest movement and positioning of the body, including the hands, legs and torso; there were even formulas for proper facial expressions, language and tone of voice. In short, behavior was so highly stylized that life was as demanding as any theatrical role.

The manner of preparing, serving and eating food, along with drinking, was prescribed in detail, as was virtually everything else in Japanese life. Because practically all Japanese behavior was carefully prescribed, institutionalized, and then ritualized, non-prescribed behavior was taboo. Behaving in a non-Japanese way was not only antisocial, it was often against the law.

In this environment, people got to the point where they could anticipate how other people were going to behave and what they were going to say and what they were going to do at virtually anytime under virtually any circumstance, because everybody followed scripted roles that everybody knew. This cultural homogenization was what gave birth to *haragei* (hah-rah-gay-e), or "the art of the belly," which referred to the ability of the Japanese to communicate and understand each other with little or no verbal communication. This was possible, it is contended, because the Japanese were conditioned to think alike and react in the same way.

One of the most important facets of this homogenized intellectual, emotional and spiritual life-style was that retainers, servants, employees and others in inferior positions could, and indeed were required to, anticipate the needs and whims of their superiors and to fulfill them without being ordered to do so. The Japanese have lost a great deal of their cultural homogeneity since the end of the feudal era in 1945, but a significant proportion of their present-day behavior remains firmly anchored in their past.

In business, one of the practices that is based on cultural homogeneity and a long tradition of mutual understanding and trust is called *mikomi hatchuu* (me-koe-me haht-chuu), which means "orders that are expected." *Mikomi hatchuu* refers to the general practice of salespeople in manufacturing companies to place orders for their customers before they actually get the orders, to make sure that the goods are available and can be delivered to the customer precisely on time.

This kind of business activity has traditionally worked well in Japan because of the intimate nature of the relationships that exist between suppliers and their customers, and the fact that there is virtually no chance that customers might not follow through with their orders. In the event that orders are not forthcoming because of something that is beyond the control of their customers, the practice is for suppliers to carry them until the situation returns to normal.

Another advantage of the *mikomi hatchuu* practice is that it makes it possible for suppliers to deliver goods early or on short notice, in the event customers unexpectedly run short of stock.

It generally takes foreign manufacturers in Japan a long time to establish a *mikomi hatchuu*-type relationship with their customers—if they ever do—and this is one of the reasons why Japanese have traditionally been reluctant to do business with foreign companies.

Until the 1990s, the Japanese had two common complaints about their dealings with foreign companies; first, they considered the quality of their goods to be poor, and second, they regarded delivery services as undependable, including the inability of foreign companies to react quickly to emergency situations. Most foreign companies have now resolved the quality issue.

禊ぎ
Misogi
(Me-soe-ghee)

Wiping the Slate Clean

In early Japan one of the most common Shinto practices was bathing in a stream or river as part of a ritual for getting rid of all spiritual defilement, or "sin" in Christian terminology, a ritual that was known as *misogi* (me-soe-ghee). This practice was, of course, based on the belief that immersing oneself in water removed guilt for misconduct as well as dirt and sweat—and was a ritualistic feature that Shintoism and Christianity shared.

In present-day Japan virtually the only people who practice this ancient ritual in its original form are Shinto priests and a few dedicated devotees. However, virtually all Japanese still believe in the purification power of water and regularly indulge in their own version of *misogi* without calling it that.

Today the term *misogi* is often used by the news media in reference to Japan's scandal-prone politicians, but in an entirely different sense. When a Japanese politician wins re-election to office after having been accused of taking bribes or of some other illegal behavior, the election is called a *misogi*, because the politician concerned considers himself cleansed of all "sin"—like Christian converts baptized in water.

Since the first post-World War II elections in Japan in the latter part of the 1940s, there have been candidates in virtually every national election who have used—or tried to use—elections for their personal *misogi*.

What is equally interesting is that the more notorious these *misogi* candidates, and the more money that was involved, the more likely they were to be re-elected and therefore "washed clean" as far as their constituents were concerned. The reason for this odd situation is that in addition to lobbying for government contracts in their districts, Japanese politicians have traditionally raised money from companies that are the recipients of the contracts, and then they spread the money around among their supporters.

Probably the most notorious example of political *misogi* in recent decades was the "cleansing" of Kakuei Tanaka (1918–1993) on several occasions during his turbulent life. Tanaka, who served 16 terms in the Diet and was prime minister from 1972 to 1974, is considered by many Japanese to have been one of the greatest political figures the country has produced.

Born to a poor family in Niigata Prefecture, often described as *Ura Nihon* (Uu-rah Nee-hoan) or the "rear (and wrong) side of Japan," Tanaka was only the third "commoner" in Japanese history to reach the highest pinnacle of political power in the country. The others were the Hideyoshi Toyotomi, who became the de facto shogun in the 16th century, and Takashi Hara, who served as prime minister for a short period just before his death in 1921.

In 1948 Tanaka was serving a term in Kosuge Prison because of his role in a bribery scandal. Eight years later, at the age of 39, he was a cabinet minister and a folk hero. By 1972, and 11 more encounters with the law, he was the prime minister of Japan. The "Great Lockheed Scandal" that began in the 1960s and culminated in the early 1980s, was responsible for the most famous *misogi* election up to that time. Tanaka was accused of taking millions of dollars in bribes as part of a deal to favor Lockheed over Boeing and McDonald Douglas, and was forced to step down as prime minister. But for the next decade he remained the most powerful politician in the country by controlling the largest political faction.

Calls for Tanaka's head had built to a crescendo by the fall of 1983, but when the elections were held in December of that year, Tanaka's Niigata constituents gave him the largest number of votes he had ever received—and more votes than were received by any of the other 848 candidates throughout the country. The elections of 1983 were appropriately dubbed "The Great *Misogi*."

There have been many political scandals in Japan since the Lockheed affair, some exceeding it in scale, but none to date have produced a *misogi* to compare with the 1983 cleansing of Kakuei Tanaka.

身内
Miuchi
(Me-uu-chee)

Insider Logic

The traditional exclusivity of the Japanese family, the work group, the community, and the clan has had a profound effect on how the Japanese perceive themselves, members of their own groups, and nonmembers. Generally, the smaller and more enclosed these social, economic and political units, the more powerful are the ties that bind the people together. The more clearly members of individual groups distinguished themselves from outsiders, the more ingrown their sense of responsibility.

In this traditional environment, the negative behavior of any individual in a group had a direct impact on every other member, and threatened the existence of the group as well. Responsibility was therefore collective, and in keeping with the Japanese trait of numbering and labeling things, it was made mandatory that community and village residents would help each other on ten specific occasions. These occasions were birth, coming of age, marriage, death, memorial services for the dead, fire, flood, sickness, making preparations for a journey (which was often a dangerous undertaking), and building or construction work of any kind.

The primary sanction used to control the behavior of group members was the threat of expulsion from the group—a practice that gave rise to the term, *mura hachibu* (muu-rah hah-chee-buu), or "eight-tenths of the village," meaning that residents would ostracize anyone who misbehaved or threatened the group in any way by refusing to help them in eight out of the ten occasions when mutual participation was mandatory. The only instances when a community or village could not refuse to help a wayward member of the group was when the individual died or when a family member died or in the event of a fire.

In this tightly knit context, virtually all Japanese were divided into precisely identified groups, resulting in the development of an insider/outsider mentality that influenced all of their attitudes and behavior.

There was one logic and rationale when fellow insiders were concerned, and a totally different logic and rationale that was applied when outsiders were concerned. This insider/outsider mentality is still a significant part of the make-up of most Japanese, and plays a significant role in every aspect of daily life in the country.

In companies, all of the various sections, departments and divisions regard themselves as exclusive groups and each has its own insider logic. In principle, every member of each of these groups is involved in decisions concerning his or her group, and each member shares in the responsibilities of the group they belong to. Universities, hospitals, government ministries and agencies, political factions, or whatever, are also made up of exclusive groups of people whose turf is carefully marked and protected.

One of the aspects of this group system is that the individual Japanese has traditionally had few if any friends outside of their own group. In the professions, doctors, engineers, technicians and others, did not have close personal relationships with other professionals. Members of a group looked upon others in the same profession as outsiders to be kept at a distance.

This syndrome still exists in Japan, although it is gradually weakening, and it is one of the many cultural factors that handicap the Japanese in their efforts to rationalize their political and economic systems, and to further humanize their social system. Because of the restrictions imposed upon the Japanese by their traditional insider/outsider mentality, the relationships they develop within their own groups are often described as *miuchi* (me-uu-chee), which literally means "inside the body."

The connotation of a *miuchi* relationship or friendship is that the individuals concerned are virtually extensions of each other, sharing the same "body." They work together, play together, and act in unison for the benefit of the body. Because of this *miuchi* conditioning over the centuries, most un-Westernized Japanese have a great deal of difficulty functioning as individuals on their own. They are particularly inept at coping with social and cultural challenges that are outside of their own exclusive group experience.

At international gatherings, the Japanese are almost always the odd people out, because their insider logic and exclusive group behavior does not cross either group or cultural boundaries well. A great deal of Japan's success abroad as an economic superpower was accomplished because of its insider/outsider mentality—a multitude of tiny groups moving in unison as one huge group, working at a frenzied pace to produce things for export, while keeping foreigners outside of their inner circles.

But this insider logic and behavior no longer works, even in Japan, where communication and interaction can no longer be limited to small, finite groups; and the Japanese will not be able to resolve their own internal problems or become true members of the global community until they overcome their *miuchi* mentality.

雅び
Miyabi
(Me-yah-bee)

Elegance in Things Japanese

One of the most conspicuous, important, and impressive facets of Japanese culture is the presence of so much grace, refinement and elegance not only in the arts and handicrafts of Japan, but also in the traditional apparel and behavior of the Japanese. Foreigners who are first exposed to the special elegance in Japanese-style homes, inns, handicraft shops, and elsewhere, are often left speechless. They know they are in the presence of extraordinary beauty, but generally they do not have the experience—or the vocabulary—to describe it.

Japan owes this special elegance to technology and standards introduced into the country by Korean artisan-immigrants during the 5th, 6th and 7th centuries. The technology was then assimilated and improved upon by Japanese artisans during the golden age of Heian (794–1185) when Kyoto reigned supreme as the political as well as cultural center of the country.

The special elegance that distinguishes so much of Japanese culture, including many modern-day products, is expressed in the term *miyabi* (me-yah-bee), which translates as "refined in taste, urbane, graceful, elegant." But the *miyabi* that is seen in Japan today is not the same that first flowered during the Heian Period. That was a kind of beauty that was bolder and far more ornate than anything seen today.

The "refinement" of *miyabi* occurred during Japan's Middle Ages following the introduction of Zen Buddhism into the country, the ascendancy of the samurai class to power, and the appearance of great tea masters as Sen No Rikyu (1522–1591).

The samurai class provided the impetus for the evolution of *miyabi* into the standard of elegance that is known today. Having mastered the arts of war and risen to the top of the social ladder, the samurai made the pursuit of culture one of the main priorities in their lives. The samurai's influence led artists to eliminate everything that was superfluous or wasteful in their products in keeping with the Zen concept that nature is the ultimate designer of beauty and that the greatest beauty lies in the simplest things.

The next, and many say the most important, contribution to the concept of *miyabi* came from Japan's great tea ceremony practitioners, especially Sen No Rikyu, the most famous tea master of his century, who taught that to be truly beautiful, a thing had to be refined down to its essence, to where the spirit of the object could be seen. This ideal of beauty became the national standard in Japan because of two other factors that were unique to the times: the fact that Japan was basically a very poor country, in which frugality had long since been second nature to the Japanese, and the fact that Zen Buddhism taught that only the frugal were virtuous.

Despite the glorious temples, shrines, palaces and other edifices that have graced Kyoto since it was founded in 794, they were not gaudy representations of great wealth. They owed—and still owe—their enduring beauty to the concept and philosophy of *miyabi*.

As the generations went by, the concept of *miyabi* permeated Japan's culture. The lowliest workman was an artisan who naturally sought to build elegance into everything he made, whether it was a pair of straw sandals, a paper fan, or the *tori* gateway of a Shinto shrine. For century after century, virtually all of the utilitarian implements made in Japan for the house and kitchen were literally works of art.

Japan's cultural impulse for elegance has suffered grievously since the country was opened to the outside world in the mid-1800s, and particularly since 1945. But enough of the *miyabi* concept remains in the traditional arts and crafts that have survived, and in the Western-type products that are created by classically oriented designers, to distinguish the Japanese and give them an extraordinary advantage.

No one can spend time in a purely Japanese setting, whether it is an office with Japanese decor, an inn, or a private home, without feeling the deep and abiding impact of the power of *miyabi*. Especially for those who are particularly sensitive, the feeling is one they never forget.

Mon
(Moan)

Wearing Company Colors

One of the distinctive customs in Japan is the wearing of corporate lapel pins or badges by company employees. Because of this custom it is possible to identify on sight the employers of many Japanese.

The custom of wearing lapel pins is a modern version of the use of the *mon* (moan), or "family crests," which originated in Japan sometime in the late Heian Period (794–1185). Japanese historians say that by the last centuries of this era, the "marks" that noble families first began putting on their carts to identify them had evolved into family crests, which were put on their kimonos, banners, gates, temples and other property. By the middle of Japan's last great shogunate dynasty (1603–1868), there were more than 12,000 *mon* in use in Japan. Not only the emperor, members of the Imperial Court, shoguns and provincial lords, but also merchants, farmers, and even prostitutes had their own crests.

Family and clan crests played a vital role during Japan's feudal samurai age (1185–1868) because of the importance of identifying the shogunate and clan affiliations of soldiers, retainers, messengers and others as they warred and moved about the cities and countryside. The honor, prestige and power of the clans and leading families was embodied in their *mon*. The crest of the emperor was virtually sacred. The crest of the Tokugawa family was so influential as a symbol of power that the most murderous miscreants, caught in the act of breaking shogunate laws, have been known to bow down to the ground and grovel when the awe-inspiring crest was suddenly displayed before them.

Mon still play an important role in Japan, now primarily as emblems of old-line companies such as Mitsubishi, Mitsui, Mitsukoshi Department Store, and numerous sake brewers. According to business sources, some 700 *mon* are in use in Japan today for commercial purposes. But there are dozens of thousands of company emblems that are the direct lineal descendants of the historical *mon*, and they play a similar role. The biggest difference between a family crest of old and a present-day company emblem is that the latter are generally worn only by male employees of the companies concerned—who pin them on the lapels of their suits.

Just as *mon* served both as identification and protection during Japan's feudal days, company lapel pins provide Japan's elite workforce with personal symbols that gives them a sense of security, and are something visible that they can rally around.

Company insignia are part of the cultural adhesive that binds the Japanese to specific groups; the company logo energizes them and inspires them to go above and beyond the call of duty. When in public with their company pins conspicuously displayed on the wings of their suits, Japanese employees are acutely aware that their appearance and their behavior reflects directly on the image and reputation of their employers. They are also aware that any misbehavior on their part may have unusually serious consequences in their careers, because their employer will take note of it, and it will become a permanent black mark in their personnel file.

Most large foreign companies in Japan pick up on the role and importance of corporate lapel pins, and have them designed, manufactured and presented to their employees as part of their employee and public relations efforts.

It would be wise for all foreign companies in Japan to follow the same custom, regardless of their size or the nature of their business.

物の道理
Mono no Dori
(Moe-no no Doe-ree)

Something New in Japan

Among the most frustrating experiences Americans and other Westerners can have is to become involved in discussions or negotiations with people who do not think or behave in a logical manner.

This means that Westerners who are engaged in international business or diplomacy spend a lot of their time in a state of frustration, because some 60 to 80 percent of all the people on earth either do not know what logic is, or they look upon logical thinking as inhuman and "irrational."

The Chinese, Japanese and other Asians are familiar with the concept of logic, but in their societies it has traditionally taken a backseat to personal, hierarchical relationships. Their beliefs and customs were—and still are to a great extent—based on personal obligations and arbitrary policies rather than universal principles.

Cultural contradictions produced by a mindset based on policies rather than principles are especially conspicuous in Japan, because clashes between the two viewpoints have become daily occurrences in almost every facet of society, and the old way is losing ground.

On an individual basis, most Japanese think logically and attempt to conduct themselves according to a precise set of principles, although the latter are not always the same principles that exist in the West. But when the Japanese act as members of groups, regardless of the size or nature of the group, they are forced by tradition to behave according to policies rather than principles, a situation that causes them, and Westerners dealing with their groups, no end of problems.

The Japanese are learning the hard lesson that policies may work well for specific purposes on a short-term basis, especially when the situation is simple and relatively isolated, but that short-term policies do not work under other circumstances. Virtually all of the political and economic problems that Japan has experienced in the past have been the result of policies that were outdated, inadequate, or invalid in the first place.

As early as the 1960s some Japanese intellectuals were preaching that the Japanese custom of living by policies rather than principles had to be reversed, or the country would eventually find itself in conflict not only with itself, but also with the rest of the world. These early voices urged all Japanese to begin conducting themselves according to *mono no dori* (moe-no no doe-ree), or "the principle of things," rather than looking out for their personal interests and trying to maintain the status quo of their groups.

By the 1980s the overwhelming majority of the Japanese had subscribed to the new and still revolutionary concept that they and the country had to begin acting on universal principles in order to put themselves in harmony with the rest of the world. The key word in this new concept was *kyosei* (k'yoe-say-e), meaning "symbiosis," or, in this case, a mutually beneficial cooperative alliance with the rest of the world.

Today most Japanese pride themselves on their strong belief in *mono no dori*, and the concept is slowly but surely working its way into the core of the culture. But progress is slow and uneven because of the enormous weight of the old baggage—the precedence and importance given to groupism which requires the suppression of individual thought and behavior, the exclusivity of each group, and the resulting tendency to treat all nonmembers as adversaries.

Japan's government bureaucrats, particularly those who inhabit the labyrinthine bureaucracies controlling the education of the Japanese, are the biggest obstacle to rationalizing the culture, and despite growing domestic and international pressure, they will no doubt make the process an incremental thing that happens over generations. In the meantime, logical Westerners who get caught up in the quagmire of Japanese personalism will have to do what the Japanese do: endure.

猛烈社員
Moretsu Shain
(Moe-rate-sue Shah-een)

Working with Violence

From the late 1940s to the early 1980s, most adult Japanese behaved very much like robots, working ten to 14 hours a day, six and seven days a week, and generating an unending bustle of activity and noise that critics of the system compared to millions of mice chewing away.

This attribute was a mindset that compelled people to work with an intensity and at a speed that was practically inhuman—a custom that had been common in Japan before World War II, but was dramatically intensified by the shock of Japan's defeat and the destruction of the country's industrial base.

In keeping with the Japanese custom of labeling everything, economic commentators began calling this particular trait *moretsu* (moe-rate-sue), which means "violence," "fury," or "ferocity," and employees who worked furiously as *moretsu shain* (moe-rate-sue shah-een), or "fierce employees." *Moretsu shain* sacrificed themselves to their companies, often working around the clock.

People like Akio Morita, cofounder of Sony, would spend days to weeks at their factories, sleeping a few hours on the floor or in makeshift cots when they could no longer stay awake. Managers went for as long as 20 years without taking a single day of their vacation time, and the news media praised the custom of working in this manner, making it a badge of honor.

When Japan's GNP began to surpass one major industrial country after the other, and it was predicted that Japan would surpass the United States and have the largest economy in the world by the end of the 20th century, the Japanese were astounded at what they had accomplished.

Part of Japan's success was based on the *moretsu* mentality that drove Japanese managers and workers. Some of it was based on the flow of American and European technology into Japan. Some of it was also based on a team-style of management, the development of more efficient manufacturing techniques, and an obsessive dedication to product quality. But predictions that Japan would be the number one economic power in the world turned out to be incorrect because of the country's astounding success.

The threat posed by Japan's economic blitz finally awoke American manufacturers from the zombie-like trance they had been in for more than 20 years. In a remarkable turnaround, American companies began adopting the Japanese-style of business management, from "quality circles" to the *kanban* (kahn-bahn), or "just-in-time parts delivery." By the early 1990s, the United States had regained its technological and manufacturing supremacy, and Japan's *moretsu*-driven economy had suffered a blowout—because it had gone beyond its limits, physically as well as psychologically.

The *moretsu* syndrome had been under siege since the mid-1980s, in part because the generation of Japanese who had sustained it since the 1950s had grown old and tired, and because the new postwar generations were not as committed to it.

The collapse of Japan's "bubble economy" jerked the Japanese up short, making it starkly clear that in order for Japan to remain an economic superpower they had to work smarter, not harder. From that point on the new orthodoxy became *kyosei* (kee-oh-say-ee), or "working cooperatively with the rest of the world for everyone's mutual benefit." This does not mean, however, that there are no more *moretsu shain* in Japan. The syndrome is so deeply embedded in the Japanese psyche that it will probably never disappear altogether, because it is powered by an indomitable pride that has nothing to do with GNP and everything to do with culture.

Foreign companies setting up business in Japan would be wise to make sure they have at least a few *moretsu shain* among their Japanese employees.

無駄、ムラ、無理
Muda, Mura, Muri
(Muu-dah, Muu-rah, Muu-ree)

Waste Not, Want Not

Until the early 1970s, sidewalks, streets, lanes and alleyways in Japan were scrupulously clean of man-made trash. There were no bottles, cans, pieces of paper, cardboard, plastic, metal, wood, or even cigarette butts to be seen anywhere.

There were two reasons for this. First, the Japanese had been conditioned for centuries to clean public areas around their homes and businesses every morning. And second, what industrial trash was being produced was quickly collected and recycled as an economy measure.

I clearly remember the first years that uncollected trash began to appear on sidewalks in Japan. The first trash to become conspicuous on sidewalks was cardboard shipping boxes and packing materials discarded by retail shops. During the following years the amount of trash discarded every day for pick-up by city workers paralleled the economic growth of the country and resulted in an island of trash in Tokyo Bay, nicknamed *Yume no Shima* (Yuu-may no She-mah), or "Dream Island."

By the mid-1980s, the traditional Japanese attitude that waste was sinful had reasserted itself, and enormous efforts were initiated to reuse household and business trash. Another factor that brought increasing pressure on the Japanese to eliminate as much waste as possible was the ever growing need to keep the cost of manufacturing down.

Domestic competition for market share was fierce, but there was a kind of unwritten rule that manufacturers would keep the prices of the goods they sold in the domestic market artificially high in order to subsidize the continuous expansion of their exports. As part of the nationwide program to maintain an export price advantage, companies became especially zealous in reducing visible material costs, and then they began to tackle costs that were not as conspicuous, or were virtually entirely invisible.

Establishment of the International Standards Organization 9000 (ISO 9000) by European manufacturers in 1987 was to have a dramatic effect in Japan, where Total Quality Control circles had reigned supreme for several decades. In 1991, 39 of Japan's largest business organizations joined forces to translate ISO 9000's requirements into Japanese, which were then adopted as "Japan International Standards Z 9000."

Two years later this joint business group established the Japan Accreditation Board for Quality Systems Registration. Fearful of being shut out of the European market, other Japanese business groups and companies began joining the new Board, and a campaign to further improve quality swept the country.

One company labeled this new effort its *Muda* (Muu-dah), *Mura* (Muu-rah), *Muri* (Muu-ree) campaign (soon shortened to the "Three M's")—a catchy phrase that was easy to remember and was something all Japanese could relate to intellectually, emotionally and spiritually. Other companies quickly adopted the same slogan. *Muda* means "waste"; *mura* means "irregularity" or "inconsistency"; and *muri* means "unreasonable, unnatural, unjust" and, in colloquial usage, "impossible." In this case the "three m's" stood for any wasteful, irregular, or unnatural behavior or process that would invisibly add to manufacturing costs.

As was also typical of the Japanese, they approached this new challenge with the kind of zeal and dedication that Westerners would more likely associate with religious fanaticism—which is interesting because from the middle of the 1700s, the Japanese were taught that working as hard as one could for as long as one could was, in fact, a religious exercise that would be rewarded in the afterlife.

In reality, the Japanese were motivated by this old concept, as well as by strong feelings of culturalism—they were sure that no one could surpass them in their dedication and efficiency in rooting out the "three m's"—and by the sure knowledge that if their company was unable to compete they would suffer the economic consequences. While not all companies officially adopted the *muda, mura, muri* slogan, they all inaugurated similar campaigns.

Thereafter, each time there was any kind of threat to the growth of Japanese companies there were renewed calls for *costodaun* (cost-down) programs, meaning measures to reduce manufacturing costs. The most widespread *muda, mura, muri* campaign effort of all was initiated by virtually every company of any size in Japan following the crash of the "bubble economy" in 1990–1991. And also as usual, one of the primary goals of these campaigns among manufacturing enterprises was to increase the quality of their products.

内定
Naitei
(Nie-tay-ee)

Hitting the Glass Ceiling

Japan has been a male-dominated society since the ascendancy of the samurai class of warrior-administrators in the latter part of the 12th century. The more powerful and important *Bushi Do* (Buu-she Doe), or "The Way of the Warrior," became, the more the status of women degenerated. Prostitution and mistress-keeping were legal, marriages were arranged, and wives were valued primarily as child-bearers and workers.

With the changeover from an agricultural-craft economy to an industrial economy in the 1870s and 1880s, Japanese women were further exploited, many becoming little better than indentured laborers.

Japan's defeat in World War II and the imposition of an American-drafted, democratic constitution on Japan in the period from 1945 to 1946 legally freed Japanese women from many of the abuses of the past. The influence of the American-led military occupation of Japan from 1945 to 1952, and the ongoing influence of American culture following the end of the occupation, did more than anything else to emancipate Japanese women.

Women began seeking higher education, finding their own jobs, dating men, and marrying for love. Huge numbers of young women became hostesses in the extraordinary nightlife of bars, cabarets and clubs that grew apace with the burgeoning postwar economy, becoming tough and independent.

By the end of the 1950s, Japanese men were having serious problems with women. One of the sayings that was popular during this period was a reference to the fact that women and stockings were getting stronger. By the 1990s, young Japanese women had virtually become a separate society; their attitudes and values were so different from those of Japanese men that it often seemed like they could not be members of the same culture.

Both the Japanese government and industry leaders have acknowledged that women are the primary pillars, not only of society, but of the Japanese economy as well. Women are still far from being equal to men when it comes to jobs, pay and opportunities for advancement, however. At the first sign of an economic crunch, Japanese women are the first to go and the last to be hired. For female college graduates seeking career jobs, one of the most important and difficult barriers is getting a *naitei* (nie-tay-ee), or "unofficial promise of employment," following interviews that take place before graduation.

Naitei are an institutionalized system in the Japanese hiring process. Companies invite large numbers of college seniors before graduation to annual meetings at which the companies introduce themselves and select students for personal interviews. Students who the companies want to hire are given a *naitei*, because it is illegal for companies to officially hire them before they graduate.

Japan's new breed of well-educated, independent and sophisticated young women must first of all compete with men in getting invitations to these company orientations. Getting such invitations is often equated with trying to get tickets to attend a superstar's exclusive rock concert.

The few companies that do not require formal invitations to their hiring orientations may be deluged by hundreds of job-seekers, and the companies may end up giving the coveted *naitei* to only a few dozen. Young women, dressed in "recruit suits" and carrying their resumes, are conspicuous among those who are turned away.

仲間
Nakama
(Nah-kah-mah)

The Personal Relations Room

The exclusive nature of Japan's group-oriented culture has traditionally put severe limitations on personal friendships. Generally speaking, nonmembers of one's group were regarded as competitors at best and enemies at worst, and in this cultural context it was not logical to make friends with outsiders. During the feudal era (1185–1945), loyalty to one's group—family, coworkers, community, clan—was mandatory, and the idea of establishing intimate relationships with outsiders was regarded as disloyal and dangerous; in general, it simply was not done.

Following the end of the feudal period, the perimeter of one's friendship circle was expanded to include schoolmates, but again, generally speaking, that is where the circle stopped expanding and where it was to stay until recent times.

As late as the 1980s, it was still uncommon for the Japanese to establish close friendships outside of their professions or occupations. The idea of an engineer from Toshiba palling around with an engineer from Matsushita was not officially taboo; it was just unthinkable. Barriers to cross-group friendships in Japan are gradually coming down, but it will probably be two or three generations before common interests take precedence over professional affiliations, particularly in the high-tech and traditional professions.

Nakama (nah-kah-mah), the Japanese word for "intimate friend, pal, colleague, coworker," and so forth, naturally has powerful cultural nuances that reflect its origin and use. *Naka* means "relations" or "relationship," and *ma* means "space" or "room." When combined they refer to people who share the same space and who have a close relationship.

Among the other expressions that use the word *naka* are *naka ga ii* (nah-kah gah ee), "a good relationship with someone"; *naka ni hairu* (nah-kah nee ha-ee-rue), "to go into a relationship," that is, "to mediate between two people"; *naka no hito* (nah-kah no shito), "an intimate friend"; and *naka yoku kurasu* (nah-kah yoh-kuu kuu-rah-sue), "to live in harmony."

Tomodachi (toe-moe-dah-chee) is a more common Japanese word for "friend," but it does not have the cultural depth or significance of *nakama*. In its Japanese context, a *tomodachi* can be an acquaintance or a casual friend. When someone is introduced as a *nakama*, however, the implication is that the relationship is long and intimate— often dating back to school days, which is generally the time that the Japanese form their most important relationships.

It is relatively easy for foreigners to establish *tomodachi* relationships with the Japanese in a short period of time. But becoming a true *nakama* requires a great deal of time and the sharing of numerous intimate experiences. This puts foreign businesspeople and others at a disadvantage in getting into the "relationship room" of any Japanese, because opportunities for them to share intimate experiences with their Japanese contacts are usually limited.

Over the decades I have known many foreigners who had what they thought were *nakama* relationships with Japanese business associates, only to discover to their shock and dismay, after 20 or 30 years, that the feelings were not mutual. These people made two mistakes. They interpreted a *tomodachi* relationship as being a *nakama*, and they presumed that their Japanese colleagues were capable of letting them into their "relationship space."

While there are exceptions, most Japanese are so conditioned in cultural and racial exclusivity that they cannot truly open a door for foreigners to enter their "Japanese room."

Among the reasons why a Japanese businessman or professional in some other field generally cannot open a door and allow a foreigner to become a *nakama* is that the space a person occupies is not private, and the person is not the only keeper of the keys; the space is shared with Japanese coworkers and colleagues.

Virtually the only recourse this leaves a foreigner on a professional basis is to establish a relationship with all of the key members in a Japanese friend's group, and to hope to be accepted by the group as a whole as someone who offers no kind of threat, as one who understands and sympathizes with the problem of the group, and as one who is a source of assistance when the other members of the group need it.

握りつぶす
Nigiritsubusu
(Nee-ghee-ree-t'sue-buu-sue)

Crushing People's Projects

The group-orientation of the Japanese is a major asset in some situations and a devastating defect in others. When a coherent, cohesive team effort is called for, a group of Japanese is formidable in whatever it sets out to do. When several Japanese groups combine forces in a coordinated effort to achieve a goal, they are even more invincible. But the first principle of any Japanese group is survival, and in routine matters, self-preservation takes precedence over virtually everything and everybody, including sister groups in the same organization.

This survive-and-grow instinct creates a constant competitive atmosphere between groups that can energize a company to achieve remarkable things as long as the mission is understood and has been accepted by all group leaders. As is so often the case in Japanese culture, however, there is a corollary negative side to the competitive relationship between Japanese groups. Group leaders, at whatever level, vie with each other for supremacy. They also compete with members of their own group in an ongoing effort to demonstrate their seniority and their mandate to lead.

It frequently happens that an individual member of a group will submit a proposal to his boss (it is customary in Japan for proposals to originate with lower-level staff) and get no reaction whatsoever from his superior. For some reason that the manager chooses not to explain, the proposal is subjected to an institutionalized action known as *nigiritsubusu* (nee-ghee-ree-t'sue-buu-sue) or "grasping and crushing." In other words, the manager kills the proposal.

A manager resorts to *nigiritsubusu* for a variety of reasons: to prevent the individual who made the proposal from getting credit for it, for example. Another reason might be that the proposal conflicts with a manager's personal agenda. Still other reasons might be that a manager disapproves of the subject of the proposal or of the companies or people that the proposal involves, and for various reasons the manager does not want to go on record as officially opposing it.

In other cases, the manager may not be competent to pass judgment on a particular proposal, and rather than make a point of his or her ignorance or lack of experience, the manager chooses to ignore the proposal.

If the individual who submitted the proposal decides to go over the boss's head to a senior director or to the president of the company, this step is known as *jikiso* (jee-kee-soh), or "making a direct appeal"—a move that can be fraught with danger. In bygone times, a subordinate who went over the head of a local magistrate or clan lord with some kind of petition was literally risking his life. Even when the petition was justified, this break in the chain of protocol was often treated as a capital offense.

A member of a Japanese company who resorts to *jikiso* to revive a *nigiritsubusu* proposal may be putting his career on the line. If a senior executive likes the proposal and wants it implemented, the boss who pigeonholed the idea is put in a bad light. If the senior man does not like it, the petitioner is in a worse spot with his boss.

Where foreigners are concerned, the *nigiritsubusu* custom can be just as upsetting. Outsiders who submit proposals to department heads or director-level contacts in Japanese companies should discreetly follow up on a regular basis to make sure that the proposals have not been buried. On some occasions, this follow-up is best done by a third party who has good connections with the company concerned.

Sitting on proposals for month after month, or even for years, is one of the ways individual Japanese and Japanese companies say "no." It is also one of the ways Japanese companies have historically used to learn more about a technology, a process, or a product without making any kind of commitment.

日本人論
Nihonjinron
(Nee-hoan-jeen-roan)

Psyching Out the Japanese

It is said that Westerners first became acquainted with Japan's now famous wood-block prints when they found them used as wrapping paper on lacquer ware, ceramics, pottery and other items taken to Europe by Dutch traders during the middle years of the Tokugawa Shogunate (1603–1868). Much to the amazement of the Japanese, the prints quickly became collector's items, and went on to have an enormous influence on the European painters of the day.

After Japan was fully opened to trade with the West in the mid-1800s, there was a period of time when virtually all of the traditional arts and crafts of Japan were regarded with disdain by the Japanese. Because the Japanese had been isolated from the rest of the world for so many centuries, their own wares had become so commonplace that they saw no particular merit in them. But they were fascinated by everything foreign.

It was not until foreigners began making a fuss over every Japanese art and craft, treating many of them as outstanding masterpieces on par with the greatest art of Europe, that the Japanese began to reevaluate them. And naturally enough, the Japanese did not have any special interest in the uniqueness of their own cultural attitudes and behavior until they began to see and experience the differences between them and Westerners.

It therefore happened that the earliest Japanologists were foreigners trying to understand the whys of Japanese attitudes and behavior in terms of their own cultures. Among the first of these was a Portuguese named Joao Rodrigues. Born in 1561, Rodrigues went to Japan when he was 16, quickly became fluent in Japanese, joined the Jesuits when he was 19, and later met and often dealt with Japan's two paramount leaders of the day, Hideyoshi Toyotomi and Ieyasu Tokugawa.

After being expelled from Japan in 1610, along with all the other Jesuits (who were notorious for their political intrigue), Rodrigues went to China where he later wrote a number of insightful books on Japanese history, etiquette and culture in general.

Among the first Japanese to look inward at Japanese culture was Kakuzo Okakura (1862–1913), an art critic and philosopher better known by his pen name, Tenshin. A cofounder of Japan's first official art academy (now the Tokyo University of Fine Arts and Music), curator of the Imperial Household Museum (the present Tokyo National Museum), and later assistant curator of the Chinese and Japanese

Department of the Boston Museum of Fine Arts, Okakura traveled widely and was a prolific speaker and writer. His English-language book, *The Book of Tea* (written in English), was the first attempt to explain the roots and nature of Japanese aesthetics and art, and was widely read throughout the world of art. The book is in print up to this day.

It was not until Japan suffered a devastating defeat in World War II that Japanese attempts to discover and understand their own cultural roots became an industry within itself—a field of study that was soon labeled *Nihonjinron* (Nee-hoan-jeen-roan), which can be translated as "comments on the Japanese people," "essays on the Japanese people," or "theories about the Japanese people."

This sudden flowering of writings on the Japanese was especially stimulated by the publication in Japanese of *The Chrysanthemum and the Sword*, the classic book on Japanese personality and culture by American anthropologist Ruth Benedict for the American War Department during World War II. Benedict had never been to Japan, but as a result of her research and interviews with Japanese-Americans and with other Americans who had spent years in Japan before the war, she was able to write a book that was to become the mother of all subsequent *Nihonjinron*. There are now hundreds of *Nihonjinron* books in print, with more coming out each year. Dozens of magazine articles are also published annually on the unique character and personality of the Japanese.

Interestingly, one of the most unusual of the theories about Japanese behavior is that the Japanese use the left side of their brains to process and deal with such things as language, sounds and mathematical calculations, in contrast to Westerners who use the right side of their brains; this, according to some, has a profound influence on the way the Japanese think and behave.

This theory, advanced by Professor Tadanobu Tsunoda in his book, *The Japanese Brain: Uniqueness and Universality*, was widely discounted by linguists and others. But since there have been no other more persuasive theories, most Japanese appear to have accepted Dr. Tsunoda's explanation.

Foreign businesspeople and others dealing with Japan need not become obsessed with reading *Nihonjinron* books, but there is no escaping their importance in understanding and interacting effectively with the Japanese.

日本的
Nihonteki
(Nee-hoan-tay-kee)

Being Japanese-Like

Japan's traditional culture was both distinctive and exclusive to the point that anybody or anything that was not pure Japanese was as conspicuous to a Japanese as black on white. Virtually all Japanese eventually became so discriminating that the slightest variation from a very narrow norm in appearance and behavior was considered un-Japanese and not acceptable. This built-in discrimination became an essential element in the Japanese concept of their own identity. Anyone who did not demonstrate the element to the proper degree was no longer considered truly Japanese.

Generally speaking, the Japanese were conditioned to reject foreign philosophies and morality offhandedly, and anything foreign had to be Japanized before it could be accepted. This conditioning in exclusivity and discrimination has been steadily diminishing for more than a hundred years, but it was such a deeply integrated part of Japan's traditional culture for so long it continues to prevail among most Japanese.

Till this day, there are probably no more discriminating people on earth than the Japanese. They automatically distinguish between what is foreign, what is Japanese, and what is *Nihonteki* (Nee-hoan-tay-kee).

Nihon means "Japan." *Teki* has the meaning of "suitable, fit, compatible, conforming to," or "similar to." When combined, the compound can be translated as "Japanese-like." Since the reopening of Japan to the outside world in the 1850s and 1860s, the Japanese have used the *Nihonteki* rationale to adopt a wide variety of foreign attitudes, behavior, customs and things by the simple process of Japanizing them.

And herein lies the source of much of the friction that continues to exist between Japan and the outside world. Outsiders too often presume that because the Japanese have adopted so many Western ways, that they think and behave like Westerners. Such is almost never the case. The point is that all of the Western ways that the Japanese have adopted are no longer purely Western. They have become *Nihonteki*, with their own special Japanese nuances. They may look the same to Westerners, but they are not. They have been Japanized.

American companies in particular were slow in picking up on the need to make their products *Nihonteki* before they tried to export them to Japan. It was well into the 1980s before this message finally got through.

Americans were even slower in picking up on the idea that the image the Japanese have of a product regarding quality, value, and the manufacturer begins with the packaging. The higher the market end a product is aimed at, the more its packaging must qualify in terms of materials, design and printing. Indeed, there have been many occasions in the past when foreign shoppers in Japan valued the packaging or container more than the product they bought.

Determining when something is Japanese or *Nihonteki* enough to be accepted in Japan requires a level of exposure to Japanese culture. This naturally eliminates virtually all foreigners who have not lived in the country for long enough years or who have not become sensitized to the subtle signs and nuances that are the necessary ingredients of Japaneseness.

Merely living in Japan is not enough to give one a sense of *Nihonteki*. *Nihonteki* is a level of awareness and insight that must be deliberately pursued, and it covers the whole world of Japanese aesthetics. Such words as *shibui* (she-booey), "restrained, refined"; *wabi* (wah-bee), "simple, quiet, tranquil"; *sabi* (sah-bee), literally "rust," but referring to the beauty of age; and *yugen* (yuu-gane), "mystery" or "subtlety," are keys to this understanding. In fact, there is no way that one could possibly understand Japanese aesthetics without a full grasp of the meanings and uses of these terms.

Among other things, these words refer to elements that make up *Nihonteki*, and as such are the foundation of all Japanese arts and crafts, including architecture, gardening, and all the other arts for which Japan is known overseas, from kabuki and Noh to woodblock prints. Even Western products that have been accepted by

Japanese consumers without any changes—and there have been some—have a different image when viewed by the Japanese.

Any company contemplating exporting a consumer product to Japan should be aware of the *Nihonteki* factor and should try to make sure that the product "fits" the Japanese image of product correctness.

ノーミス

No Misu
(No Me-sue)

Second Best isn't Good Enough

Japan owes its rise to superpower status to a variety of internal and external factors. But no matter how much help the Japanese got from foreign technology, the huge, rich and open American and European markets, and the American wars in Korea and Vietnam, there would be no Japanese superpower if it had not been for a number of cultural factors that literally made the Japanese a superior people.

One of the cultural factors that became a primary pillar in the economic edifice built by the Japanese was their obsession with quality. From around the 5th and 6th centuries, when Japan first began to import handicraft technology and artisans from Korea and China, the Japanese were increasingly exposed to arts and crafts that were made by masters.The Japanese also adopted and elaborated on the already ancient Chinese custom of using the master–apprentice approach to training artists and craftsmen. Boys, sometimes from the age of seven or eight, were routinely apprenticed to skilled artists and craftsmen for ten to 30 years. This system, continued for generation after generation, produced great numbers of master carpenters, carvers, painters, potters and other artisans, gradually raising the level of the quality of everything produced in Japan, and imbuing ordinary Japanese with what may well have been the highest quality standards in the world.

When Japan was industrialized between 1870 and 1895, and the country began producing Western products, generally under the direction of foreign importers, they were unable to apply their traditional quality standards as the products were new to the Japanese and were made with unfamiliar equipment and were mass-produced.

This phenomenon was repeated following the end of World War II, but this time there was a different ending. In the late 1940s and early 1950s, Japanese engineers, in collaboration with American occupation authorities, resolved to introduce the latest quality control methods into Japan.

In 1950 the American statistical control expert W. Edward Deming was invited to lecture in Japan. He was followed in 1954 by J. M. Juran, another well-known American quality control authority. Over the next decade the Japanese wedded the quality control methods learned from these American experts with their traditional master–apprentice approach to training and with their obsession with neatness, precision and quality, to engineer and produce a stream of high-quality products that took the world by storm.

For want of a simple way of describing both the attitude and process that led to high-quality products, the Japanese began using the term *no misu* (no me-sue), from the English "no miss," meaning "no mistakes." By *no misu* the Japanese meant that absolutely no mistakes should be made in design, engineering, or production, resulting in virtually zero defects and eliminating claims, costly repairs or replacements, downtime, and so on.

This philosophy and approach was in stark contrast to the American policy of that time, which was to aim at a balance between defects, quality and cost. In the United States, if a product proved to be a success, it was additionally refined and any engineering bugs were removed over a period of months or years—but only if a company could not avoid doing so. The disparity between the Japanese *no misu* approach and the American system was a key factor in the success of Japanese-made products in the United States, and the failure of many American-made products in Japan.

But by the mid-1980s most American business leaders had finally gotten the message: They had to clean up their factories and get their act together, or go to work for the Japanese. For the first time in the history of the United States, American industry found itself behind a competitor and playing catch-up.

But in typical American fashion, company after company met the challenge, and in the next five to ten years American manufacturers turned themselves around. These companies did so by going back to the roots of American business, by adopting Japan's *no misu* philosophy, and by improving on both of them.

Today, pressure from cheaply made Asian as well as American imports is bringing increasing pressure against Japan's *no misu* approach to manufacturing, and there are signs that some Japanese companies are being forced to cut corners.

乗り気
Noriki
(No-ree-kee)

A Japanese Ingredient

There is often some rather ironic humor in the behavior of Western businesspeople who are "old Japan hands" and who at the same time are known for being especially critical of the Japanese. In fact, the more experience such Westerners have had in dealing with the Japanese, and the more critical of the Japanese they are, the more humorous these situations can be.

On so many occasions that I can no longer estimate the number, I have heard this category of foreign businesspeople become eloquent in their enthusiastic description of the intelligence, commonsense, energy and ambition of a Japanese they had recently met and with whom they had, or were seeking to have, a business relationship. These glowing descriptions invariably included the statement, "He's not like other Japanese!"

The kind of Japanese these old Japan hands are describing are, in fact, very special, but they are also very common, especially among young and middle-aged men who have opted out, or who have been kicked out, of the corporate establishment and have set themselves up as entrepreneurs.

Among other things, these Japanese exhibit a character trait that is described in Japanese as *noriki* (no-ree-kee), which means "interest," and "enthusiasm." But in its

Japanese context *noriki* has far more powerful implications than that which is normally suggested by its English definition. A more accurate translation of *noriki* would be "burning interest," and "enthusiasm to the nth degree."

When Japanese corporations interview employee candidates, they look for the *noriki* trait and, the degree to which the candidates "show their interest" or "become enthusiastic," or *noriki ni naru* (no-ree-kee nee nah-rue). There is probably no better example of young Japanese who are literally brimming over with *noriki* than the annual crop of high school and university baseball and soccer players—which is the reason why the more successful players are enthusiastically courted by major corporations long before they finish school.

One of the biggest complaints of professional American baseball players who join Japanese ball clubs is that the Japanese players are so enthusiastic, so dedicated to training, and generally so obsessed with the game, that it takes the fun out of playing. Some of the American baseball players have eventually found this constant gung-ho attitude and behavior so infuriating that they rebel and either leave on their own or are sent away to "rest"—permanently.

Noriki ni naru Japanese are especially conspicuous because they do stand out from the stereotypical image of the Japanese as quiet, passive and polite—characteristics that Westerners, who are used to a more aggressive manner, generally regard as weak. Japanese employers know that the best kind of staff to have is one that has a balanced combination of *noriki ni naru* members and the less colorful and exciting type that works quietly and consistently.

Foreign employers in Japan who are lucky enough to find and hire *noriki ni naru* staff should keep in mind that such people are acceptable to other Japanese only in certain, specific categories of work, particularly sales, customer relations, public relations, and so on. As a general rule, people with this kind of personality do not make good envoys or agents with responsibilities for making and keeping good relations with government offices, or for negotiating with other companies.

Virtually the only exceptions to this rule are when the *noriki ni naru* members of a company are well known to the public because of successful sports careers or other accomplishments that have won them celebrity status.

入社式
Nyushashiki
(N'yuu-shah-she-kee)

The New Corporate Baptism

In the 1870s Japan's ancient clan fiefdoms were legally abolished, and were, in effect, soon replaced by family-owned industrial combines or *zaibatsu* (zigh-baht-sue), which literally means "financial cliques" or "financial factions." Over the next several decades, a number of these *zaibatsu* grew to incredible size, and together they dominated Japan's economy. The Mitsui *zaibatsu*, for example, at its pre-World War II peak, had in excess of three million employees and was the largest corporate entity the world had ever seen. These huge industrial combines, as well as Japan's larger independent corporations, were structured and managed very much like the clans.

Hierarchical to the extreme, each had its own "house rules" and "crest" and demanded absolute conformity from its employees.

Following Japan's defeat in World War II, the owners of the *zaibatsu* were purged, and the conglomerates were divided up into relatively independent pieces. But the clan-like nature of individual Japanese corporations remained an essential element in their management philosophy and system, one feature of which was the hiring system.

New employees were brought into the companies in large groups once a year. Upon completion of the hiring process, each new annual draft of recruits was formally initiated into the companies in a ceremony known as *nyushashiki* (n'yuu-shah-she-kee), which can be translated as "corporate entrance ceremony."

The *nyushashiki* were more than just formalities. In many ways, they were similar to the initiation rituals typical of many religions, cults and exclusive clubs. The highlight of each ceremony was an address by the president of the company in which he detailed the philosophy of the company and what was expected of each new employee. Recruits were required to give up their individuality and independence and to master and abide by the corporate culture, with its absolutes of hierarchical harmony and teamwork.

This system turned Japanese employees into obedient soldiers who performed with extraordinary efficiency from 1945 to the latter part of the 1980s, during which time they transformed Japan into an economic superpower.

By the end of the 1980s, however, conditions had changed so much in Japan and internationally that this ant-like approach to management was no longer compatible with the new world. Younger Japanese were no longer content to sacrifice their individuality to stifling corporate cultures. Domestic as well as international competition made it imperative that company employees be freed from the age-old cultural restraints and be allowed to develop their innovative and entrepreneurial abilities.

Almost overnight, a significant number of the homogenized attitudes and much of the conformist behavior that had historically been held up as the glory of the Japanese were recognized as serious handicaps that were threatening to destroy all that they had accomplished.

This sea change in the overall Japanese image of themselves and of the world at large was dramatically conspicuous at the thousands of *nyushashiki* held throughout the country in the spring of 1995. Instead of emphasizing the suppression of individuality and the traditionally mandatory group mentality, most of Japan's corporate presidents emphasized such things as independent thinking, creativity, flexibility, specialism, professionalism and internationalism—all things that previously had been totally taboo.

By this time, many Japanese companies had already significantly altered their management philosophy and systems, generally in the direction of those in the United States and in other Western countries—and the pace of these changes has been picking up ever since.

However this is not to suggest that Japanese management will ever become "Westernized" in the fullest sense of the word. Japan's traditional culture is far too tenacious, too powerful and far too pervasive for that to happen in the foreseeable future. No matter how "Westernized" the speeches at Japan's annual spring *nyushashiki* rituals, there will continue to be a strong Japanese element in corporate management in Japan that makes it fundamentally different from the management style of the West.

What, in fact, is happening is that little by little Japanese executives are eliminating those aspects of their traditional management culture that are no longer effective—and which in some cases are seriously detrimental—and they are adding Western-type elements that are positive. The overall effect of these changes may very likely be that Japan once again will end up with a management system that will provide its companies an edge over their foreign competitors.

大風呂敷
Oburoshiki
(Oh-buu-roe-she-kee)

The Big-Mouth Syndrome

Among the most practical and versatile of the traditional artifacts of Japan is a square piece of cloth that generally comes in two sizes: approximately two feet by two feet, and four feet by four feet. The smaller-sized cloth is known as a *furoshiki* (fuu-roe-she-kee). The larger-sized is called an *oburoshiki* (oh-buu-roe-she-kee).

Furoshiki are said to have originated as accessories for use in public bathhouses, which most Japanese used until the coming of affluence and homes that included baths and showers, from about 1960 on. *Furo* means "bath," and *shiki* means "threshold" or "something to stand on."

After undressing, bathers placed their clothing on a *furoshiki*, folded the four corners up and then tied them together, making a neat bundle. After bathing it was customary to stand on the *furoshiki* to keep from dripping on the floor while drying off and dressing. As time went by, *furoshiki* gradually came to be used as all-purpose carrying cloths because they were instantly adaptable to objects of any shape, could be folded up and carried in a pocket or purse when not in use, would last for decades, and were inexpensive.

Large objects and several items bundled together required larger carrying cloths, giving birth to *oburoshiki*. When loads were too bulky or heavy for the *oburoshiki* to be carried by hand, they were slung on the individual's back, like a back-pack, with two of the corners wrapped around the shoulders and tied across the chest.

The most common use of *oburoshiki* was by traveling salesmen, who would bundle their goods into them and trek throughout the urban and rural areas of the country, going from house to house. These traveling salesmen were a familiar and famous part of Japanese life for many centuries. Younger, stronger peddlers were proud of their ability to carry huge *oburoshiki*, and made a great show of their strength and the number and variety of items they could carry and spread out for customers to inspect and buy. Eventually, it became common to refer to people who talked big and bragged a lot as spreading *oburoshiki*.

Another historical practice that turned into a colorful figure of speech was the custom of Buddhist priests who lived in remote mountains to use conch horns, *hora* (hoe-rah), to communicate with each other. Blowing on a horn, *hora wo fuku* (hoe-rah oh fuu-kuu), came to mean "talking big." Both *oburoshiki* and *hora wo fuku* are still frequently heard today, and not surprisingly, they are often used in reference to foreigners, particularly Americans, who tend to talk big and blow their own horns.

But the negative overtones of *oburoshiki* and *hora wo fuku* are gradually diminishing, as the Japanese themselves become more outspoken and aggressive—an evolutionary cultural movement that is, in fact, being promoted by a growing number of people in highly visible positions who see the traditional low-key, indirect, and behind-the-scenes behavior as a serious handicap in international affairs.

Generally speaking, it is not advisable for Americans or other foreigners to try to behave in the traditional Japanese manner—which the Japanese themselves are trying to give up. Japanese behavior requires extraordinary skill that comes only with growing up as a Japanese, and therefore is difficult for the foreigner.

Foreigners should tailor their behavior toward Japanese by being a bit more formal in introductions, in exchanging name cards, arranging seating, conducting meetings, and so on. And they should restrain any impulse to be extra loud, or to brag, or to be repetitive or overbearing. But they should be frank, clear, direct and decisive, and diplomatically request that their Japanese counterparts take the same approach.

煽てる
Odateru
(Oh-dah-tay-rue)

Applying Soft Soap

The grand opening ceremony of an American company's marketing operation in Japan, held at the huge Events Hall in Makuhari on the outskirts of Tokyo, was a conspicuous example of the ongoing cultural differences that separate and often confuse Japanese and Western businessmen. The Americans chose to emulate a rock concert, with an elaborate production of laser lights and loud music accompanying the introduction of the president and vice president of the American firm.

In keeping with this approach, the Japanese master of ceremonies shouted out his lines with all the bombast of a circus announcer—all behavior that was totally alien and inappropriate to the Japanese.

The president and vice president of the American company made speeches in English that were translated into Japanese. Both of the VIP visitors incorporated short Japanese phrases into their talks, a common practice that can add a nice touch if the phrases are appropriate and the speaker pronounces them well enough that they can be understood.

In this case, neither of the speakers did well at pronouncing the Japanese words they used, and one of them really butchered the expression he chose: *yoroshiku onegaishimasu* (yoe-row-she-kuu oh-nay-guy-she-mahss). This is an institutionalized and very important expression that means something like, "please. . .," "please take care of it," "I leave things in your hands," "I ask your indulgence," or "I ask for your support." Yet the emcee heaped loud praises on the visitors' "beautiful Japanese."

The behavior of the emcee was not an isolated incident. It was, instead, symptomatic of a deeply ingrained Japanese habit of praising people for actions or accomplishments that are totally undeserving of any accolade. Foreigners who manage to use chopsticks well enough to get a few tidbits of food into their mouths are praised effusively. Being able to actually pronounce a few words in Japanese properly invariably elicits high praise.

The Japanese habit of praising indiscriminately no doubt grew out of a social etiquette which demanded that people stay on good terms with superiors by strictly avoiding any words or behavior that might be construed as criticism or arrogance, and by the need to maintain a careful harmony by following an extraordinarily strict code of politeness.

Japan's samurai warriors, who were the arbiters of acceptable manners for some 700 years, played a key role in conditioning the Japanese to compliment rather than criticize. Not only were they severe taskmasters in their own standards of behavior, they demanded as much from commoners as well. Punishment for those who offended them was sure and sometimes fatal.

During this long warrior-dominated feudal age, it paid to polish everyone's apple, regardless of how rotten it might be, and the custom eventually became so ingrained that it was done automatically at every level of society. One of the special words that came into use during this period to describe unwarranted praise was *odateru* (oh-dah-tay-rue), which literally means "to flatter," "to butter up"; the meaning of "cajole" and "wheedle," might also be included.

The Japanese still habitually use *odateru* in all of their relationships, and are extremely sensitive to this deeply ingrained form of behavior. Professionals, in particular, are accustomed to being buoyed up by a constant flow of *odateru* from outsiders, their clients and junior associates.

Foreigners working in Japanese companies often have an especially hard time because they are either not familiar with this buttering up syndrome or its importance, or they downplay it or ignore it altogether. More traditional Japanese consider failure to follow this custom a serious transgression, marking one as insincere, selfish and arrogant.

小田原評定
Odawara Hyojo
(Oh-dah-wah-rah H'yoe-joe)

A Delaying Tactic

I was once retained by a Japanese publishing company to help restructure its management system and to plan for the introduction of a number of new publications—something that I knew would be a challenge because the company was not making a profit and had a reputation of being poorly managed.

I spent the first two weeks in my work asking questions and listening to comments from people in all of the sections and departments, on all levels of management. This included talking to each of the senior managers in the company in private sessions over lunches and dinners. I spent another week, detailing the strengths and weaknesses of the company; I then came up with a list of recommendations, then asked the president to schedule the first meeting. The president, all of the directors and all of the *bucho* (buu-choe) or "department heads" or "general managers" (and in larger companies the equivalent of vice presidents) took part in the meeting.

As the outside foreign "expert," I was invited to present my ideas first—which I did. My recommendations required the shifting of authority and responsibility among the department managers, changing the accounting system, updating the circulation system, hiring some new personnel, and letting a few people go or reassigning them. In short, I recommended a complete overhaul of the company.

The president then asked each of the other members to give their views. Everyone talked at some length; the sales director spoke for nearly an hour. No one disagreed outright with anything I had said because everyone knew that the president wanted to make the changes I had recommended, and I was being used as an outside authority to substantiate the position of the president.

But it was clearly obvious that none of the *bucho* were willing to give up any authority, that none of them wanted to introduce any new system with which they were not familiar and could not dominate, and that they did not respect the president or appreciate his bringing in a "hatchet man." As was typical, the first meeting ended without anyone giving an inch, and without any decisions being made.

Thereafter, we held meetings once or twice a week for the next six months. On each occasion, I tried to strengthen my argument that the fundamental changes I had recommended were essential if the company was going to survive, much less launch any new publications.

At the end of this period absolutely no progress had been made. The *bucho* had dug their heels in and would not move. The company had become a victim of the traditional Japanese syndrome known as *Odawara hyojo* (Oh-dah-wah-rah h'yoe-joe), or, in colloquial terms, "the Odawara impasse," an expression that is derived from an event that took place in 16th century Japan.

In 1590 Japan's paramount warlord Hideyoshi Toyotomi sent an army to attack the Odawara Castle, the headquarters of Ujinao Hojo, one of his opponents. Hojo called in his generals and advisors for a war council to decide what they should do: fight to the death or negotiate a truce. The debate went on day after day until it was too late.

Toyotomi's forces easily took the castle. Since that time it has been common to refer to the meetings held by Japanese politicians, academics, scientists, and sometimes by businesspeople as well, which go on for weeks, months and years without reaching any decisions as *Odawara hyojo*.

There is something of the *Odawara hyojo* syndrome in most Japanese meetings since a consensus is usually required before any action can take place, and achieving a consensus typically takes time. It is also common for the Japanese to deliberately resort to *Odawara hyojo* tactics in both domestic and international affairs when they do not want to make decisions or take action for whatever reason.

The only recourse that a participant in an *Odawara hyojo*-delayed decision has, is to bring some kind of pressure or force against the opposing side. Generally the only effective pressure is a clear threat that the obdurate side will suffer a significant loss of some kind if it does not move.

お彼岸
Ohigan
(Oh-hee-gahn)

Keeping in Tune

Life in Japan, prior to industrialization in the closing decades of the 19th century, was controlled by the rhythm of the seasons—to the extent that Japanese culture was sometimes referred to as "a four-season culture." There were special foods and clothing as well as seasonal work, seasonal customs and festivals that marked the passing of time and gave a precisely structured form to the Japanese life-style. The most important of these seasonal changes occurred in the early spring, around March 21, and in the early fall, around September 23, in conjunction with the vernal and autumnal equinoxes.

In addition to marking the end of winter and the beginning of fall, these two periods had historically been set aside for Buddhist memorial rites known as Ohigan (Oh-hee-gahn), apparently because during the equinox, the sun sets directly in the west, the direction that the spirits of the dead had to go to enter the "western paradise." Ohigan is the Buddhist word for the nirvana that the spirits of pious people are believed to enter upon death. It literally means "the farther shore," while the physical sphere is known as *shigan* (shee-gahn) or "this shore."

During Ohigan, Buddhist temples held memorial services, and people placed special offerings of *mochi* (moe-chee), "rice balls," before the miniature altars in their homes, and they visited family graves.

Shortly after the beginning of the Meiji Era (1868–1912), the two equinoxes were designated as official national holidays. Soon after the end of World War II, the two days were given their present names, Shunbun no Hi (Shoon-boon no Hee), "Vernal Equinox Day" and Shubun no Hi (Shoo-boon no Hee), "Autumnal Equinox Day."

Even today Ohigan, along with Obon (Oh-bone), or the "Festival of the Dead," in August, remain the most important Buddhist celebrations in Japan. On Shunbun no Hi, millions of people visit Buddhist temples to pray for good luck and happiness.

Generally speaking, most Japanese do not take Buddhism or any other religion seriously, although it is common for them to bow before temples on such special occasions as Ohigan, Obon and New Year's. But the events themselves are important both socially and economically as cultural observances that involve millions of people and the expenditure of huge sums of money for traveling, accommodations, food and gift items.

Foreign residents and visitors who are in Japan during the two Ohigan holidays, can make use of these two celebrations to actively participate in Japanese culture on the inside. Foreign managers in particular can benefit by joining their Japanese employees in visits to temples, and, later, eating and drinking with them at outdoor food stalls on the temple grounds or in nearby restaurants.

Invariably it is those foreigners who make themselves aware of Japan's cultural events and participate in them who end up learning how to survive and succeed in Japan, and who enjoy the challenges and the rewards in the process.

お見合い
Omiai
(Oh-me-aye)

Love Takes a Backseat

Marriage in the contemporary sense is a relatively recent phenomenon in Japanese history. During the Heian Period (794–1185), "marriages" were not seen as permanent arrangements. Higher-class men generally had several mates during their lifetime. Lower-class men generally could not afford to keep more than one wife at a time, but they could change wives easily if the existing wife's families were of a lower status and not in a position to bring political pressure against them.

Men could avoid getting "tied down" to specific "wives" by not bringing them into their ancestral households and not building or maintaining private homes for them. Mating was more of a "household" or "family" thing than a private union between two people, and children belonged to the household rather than to either parent.

Between the 11th and 15th centuries, marriages in Japan became even more politicized and controlled by local authorities. The main purpose of marriage shifted from producing offspring to guaranteeing the continuity of households, providing guarantees for the social status of families, and ensuring their cooperation. Families took great care to make sure their sons and daughters married at or above their own social level. Multiple wives became less common among the upper classes, and their marriages became more like political alliances.

During the early decades of the Edo or Tokugawa Period (1603–1868), the shogunate totally bureaucratized society, permanently fixing the people in the class of their birth—as samurai, artist-craftsmen, merchants and farmers.

All families were required to register with local authorities, and copies of *koseki* (koe-say-kee), or "family registers," were provided to the shogunate government. The social status of every family was fixed by these registers.

A marriage had to be approved first by a go-between, a role played by local government officials, to make sure that the proper social relationships were maintained, and then the marriage had to be further cleared with higher authorities.

Generally speaking, the only young people who had any choice in their marriages were the sons and daughters of farmers, who over the ages had continued the early aristocratic practice of multiple premarital relationships and finally settling on a mate only after a partner became pregnant.

Young unmarried rural men and women traditionally met in *wakamono yado* (wah-kah-moe-no yah-doe), or "young people's huts," for sexual purposes. Young men also traditionally engaged in *yobai* (yoe-by), or "nighttime visiting," of the homes of young women. If a young woman allowed a particular youth to continue *yobai* visits and, as a result, became pregnant, the pair would be united in marriage.

After the downfall of the shogunate system of government and elimination of the fixed social classes in 1868, marriages were no longer subject to official government approval. But the system of family registration was continued, and families on their own continued to arrange the marriages of their sons and daughters.

Arranging for two marriage candidates to meet for the first time was known as *miai* (me-aye) which literally translates as "meet and see," or more formally as *omiai* (oh-me-aye), "honorable meet and see." *Omiai* meetings were generally arranged by a relative, an employer, or a professional go-between—after the families concerned had been thoroughly investigated to make sure their social status was compatible, and photographs had been exchanged.

Arranged marriages, or *omiai kekkon* (oh-me-aye keck-kone), continued to be the norm in Japan until well up into the 1960s, some 20 years after the old feudal household law was abolished following the end of World War II.

It was not until the mid-1950s that single Japanese boys and girls began dating Western-style for the first time in the history of the country. This naturally led to the growth of love-marriages, or *ren'ai kekkon* (ren'aye keck-kone).

Arranged marriages are still common in Japan today, however, especially among the upper classes, where marriage continues to be an economic and political as well as a social union. The tradition of *wakamono yado* continues in the form of "love hotels," and the *yobai* custom has been replaced by visits to hot-spring spas and other resorts.

Dozens of marriage bureaus, some of them operating on a very large scale and using the latest technology, have replaced most of the professional *nakodo* (nah-koe-doe), or "go-betweens," and the traditional *omiai* held in coffee shops, restaurants, and hotel lounges.

Indications are, however, that *omiai kekkon* will continue to be a significant feature of life in Japan for the foreseeable future.

お土産
Omiyage
(Oh-me-yah-gay)

Creating Obligations

There is an old saying in Japan that reveals a great deal about Japanese culture: *Ebi de tai wo tsuru* (Eh-bee day tie oh t'sue-rue), or literally "Use a shrimp to catch a sea bream, or red snapper." The English equivalent of this adage is, of course, "Use small fry to catch a big fish."

The saying refers to the institutionalized role that gift-giving has traditionally played, and which it continues to play, in Japanese life. *Omiyage* (Oh-me-yah-gay) or "gifts," have, in fact, been the "oil of life" in Japan since ancient times.

Formalized gift-giving began in Japan as religious offerings to the many Shinto gods in order to obtain good crops, good health, to ward off evil spirits, and so on. Because Japanese society was authoritarian in nature, with rulers exercising godlike power over their subjects, it also became customary for people to give gifts to those in authority when they wanted favors or help of any kind, or just to stay on good terms with them. The higher the authority figures, the more important it was to give them gifts, and the more protocol there was in selecting, wrapping, and presenting the gifts.

By the Middle Ages, gift-giving had become institutionalized at every level of Japanese society. It was not only a major facet of social behavior; it was also a key factor in the overall economy of the country. Rules governing the selection and presentation of gifts to the emperor, the shogun, their ministers and other high-level officials were so voluminous and detailed, that every business and family had at least one individual who acted as the in-house authority on the subject. Clan lords and others who dealt regularly with the shogun and imperial courts maintained instruction books on gift-giving, because giving a gift that was inappropriate, that was not wrapped properly, or that was not presented in the right way, could be disastrous.

Until contemporary times, the biggest gift-giving occasion in Japan was Chugen (Chuu-gane), in the middle of the year, in conjunction with Obon (Oh-bone), the Buddhist All Souls' Day Festival, in August.

In earlier times Obon gifts were presented to the souls of the dead, and were generally special foods. Now they are given to bosses, other superiors, clients and others—but not to individual family members—and often consist of apparel, accessories, sporting goods, cases of beer, sake, fruit baskets and other gifts of food.

The largest gift-giving period in present-day Japan is Seibo (Say-e-boe), which means "End of the Year," when individuals and businesses give gifts to demonstrate appreciation for favors received during the year. In the case of individuals, Seibo gifts are traditionally from "inferiors" to "superiors"—from families to teachers, doctors and others seen as benefactors. Companies send Seibo gifts to valued customers as well as to other companies with which they do business.

In addition to being used as expressions of appreciation, gifts given during both Chugen and Seibo are also used as a means of building up obligation that can be drawn on later when some kind of favor is needed.

When the Japanese visit private homes for social or professional reasons, they generally take some kind of *omiyage* to their hosts—usually food or drink. When the Japanese travel, they are obligated to bring back gifts for family members and coworkers. In this case, the custom is to bring back items that are produced in the area they visit, especially things that are known as *meibutsu* (may-e-boot-sue), "famous products," of that region.

Japanese travelers also take small gifts with them to give to people along the way who are helpful to them or from whom they want something. These gifts range from folding fans and small wrapping cloths, *furoshiki* (foo-roe-shee-kee), to tiny calculators.

Japanese businesspeople are also masters at using the country's extensive *mizu shobai* (me-zoo show-by), literally "water business," figuratively, "nighttime entertainment," as "gifts" to help them develop personal relationships with customers, potential clients, and partners, and to obligate them.

In recent years there has been growing talk about reducing the role of gifts in Japanese society because it is a costly and often wasteful custom, but the practice is now fueled by commercial interests that so far have proven irresistible.

思いやり
Omoiyari
(Oh-moe-ee-yah-ree)

Japanese-style Sympathy

Japan has traditionally been noted for the extraordinary exclusivity of its culture—a factor that is now recognized as one of the country's most serious handicaps in its dealings with the outside world. The exclusivity of the Japanese mindset goes beyond the intangible features of culture, such as philosophy, morals, ethics, values, and so on; it also includes race, food and other aspects of life.

To make things even more complicated, Japan's exclusivity complex is based on group membership; that is, every group in Japan tends to see itself as an exclusive entity—one that would like to be, and tries to be, independent and self-sustaining. It is therefore very difficult, and often impossible, for the Japanese to put themselves in the shoes of someone who is not a member of their group; as a result, it is difficult for the Japanese to personally relate to strangers, including other Japanese.

This group exclusivity is one of the primary reasons why communication in Japan is so difficult, and why it generally takes so long to get things done in that country. The exclusivity protocol makes it mandatory that communication follow a precise, hierarchical path within groups and between groups, making communication time-consuming, cumbersome, and often inexact. In addition, the more bureaucratic the group or organization is, the more effort is required to communicate with it. Japan's political factions, government ministries and administrative agencies, all of which are made up of vertically ranked members, are good examples of groups with which communication can be difficult.

Because of the intensity and importance of personal relationships within Japanese groups, empathy and sympathy are essential ingredients for functioning in Japan. These ingredients are generally not used beyond the group, however, unless special circumstances are in effect. The Japanese are, in fact, proud of the depth and scope of the *omoiyari* (oh-moe-ee-yah-ree), or "sympathy," in their culture, but they are not naturally conscious of its limitations, particularly in relation to non-Japanese, nor are they often aware of how selectively it is used.

This lack of universal sympathy in Japanese culture has long been a topic of spirited debate among Japanese intellectuals, and even politicians and businesspeople join the discussions when matters of international concern are involved. As a result, Japan's foreign policies, both political and economic, are increasingly being designed with an element of *omoiyari* for international causes and for foreign people. This sympathy ranges from concern for the health and the physical hardships of the non-Japanese to their concern for the economic future.

One of the special occasions when the Japanese automatically extend extraordinary sympathy is when tourists or other guests of the country experience a mishap—when they are robbed, lose a camera, or incur some other misfortune. On such occasions it is typical of individual Japanese to take extreme measures to see that the lost items are returned or that the people are compensated in some way. A taxi driver, for example, will spend hours of his own time trying to locate a passenger who left something in his vehicle.

Of course, there is more than just *omoiyari* in these actions. There is also pride. When any short-time foreign visitor who is in Japan legally has any kind of problem, the Japanese feel honor-bound to remedy the situation so the visitor will not leave with a negative image of the Japanese or of the country.

Ultimately, a universal concept of "the good Samaritan" will not develop in Japan until this concept is institutionalized in the child-raising and educational systems and becomes an integral part of the learning process.

表、裏
Omote / Ura
(Oh-moe-tay / Uu-rah)

Telling the Front from the Back

During most of Japan's pre-democratic history, prior to 1945, etiquette prohibited the Japanese from making blunt, candid comments on virtually any occasion, and it was especially important to disguise one's thoughts and intentions in business and in political matters.

The reason for this custom was bound up in the vertical structure and group orientation of the society, in the allegiance and obligations individuals owed to those above them, in severely enforced sanctions against people acting according to their own personal desires or inclinations, and in the fact that everyone, one way or another, was in competition with each other, as were all groups of whatever size.

Avoiding any comment or behavior that might be construed as arrogant, self-serving, individualistic, aggressive, or disapproving, was programmed into the Japanese until such conduct became second nature; sanctions enforcing this kind of interpersonal behavior were very severe, and usually they were implemented swiftly. Generally, the only people who were permitted to break these taboos were people in positions of authority when they were dealing harshly with subordinates.

In this environment, particularly in business and politics, it became natural for the Japanese to speak in indirect terms, and to leave it up to the other side to divine their intent. Whatever people said publicly was regarded as their *omote* (oh-moe-tay), or "front," while their real intentions, or *ura* (uu-rah), "back," remained concealed. Thus, it came about that virtually every discussion or negotiation in Japan had its *omote* and its *ura*—its front and its back—and nothing was settled or accomplished until both parties were satisfied that they understood each other's *ura*; a process that was usually time-consuming, and often costly.

Given this situation, very little of real substance was ever discussed publicly in formal Japanese meetings. Two sides would speak in general times, present their *omote*, and leave their real goals to become apparent later during behind-the-scenes meetings, or to become obvious from their actions—as was typically the case in diplomatic affairs.

The *omote–ura* way of interacting is still the prevailing custom in Japan; however, a growing number of Japanese businesspeople, as well as some politicians and diplomats with international experience, are able to dispense with this roundabout way of negotiating, and they use the Western approach when dealing with foreigners.

Westerners who are not familiar with the *omote–ura* way of doing things are naturally at a serious disadvantage when dealing with the Japanese, because it is generally the custom for Westerners to reveal their entire position at the first meeting. However, once the foreign side has "tipped its hand," it has much less leverage than the Japanese side.

The Japanese often never fully explain their intentions and goals—sometimes because they do not really know what their goals are; other times because they assume goals will change; and still on other occasions as a ploy to keep the other side guessing. Foreign diplomats know only too well that the Japanese are masters at using the *omote–ura* technique as a delaying tactic, oftentimes keeping discussions going on for years without ever making a commitment.

As a general rule, outsiders negotiating any kind of arrangement with Japanese companies or with the Japanese government would be well advised to take a page from the Japanese manual, speaking first in broad, general terms, and then getting down to the nitty-gritty step-by-step, introducing and covering one point at a time.

Another rule in negotiating contracts and agreements with the Japanese is to do the negotiating on your own home ground rather than in Japan, if at all possible. And if some of the negotiating has to be done in Japan, keep in mind that it is better to do the first part there and the final part in your home country or at some neutral place. The reason for this is that the farther the Japanese are away from Japan, and the longer they have been abroad, the more vulnerable they become, or I should say, the more understanding and flexible they become.

The words *omote* and *ura* are also used in the sense of "the front side of Japan," *omote Nihon* (oh-moe-tay Nee-hoan), in reference to the eastern seaboard, where the bulk of the population and industry are located, and "the back side of Japan," *ura Nihon* (uu-rah Nee-hoan), the western seaboard, which is generally considered the "wrong side of the tracks" in Japan.

恩、恩返し
On / On Gaeshi
(Own / Own Guy-she)

Covering with Obligation

There are probably few people who depend as much on personal obligation as the basis of their interpersonal relationships as the Japanese. With only a few exceptions, virtually every interaction of any kind begins with, and is based on, a personal obligation as opposed to a loftier principle. The Japanese have traditionally been known for the generous hospitality they typically bestow upon visitors and on people with whom they want to develop a professional or business relationship.

The extraordinary gift-giving that is so much a part of Japanese life is also one of the facets of creating and repaying obligation. When the Japanese travel abroad they normally take small gifts for everyone who befriends them or for those from whom they want some kind of assistance or cooperation.

Practically all foreigners who have been involved with the Japanese to any extent have had experience with this *on* (own), or "obligation," aspect of Japanese culture—which sometimes is so overwhelming that it is upsetting. *On* has traditionally been the "glue" that bonded the Japanese to the Japanese Way, controlling relationships between children and their parents, between students and their teachers, between workmen and their employers, and between warriors and their clan lords.

Once *on* has been accepted, the powerful sense of debt that compels people to repay the obligation with some kind of cooperation, favor, or assistance is referred to as *giri* (ghee-ree), which is translated as "duty, justice, obligation."

In traditional Japanese culture, *on* and *giri* were the very foundations of existence. They controlled the lives of the Japanese more definitively than the moral precepts of Christianity and the civil laws of the Western world affected the lives of Westerners, because the failure to fulfill personal obligations could not be disguised, and the sanctions for not fulfilling obligations could have an immediate effect on one's livelihood.

On has a number of facets and degrees. There are great numbers of Japanese who display great generosity and expect nothing in return. There are, on the other hand, many who deliberately place *on* on a person in order to get something in return—an act that is referred to as *on wo uru* (own oh uu-rue), meaning "to sell obligation." And there are large numbers of people who specialize in *on wo uru* as a key part of their work and existence. Forcing people to accept obligation and then maneuvering to get them to repay it is known as *on ni kiseru* (own nee kee-say-rue), or "to cover someone with obligation."

Repaying *on* is known as *on gaeshi* (own guy-she) or "returning obligation." Refusing or neglecting to repay *on* is a serious transgression in Japanese society, and earns one the disreputable reputation of *on shirazu* (own she-rah-zuu), "not knowing obligation" or "not honoring obligation."

Today *on* is still one of the most important cultural factors in Japanese society, and it will obviously remain so until it is replaced by a more objective system of morality. Interestingly, most Japanese are in favor of discarding the traditional *on* morality because it is an extraordinary emotional burden, takes up a lot of time, and is expensive.

Foreigners interacting with the Japanese should beware of incurring obligations that they cannot readily and willingly repay. This means developing enough insight to know the difference between a gift or a favor that is extended out of a sense of goodwill and friendship, and one that is designed to gain some favor in return.

Also, foreigners should be aware that the difference between a social obligation and a business obligation is often blurred.

お得意さん
O'tokui San
(Oh-toe-kuu-ee Sahn)

Mr Honored Customer

During Japan's feudal period, the bond between samurai warriors and their fief lords transcended all normal human relationships. The warriors had to be prepared at all times to give their lives, and the lives of their families, at a moment's notice, to protect or to serve the needs of their lords.

There are numerous historical records of samurai being called upon to provide this ultimate proof of their loyalty to the samurai code and to their lords—in some instances dispatching their own families before committing ritual suicide. This traditional relationship between the samurai and their lords is often used to emphasize the depth and importance of the relationships that exist between many Japanese manufacturers, suppliers and distributors.

In fact, some of these modern-day relationships do go back to the feudal era, and have become sanctified by time as well as tradition. And although some of the relationships have long since ceased to make economic sense, they are continued out of deep feelings of loyalty and obligation.

Customers who have long histories with retailers, wholesalers, or manufacturers are often referred to as *O'tokui San* (Oh-toe-kuu-ee Sahn), which means "Mr (or Mrs) Honored Customer." They are especially valued and get special treatment, particularly if their patronage is exclusive.

Over the decades, the samurai-like bonds between Japanese companies, especially those between manufacturers and distributors, have served as obstacles—and sometimes as insurmountable barriers—to foreign enterprises attempting to gain footholds in Japan or attempting to do business with Japanese companies outside of Japan. The bonds have regularly prevented Japanese companies from changing or adding suppliers, or from taking on new distributors or new product lines even when new relationships would have been good business.

Times have changed, however. The importance of the *O'tokui San* relationship began to wane in the 1980s in concert with fundamental changes in Japan's economy. These changes included growing consumerism and more liberal trade practices, most of which were brought on because of pressure from foreign governments, and many of them made it easier for foreign companies to do business both in the Japanese market and with Japanese companies overseas.

At the same time, some Japanese companies became so international that they lost much of their Japanese identity and any need for maintaining meaningless O'tokui San relationships. Other companies were forced by competition to rationalize their policies to the point that their old ties no longer have such a strangle-hold on their business activities.

But the *O'tokui San* factor is far from dead in Japan's business world. It is much too deeply entrenched in the social and corporate culture to disappear in one or two generations. The older the Japanese company, the more likely it is to have "honored customer" relationships, and the larger the company the more of these relationships it is bound to have. The question now is whether or not these companies have evolved to the point that they are able to reduce or eliminate the negative aspects of such ties. Foreign companies contemplating doing business with specific Japanese firms should identify any and all of their *O'tokui San* relationships, and find out what impact those relationships would have on their own proposed arrangements.

Gaining the position of an *O'tokui San*, even in a much watered down sense, is still a valuable asset in Japan, whether the business involved is a neighborhood fish market, a favorite bar, or a multibillion-dollar-a-year conglomerate.

お疲れさま
Otsukare Sama
(Oh-tsu-kah-ray Sah-mah)

Above and Beyond the Call

Foreign employers in Japan often run afoul of their Japanese employees because they are either not aware of, or do not appreciate, a number of customs that are a significant part of the social behavior of the Japanese.

Most of these customs, which just as often appear unimportant and overdone to the average foreigner, involve catering to the culturally conditioned sensitivities of the Japanese by bowing at the right time and in the right way, expressing thanks, paying compliments, apologizing—even where there is no real reason to do so, and following other etiquette rituals that remain deeply ingrained in the Japanese.

Over the centuries the Japanese were conditioned to conduct themselves in a precise, detailed manner in all of their social relationships. There was a prescribed behavior, including the language to be used, for virtually every situation. Training in this formalized etiquette began when infants were still strapped to their mothers' backs. By the time children were two or three years old, bowing was an automatic reflex. By the time they reached their teens, their physical and mental programming was complete. Practically all behavior was automated. Conditioning in traditional etiquette continued in full force throughout Japanese society until the latter part of the 1950s, when parents began to slack off in the intensity of their efforts.

Over the decades since, there has been a slow but steady decline in the formal efforts to program the behavior of the Japanese. However, Japanese etiquette was so pervasive in the past that it is still strong and persistent enough to continue to mold most Japanese in the traditional image.

Foreigners who study the Japanese language and become intimately involved with the Japanese for as little as two or three years subconsciously absorb many of the Japanese patterns of behavior, particularly the bow. I was in my late teens when I took up residence in Japan, and I vividly recall that within a few years I regularly caught myself bowing furiously during telephone conversations, just as if the party I was talking to was standing in front of me.

Otsukare Sama (Oh-t'su-kah-ray Sah-mah) is one of the more important "code" words used in Japanese etiquette. The "O" in *otsukare* is honorific. *Tsukare* means "fatigue" or "weariness." *Sama* is a very polite form of *san* (sahn), which is the equivalent of Mr, Mrs and Miss. Put together, they all literally mean something like "Honorable Fatigued Person."

In usage, *Otsukare Sama* is a ritualized way of expressing thanks and gratitude to people who have worked especially hard—and usually overtime—when they finally leave the office for home. It means, "Thanks for working so hard—for the extra effort—for persevering—for going above and beyond the norm." The ceremonial use of *Otsukare Sama* is not limited to employers or superiors, however. Employees may also use it among themselves. Foreign company managers in Japan may get by with expressing their thanks in English or with using the Japanese equivalent of "thank you very much," *domo arigato gozaimasu* (doe-moe ah-ree-gah-toe go-zie-mahss), but they will gain more stature with their Japanese managers, employees and coworkers if they add *Otsukare Sama*!

廉恥心
Renchishin
(Ren-chee-sheen)

Avoiding Shame

The Japanese have never been morally burdened by any sense of original sin, which is one of the reasons why they have never been very much attracted to Christianity. The moral foundation of Japanese society was based on shame, which apparently originated in the Shinto concept that all Japanese were the direct earthly descendants of gods and goddesses, and that any behavior that would displease their godly ancestors was shameful.

There is a little catch to this theology, however. All of the gods and goddess in the Shinto pantheon were not good gods and goddesses. As on the human plane, there were some real stinkers among the heavenly hosts of Japan—with one of the results being that the Japanese had more than one role model to imitate, or to blame, depending on the circumstances.

In any event, sin in Japan became equated with social shame, not with spiritual guilt over such things as sex out of wedlock, killing, worshipping other gods, and so on. Thus, the primary goal of the Japanese was to avoid *haji* (hah-jee), "shame," and *renchishin* (ren-chee-sheen), "feelings of shame," and avoiding shame meant behaving in the manner that had become customary and accepted in Japanese society.

This meant that if there was no shame—if one was able to maintain his or her honor according to the standards of Japanese society—there was no sin. In its Japanese context, shame resulted when one lost face or when one's honor was sullied by the words or actions of others. Losing face could be caused by failing to keep a promise, by failing at some task, by being insulted or criticized, by being outdone by someone, or by committing a crime and getting caught. Face or honor was also lost when someone said something or did something to a member of one's family that was not quickly avenged.

In part, at least, shame became the primary arbiter of behavior in Japan because virtually all activity was based on specific, exclusive groups working closely together, all mutually responsible for the behavior of the others. What one did, had an effect on all of the members of the group.

Being ostracized within a group or, even more serious, being ostracized from a group, was a very serious matter because it was generally impossible to get into new groups, and as a result, ostracization often meant economic catastrophe. This made it extremely important for everyone in a group to stay on good terms with each other, and to be especially concerned about one's image and reputation.

Renchishin continues to be the primary force governing Japanese behavior, though inroads have been made by the Western principles of good and bad rather than personal emotional reactions. But because of these differences, people from Western cultures who are taught to believe in spiritual as well as secular guilt have difficulty dealing with people from shame cultures, and vice versa, because both sides routinely do things the other side regards as immoral and unacceptable.

One of the reasons why friction develops between the Japanese and Westerners is that the Japanese are exceptionally easy to insult by Western standards. Another reason is that a great deal of Western behavior that is natural and benign in its Western context is regarded by the Japanese as insulting. This includes being aggressive, being candid, flaunting individual knowledge or ability, taking personal credit for accomplishments, being disrespectful toward superiors, and ignoring chain-of-command protocol.

For the present moment, it seems that the only practical recourse for people doing business with traditional Japanese is to do their best to follow Japanese standards of behavior in all of their relations, and to apologize frequently for unintentional slips, including those one is unaware of.

流行
Ryuko
(Ree-yuu-koe)

Fashions and Fads

During most of Japan's long feudal Shogunate Period (1185–1868), people were divided into clearcut social classes: samurai warriors and their families, farmers, craftsmen-workers and merchants. Each of these classes of people tended to wear the same or a similar kind of clothing which identified them with their class.

As part of the government's overall social and economic control system, the Tokugawa Shogunate (1603–1868) went so far as to officially decree that people were to dress in a certain manner according to their class.

These efforts, along with the enforcement of a variety of other laws and national customs, had a significant homogenizing affect on Japanese attitudes and behavior. Over the generations, this kind of life-style conditioned the Japanese to be extraordinarily sensitive to what other people wore, owned, used, or whatever, and to immediately notice anything that was not common or familiar.

When the shogunate system fell in 1868, and the life-style restrictions that it had imposed upon the Japanese for centuries went with it, the Japanese became free for the first time in their history to experiment with new fashions and new ideas of all kinds.

But the centuries of conditioning that had gone into the making of the Japanese mindset had made the overwhelming majority of them more prone to copy other people than to originate new styles or ways of doing things.

From 1868 on, young people in Tokyo—never more than a small group, however—became the trendsetters, adopting one new Western *ryuko* (ree-yuu-koe), or "fashion," and custom after the other, which then swept the other urban areas of the country. *Ryuko-shugi* (Ree-yuu-koe-shuu-ghee), or "the appeal of fads," has continued to be a primary factor in Japanese society since the 1870s, applying not only to apparel and accessories, but to virtually every other aspect of Japanese life, from hobbies, such as photography, to outdoor recreational activities and professional equipment.

By the 1970s this phenomenon had been subsumed by the mass media as its special province. From that time on the media reacted in herd-like concert, catering to as well as creating national fads by hyping them up day after day. These fads ranged from items of clothing and accessories to travel destinations, magazines and books, household pets, character wristwatches, golf clubs, and included giving chocolate candies on Valentine's Day and wearing platinum rather than gold wedding bands. New businesses were started for the specific purpose of taking advantage of the fad syndrome in the Japanese character, with the main focus of attention on young children and teenagers.

The decade of the 1980s, which was the heyday of Japan's "bubble economy," was also the high point of *ryuko-shugi* in Japan. When the economy fell flat in 1990 and 1991, the average Japanese became significantly more selective in what they bought on a whim.

But the Japanese remain far more *ryuko*-conscious than most people, and they continue to be more homogenous as a market than Western countries, a factor that plays a significant role in the promotion and marketing of consumer goods.

Market research done by foreign companies proposing to introduce a consumer product into Japan should include a careful, detailed look at whether or not the Japanese perceive the product as a fad or fashion item, which has a longer market life than a fad.

差別語
Sabetsu Go
(Sah-bate-sue Go)

Taboo Language

The concept of free speech, a purely Western invention, is guaranteed in Japan by the country's made-in-America constitution, but neither the principle nor the practice of freedom are fully accepted.

Prior to the beginning of the modern era in Japan, there was no legal concept of free speech. It was dangerous to publicly criticize clan authorities or the shogunate government, and there were words, especially pertaining to the emperor, that were taboo. The idea of free speech was one of the many Western concepts imported into Japan in the 1870s, and for a brief period of time it flourished like wind-driven wildfire, resulting in the appearance of a number of magazines devoted to analyzing and criticizing the new government and its policies.

As the decades passed and Japan became more deeply involved in attempting to colonize the whole of Asia, official censorship grew to the point that virtually nothing could be printed or broadcast without government approval. In addition to prohibiting the publication of statistical information about the economy, information about virtually all other areas of Japanese life was classified and controlled. Finally, from the mid-1930s to Japan's defeat in World War II, virtually the only "news" that could be published was the propaganda of the military-dominated government.

Political freedom introduced into Japan by the American occupation forces, removed all of the official restrictions on the freedom of speech, once again allowing critical publications of every type and persuasion to flourish. But ages of conditioning in the suppression of information and news that might be damaging to the elite Establishment, or which might discolor the national image of the country, continued to influence the behavior of the leading news media. From the beginning of the modern publishing industry in Japan, the news media and many book publishers had their own list of taboo words.

Another type of censorship was practiced by the news media through their system of "reporter clubs." In this system, which still prevails, specific reporters are exclusively assigned to each of the major news sources, resulting in opportunities for these reporters to mold the news to fit their own agendas.

Prior to the early 1990s, most publishers and broadcasters censored themselves. But early in the decade, one private group after the other joined the battle to get more and more words declared taboo, and for the first time the public began to have a dramatic impact on the language that the news media used.

Among the first and largest of these groups were residents of former *buraku* (buu-rah-kuu), or "outcast communities," who began to demand that the news media not use words that they regarded as demeaning. These demands resulted in the rapid growth of lists of *sabetsu go* (sah-bate-sue go), or "discriminatory language," that the news media was enjoined not to use. By the mid-1990s a national debate was raging on the topic of *sabetsu go* in such areas as gender, age, illness, physical impairments, and ethnic background.

A number of foreign books that had been published in Japanese, including *Little Black Sambo* and *Pinocchio*, were brought into the fray. Other books about blacks, Jews and other racial and ethnic groups were also on the list of books that various groups claimed contained *sabetsu go*. With the subject of *sabetsu go* brought out into the open by complaints about these publications, the list of words not to be used, or to be used only "with discretion," grew rapidly.

Japanese opponents of the movement to avoid discriminatory language point out that Japan has traditionally hidden behind its language and used words both as shields and as weapons in its encounters with foreigners. They add that if the Japanese are ever going to become less xenophobic and be understood by foreigners, they are going to have to start by developing a tolerance for words.

Foreign companies in Japan must exercise special caution to avoid using words that the Japanese find offensive, a circumstance that makes it vital for them to "run their copy by" trusted Japanese associates before releasing anything to the public.

The other side of this coin is that Japanese sensitivity to words can be a special boon to marketers who hit on the right ones to sell their products. Terms that have been the most successful in the past were invariably soft, romantic, and often suggestive of things that had little or nothing to do with the product.

サービス

Sabisu

(Sahh-bee-sue)

More than Service

One of the cultural factors that contributes to an "understanding gap" between Japan and the rest of the world is the Japanese custom of Japanizing virtually everything they import from the outside world.

Generally speaking, it does not make any difference what the import is; nothing from abroad will be fully accepted by the Japanese until it is given a Japanese touch of some kind. This can be applied to the size, shape, color, or weight of a product, or to a product's taste, its packaging, or whatever. Sometimes the change is subtle; other times it is a complete makeover.

English words imported into Japan are no exception. The first thing that happens is that the sounds making up the English words are converted to Japanese syllables so they can be pronounced as if they were Japanese. "Milk" becomes *miruku* (me-rue-kuu), and "bread" becomes *buredo* (buu-ray-doe), for example.

Meanings of imported words may be changed totally, or they may just receive a slight Japanese flavoring, the result of which is that foreigners may not presume that a familiar English word necessarily has a familiar meaning.

A commonly used Japanized English word that frequently misleads foreigners who have little or no experience in Japan is *sabisu* (sah-bee-sue), from the English word "service." I say from the English word, because in this case the most commonly used Japanese meaning of *sabisu* is totally different from the original English word "service."

From ancient times the Japanese have equated the traditionally meticulous and elaborate "service" that they provided to inn guests, restaurant diners and retail store customers, as something that was an integral part of their duty to clients—not something they could or should charge for. In other words, "service" was something that was free. So when the English word "service" was Japanized, it was given the additional meaning of "free" or "without charge." Later, the word also came to mean "giving a discount."

Part of the reason why "service" was imported and Japanized is that the traditional Japanese word that is closest to it in meaning, *sewa* (say-wah), has too many other meanings, including "annoying," "troublesome," "kindness," "help," and "assistance." In addition, the Japanese like the foreign flavor of imported words.

The original meaning of "service" has been retained in the phrases *ii sabisu* (ee sah-bee-sue), or "good service," and *warui sabisu* (wah-rue-e sah-bee-sue), or "bad service." But in other contexts the word means that something is free or discounted. *Sabisu kohi* (Sah-bee-sue koe-he) means "a free cup of coffee." Stores often give away small novelty or sample items as *sabisu*.

A customer asking for a discount would say, *Sabisu shite kudasai* (Sah-bee-sue-ssh-tay kuu-dah-sigh), or "Please give me a discount." Ordinary green tea is a "service" item in Japanese-style restaurants, meaning that it is free if you order something else. However, going into a restaurant and asking for only green tea, *bancha* (bahn-chah) or *Nihon cha* (Nee-hoan chah), is unthinkable to a Japanese.

Because of the historical importance of "service" in the English sense in Japan, the newly imported word quickly took on special significance in the world of Japanese business, and since the 1980s, the Japanese emphasis on "service" has had an equally significant impact on the way foreign companies service their own clients. Newcomers to the Japanese scene should keep the two meanings of *sabisu* in mind and be careful not to confuse them.

Another term that comes in handy is *omake* (oh-mah-kay), which refers to something thrown in a deal for free, as an extra or premium—something that the Japanese do regularly in the final stages of negotiations to make the other side feel good. A term that looks and sounds very much like *omake* is *ohmake* (ohh-mah-kay), meaning a "big discount," "a big reduction," or "a major defeat."

探る
Saguru
(Sah-guu-rue)

Probing Your Partners

Among the more costly mistakes that foreign companies make almost routinely is not spending enough time, effort and money checking out potential Japanese agents, affiliates, or partners before going into business with them. Foreign companies are especially susceptible to making this mistake because it is time-consuming and costly to thoroughly investigate a Japanese company, and very difficult to evaluate a company after going through all the routine research.

However, going into a relationship without proper research is a major gamble, because Japanese companies often are not what they seem to be, and any mistake may not be recognizable for two or three years.

Furthermore, it is just as important, if not more so, for foreign companies to investigate and evaluate Japanese companies that approach them, including large, internationally known firms—especially trading companies, which may have agendas that are totally different from that which would serve the best interests of the foreign side.

In some cases, foreign companies ignore the importance of researching and qualifying Japanese firms for strictly monetary reasons. Either the money is not available, or money spent in this manner is not considered a good investment. In other instances, foreign firms ignore this important step because they are inexperienced in dealing with people who have different customs and values, and they go into business relationships with the Japanese out of a misplaced sense of trust and wishful thinking.

The Japanese, on the other hand, have a highly honed sense of mistrust and are extremely cautious about getting into situations where they might lose. This built-in wariness results in the Japanese generally going to extremes to qualify any company they expect to do business with. This caution has become institutionalized in the term *saguru* (sah-guu-rue), which means "to spy on," "to sound out," "to fathom." The word is also used in the expressions *saguri wo ireru* (sah-guu-ree oh ee-ray-rue), which means "beating around the bush" or "to sound a person out," and *saguridasu* (sah-guu-ree-dah-sue) which means "spy out," "ferret out," or "smell out."

The Japanese automatically think in terms of *saguru* in virtually every situation involving a business or professional relationship. The larger and more important the potential relationship, the more time and effort they spend researching and evaluating the risks and the rewards.

Foreign companies should be wary of Japanese firms which indicate an interest in doing business without going to considerable length to qualify the foreign company, to learn a lot about the company, and to get solid commitments from the company. The Japanese firm may be seeking something that does not appear to offer any risk to them, but affiliation with the Japanese company may be very risky for the foreign side.

In addition to financial stability, market standing and the product or service concerned, *saguru* always includes a human element—and the smaller the company the more weight that is given by the Japanese to the character and personality of the people involved.

If the initial *saguru*, or "probe," by the Japanese of the first foreign representative to make contact with them is conspicuously negative in any way, the chances of a relationship developing are greatly diminished. And, of course, unless the Japanese involved have been Westernized, this "probe" evaluates the foreign contact using Japanese values and standards.

The lessons to be learned from the Japanese compulsion to subject all new contacts to intense *saguru* is that it is important to prepare in advance for such meetings, and it is just as important for the foreign side to be equally diligent in probing any Japanese company they propose to do business with.

災害
Saigai
(Sigh-guy)

Land of Disasters

Like the fabled Phoenix, Japan rose from the rubble of World War II to become the world's second largest economy in less than 30 years. During that brief but remarkable period, memories of the great *saigai* (sigh-guy) or "disasters" that had regularly struck the country throughout its history became faint and far away. The Kobe earthquake (or, the Great Hanshin Earthquake, as it has been officially named) of January 17, 1995, in which more than 5,200 people died and over 300,000 were left homeless, was therefore an especially shocking reminder to contemporary Japanese of the folly of ignoring nature.

Since the beginning of Japan's history, the country has been plagued by *jishin* (jee-sheen), "earthquakes"; tsunami (t'sue-nah-me), "tidal waves"; *kaji* (kah-jee), "fire"; *taifu* (tie-fuu), "typhoons," and *kazan* (kah-zahn), "volcanoes," earning it the wry title of *saigai guni* (sigh-guy guu-nee), or "land of disasters."

Japan sits on top of one of the earth's most active earthquake zones, and over 500 major quakes have struck the islands during recorded history, mostly in the vicinity of Kyoto, Osaka, Kobe, Tokyo and Yokohama. Between 1880 and 1990 there were 23 earthquakes in Japan that measured above six on the Richter scale and caused massive damage. The greatest of these occurred on September 1, 1923, destroying much of Tokyo and Yokohama, and killing over 100,000 people.

Earthquakes occurring as far away as Chile have caused huge tidal waves that have struck Japan's eastern shores. One such wave that occurred in 1495 rushed inland through the former shogunate capital of Kamakura and swept away the huge temple hall enclosing the famous Kamakura Buddha, which had been cast more than 200 years earlier.

Fires, *kaji*, have been so common in Japan's history that until the modern era and the use of natural gas for cooking and heating, and electricity for lighting, fires virtually came with the seasons. Much of the destruction resulting from the Kobe earthquake of 1995 was caused by fires.

Annual typhoons have traditionally been both a blessing and a curse to Japan, bringing heavy rains that feed the rivers and fill rice paddies, but which have also caused extensive damage to the country's infrastructure, resulting in loss of life. Landslides triggered by earthquakes and heavy rains and massive snowslides on the Japan Sea side of the main island of Honshu, have regularly worked havoc with the nation, adding to the *saigai* mentality of the people.

The Japanese credit the regular occurrence of natural disasters for much of the character and flavor of their traditional culture, from their architecture to their cult-like emphasis on the kind of beauty that epitomizes the fragility of life. Any discussion of Japanese philosophy, including contemporary attitudes and behavior that have to do with business or other subjects, invariably brings up *saigai* as being a fundamental influence. The constant threat of disaster under which the people have lived throughout their history is one of the stock explanations given for both the resilience of the Japanese and for their compulsive work ethic.

Foreigners who are resident in Japan, or who are visiting there for whatever purpose, need not be paranoid about being caught up in a disaster. But, continuing earthquakes and other disasters made it starkly clear that some forethought should be given to the possibility. Some travelers visiting Japan refuse to accept rooms above the eighth or tenth story level in high-rise hotels—a precaution that strikes some as foolish because of all the various and unpredictable factors that are involved in a disaster situation.

Businesspeople in particular should make a point of creating a contingency plan for *saigai*, particularly earthquakes and fires, circulate it to all employees, and post the plan in prominent places. It also pays to know what kind of contingency plans your major customers or suppliers have, and it is important to share plans with them.

細工
Saiku
(Sigh-kuu)

The Small-is-Cute Syndrome

Among the most provocative–and often contradictory–facets of Japanese culture is an extraordinary emphasis on creating very large things as well as very small things.

Japan boasts the largest wooden building in the world, the Todai Temple in Nara; some of the largest gates in the world—at the Tokugawa Mausoleum in Nikko; as well as some of the world's longest bridges and tunnels. The battleship Yamato, completed in December 1941, was the largest warship ever built. But it was in the reduction of things—taking ordinary-size things and making them dramatically smaller—that the Japanese genius came to the fore.

Early in the history of the country, the Japanese developed an amazing talent for *saiku* (sigh-kuu), or "delicate workmanship," which was followed by a powerful impulse to reduce things down to their essence—not just as miniatures that could be viewed and marveled at, but as fully functioning accessories and utilities.

The impulse to reduce things is visible in virtually every area of Japanese culture, including *haiku*, (hi-kuu), the world's shortest form of poetry; short stories of only two or three pages in length; bonsai, "miniature trees"; fans made to fold down; umbrellas that collapse down to a small rod; tiny gardens that depict mountains, forests and the sea; and more recently, miniature radios, TV sets, tape recorders and other electronic devices.

In practically all cases, historical and modern, the Japanese began by importing standard-size products from abroad, miniaturized and improved on them, and then exported the new versions to the countries they originally came from—often with unexpected consequences.

In fact, one of the world's first trade wars came about because of the folding fan. Rigid fans were in use in China long before Japan appeared in the pages of history; fans had become an important cultural artifact in China, and were used not only for moving air, but also as a fashion and dance accessory.

These early Chinese fans were first brought into Japan sometime between the years 200 and 300, and legend has it that the Empress Jingu (201–269) had her court craftsmen make fans that would fold down so they could be more easily stored and carried when not in use.

Some time after that, the Japanese began exporting folding fans to China. By the 1400s, the volume of Japanese-made folding fans exported to China had grown so large that it had become a threat to the Chinese domestic fan industry. The Chinese began boycotting the Japanese made fans, resulting in a great deal of ill will on both sides, and according to some historians, the Japanese made attempts in the 15th century to force the Chinese to continue importing the fans.

Part of the Japanese compulsion to make things small is what appears to be a traditional sense of seeing a special kind of beauty in tiny things. Historically, the Japanese have been fascinated by a size-related "cuteness" in things, and the Japanese word for beautiful, *utsukushii* (uu-t'sue-kuu-she-e), strongly suggests something is pretty because it is small. This "cuteness" syndrome in Japanese culture is still as strong as ever, and is manifested in a variety of ways, from the use of "small" babyish voices in television commercials to TV sets that can be held in the palm of a hand.

The Japanese penchant for reducing and abbreviating things is particularly notice-able in their use of language. Abbreviations of all kinds abound. Even the common day-to-day greetings are all abbreviations. Japanese for "good afternoon," *konnichi wa* (kone-nee-chee wah), literally means "today is ---" which is short for "today is a fine day, isn't it!" "Good evening," *komban wa* (kome-bahn wah), literally means "this evening ---," and is an abbreviation of "this evening is a fine evening, isn't it!"

Hundreds of other common expressions and single words are routinely abbreviated down to an initial one or two syllables, and new words and new phrases are regularly created by joining the first syllables of two or more words.

The role of the *saiku* factor in Japanese culture is more than obvious to the rest of the world today.

盛り場
Sakari Ba
(Sah-kah-ree Bah)

The Business of Having Fun

Japan's recent history has given much of the world the impression that the Japanese are workaholics, or "economic animals," in the eyes of many foreign critics. And, of course, it is true that since the beginning of the industrial age in Japan in the 1870s, most Japanese have toiled like bees, or "like ants" in the terminology of social critic and author Michihiro Matsumoto.

But this image of the Japanese is totally wrong. Despite having been dominated for nearly 1,000 years by a class of warriors famed for their economy and the stern standards of etiquette which they forced upon the people, the Japanese have historically been one of the most pleasure-prone, fun-loving people in the world.

The long and colorful reign of Japan's Tokugawa shoguns was especially remarkable for the volume and variety of pleasures available to the people—and the extent to which they took advantage of them. During the Tokugawa Period, virtually every town and city in the country had its *sakari ba* (sah-kah-ree bah), or "lively place," and during most of this period, Japan had more towns and cities than any country in the world except for China and, maybe, India.

In more colloquial terms, *sakari ba* translates as "entertainment district," and anyone who has been to Japan since the 1950s knows what that means.

By 1955, only ten years after the end of the war and the almost total devastation of Japan, such large cities as Tokyo, Yokohama, Nagoya, Kyoto and Osaka each had from dozens to hundreds of *sakari ba*. In fact, entertainment was the first of Japan's major industries to fully recover following the debacle of World War II, and it was to create some of the country's first postwar millionaires.

By the mid-1960s, it was estimated by the Japanese government that over five million people were employed in the entertainment trades in Japan, which at that time was close to five percent of the population.

In its Japanese context, a *sakari ba* refers to a dense concentration of restaurants, bars, cabarets, night clubs, pachinko parlors, and, sometimes, geisha houses, which in modern times refer mainly to exclusive Japanese-style restaurants that call in geisha when they are requested by patrons. And until recent times, all of Japan's major- and many medium-sized cities had large geisha districts that were *sakari ba* in their own right. Some of the *sakari ba* in Tokyo and Osaka, Japan's two largest cities, cover dozens of square blocks and are virtually cities within themselves, with shops, department stores and hotels mixed in among the bars, bathhouses, cabarets and restaurants.

Many of the operators of Japan's *sakari ba* businesses have been in the entertainment trades for generations and have their own folk history, including distinctive work costumes and a special language they use among themselves and with patrons of the areas.

In Tokyo some of the most popular *sakari ba* include Akasaka, the Ginza, Harajuku, Roppongi, central Shibuya, kabuki cho in Shinjuku, Asakusa and Ueno, the latter district having been in existence continuously for more than 300 years.

All of these places, and several hundred smaller ones, live up to their reputations as "lively places."

Their narrow streets, lit by a maze of neon signs, are massed with young couples, company employees, cabaret and bar girls, street vendors, customer touts, professional hoods, strollers and tourists. The scene is a kaleidoscope of contemporary Japan at play, and once experienced, it is something that one never forgets.

桜前線
Sakura Zensen
(Sah-kuu-rah Zen-sen)

The Cherry Blossom Culture

Spring, summer, fall and winter are very pronounced seasons in Japan. Each has its own harbingers and its own special pleasures that have traditionally played key roles in the lives of the Japanese.

Fall is especially welcomed in Japan because it brings relief from the heat and humidity of summer and paints the forests of Japan with great swatches of brown and gold. But no season is as eagerly anticipated or as fully enjoyed as spring. Besides marking the end of a cold and often wet and windy period, which is the most physically demanding time of the year, spring is heralded in a glorious and delightful manner by Japan's famous cherry blossoms, which have been something of a national treasure since ancient times.

Cherry trees, or *sakura no ki* (sah-kuu-rah no kee), grow wild in mountainous Japan and have been widely cultivated since the dawn of Japanese civilization. History books and anthologies of poetry compiled in the 8th and 9th centuries make mention of the fragile flower.

By the time of the appearance of the samurai class of professional warrior families in the 12th and 13th centuries, the cherry blossom had become intimately linked with Japanese culture, and equated with the values of simplicity and purity. Cherry blossoms were also seen as symbolic of the samurai, whose fate was in the hands of their lords. Like fragile cherry blossoms, their lives could be wafted away as if by a breeze.

By the Middle Ages, the viewing of cherry blossoms each spring had become institutionalized into a national event that was called *hana-mi* (hah-nah-me), or "cherry blossom-viewing." Millions of people gathered in cherry tree groves and along the banks of streams and rivers flanked by the trees to view the blossoms, drink sake, eat picnic foods, sing, compose poetry, and otherwise enjoy themselves. The custom of *hana-mi* has survived the passage of time in Japan, and is now something that attracts tens of thousands of foreigners annually as well. In late March of each year, Japan's weather forecasters and news media begin to announce one of the most honored rites of spring—following the progress of the *sakura zensen* (sah-kuu-rah zen-sen) or "cherry blossom front," as the front moves from the southern island of Kyushu northward to Hokkaido.

The *sakura zensen* usually begins on March 24 on the plains of southern Kyushu. From there it proceeds northward at the rate of about 18 miles each day. The front passes through Kobe, Osaka, Kyoto and Nagoya in about one week, usually reaching the Tokyo area around the first of April, Sendai in the Tohoku region between April 17th and 19th, and the northern island of Hokkaido on about May 10.

Something quite remarkable happens in Japan as the *sakura zensen* approaches. The mood of the people changes from sedate and sometimes grim to a more open and sunny disposition. Glimpsing a single tree in full bloom is enough to soften one's countenance and bring a contemplative smile. A few hours beneath a canopy of *sakura* blossoms is enough to create a spiritual high that lasts for days—if you go easy on the sake, that is.

The most conspicuous cherry trees in central Tokyo are those lining the moat that surrounds the Imperial Palace grounds, but the largest grove within the city is in Ueno Park, about 12 train or subway minutes from Tokyo Central Station. There are some 2,200 cherry trees in Ueno Park. In the evenings during the main *hana-mi* season, hundreds of colorful paper lanterns are hung on the branches of the trees, giving the scene a nostalgic look that evokes powerful images of traditional Japan.

Foreigners contemplating a springtime visit to Japan would be well advised to coordinate their travels with the *sakura zensen* to take advantage of this extraordinary time of the year. Those who reside in Japan can get extra points with their Japanese friends, employees, and contacts by displaying knowledge of the annual *sakura zensen* phenomenon, and participating in the ritual of *hana-mi*.

産業スパイ
Sangyo Supai
(Sahn-g'yoe Spy)

Industrial Espionage

During the 1950s and 1960s, thousands of Japanese businesspeople traveled throughout the United States and the industrialized countries of Western Europe on study missions that were often sponsored and financed by the host countries. Participants in these missions had one goal: to learn everything possible about the economy and business of the countries they visited—from the arrangement of product displays in department stores and supermarkets to the latest technology in every field of endeavor.

Governments and businesspeople in the host countries were incredibly open to the Japanese, allowing them to bring back to Japan as many photographs, samples, manuals, and data as they wished. American and European businesspeople who visited Japan during this period were equally open and cooperative in helping the Japanese satisfy their insatiable appetite for information and knowledge about anything foreign that might be of any value to them.

During this same period, Japan's great prewar *zaibatsu* (zigh-baht-sue) firms, Mitsui, Mitsubishi, Sumitomo and Itoh-Chu in particular—all of which were reincarnated after the war as *keiretsu* (kay-ee-rate-sue) firms. This means that they had realigned themselves with their former member firms and affiliates—reestablished hundreds of overseas office around the world to engage in trade, to monitor events, and to collect business intelligence. By the 1970s, the intelligence networks of these companies were often compared to the finest national intelligence gathering services in the world.

All of this was just the public face of the *sangyo supai* (sahn-g'yoe spy) or "industrial espionage" that was being carried on in Japan and abroad by industrial spies that included employees of Japanese firms, detective agencies and freelance spies, as well as foreign agents that included American and European lobbyists and public relations firms.

The subject of *sangyo supai*, also called *kigyo supai* (keeg-yoh spy), is practically taboo in Japan, not because it is an unsavory and often illegal activity, but because it is one of the many things which most people publicly pretend do not exist. Shortly after the end of World War II the notorious Nakano Spy School in Tokyo was back in business training industrial espionage agents.

Japanese companies have traditionally engaged in "information gathering" since industrialization began in Japan the 1870s, and for many decades thereafter it was a normal part of their activities, and it was supported by their foreign contacts. It was not until the Japanese began their military hegemony in Asia and later in the Pacific that such technical and data gathering became a surreptitious activity specifically designed to enhance Japan's war machine.

Total defeat in World War II rid Japan of its dream of world conquest by force, and the new constitution that went into effect in 1947 outlawed war as a legitimate instrument of the government. Japan's surviving military, government and corporate leaders resolved from that time that Japan would take the economic road to success at home and abroad, and they immediately turned their considerable talents and experience to building and maintaining a reservoir of intelligence to contribute to that end. Thus, intelligence gathering became a major—but generally unstated—focus of Japanese business activity at home and abroad.

Over the years there have been occasional "industrial spy scandals" reported by the news media, along with exposé-type stories about the widespread use of *sangyo supai,* including rumors that first-class coaches on Japan's famous bullet trains were bugged as a means of listening in on the conversations of businessmen. But the subject of *sangyo supai* remains very much like so many other facets of Japanese society; it is there and everybody does it to the best of their ability, but nobody talks about it.

Most Japanese businesspeople have long been raised on the strategy and tactics taught by China's great 4th century B.C. military strategist Sun-tzu (Sonshi in Japanese), who based his philosophy on knowing everything there was to know about one's enemies, then using deception to undermine the enemy's position and to lead the enemy into making fatal mistakes.

This is not to suggest that all Japanese negotiations and business relationships are based on false pretenses, but it should serve as a warning that the Japanese are likely to know far more about a potential partner than they let on, and that one should be far more prepared for an encounter than one might think would be necessary.

三磨の位
San Ma no I
(Sahn Mah no Ee)

The Three Doors to Success

One of the most important lessons that the Japanese learned from Zen Buddhism, primarily propagated in Japan by Eisai (1141–1215) and the even more famous Dogen (1200–1253), founder of the Soto sect, was the importance of spirit in all human endeavors. They learned that there was a spiritual element in all achievement, and that the greater the achievement the greater the role of spirit.

Japan's samurai warrior class, which arose during the 11th and 12th centuries, became great advocates of Zen Buddhism, because the religion taught an austere lifestyle combined with an almost obsessive dedication to training in life skills and in the arts. Since the lives of the samurai depended on extraordinary skill in the martial arts, and eventually an equally extraordinary degree of skill in precise social etiquette, Zen became their spiritual guide as well as their training manual.

The samurai were Japan's ruling class from around 1185 to 1868. Although they made up only around ten percent of the population, they set the standards in every facet of Japanese life: in language and literature, in aesthetics, in the arts and crafts, in everyday behavior, and in morality.

The samurai also imbued Japanese culture with a strong martial nature that conditioned the Japanese to do things in a precise, regimented order and to abhor weakness or failure of any kind. Till this day there is no area of Japanese life that is not affected by the legacy of Zen, and there is still a significant Zen element in the character of every Japanese. Zen is still the heart of all of the martial arts for which Japan is famous, from aikido and karate to kendo; and the Zen rules that apply to learning these arts are taught as guidelines for success in business.

Nobuharu Yagyu, the 21st *iemoto* (ee-eh-moe-toe), or "headmaster," of the Yagyu School of Kendo, explains that the secret to achieving skill in kendo is in the spirit that derives from repetition of *san ma no i* (sahn mah no ee), or "the three exercises." The three exercises are receiving the right teaching, dedicating oneself to the teaching, and applying one's own ingenuity to what is learned from the teachings.

One of the key aspects of both absorbing and using the right teaching is emptying the mind of other matters, striving for complete detachment, and opening the mind fully in order to perceive completely and accurately whatever situation is at hand.

Yagyu says that it is essential that one nurtures *ken* (ken), "sight," and *kan* (kahn), "insight," in order to perceive reality and to be able to read an opponent's intentions—including the slightest movement or no movement at all, a lesson that applies to all human behavior, not just kendo.

As all masters learn, once having reached a high level of skill in any art or craft, training and practice must continue in order to maintain the skill, a feature of the *kaizen* (kie-zen) philosophy of the Japanese. This philosophy holds that one never totally masters anything and one must therefore continually strive for improvement.

There is a well-known saying in Japanese that expresses the ongoing belief in continuous improvement: "Today I must beat the me of yesterday."

さっぱり、爽やか
Sappari / Sawayaka
(Sop-pah-ree / Sah-wah-yah-kah)

That Oh-So-Sexy Feeling

Traditional Japanese culture is very sensual. Japanese-style kitchen utensils, home furnishings, the *yukata* (you-kah-tah), the kimono, *tatami* reed-mat floors, *shoji* (show-jee) paper doors—all exude an aura of sensuality that has an immediate conscious and subconscious effect on anyone exposed to them, including most non-Japanese. The sensual quality that is built into traditional Japanese things is one of the elements that give these things their Japaneseness, and this quality is therefore a vital but hard-to-explain facet of what the Japanese see and admire in their arts and crafts.

The older Japanese can almost always instantly distinguish between Japanese arts and crafts and those that are of Chinese, Korean, or other origin. But generally, only the Japanese who are professionally trained in Oriental aesthetics can explain what it is exactly that makes something "Japanese" and not "Chinese" or "Korean." In many instances the difference between Japanese, Chinese and Korean aesthetics is so subtle that it can only be perceived intuitively, and even the experts in the various cultures differ in their explanations.

This same subtle factor often exists in the shadings of meanings in Japanese words, making it extremely difficult—and sometimes impossible—to translate many Japanese words into other languages and retain their original flavor. It is usually possible to get around this problem in ordinary conversation because precise shades of meaning are not so critical. The translation of fiction is another matter, however, and the full power of the original author's skill is often lost in translation, doing an injustice to both the author and to foreign readers.

Where fiction is concerned this problem seldom attracts any attention unless a reviewer of the translated edition happens to be totally fluent in Japanese and has read the original. But the subtle meanings of the Japanese that is used in advertising, especially in advertising foreign products, is another matter altogether.

Over the decades some of the biggest battles between foreign companies and Japanese advertising agencies have been in selecting the Japanese equivalents of foreign words, and in selecting original Japanese words and phrases to get exactly the "right" message to consumers.

Two of Japan's most frequently used cultural code words in the advertising field are *sappari* (sop-pah-ree) and *sawayaka* (sah-wah-yah-kah), which are often used as if their meanings were exactly the same. Japanese dictionaries define *sappari* as "fresh, refreshing, clean, neat, frank, feel good," depending on the context of the word. *Sawayaka* is defined as "delightful, refreshing, reviving, bracing, crisp, clear, resonant, sweet, eloquent," also depending on how it is used.

Both of these terms impart feelings of sensuality, especially *sawayaka*, and both are favorites in the soft drink industry. In fact, a great deal of the phenomenal success of Coca-Cola in Japan was based on the inspired advertising phrase *Sukkatto* (Scot-toh) *sawayaka*! *Sukkatto* by itself means "completely, perfectly," but it also suggests the release of something that is under pressure, like the little hissing sound of escaping carbon dioxide when a bottle of Coke is opened. When *sukkatto* and *sawayaka* are put together, they create an image that has several dimensions and which is almost irresistible. The closest equivalent in English is, "Something that is completely refreshing," or "The refreshment that refreshes."

Sappari describes more of a physical feeling that is both refreshing and satisfying at the deepest level. One occasion when I feel *sappari* is on a hot, muggy evening in Tokyo when work is done, and I join friends in an air-conditioned setting for a beer. Another occasion that invariably creates a *sappari* feeling for me is when I ease myself down into a Japanese-style bath—especially if it is in a *ryokan* (ree-oh-kahn) inn away from the city in some mountain setting. All the tension leaves my body, and my concerns melt away as if by some miracle.

サラ金
Sarakin
(Sah-rah-keen)

The Loan Shark Business

In the 1950s, when Japan was just beginning to emerge from the devastation of World War II, members of the country's infamous yakuza (yah-kuu-zah) gangs and other unsavory types set themselves up in the loan business, catering primarily to salaried employees wanting to repair or rebuild their homes.

Because the borrowers generally had no collateral or assets other than their salaries, these loans came to be known as *sarakin* (sah-rah-keen), which was a combination of "salary" and *kin*, which means "gold" or "money"—"a salary loan." *Sarakin* loan companies charged substantially higher interest rates than banks, so the business was very profitable, resulting in a fantastic proliferation of these companies over the next two decades.

By the early 1980s there were over 220,000 *sarakin* companies in the country. Over the years, large numbers of salaried workers defaulted on their payments because of the high interest rates, and suicides, sometimes including whole families, became common. Other individuals and their families resorted to what the Japanese call *yonige* (yoh-nee-gay), which means "fleeing during the night," to escape from the debt they owed.

This caused a public outcry that resulted in the government passing the Sarakin Regulation Law in 1983, which limited the interest rates that could be charged on *sarakin* loans, required all *sarakin* loan companies to register with the government, and prohibited them from using force to collect payments that were due. Prior to this law, many of the *sarakin* companies were being financed by banks and other loan institutions. When most of these institutions stopped loaning money to the *sarakin* firms, thousands of the yakuza-run businesses went bankrupt.

By the mid-1990s there were fewer than 50,000 *sarakin* companies in Japan, and the numbers were continuing to slowly decrease. While there are no precise statistics, indications are that many of the surviving *sarakin* firms are controlled by yakuza gangs that do not have to depend upon banks for financing. They have their own ways of charging interest rates above the legal limits and their own ways of collecting unpaid debts.

左遷
Sasen
(Sah-sen)

Moving Down a Step

Two of the many things the Japanese imported from China between the years 400 and 800 were the custom of using different kinds of headgear and hairstyles to distinguish among the ranks of nobles and provincial lords, and a ranking system of seating arrangements at official functions.

In the Chinese seating system, the emperor was positioned at the top of a pyramid-like structure that had a long line of descending stairs. Princes, ministers, generals and others were assigned seats on the descending stairs in the order of their rank. But the Japanese did not import the pyramid structure because it did not fit their style of architecture.

When meetings occurred inside buildings, the Japanese emperor, the shogun, or other ranking individual sat on a platform, at the head of the room or hall, that was usually no more than 20 inches high. Other attendees were assigned positions on the floor in two rows, one to the left and one to the right of the platform, with those of the highest rank seated the closest to the dais and the lowest ranking members seated the farthest away.

This method of seating was called *sasen* (sah-sen), which in its original Chinese context meant something like "the following order or choice." When an individual lost rank, his *sasen* changed; that is he was moved farther down the steps and farther away from the dignitaries. In Japan, *sasen*, which is translated as "lowering the seating order," came to mean a demotion in rank or a transfer to a less desirable location without any change in rank. At first the term was applied only to imperial and clan officials. After the beginning of the shogunate form of government in 1185, it was also applied to samurai warriors as well.

Sasen has survived into modern times and is now the term used in business to denote both demotions and transfers. Generally, Japanese companies do not directly demote employees in rank or grade. They "lower their seating order" by assigning them a job in which they have no staff or assistants and no authority, or by transferring them to regional or local branch offices.

When either of these two moves occur, the message is starkly clear. The employee has been removed from the promotion escalator and shifted away from the center of power—which is the modern-day equivalent of being banished to some faraway island, as often happened to people during Japan's feudal age.

The *sasen* way of getting rid of people who mess up or get on the wrong side of senior managers or executives sometimes has a direct impact on foreigners doing business in Japan. In some cases, the *sasen* occurs because an individual made what the company regards as a serious mistake in dealing with foreign entities. A *sasen* may also occur if section or department managers become too personally involved in business deals; if they begin acting more individualistic than the Japanese culture allows, or if they try to profit personally from any transaction.

Foreign businesspeople whose Japanese contacts have been the victim of *sasen* may find their relationships with their companies fatally damaged if it is thought that the foreigner played any role in the unacceptable behavior of the demoted employees. Businesspeople approaching a Japanese company for the first time should make sure that their primary contact in the company is not someone who has already been banished to a meaningless position by *sasen* and is being used as a barrier to keep outsiders at bay—something that is fairly common. This situation can usually be determined easily and quickly by noting whether or not the individual concerned has a staff and whether the person's desk is located in a center of activity or whether it is aside from others.

The best safeguard foreigners can have against getting caught up in *sasen* situations, and one that applies across the board where all relationships with Japanese companies are concerned, is for them to make sure that they have several contacts in the companies involved, and that all of the contacts are kept aware of any negotiations going on and the status of the business relationship.

悟り
Satori
(Sah-toe-ree)

Seeing the Light

Over the decades I have known many Westerners who worked for Japanese companies—in numerous cases, for 20 or more years—whose most common complaint was that they could not truly understand what was going on in their respective companies, and could not anticipate what was going to happen from one day to the next. In some cases, the people involved did not speak or understand Japanese fluently. In other cases, they were not only fluent in the language, they were also intellectually aware of most if not all of the nuances of Japanese behavior—two skills that are not necessarily dependent upon each other.

The one thing that all of these people lacked was a Japanese psyche—the spirit and soul of the Japanese that is a product of subconscious absorption, not intellectual effort. These long-time employees of Japanese firms could think like a Japanese if they desired to, and with conscious effort they could react like a Japanese. But if their Japanese "software" was not turned on, their cross-cultural screen remained blank and they remain clueless.

In contrast, the mental software of their Japanese colleagues was not only built-in, it was their only medium of thought. Furthermore, all of the Japanese mental computers were linked by the same cultural umbilical cord. Because their Japanese coworkers shared a common reservoir of cultural knowledge and experience, they did not have to explain their values or feelings or actions to each other. Because it was taken for granted that the Japanese all shared the same goals and were aware of the methods to be used in achieving these goals, they did not have to discuss them at any length. Furthermore, because of the traditional commonalty of attitudes and experience in Japan, the Japanese have a built-in dislike of detailed instructions about how to do things; they regard such instructions as patronizing if not insulting. As a result, Japanese executives, managers and supervisors generally do not give detailed instructions to employees on a regular basis.

New employees receive basic orientation in the corporate philosophy and refresher training in groupism, cooperation and team work. Then it is up to them to discover what is going on and how things are done, first by observing and then by doing.

There is another key factor that makes much of what goes on in Japanese companies "invisible," and therefore extremely difficult for non-Japanese eyes to see. This hidden dimension of Japanese behavior has to do with the Japanese language and how it must be used to be culturally acceptable. Japanese does not always allow for absolutely precise, clear expression. Much of the everyday vocabulary is vague and allows for a variety of interpretations.

A professor of Japanese at Tokyo University once estimated that the Japanese are able to understand only about 70 percent of what they say to each without asking for clarification. The built-in vagueness of many terms require additional explanation that can sometimes be accomplished only by indicating the kanji (kahn-jee) ideogram used to write the word. All old-timers in Japan have had the experience numerous times of seeing Japanese write out kanji characters on paper, in the palms of their hands, or in the air, in their attempts to explain what they are talking about.

Equally important, if not more so, cultural requirements and taboos call for language to be used in an indirect and often very vague manner—to avoid offending anyone, to avoid the appearance of taking a firm stand, to avoid appearing arrogant, and for other similar reasons.

All these things combined make it difficult for the Japanese to speak plainly and clearly, a circumstance that has resulted in them leaving a great deal unsaid and relying on the listener to infer the meaning, a process that is often described as *satori* (sah-toe-ree). *Satori* is a Buddhist term that means "spiritual enlightenment" or "spiritual awakening." In more practical usage, it refers to comprehension or understanding that seemingly comes out of the blue. In Japanese companies, employees are generally expected to understand what is going on through an ongoing process of *satori*, something that most non-Japanese employees simply cannot do.

The *satori* syndrome, along with all the cultural guidelines the Japanese must follow to stay in harmony with each other, are reasons why un-Westernized Japanese usually do not ask questions during or after meetings and presentations.

青春
Seishun
(Say-ee-shuun)

The Trials of Youth

In addition to the wintertime view of snowcapped Mt Fuji, the annual spring show of cherry blossoms, the Great Buddha in Kamakura and other distinctive sights, Japan has also long been famous for the beauty and vivaciousness of its young children.

It was often said in the past that because adult life in Japan was so confining and so precarious, parents went to extremes to make sure their young children lived in a kind of paradise. There was no doubt some truth to that rationale in the past, particularly where children of preschool age were concerned. But by the 1960s, competition to get young children into the most desirable schools, from kindergarten onward, was so fierce that many mothers began turning the lives of their young children into a kind of hell rather than a heaven.

From junior high school on through senior high school, especially, the lives of most young Japanese became a never-ending struggle to memorize massive amounts of information that would allow them to pass university entrance examinations. The demands of this system were so severe that one generation after another of young Japanese passed through their formative years in what amounted to social isolation.

Every day after school they went to a prep school and then home to study some more—this kept them busy from ten to 14 hours a day. This regimen made a mockery of what the Japanese had historically referred to as *seishun* (say-ee-shuun), or "the spring of youth," which was regarded as the best time of a person's life, coming before adulthood descended upon them and imprisoned them for the remaining of their years.

But the images of youthhood as a carefree time in Japan had always been greatly exaggerated. From the earliest times, children began to shoulder a variety of responsibilities by the time they were six or seven years old. From this age, members of the samurai class were required to study and engage in the practice of martial arts for several hours each day.

Among the common people, most young boys who did not work in family businesses were apprenticed by the time they were ten or 11 years old. In keeping with the traditionally male-oriented culture, boys and girls generally went separate ways from an early age, with the training of girls centered in the home, and the boys outside the home.

Today when the word *seishun* is used it carries an additional nuance. It no longer just means "the spring of youth." It also refers to the fact that most young Japanese are growing up isolated from the realities of the world. Japanese sociologists say that most young Japanese grow up innocent, and ignorant of the evils and ills of the world at large, and are therefore handicapped in coping with the problems they encounter as adults.

A significant part of this problem results from the fact that young boys and girls still live in separate worlds, divided by sports, clubs, and various other institutions and customs that have been held over from the past. Despite all the dating couples that one sees in Japan today, the culture still does not provide for bringing young boys and girls together during their formative years. As a result, the majority grow up unable to communicate well with each other.

The adult world in Japan is even more segregated by sex than the world of pre-teens and teenagers, so the separation of young men and women not only continues, it is reinforced. There does not appear to be any serious movement to overcome the cultural separation of males and females in Japan, regardless of their age.

Generally speaking, both Japanese males and females seem to be content with keeping their distance from each other. Given this situation, there are surprisingly few feminists in Japan, but one very conspicuous trend is for women who are held down by the "glass ceiling" in Japanese companies to quit and go into business for themselves, and often hiring only other women.

正座
Seiza
(Say-ee-zah)

Sitting Correctly

One of my earliest and most vivid memories of Japan is the sight of thick, unsightly calluses near the ankles—particularly on the feet of women. It did not take long to discover that the calluses were created by people sitting on their lower legs and with the tops of their bare feet against reed-mat floors; the calluses were more common and more pronounced on women than on men because women spent a great deal more time than men sitting in that manner. I also discovered that this style of sitting becomes excruciatingly painful very quickly for adults who are not conditioned to it from childhood.

The Japanese have always sat on the floor because chairs did not developed as household furniture; but this particular style of sitting, called *seiza* (say-e-zah), or "correct sitting," was a legacy of the tea ceremony. In the 15th and 16th centuries, conducting and attending tea ceremonies became a national vogue among the samurai and merchant classes. The etiquette associated with the ceremony became more and more stylized, and how one sat and moved was precisely programmed. Under the influence of Sen no Rikyu, generally regarded as Japan's greatest tea master, tearooms also became smaller and smaller, requiring participants to sit close together to take up as little space as possible.

Another factor that led to the *seiza* style of sitting was that the movements of tea masters were less restricted when they were sitting on their legs and feet, rather than kneeling, sitting in some other style. And since absolute control and economy of movement became key elements of the ceremony, Sen no Rikyu and other masters made the *seiza* style of sitting a fundamental part of the ceremony itself.

The influence of the tea ceremony on Japanese culture in general was so powerful that *seiza* gradually became the formal way of sitting on all occasions for people in all classes. And since so much of life in Japan was formal, "correct sitting" eventually became the natural way for people to sit, with the result that foot calluses became virtually an identifying mark of the Japanese.

Sitting *seiza* style is natural for all very young children, not just for the Japanese. Children take the position unconsciously and regularly until they are three or four years old. But the older one gets, the more discipline the position requires, and it was this aspect of *seiza* that made it an important element in shaping the character of the Japanese from this early period on.

Just as the Japanese were meticulously trained in sitting correctly from childhood, so were they programmed to follow a precise form of behavior in all other areas of life.

But Japan's defeat in World War II, the end of the feudalistic family system, the introduction of democracy, and Western customs imported into Japan wholesale from 1946 were to have a major impact on *seiza* in particular. By the end of the 1950s, most postwar parents had stopped forcing their children to sit in the formal way. Teenage girls, striving for Western standards of beauty, began refusing to sit *seiza* style not only to avoid callusing their feet, but also because the posture was said to be one of the primary reasons why people's legs were shorter in Japan than in Western countries.

In present-day Japan virtually the only people who regularly sit *seiza* style are professional performers of the tea ceremony, priests, and a few other categories of people who practice traditional activities—examples are geisha and maids in *ryokan* (ree-oh-kahn) inns. However, most Japanese are called upon to sit in the style on a number of special occasions, such as at funerals and at other formal functions that take place on *tatami* reed-mat floors. And on these occasions most of them suffer serious pain if the proceedings last for more than a few minutes. Being able to sit *seiza* style is now regarded as ultimate proof of whether one is traditional or modern and Western-minded.

The Japanese are aware that the *seiza* style of sitting is unique to Japan, and they do not expect foreigners to sit in that position. They know that it is literally impossible for many foreigners, particularly those who are large and heavy, to even assume the position, much less remain in it for any period of time.

In situations where foreigners are required to sit on the floor, they are invariably invited to sit *agura* (ah-guu-rah) style, which refers to the "Indian" way of sitting, with the legs folded, and usually crossed, in front of the body. Foreigners who cannot manage even the *agura* style are allowed to sit with their legs folded and tucked alongside the body, or if they are at a Japanese short-legged table, to extend their legs beneath the table.

At the same time, the rare foreigner who can "sit correctly" is regarded with some disbelief, because it is another one of those things the Japanese have traditionally believed only Japanese could accomplish.

世間知らず
Seken Shirazu
(Say-kane She-rah-zoo)

Babes in the Woods

The Japanese have presented both a mystery and a challenge to the outside world ever since they first became involved in international affairs. A significant percentage of the American occupation forces in Japan in the late 1940s and early 1950s habitually described the Japanese as stupid and incompetent.

From the mid-1950s this refrain was picked up by American importers who began visiting Japan by the thousands to get consumer products copied at low prices. Unable to see beyond their own cultural blinders, many of these frequent visitors carped continuously, accusing the Japanese of not being able to do anything right without detailed instructions and of making mistakes that were so irrational they were unbelievable.

By 1960, however, the Japanese had already been successful enough that this breed of critic was having trouble accepting all of the success he saw around him. Then critics began creating one rationale after another to explain Japan's growing economic might, with the Japanese themselves getting little if any of the credit for this progress.

This misreading of the Japanese by so many people, and which continues today on a vast scale, resulted from a combination of many factors, including the inability of the foreigners to recognize and appreciate the overall cultural differences that made the Japanese appear inadequate, including a variety of specific Japanese manners and customs that struck uninitiated outsiders as childish.

A key Japanese trait that then and now contributes to underestimating the abilities of the Japanese by outsiders is expressed in the term *seken shirazu* (say-kane sherah-zoo), which means "to know nothing of sophistication," and which is usually translated as "to be naive." Japanese culture traditionally valued naivety, real or feigned, more than knowledge and sophistication. In a group-oriented society, the exceptionally intelligent and capable person inspired envy and ill will, not admiration, because he or she represented a threat to the rest of the group.

As a result of this, it became socially obligatory for outstanding people to behave in a naive manner in order to maintain good relations with other members of their group. Failure to do so invariably resulted in serious consequences, ranging from non-cooperation to ostracization and physical attacks.

Foreigners encountering the Japanese for the first time, particularly in earlier years, were therefore confronted with two kinds of naivety, both of which they often misunderstood. The first was the culturally conditioned naivety that each Japanese was forced to wear as a protective cloak. The second was genuine naivety about the outside world, about foreign thinking and foreign ways of doing things.

It is still characteristic of un-Westernized Japanese to adopt a humble and naive mode when interacting with each other as well as with foreigners, in order to give the impression that they are very ordinary people and not a threat to anyone. This conduct requires a lot of polite denials, bowing and other forms of subservient behavior that foreigners generally take as a reflection of the real person.

In typical social and informal Japanese settings involving groups of people, it is virtually impossible to separate the real naive people from the people who are feigning naivety. Even in formal situations, such as business meetings in which two or more Japanese from the same group are involved, feigning naivety is common.

Among the few times when the Japanese can safely dispense with feigning naivety—if they wish to do so—is when they are on their own in meetings with foreigners, in informal one-on-one conversations, when the subject is technical and they are the acknowledged expert, and when they are the boss and run a one-man show.

Of course, one of the reasons why most foreigners cannot judge the intelligence or abilities of the Japanese is their inability to speak or understand the Japanese.

世間ずれした
Seken Zure Shita
(Say-kane Zoo-ray Ssh-tah)

Too Wise for the World

One of the most insightful and memorable comments I have ever heard was made in the early 1950s by a Japanese bar hostess and prostitute. She said (to me!), "Men with brains are no good in bed!" We were having an intellectual discussion!

Of course, this comment may be disputed by some men, but it takes no special intelligence to recognize that what the girl said is no doubt generally true. In any event, she was an expert on the subject.

I was to learn later that the Japanese traditionally tended to have a culturally induced prejudice against people who were more experienced or more intelligent than average, and who made no effort to disguise their superiority. This prejudicial syndrome grew out of the fears of ordinary people that those who were more capable would rise above them and would eventually have more than they had. Furthermore, this prejudice was promoted by the Japanese government as a means of reducing the possibility of envy and dissatisfaction among the people, which could threaten the stability of the state.

During the decades of the 1960s and 1970s, most Japanese still regarded individualism and the overt demonstration of personal intelligence and practical skills as disruptive and un-Japanese. Particularly in non-technical and social disciplines, such people were often described as *seken zure shita* (say-kane zoo-ray ssh-tah), figuratively, "too wise in the ways of the world." The ideal character and personality continued to be one who did not stand out from the crowd.

It was not until the 1980s that the Japanese in practically all fields began to champion the idea that individual ability and initiative were not only acceptable, but that they were essential for the continued survival and success of Japan. Books written by people who were *seken zure shita* became bestsellers, and their authors became role models for the new generation of Japanese.

But while the majority of Japanese appear to have intellectually accepted the new idea that individualism, initiative and personal superiority are in, the application of this new attitude to the overall social, economic and political culture of Japan is only in its infancy. It will no doubt take one or two full generations before the deeply embedded cultural attitude of *seken zure shita* will weaken to the point that it is no longer a significant factor in life in Japan.

Until that time approaches, foreigners dealing with the Japanese should be aware that aggressive displays of expertise, with one or two exceptions, can and probably will have a negative impact on their Japanese counterparts if the expertise is flaunted too openly.

One area where Japanese culture is generally accepting of the personal acknowledgment of one's expertise is in the world of *mizu shobai* (me-zoo show-by), literally "water business," a term which is used to refer to bars, cabarets, night clubs, massage parlors and similar establishments. Because of the important role drinking and sex traditionally played in all areas of Japanese life, men have long had the privilege of participating in these activities, and were accorded enviable status if they excelled in either or both of these pursuits.

The ability to drink huge amounts, and success with *mizu shobai* women have lost a lot of their luster in recent years, but knowledge and some experience in the "water business" are still important assets that most Japanese men cultivate with the same care and dedication that they apply to their technical specialties. Foreigners visiting or living in Japan are at a disadvantage in their business relationships if they do not know their way around in the *mizu shobai* business and do not have a few special places where they can take guests for entertainment.

It is still advantageous in Japan to maintain a humble, naive mode in order to avoid being labeled as "too smart, too wise in the ways of the world"—which is synonymous with being untrustworthy.

先生
Sensei
(Sen-say-ee)

Polishing the Apple

Despite the democratization that has taken place in Japanese society since 1945, rank and titles still play an especially important role in Japan. People with managerial business titles like *kacho* (kah-choe), "section chief"; *bucho* (buu-choe), "department chief" or "general manager"; *senmu* (sen-muu), "senior managing director" or "executive vice president"; *shacho* (shah-choe), "president"; and *kaicho* (kigh-choe), "chairman of the board," are always addressed by their titles, not by their names.

But the most common title of all in Japan with the exception of *san* (sahn), which is the equivalent of Mr, Mrs or Miss, is *sensei* (sen-say-ee), which literally means "the first born," but which is used colloquially to mean "teacher, master, professor," and is sometimes the equivalent of "sir" or "madam." *Sensei* is a title of respect that the Japanese use to address people with any professional skill or position, including school teachers, scientists, medical doctors, sports trainers, painters, composers, tea ceremony and ikebana masters, potters, marketing and sales experts—as well as politicians and authors.

Not surprisingly, people commonly use the term *sensei* to flatter people who truly do not qualify for the title, and generally this is taken with good humor. But one has to be very careful about using the title in this way because it can paint one as being a sycophant or something worse. The Japanese achieve their aim of flattering people by calling them *sensei* without making themselves look bad by letting the other person know that the use is intended as good-natured flattery. At the same time, they make it clear that they want something from the person, such as the other person's goodwill, support, or cooperation.

Foreigners in Japan who are not used to being addressed by a formal title—technicians, engineers, journalists, advertising copywriters, successful salesmen, and so on—sometimes let the title of *sensei* lower their critical faculties and make them much more susceptible to being influenced and led on by their Japanese contacts and hosts. This kind of usage by Japanese who have not had that much experience with foreigners is usually not deliberately insidious, but those who are experienced with the reactions of foreigners to such flattery have learned to take advantage of the power of the *sensei* title.

Of course, two can play at this game, and foreigners who are tuned into Japanese culture routinely use the title *sensei* to build and sustain relationships with their Japanese friends and associates. A word of warning is due, however. People who are not very bright, or who are klutzes at something or other, are frequently referred to as *sensei*—in a non-serious and joking manner when it is to their faces, and as a way of putting them down when the title is applied to them behind their backs. The point is that when the title is used in a humorous vein to refer to someone directly, the intention should be clear. Incorrectly used, the term can be insulting.

When middle-aged Japanese men are out drinking, they will often refer to each other as *sensei* as a parody on the misuse of the word at other times, and to show contempt for people who like to be called *sensei*, but who do not deserve the honor.

Foreigners who are tempted to play this game should be fluent enough in the language and culture to be certain that they are playing it the right way at the right time.

節約
Setsuyaku
(Say-t'sue-yah-kuu)

The Saving Syndrome

A mid-20th century Japanese historian, Shozaburo Kimura, wrote that one of the primary reasons why the Japanese liked to travel abroad was because American- and European-made towels and quilts were far superior to Japanese towels and bedding, and Western toilets were more comfortable than pit-style Japanese toilets. Kimura's comments on the relative merits of Japanese towels and bedding were contained in an article in which he said that the quality of life in Japan had declined for the first time in over 100 years.

Kimura said that while Japan's technological civilization had matured and was one of the highest in the world, housing and "personal comfort" had not kept pace. He was especially critical of the lack of efficient central heating in many Japanese homes, and the failure of the hospitality industry to show sufficient concern about such simple things as damp towels and chilly toilets.

The reason for this failing, Kimura continued, was the Japanese concept of *setsuyaku* (say-t'sue-yah-kuu), which in its straightforward meaning refers to saving and practicing economy. Unfortunately, Kimura added, the traditional Japanese interpretation of *setsuyaku* virtually ignored the health and welfare of the people.

Kimura was referring to the age-old traditional custom in Japan of making no attempt to heat homes or workplaces during the frigid months of winter, and of enduring numerous other life-style customs that ranged from uncomfortable to painful and detrimental to the health. Well up into the 1950s, most buildings in Japan had no heating systems other than charcoal burning pots and, in some homes, sunken floor pits. The pots warmed only the hands and the pits, only the feet and legs.

Apparently one of the reasons why the early Japanese did not adopt the ancient Korean and Chinese method of heating rooms and buildings with hot air ducts beneath the floors was due to the belief that enduring the discomfort and dangers of cold contributed to strengthening one's spirit. For both pragmatic and religious reasons, the Japanese were imbued with the notion that there was great merit in an austere life-style. This concept eventually permeated the culture to the extent that it became directly associated with being Japanese.

Another reason why so-called "clean poverty" flourished during Japan's long feudal age—and was still the standard in the early 1950s—was because of government policy. From 1185 to 1868 the samurai-administered shogunate and clan governments generally followed a taxation policy that left the bulk of the population with just enough of their income and produce to survive.

Japan's last great shogunate dynasty, the Tokugawa, which began in 1603 and ended in 1868, made the policy of keeping the life-styles of the people at a subsistence level a key part of its military strategy. These religious and political influences, over a period of many generations, combined to make economizing and enduring hardships second nature to the Japanese, and it was not until the introduction of democratic and free-market principles into Japan following the end of World War II that the majority of Japanese had any choice in the matter.

Present-day Japanese are still far more committed to *setsuyaku* than their American and European counterparts, but the concept of "clean poverty" no longer appeals to most of the younger generations. Interestingly, however, in the early 1990s there were signs that the stark materialism that had virtually replaced the old idea of clean poverty had reached its zenith, and that a small but growing number of middle-aged and older people were choosing to go back to the old way—giving up their appliance and gadget-filled apartments for rustic homes and a simple life-style in rural and mountainous areas.

Demands by foreign governments that the Japanese save less and spend more strike a very sensitive place in the Japanese psyche, and these voices might be more effective if they addressed the concepts of consumption and life-styles in terms that the Japanese understand.

社畜
Sha Chiku
(Shah Chee-kuu)

A Nation of Corporate Sheep

Watching the behavior of groups of Japanese in movies, especially in *jidai geki* (jee-die gay-kee), or "period films," depicting life from the 17th through the 19th centuries, I have often been reminded of the behavior of some species of birds and wild animals. In many of these Japanese films, groups of people, from half a dozen to several dozen; frequently behave in the same manner as a flock or herd, bunching together and moving in unison, often behind a leader. It is as if each of the groups of people is a single organism, made up of virtually identical parts, and controlled by a single will.

Such herd-like behavior has, in fact, been a conspicuous part of life in Japan for centuries. The Japanese were conditioned intellectually, emotionally and physically to conform to a highly refined etiquette system and to function as a member of a group rather than as an individual. Eventually this group mentality became the norm.

Both the form and process of politics and economics in Japan, from the feudal age down to the present time, have naturally been manifestations of this cultural conditioning. Military leaders, politicians and businesspeople have traditionally taken advantage of this robotization of the population in the pursuit of their goals—good and bad.

Despite the growth of individualism in Japan since 1945, the legacy of this robot-like behavioral and psychological programming lives on in schools, in government offices and in large corporations, where business leaders prefer a docile and obedient workforce and often go to extremes to mold their employees into what some critics now call *sha chiku* (shah chee-kuu), or "corporate sheep."

Till this day, joining one of the large and traditional companies in Japan is like being initiated into a herd, where conformity in both attitude and behavior are the guiding principles and the only means of survival. The employee who deliberately marches out-of-step with the group is brought under severe pressure to conform. Anyone who persists in "misbehaving" is eventually ostracized.

The extent that many Japanese companies go to control the corporate and private lives of their employees sounds like Orwellian fiction to most Westerners. The *sha chiku* conditioning process in these companies begins even before new employees are hired; it continues formally for 20 to 30 years, and informally thereafter.

Until recent times, many company labor unions as well as company managers participated in perpetuating the *sha chiku* syndrome. One of the most notorious examples was the "Total Lifetime Plan" endorsed by Toyota Motor Corporation's labor union for all of the company's employees. In addition to mandating uniform behavior, the Toyota lifetime plan specified when each employee should buy a car, take out a company loan to buy a house, get married, have the first child, pay for a vacation trip for their parents to go to a hot springs resort, and so on.

The *sha chiku* syndrome was so strong in many companies that employees who were courageous or reckless enough to participate in activities outside of the company were harshly criticized by coworkers, who accused them of wasting time and of being disloyal to the company. If an outside activity resulted in some sort of financial benefit for the person, the criticism was even harsher.

Company regulations designed to force *sha chiku* behavior onto female employees were generally more strict than those applying to men, reflecting the ongoing sexual bias of Japan's male-dominated workplace.

Since the early 1990s, there has been growing economic, political and social pressure for Japanese schools and corporations to encourage rather than suppress independent thought and action. But the *sha chiku* syndrome will no doubt remain characteristic of the behavior of a majority of Japanese for two or three more generations, and continue to impact Japan's international political and economic relations.

借景
Shakkei
(Shock-kay-ee)

Creating Japaneseness

As I have mentioned in other contexts, there is a special quality about many of Japan's arts and crafts that is unique and reaches a new level of aesthetic beauty. One of the reasons for this extraordinary beauty is a mysterious ingredient that is usually unfathomable to the average Westerner, at least in terms of articulating its source and its power.

The uniqueness, or "Japaneseness," of this special aesthetic quality drives from what Korean author O-Young Lee describes as "contracting nature" by a technique known as *shakkei* (shock-kay-ee), or "borrowed scenery"—that is, the sea, mountains, forests, clouds, rain, snow and other features of nature. The concept and practice of "borrowing nature" to achieve a particular aesthetic effect has origins in China as well as in the West, but as usual, Japanese artists and craftsmen took the concept further and created something that was original as well as distinctive. Instead of being satisfied with using *shakkei* as coincidental or auxiliary parts of a garden, Japanese landscape designers made the "borrowed scenery" the main elements and the central theme of their gardens.

A Japanese garden is a vast panorama of nature reduced down to where one can stroll through it and see it in a matter of minutes; in nature, on the other hand, the scale of the original is so large that no one can ever comprehend it all because it can be seen and enjoyed only in tiny portions of the whole. Japanese gardens are designed in such a way that one can absorb the ambiance of a whole ocean, a huge mountain, and a great forest in just a glance or two, or one can contemplate a scene endlessly and never be bored.

By the 1700s, all of Japan's important clan lords had their own *kaiyushiki teien* (kigh-yuu-she-kee tay-e-en), or "strolling gardens," that were said to depict scenes from the marvelous vistas the clan lords saw while traveling between their fiefs and the shogunate capital of Edo, where they spent every other year in attendance at the shogun's court, and where they maintained their families in mansions the year round.

The goal of a "contracted scenery garden" is to utilize rocks, water, trees and mounds of earth in such a way that the image that is presented to the viewer is not that of a miniature but of the real thing—a whole mountain with its trees, rushing streams, and rocks, or the vastness of an ocean with its waves and shoreline. Such a view is also designed to recall to the viewer's mind any paintings and poetry depicting the scene, and thereby allowing the viewer to simultaneously take pleasure in all of those images as well.

The Japanese incentive for creating *shakkei* gardens is the same one that motivates them to continuously strive to reduce the size and refine the appearance and operation of such mundane products as calculators and cameras. I have always believed that no outsider can fully understand and appreciate Japanese culture and Japan's economic accomplishments until he or she has grasped the full essence and meaning of the Japanese ability to create a universe in a tea cup, so to speak.

The Japanese themselves often say their impulse to reduce or contract things comes from the fact that Japan is a small country. But I do not believe that. As I have also mentioned elsewhere, one does not have a sense of being in a small country when in Japan. The length of its shorelines and the vastness of its mountain ranges present grand panoramas that seem to go on forever. The reduction impulse of the Japanese must come from somewhere else—perhaps from Shinto beliefs, in which every rock, tree, hill, body of water and other feature of nature is an embodiment of the entire cosmos.

In any event, this Japanese compulsion and special talent has been a key factor in the development of Japanese culture. Even Japanese etiquette is based on reductionism—on accomplishing the most with the least amount of movement and energy. This peculiar drive and skill is something that outsiders should be aware of when dealing with and when competing with the Japanese.

しぶとさ
Shibutosa
(She-boo-toe-sah)

Fight to the Death

The Japanese attribute many of the most distinctive aspects of their traditional attitudes and behavior to the contrasts, the unpredictability, and the frequently destructive nature of the climate that prevails upon the island chain.

While the climate is not that extreme even on Hokkaido, the northernmost of the four main islands, the archipelago is subjected to wide variations of heat, cold, rain and wind from one season to the next. Typhoons regularly batter the southern islands of Okinawa and Kyushu in the late summer and early fall. Heavy snows regularly blanket the central mountains and Japan Sea side of the main island of Honshu as well as Hokkaido during the winter months.

Over the centuries, the islands of Japan have also been systematically ravaged by earthquakes, tidal waves and great fires that regularly consumed whole towns and huge parts of cities—all circumstances that conditioned the Japanese to be tough and resilient, and which imbued them with the quality of *shibutosa* (she-boo-toe-sah), or "stubbornness."

Shibutosa was one of the most prized traits of the elite samurai class that ruled Japan for some 700 years. Since they were young, the samurai as a class were taught to persevere in the face of all odds—and to die rather than retreat or surrender to the enemy. They were also taught that in any contest or battle, spirit was the ultimate key to victory.

Other cultural influences that shaped the character of the Japanese, including the highly stylized etiquette system, the institutionalized apprenticeship system of training that could last for as long as 30 years, and the extraordinarily demanding ideographic writing system, also contributed to the importance and power of *shibutosa* in the lives of the Japanese.

Perhaps even more important than the rules and processes of the Japanese Way, however, was the fact that the Japanese had few options in where and how they lived. Throughout most of Japan's feudal history, farmers, who made up the bulk of the population, were prohibited from moving or changing their occupation. Town and city dwellers were also hemmed in by a variety of traditions and regulations that forced them to endure a life-style that was carefully controlled, often down to personal details such as the clothing they wore, the homes they lived in—even the height of doors. The Japanese had to be stubborn to survive and to make the most of the material possessions they had or were allowed to have, and to stay right with both sanctified customs and their political overlords.

Shibutosa has remained one of the primary characteristics of contemporary Japanese, in spite of the people's newfound freedoms to come and go, to change occupations, and to indulge themselves in all kinds of personal activities. Today this trait is more likely to be referred not to as stubbornness, but in more positive terms, such as "diligence," "dedication," or "determination," especially when the trait is used with regard to students, employees of large Japanese corporations and government bureaucrats. There is no question that the stubborn persistence of the Japanese continues to play a key role in all of their endeavors, and it is especially conspicuous in their economic history since the mid-1900s.

The Japanese are acutely aware of their reputation for being stubborn and regard *shibutosa* as one of the most admirable qualities, giving it appropriate credit for the extraordinary successes they have had. It is unlikely that this Japanese trait will significantly diminish anytime soon. On the domestic front, most Japanese continue to have a "do or die" attitude because they have few attractive educational and employment opportunities, and they face fierce competition in those that do exist. Internationally, the Japanese see themselves as surrounded by and competitors who will swallow them if they drop their guard, and *shibutosa* is their first line of defense.

指導
Shido
(She-doe)

A Word from Big Brother

In traditional Japan there was a precise way of doing everything, and form often took precedence over substance. Doing things in any way other than the established way was not only culturally taboo, but often illegal as well, and government authority to control all activity was absolute.

This system prevented the development of individualism and the capacity for self-directed innovation. People were literally programmed to act like everyone else, and to work in groups for the benefit of the whole. At a personal level this system was sustained by the apprenticeship approach to all of the arts and crafts, as well as to all other professions requiring special knowledge and skills. At a governmental level, it was sustained by licensing and other requirements.

Japan's shogunate governments, as well as the parliamentary governments that took over the country after the fall of the shogunate system, had the legal right to totally control many categories of business, and government assumed the right to offer *shido* (she-doe), usually translated as "guidance," to all business enterprises.

But translating *shido* as "guidance" gives a misleading impression of both the legal role of the government in business affairs in Japan and the practical application of the term. A much more accurate translation of *shido* is "to instruct," to tell someone or some organization exactly what to do and often how to do it—with all of the connotations this concept conjures up. The recipient of government "instructions" may have the legal choice to follow or ignore them, but culturally and in practical terms, there often is little or no choice.

The *shido* factor not only continues to exist in the area of government and business in Japan, it also permeates the academic and professional worlds.

One of the more Japanese-like characteristics of *shido* is that it is generally not "issued" in any formal or explicit way. It is almost always informal, unofficial, and frequently it is made known only in general terms, leaving it up to recipients to know what they are expected to do.

Government ministries give the country's corporations, as a group as well as individually, guidance or instruction, and these corporations in turn send *shido* signals to their subsidiaries and suppliers. Students follow the *shido* of their professors or art and craft masters, and politicians follow the *shido* of their faction leaders. It is *shido* that provides much of the essence and character of Japanese business, politics and behavior in general, and without considering this factor, it is impossible to fully understand how things work in Japan.

The *shido* system survives because most Japanese still feel compelled by generations of cultural conditioning to maintain the vertical relationships of society by obeying and supporting superiors. *Shido* also continues to work because ignoring it invariably results in sanctions of one kind or another. The company that refuses to follow a discreet suggestion by the Ministry of International Trade and Industry may be denied a license or face some other governmental roadblock in the future. The student who ignores the *shido* of a professor or master may be locked out of the most desirable job market.

Many of the obstacles that foreign companies must overcome in doing business in Japan are a result of complications caused by *shido*. And not surprisingly, Japanese companies also regularly use the threat or the reality of government "instructions" as a bargaining chip in their dealings with foreign companies.

See *Danryokuteki Un'ei*.

しきたり
Shikitari
(She-kee-tah-ree)

The Herd Instinct

It has often been observed by Westerners that Japan is a land of contradictions. From the Western viewpoint, everything good or positive about Japan always seems to have a flip side that is negative or unfavorable.

One of the apparent contradictions that has been especially difficult for foreign businessmen, particularly Americans, to deal with is the Japanese management custom, in large companies, of rotating employees. Virtually all administrative and technical employees in large Japanese firms are transferred every two or three years to different sections, departments, or divisions as a key part of their ongoing training.

Many Japanese employees do not like this system because it takes them away from jobs just when they feel they have mastered them, and for other obvious reasons as well; they are often in the middle of major projects of one kind or another that they would prefer to continue; they are forced to leave coworkers with whom they have developed a good working relationship; and they are frequently required to transfer to a new site, sometimes in distant cities or in rural areas.

In virtually every instance, Japanese employees who are transferred have to start over again in establishing and nurturing the kinds of intimate personal relationships that are essential to surviving and functioning effectively inside a Japanese company.

For foreign businesspeople dealing with Japanese companies, this rotation policy means that they have to accommodate themselves to dealing with new and inexperienced people every two or three years—a predicament that is almost always frustrating and is frequently a serious handicap for the foreign side, because it is time-consuming and expensive to recreate the necessary degree of awareness and trust with new and unfamiliar people.

Japanese companies attempt to mitigate the disruptions caused by rotating employees in and out of job slots by requiring that individuals being transferred act as temporary mentors to their replacements, joining them for the first few times they meet customers. This naturally helps smooth the transitions to some extent, but it cannot possibly keep the quality of the work performed in each job slot at the level that would be possible if employees were not regularly rotated.

The purpose of the rotation policy is to familiarize all management and technical employees with all of the functions of the company so that they can make better informed decisions and eventually contribute more to the success of the company. This makes a lot of sense, despite the problems it causes. A point that senior Japanese managers also make is that an engineer or designer can perform his job better if he knows something about manufacturing or about the problems encountered by the sales department.

The very conspicuous success of so many Japanese companies indicates that the plusses of the rotation system have so far outweighed the minuses, at least as far as the Japanese are concerned.

One of the reasons why the rotation system works as well as it does in Japan is a cultural factor known as *shikitari* (she-kee-tah-ree), which is another word for *kanrei* (kahn-ray-e), which means "custom," "convention," or "how things are done."

Shikitari incorporates all of the values, standards and rituals that make up the prevailing beliefs and behavior in a particular Japanese company. These features differ to some degree from company to company because they are primarily the creation of the executives running the companies; nevertheless, the features of the *shikitari* of a company are all rooted in the culture of Japan and are therefore similar.

Generally speaking, the *shikitari* of a company are not written down and are not explicitly taught to new employees. The *shikitari* are things that newcomers are expected to absorb by osmosis, by listening, watching, imitating, and only rarely by asking questions during their first years with the company. Because so many of the *shikitari* of a company are subtle and often invisible to the outsider, foreigners who work for Japanese companies typically find themselves working blind. They often do not know what they are supposed to do, or how they are supposed to act. The result is that they tend to be in a constant state of uncertainty and frustration. Within a company in which everyone knows and abides by *shikitari*, it is taken for granted that everyone understands and appreciates what everyone else is doing, and that there will be little or no disagreement because compromise and cooperation are built into the system.

Another aspect of the *shikitari* factor that plays havoc with the mentality and expectations of foreigners is that it does not tolerate differences of opinion or things being done differently. It demands absolute conformity.

In a purely Japanese context, *shikitari* binds the company into a highly directed, highly drilled team that is formidable when it plays against other teams, including foreign companies which are not so tightly structured or focused in their behavior.

仕込む
Shikomu
(She-koe-muu)

The Spiritual Dimension of Work

The Japanese have traditionally had their own "Protestant Work Ethic," but as in virtually all other areas of life, their spiritual emphasis on work went much farther than anything experienced in Europe or the United States.

In old Japan, developing the proper skills and the right attitude toward work was not left to personal inclination or chance. Lessons in the moral and ethical dimensions of work were a key part of the on-the-job training that everyone had to go through, regardless of their social position or occupational status. The higherthe social position of the person, the more emphasis there was on morality and ethics in everything they did, but even the lowest laborer was schooled in the social and spiritual implications of his work.

This training involved not only the straightforward lecturing of journeymen or masters instructing their apprentices. It also included such things as a carpenter sending his apprentice to the theater to learn ethics and proper social behavior.

Midway through the Tokugawa Shogunate (1603–1868), it was formally taught that work should be regarded as a religious experience, and that work was the road to spiritual fulfillment—to heaven, in other words. The Japanese had no problem accepting this "new" economic theory, because it was nothing more than formal recognition of something they had been practicing since the beginning of their civilization. The curriculum of this new school of thought came under the heading of *shikomu* (she-koe-muu), or "training in ethics and morality." *Shikomu* remains a key element in the molding of the Japanese, not only in their academic schooling, but in their workplace training as well.

In fact, virtually all of the early indoctrination and training administered to new employees by Japan's large firms is in the *shikomu* of that particular company—not in on-the-job performance. Japanese employers recognize that, in the long run, beliefs and attitudes are more important than any manual skills new employees might bring into the firm, and that beliefs and attitudes generally also outweigh technical knowledge, as far as the company is concerned.

Shikomu is one of the "secrets" of the success of Japanese companies because it affects every facet of every enterprise, from the morale, the diligence and the loyalty of employees to the management–employee relations.

Some Japanese companies send their new recruits to military-style "boot camps," where they are drilled in how to work together, how to respond to superiors, and how to give their all for their companies—just like soldiers being trained for battle. The results of this kind of training are very conspicuous. Generally speaking, the employees of Japanese companies do, in fact, behave exactly like well-trained soldiers. They are formal and courteous in their speech. They do not "horse around" while on the company premises. They take their duties and responsibilities seriously. They keep their workplaces clean and well ordered. Foreigners, particularly Americans, visiting Japan for the first time are invariably impressed, if not amazed, by the discipline and order they see in Japanese companies, including hotels and department stores.

Not surprisingly, Western influences are gradually undermining the role of *shikomu* in Japanese life. Outside of the school environment, the youth of Japan are more and more demonstrating the kind of attitudes and behavior one sees among children and teens in the United States and Europe. However, the Japanese must still conform to a significant degree to get into Japan's better companies, and the *shikomu* system is so powerful that Japanese enterprises are not likely to shed their traditional skins anytime soon.

指名
Shimei
(She-may-ee)

Picking Your Bed Partner

The Japanese custom of structuring behavior and controlling relationships is deeply and widely embedded in the culture, traditionally applying to every social and economic activity, from the protocol of the imperial and shogunate courts, to what was required of the customers patronizing the great courtesan quarters during the last shogunate dynasty.

After customers became regular patrons of the country's ubiquitous red-light districts, they were no longer free to choose different women as partners. They were required by regulations governing the quarters, self-imposed by the association of operators, to designate specific girls or women as their partners and thereafter to consort only with them. This system came to be known as *shimei* (she-may-ee), which literally means "named person," or "nominated person."

When thousands of cabarets featuring female hostesses appeared in Japan following the end of World War II, the larger and more professionally run clubs adopted the *shimei* system, primarily because of pressure from the more attractive and most popular of the hostesses. The point made by these hostesses was that, since it was their charms that resulted in big-spending customers becoming regular patrons of the cabarets, they deserved to have first claim on them every time they showed up.

Most Japanese patrons of cabarets obediently followed the *shimei* system, but when thousands of foreign importers began flocking into Japan beginning in 1952, many of these people ignored the *shimei* custom, preferring to sample different hostesses on each visit.

The *shimei* system was not limited to the so-called *mizu shobai* (me-zoo show-by), "water business" or "nighttime entertainment business." It was also an important aspect of regular business in Japan, applying to relationships between manufacturers, wholesalers, retailers and consumers. In the business world, the *shimei* principle tied retailers to wholesalers and wholesalers to manufacturers, and the older the relationships were the more powerful and unbreakable they were. The *shimei* relationship between consumers and retailers was less subject to control and therefore less likely to be absolutely exclusive.

Generally the principle of *shimei* was followed by all Japanese, regardless of their position or role in the economy. For example, families shopped at the same neighborhood shops generation after generation, and every shop owner knew which customers "belonged" to whom.

The *shimei* system, on a neighborhood as well as on a national basis, was thus a major barrier to any outsider trying to break into the market at any level. The moral obligation that *shimei*-bound retailers had to wholesalers and that wholesalers had to manufacturers was so powerful that it took precedence over virtually everything else.

Among the advantages of the system was that all of the players knew each other intimately, and because they were so dependent upon each other, none would dare rock the boat by breaking the relationship. They were therefore, individually and as a group, safe and secure. Obviously there were many disadvantages to this system. Neither retailers nor wholesalers were free to shop around for better prices or better service. The incestuous relationships prevented competition and tended to have a stagnating effect.

The bursting of Japan's "bubble economy" in 1991 and 1992 was the first really serious setback for the *shimei* system. The various disadvantages of being tied to the same suppliers and customers became acute, causing many of the relationships to be discarded. Automobile parts manufacturers that traditionally had only a single automobile company as a customer were among those most severely hurt by the sudden depression in Japan's economy. When they began breaking their life-long *shimei* ties and offering their products to other users, the shock reverberated throughout Japan for several years.

The *shimei* system, sometimes also referred to as *tokumei* (toe-kuu-may-ee), has not disappeared from Japan, however. It remains a formidable factor in doing business in Japan, and continues to have a direct and sometimes fatal impact on the efforts of foreign companies to penetrate the Japanese market.

Shinbo
(Sheen-boe)

You Must have Patience!

Westerners have been taught to view life as consisting of a precise number of years, months, days, and hours for each individual—a limited amount of time that is not going to be repeated and should therefore not be wasted. In recent times, especially after the Industrial Revolution, Westerners came to believe that not using time in some profitable or productive enterprise was sinful. We eventually became so time-conscious that we began measuring time and our activities in minutes and seconds.

The Japanese, on the other hand, were traditionally conditioned to believe that life was more-or-less a circle, with one reincarnation after another, until one reached a state of grace in which rebirth was no longer necessary and one entered into nirvana. Time was therefore a relative thing. If a task was not completed in this lifetime, there would be another chance.

At a more practical level, the Japanese of old viewed time as related to the seasons, to the aging process, to the various stages of life, and to the overall importance of keeping pace with the natural rhythms. In the Japanese view, doing things rapidly became impolite, unrefined, and in many circumstances, insulting.

Japanese etiquette came to be based on precise movements and rituals that could not be hurried. Important conversations and the exchange of vital information had their own pace and studied style. The formalities followed in meetings and various proceedings were part of the ritualization of life, and the slow, measured use of time was a positive and important aspect of the relationships involved.

Industrialization and the adoption of many Western ways have dramatically changed life in Japan since 1868, but enough of life in present-day Japan still operates under the old system of etiquette and morality that the pace of life there becomes a problem for foreigners whose attitudes and behavior are determined by the clock.

Not surprisingly, one of the criticisms the Japanese most often lodge against Westerners is that they are in too much of a hurry to get things done, and as a result they make too many mistakes and fail too often. Because of this Western syndrome, the Japanese begin almost every international business or political discussion with the admonition to the foreign side that they must have *shinbo* (sheen-boe), or "patience," and they generally repeat this cautionary advice at frequent intervals.

In the Japanese context of things, those who are the most patient ultimately end up as the winners. One of the more colorful proverbs that expresses their view of patience is *Ishi no ue ni mo san nen*, which means, "Even if one sits on a rock for three years . . ."—meaning it is better to wait as long as necessary and win than to be impatient and lose.

Shinbo has traditionally been seen as a Japanese virtue—as something that sets them apart from other people and makes them stronger and more effective than people who are always in a rush. Most of Japan's traditional arts, crafts and aesthetic practices are based upon the generous use of time to achieve the highly refined goals of emotional, spiritual and intellectual harmony.

The Japanese are now in the throes of ongoing cultural shock as they strive to maintain some kind of balance between the increasing demands of Western time frames and the nurturing benefits of using time the traditional way.

Unfortunately, time is not on the side of the Japanese in this battle. The best that they can hope for is that they will be able to continue to preserve some of the old ways in the private dimensions of their lives—in eating, bathing, practicing aesthetic arts, engaging in traditional hobbies, dressing in kimono and *yukata* (you-kah-tah), and in participating in Zen and other in philosophical and religious experiences.

Foreigners dealing with Japan would benefit greatly from a few lessons in how to slow down their clock. I recommend Zen meditation as the first step in this process. It can be practiced anywhere, requires no equipment, costs nothing, and offers immediate benefit.

審議会
Shingi Kai
(Sheen-ghee Kie)

Japan's Shadow Rulers

One of the cultural concepts that the Japanese learned from China sometime between the years 400 and 700 was the idea that leaders, at whatever level, can often be more effective if they distance themselves from those below them, if they keep their own counsel, and if they present an air of mystery.

In the year 1158, Emperor Go-Shirakawa abdicated after only three years on the throne, but he continued to control the affairs of state for the next 34 years. This set a precedent that was to become institutionalized in Japan, and till this day remains characteristic of politics, business and most of the professions.

From Go-Shirakawa's time onward, it became common not only for Japan's shoguns, who had totally usurped the power of the Imperial Court by 1200, but for provincial lords and even shopkeepers to ostensibly retire early, remove themselves from day-to-day obligations and responsibilities, and rule from behind the scenes. In addition to avoiding time-consuming ceremonial activities and giving themselves time to contemplate and plan, relinquishing all official titles also relieved the individuals concerned of any direct responsibility for the results of their policies and plans.

Most of the notorious government scandals of the 1980s and 1990s grew out of the activities of these "shadow emperors," whose power was based almost entirely on their ability to raise enormous amounts of money from the business community for use in financing the political campaigns and agendas of their supporters. Although these scandals precipitated public outrage and pressure for political reform, Japan's government continues to be dominated by men who stay in the background and have the power to make or break prime ministers, cabinet ministers, and any other political appointee in the country.

One facet of this "shadow emperor syndrome" involves the practice of government ministries utilizing special advisory groups known as *shingi kai* (sheen-ghee kie), which may also be translated as "inquiry committees," to ostensibly help them formulate policies.

The term *shingi kai* is especially meaningful because its inherent connotations are that the people making up such advisory groups are outstanding individuals who exemplify the best virtues. The problem is that the ministries select the members of their *shingi kai* from among their own retirees and their circle of political supporters who can be depended upon to protect and preserve their prerogatives and policies. Over the decades the practice of using *shingi kai* has become institutionalized to the point that critics say these groups are one of the primary reasons why Japan's political system resists virtually all efforts for reform.

As of this writing there were some 215 publicly known *shingi kai* in Japan, representing virtually every political, social and economic activity that involves the government, from animal protection to space activities. *Shingi kai* members typically include retired government bureaucrats, scholars, business and media executives, and representatives from consumer groups—all of which sounds legitimate enough.

But, say critics, the names and positions of the individual members are generally not made public, their deliberations are behind closed doors, and they always support the views and actions of the ministry or agency they are supposed to advise. Critics add that the *shingi kai* have played a key role in preventing the prime minister and cabinet ministers from reacting positively and effectively to Japan's ongoing trade problems with the United States and other countries.

The role of the *shingi kai* came to international attention in 1993 when then Prime Minister Morihiro Hosokawa, the least traditional of Japan's leaders up to that time, called for national regulations to reform the *shingi kai* system as part of his attempt to reduce the power of the bureaucracies. The following year, the Ministry of International Trade and Industry (MITI), in a gesture toward reform, appointed the first foreigner ever to become a *shingi kai* member. The American president of Mobil Seikiyu (Mobil Oil) was made a member of the *shingi kai* attached to the Ministry's Petroleum Council.

Given Japan's historical background of both government and business management by "shadow" leaders and advisors, and the inherent nature of the bureaucracies, it is not likely that the nature of the *shingi kai* will change very much in the foreseeable future.

新発売
Shinhatsubai
(Sheen-haht-sue-by)

The New Product Syndrome

It can be said with a great deal of accuracy that during most of Japan's early history there was nothing new under the sun. Following the importation of Buddhism, Confucianism, and virtually all of the arts and crafts of China between the years 300 and 700, very little in the way of new ideas or new products entered Japan for the next 800 years. Then again from 1637 to the 1850s, Japan was tightly closed to the outside world, and only tidbits of Western technology and products were allowed into the country through a tiny man-made islet called Dejima, "Exit Island," in Nagasaki Harbor. Dejima was only 125 feet wide and 600 feet long, and was connected to the mainland by a causeway blocked by a huge gate that was manned around the clock by samurai warriors.

Dutch traders stationed on the islet were allowed to receive one ship a year, and to spend a short time on the mainland once a year. Because of this virtual isolation from the rest of the world during most of their history, the Japanese developed an insatiable curiosity about foreigners, foreign ways, and foreign things. After America's Admiral Perry and his fleet of tar-coated black ships forced Japan to open its doors to foreign trade in the 1850s, the Tokugawa Shogunate gave its approval for a foreign settlement in what is now Yokohama. This resulted in many Japanese traveling from distant parts of the country in the hopes of catching glimpses of the strange people who lived in the walled-off and guarded settlement.

Even after Japan began manufacturing Western-type products in large volume from the 1880s on, virtually all of the products were exported. They quickly gained the reputation of being cheap and shoddy and unfit for Japanese consumers, and within a short time they also came to be known derisively as *Yokohama hin* (Yoh-koe-hah-mah heen), or "Yokohama products," suitable only for foreigners, the standards of which were far below those of the Japanese.

It was not until the post-World War II years, especially from 1960 on, that Japanese manufacturers began to mass-produce well-made products designed to fit the rapidly changing life-style of the Japanese.

In the years that followed, a variety of high-quality American and European products, including perfumes, jewelry, clothing, fashion accessories and gourmet foods, began flooding into Japan. For the first time in the history of the country, the Japanese had a wide variety of well-made products to choose from—and the money to buy them. The Japanese went on a buying spree that was to last for some 30 years.

Japanese manufacturers and importers continued to fuel this lust for buying by bringing out new products in a steady stream, hawking them vigorously as *shinhatsubai* (sheen-haht-sue-by), or "newly on sale" products. From the 1970s on, it seemed that every radio and television commercial in Japan ended with the magic phrase, *shinhatsubai*. The phrase became so intrusive on the airwaves that it became a joke.

Japanese importers began scouring the world for new, novelty-type items. They also began demanding that their foreign suppliers keep coming up with new products and new designs. According to marketing specialists, any manufacturer or importer who introduced a new product and promoted it nationally could expect to sell close to half a million units to impulse buyers. The *shinhatsubai* syndrome became so strong that it resulted in manufacturers and importers basing their entire business approach on introducing new items every few weeks. Hundreds of these new products were born and hundreds died within a matter of months.

By the end of the 1980s, the seemingly insatiable Japanese appetite for new things had become a monster that was driving the economy, and it contributed significantly to the bursting of the "bubble economy" in 1990 and 1991. Following the collapse of the economy, Japanese manufacturers scrambled to reduce the number of new products and new variations of products that they introduced each year, and importers began concentrating on price, bringing in staple items from China and Southeast Asia.

Shinhatsubai products have not lost their appeal to the Japanese and they still play a significant role in Japan's consumer market. But having the latest product is not the fad that it once was, and makers now must be able to claim some real benefits in order to attract large numbers of buyers. Nevertheless the appeal of *shinhatsubai* products in Japan can be a plus for foreign companies if they present themselves effectively in the Japanese marketplace.

新人類
Shinjinrui
(Sheen-jeen-ruu-ee)

Japan's New Aliens

When the first Westerners began showing up in Japan in the mid-1500s, the differences between Japanese and Western cultures were so profound that friction, misunderstandings, conflicts and often deep animosity were daily occurrences. In so many areas of thought and behavior the two cultures were so far apart that no amount of exposure to each other could eliminate the barriers. One side either gave in and became non-Japanese or non-foreign, or the two cultures remained separate, each existing in its own separate sphere.

Less than 100 years after the arrival of the first Westerners in Japan, the cultural differences and friction had become so burdensome and problematic to the shogunate government that foreigners were banned from the country for the next 200-plus years. Given this historical background, one can perhaps begin to imagine the intellectual, emotional and spiritual turmoil the Japanese had to endure when they were defeated in World War II and were subsequently occupied by a huge army of foreign soldiers and civilians. To add to the impact of this foreign occupation, most of the troops and civilians stationed in Japan, with virtually absolute authority over the Japanese, were Americans, who were more culturally removed from the Japanese than most foreigners.

The influence of the short-lived America occupation of Japan was profound—politically, economically and socially—and was to result in fundamental changes in the lives of all Japanese. However, the American years could not and did not transform the Japanese into Westerners.

One of these changes, which did not begin to conspicuously manifest itself until the early 1960s, was to become one of the greatest ironies regarding the basically xenophobic Japanese. The very first postwar generation of young Japanese were so different from their elders that they were labeled *shinjinrui* (sheen-jeen-ruu-ee), which means "new breed of people" or "new kind of people." They were, in effect, Japanese who did not think or act like Japanese, but could not be expelled from Japan as the foreigners of old could.

In the intervening years, the number of Japanese who are regarded as *shinjinrui* has continued to grow along with the population. But the overall number of "new people" within the whole population has not progressed percentage-wise from one decade to the next, because the traditional culture forces most of the young people to drop their un-Japanese ways when they enter adult society. Still, the *shinjinrui* from each year have retained some of their un-Japanese attitudes and ways as they aged and moved into adult society, and their accumulated effect on Japan is becoming more and more important.

As early as the 1980s, the non-traditional attitudes of virtually all Japanese in their teens and twenties had resulted in dramatic changes in the Japanese marketplace. Manufacturers could no longer automatically assume that they knew what young Japanese consumers would buy. The whole approach to market research, public relations and advertising had to change. Companies had to revamp their hiring practices and implement new training programs in order to literally remake their new recruits to fit their corporate cultures.

By the 1990s the first and second generations of postwar *shinjinrui* were in their thirties, forties and fifties and made up the majority of the middle management in Japanese companies, and were primarily responsible for implementing the policies of the companies as well as for providing the information on which policies are based.

Today, older generations of *shinjinrui* say that the youngest "new people" are so different from what they were when they were young that they cannot understand them, and they have difficulty dealing with them. There are ongoing studies of the attitudes and behavior of the *shinjinrui*, and every year the bottom line is that they are becoming more and more un-Japanese in the traditional sense.

In essence, they are becoming more and more Western-like in their thinking and in their aspirations. But this does not mean that all of Japan's traditional culture is doomed to disappear. A great deal of it is both rational and human oriented, and will survive, even though it often differs fundamentally from Western cultures.

信頼
Shinrai
(Sheen-rye)

Relying on Japaneseness

Years ago when I was the editor of a trade magazine in Tokyo, I accompanied one of our advertising salesmen to a meeting with the president and managers of a company in mountainous Niigata prefecture. The president had agreed to advertise in the magazine, and had specifically asked that one of the foreign staff on the magazine accompany the Japanese advertising salesman on the visit.

I knew without asking that the company president could not feel comfortable in doing business with the magazine until he had personally met one or more of the foreign staff and developed a *shinrai*-type of relationship with them.

Shinrai (sheen-rye) is normally translated into English as "reliance" or "trust," but in its Japanese context *shinrai* means a lot more than these two words suggest.

The president wanted to know—but did not ask directly—if the foreign owners and operators of the magazine could be trusted in the Japanese sense of *shinrai*. The basis for "trust" is adherence to a code of ethics that is universal—one that is fixed and unchanging. *Shinrai* is based on behavior that is relative or situational, but which is culturally approved and accepted.

In the Japanese context, there are no absolutes in human relationships. Behavior changes as the circumstances change, and if individuals follow the Japanese Way, no one will be surprised, disappointed, or hurt. The Japanese Way is for both parties to an agreement or in a venture to stay in constant contact, to keep each other informed of changing circumstances, and to adjust their behavior to meet new circumstances through "revised" understandings arising out of joint discussions. Within the "loose" confines of this Japanese-style agreement, *shinrai* can flourish in situations that are in a constant state of change because each side can trust the other to do what is culturally right, without making a big fuss or burning any bridges.

There is, however, a major weakness in the *shinrai* philosophy that has traditionally plagued the Japanese and frequently upsets their foreign relations—which is that there are invariably people who will not honor the unwritten rules of *shinrai* behavior.

It is common for one side to break the rules of *shinrai*, and then take advantage of the culturally approved behavior by explaining their deviation, apologizing and agreeing to make amends—a response that Westerners find ludicrous because it makes it possible for unethical individuals or companies to repeatedly change circumstances or obligations to suit themselves, and to get away with it.

In the past, common instances of this have included registering the trademarks of foreign companies that were not yet doing business in Japan, and then forcing a company to buy a trademark back if it wanted to do business in Japan; another example is the licensing of new technology for the specific purpose of copying it.

The best foreign response to the problem of establishing and maintaining a trusting relationship with a Japanese company is to nurture close relationships with as many executives as possible in order to morally obligate them, and also to take the time and make the effort to get a detailed contract signed.

知らん顔
Shirankao
(She-rahn-kow)

Keeping a Straight Face

As far back as the last centuries of Japan's famous Heian Period (794–1185), educated Japanese were already so culturally homogenized that much of their interpersonal communication had become nonverbal. This homogenizing process became even more pronounced and the role of nonverbal communication became greater and more important during the long centuries of the samurai-dominated Shogunate Period from 1185 to 1868.

By the time Japan opened its doors to the outside world in the mid-1800s, the nonverbal aspect of social intercourse had taken on a life of its own, and nonverbal communication often took precedence over the spoken word. All behavior was prescribed down to the smallest detail, and stylized to the point that it was as precise and as demanding as the most carefully crafted stage role. To function effectively within their society, the Japanese had to be consummate actors. Among the more critical aspects of this role-playing was the vocabulary that one used, the tone of voice, and the facial expression. The slightest deviation from what was expected in each situation was noticeable, and in situations involving immediate superiors or others in power positions, the consequences of deviations could be very serious.

Some three generations later, these very same characteristics remain primary features of Japanese culture—weakened considerably from their apex during the 18th and 19th centuries, but still sufficiently strong enough to set the essence and the tone of Japanese behavior.

One facet of this traditional Japanese behavior that continues to have an impact on outsiders, particularly on Westerners, is the facial expression known as *shirankao* (she-rahn-kow), which literally translates as "an I-don't-know face" or "a face that doesn't know." By extension, *shirankao* also refers to a face that shows nothing—a face that does not reveal an individual's feelings or intentions—in other words, a "poker face."

From day-to-day personal relations to business and political matters, it is still important and frequently vital for the Japanese to put on a *shirankao* to protect themselves from their custom of not clearly verbalizing their opinions, goals, or objections, and from the behind-the-scenes activities that characterize their relationships.

The common use of *shirankao*, combined with these other modes of conduct, are among the many reasons that Westerners generally have difficulty in anticipating and understanding Japanese behavior.

Fortunately, the use of *shirankao* is generally limited to official or formal occasions, and one of the secrets to dealing effectively with the Japanese—in personal as well as business and professional affairs—is to engage them in discourse when they are not wearing their *shirankao*.

For example, Japanese culture allows people to dispense with the *shirankao* mode when they are drinking in after-hours situations in bars, clubs and restaurants, and generally speaking, it is only in this environment that the Japanese can let their facial expressions and comments actually reflect their personal feelings and opinions.

Drinking is the key element in the process of dispensing with other aspects of traditional Japanese protocol as well. This means, of course, that Western businessmen and politicians who want to get down to the nitty-gritty with the Japanese have to engage them during after-hours when the Japanese remove their *shirankao* masks.

Women in Japan's nighttime "floating world" have also traditionally played an important role in allowing men to dispense with daytime protocol, and in solving disagreements and other barriers to personal, business and political relationships. But that is another story.

使途不明金
Shitofumeikin
(Ssh-toe-fuu-may-e-keen)

Company 'Slush' Funds

In the 1970s it became vogue to refer to Japan as "Japan Incorporated" because it was virtually impossible to tell where the government left off and the business world began. The government's infamous *gyosei shido* (g'yoe-say-e she-doh), or "administrative guidance," permeated every facet of industry.

This was not something new as far as Japan was concerned. The government provided both the direction and, often, the financing for the industrialization of the country between 1870 and 1895, and during World War II, absolute government control of industry was extended across the board. The end of the war, the military occupation of Japan, and the introduction of numerous social, political and economic reforms into Japan by the United States in the latter part of the 1940s did not sever the traditional government–industry ties, particularly those that were cultural as well as regulatory. In fact, a spate of new government regulations were passed during the first decade of Japan's recovery from wartime destruction.

One aspect of the government–industry relationship that was to have a fundamental political, economic and social effect on the country was a Ministry of Finance regulation that allowed corporations to use large amounts of money for any purpose without accounting for it, as long as a 37.5 percent tax was paid on it. The unstated reason for this law, pushed through the Diet by the ruling Liberal Democratic Party (LDP), was that it provided corporations with a legal means for donating huge sums of money to political factions and to the individual politicians of their choice—invariably the politicians that provided them with the most government contracts.

Money donated under this law came to be known as *shitofumeikin* (ssh-toe-fuu-may-e-keen), which literally means "unaccounted for money expenditures." Under the cloak of this law, Japan's top corporations annually donated over half a billion dollars to the various political factions, with most of it going to the LDP, which used the funds to finance its hold on the government.

With such huge amounts of money involved, financial scandals became routine during the 1970s. One such scandal, the Sagawa Kyubin Scandal, which began in the late 1980s and did not play out until 1993, brought down Shin Kanemaru, the most powerful politician in the country, and a host of others. When Kanemaru was arrested, the police raided both his office and his home. For the next several days the news media had a field day as the TV cameras showed a hoard of gold bullion being removed from his office and from beneath the floorboards in his home.

Altogether, the authorities found nearly $40 million in undeclared *shitofumeikin* funds that Kanemaru had squirreled away. It was also revealed that Kanemaru, along with other leading politicians, had accepted large donations from Japan's infamous yakuza mobs.

This and other scandals brought increasing demands from opposition parties, the public, and the press for political reforms in Japan. Eventually a law was passed limiting the amount of money individual corporations could donate to politicians, but the law did not put a stop to *shitofumeikin*, which had long been institutionalized within Japan's corporate world.

Since the beginning of Japan's industrial age in 1870, all of Japan's larger companies had kept special funds in reserve to pay off a variety of debts or obligations that had nothing to do with regular business operations. Traditionally, some of these funds have been used to pay for unofficial entertainment and special gifts. Some have been used to pay for "unofficial" advertising—advertising that department managers were virtually "forced" to place because of "social debts" they owed someone.

Some of these *shitofumeikin* funds have traditionally gone to pay off yakuza gangsters to keep them from sabotaging company property or products and to prevent them from disrupting stockholders' meetings.

With the custom of maintaining and using *shitofumeikin* so deeply entrenched in Japanese culture—not just in business and politics—it is not likely to disappear, regardless of any political reforms.

淑やかな
Shitoyakana
(Shh-toh-yah-kah-nah)

Gracefulness as Morality

During the Shogunate Period in Japan, the ruling professional samurai warriors went well beyond training their male and female family members in martial arts. From the first generations of this elite ruling class, all samurai were trained from early childhood in a precise style of manners that eventually became a science, and then a morality all its own.

This highly refined behavior covered sitting, standing, walking, bowing, eating, drinking, handing things to and receiving things from others, writing, working, bathing, and more. All of these very mundane actions were refined and detailed until they took on the form and essence of ritual ceremonies.

According to Japanese commentary on samurai etiquette, such attention to the details of ordinary life might seem to be both irrational and a waste of time, but in actuality it was discovered that they saved time and resulted in extraordinary improvement in the various physical skills involved. Furthermore, cultural historians noted, ritualizing ordinary behavior proved to be the most economical and graceful way of learning how to apply force in any kind of combat.

According to one historian, the purpose of all etiquette was to cultivate one's mind to the point that even when a person was seated, an opponent would not have any kind of advantage. In this line of thought, mastering the etiquette prescribed for samurai meant harmonizing one's self with the environment and thereby mastering both the spirit and the flesh.

In this context, the mastery of samurai etiquette was represented as achieving *shitoyakana* (ssh-toe-yah-kah-nah), or "gracefulness," which was seen as a reservoir of force—of power that could be precisely controlled and directed according to one's will. *Shitoyakana* was not just a source of aesthetic pleasure to the eye, or subservient to the egoistic emotions of all-powerful lords and warriors. It was a source of spiritual, intellectual and physical power.

Till this day, one of the things that invariably impresses visitors to Japan the most is the gracefulness that is inherent in traditional Japanese etiquette, particularly when it is in such traditional Japanese settings as *ryokan* (ree-oh-kahn) inns and *ryotei* (ree-oh-tay) restaurants. While foreigners may be impressed by *shitoyaka*, "graceful," behavior by the Japanese, they generally do not think about what it really means— how much energy and effort went into the training. And foreigners all too often regard Japanese etiquette as little more than an attractive but quaint vestige of the past.

What is important, however, is the fact that extensive training in very precise, very detailed etiquette today influences the morals and ethics of the people who undergo the training, just as it did in the past. In other words, being *shitoyaka* is not just simple physical mannerisms. It is a reflection of the self-discipline, the study, and the practice that was necessary to achieve it—all of which affect a person's character.

Extrapolating a bit further, one of the advantages that the Japanese, as a rule, have over Americans and other less-mannered foreigners is their *shitoyakana*—their gracefulness, as it is manifested in their etiquette. Subconsciously and otherwise, the formalized behavior of the Japanese significantly influences how foreigners view and treat them, regardless of what the real character of a person might be. Time and again I have seen otherwise rough and ill-mannered Westerners make a gallant attempt to become as polite and as courteous as the Japanese in their encounters in Japan.

Good manners do not, of course, necessarily make the man. A well-mannered person can be as much of a rogue or heel as anyone. But people who have had conspicuously good manners instilled in them when they were young, generally also pick up good moral standards on the way.

As long as the Japanese continue to make a valiant effort to preserve the *shitoyaka* aspect of their culture, they will continue to have a special advantage in their relationships with others, whether in social or in business settings.

勝負
Shobu
(Show-boo)

A Fight to the Finish

One of the distinguishing characteristics of the Japanese is that once they set out to do something, there is almost never any turning back. The challenge becomes bigger than themselves, and bigger than anything in their store of values.

Hideyoshi Toyotomi's attempts to conquer Korea and China in the 16th century, and Japan's war against China and the United States in the 19th century are the two most prominent examples of this characteristic of the Japanese. In both cases, the invasions were launched with virtually no regard for the scale of the challenges. And even after it became obvious that there was no way that Japan could be victorious, the attacks continued until they ended in disaster for the Japanese forces.

Throughout Japan's feudal age (1185–1945), some of the most dramatic and exciting events of the times were duels between master swordsmen whose reputations had forced them to meet in combat to determine once and for all which was the best—not unlike gunfighters in Hollywood Westerns. The most interesting and memorable of these death duels occurred when one of the swordsman was ill, had suffered some kind of injury, or had aged and lost some of his skill, but refused to back down from a younger and stronger challenger.

The Japanese regarded this kind of ending to the life of a swordsman as the epitome of sincerity, courage, spirit and honor. Fighting to the death was a matter of face.

This kind of confrontation is known as *shobu* (show-boo), which means "victory or defeat," or "fight to the finish," and is a mindset that has been so deeply embedded in the Japanese character that it is discernible in virtually all of their endeavors.

Japanese businessmen characteristically view their battles for market share in terms of *shobu*. Every member of a company, from individual salaried workers to top executives are expected to work as if their very survival depended upon their efforts.

Japan's extraordinary rise to economic superpower status following World War II was due in considerable part to the *shobu* element in the character of the Japanese. And the virtual epidemic of *karoshi* (kah-roe-she), or "death from overwork," that appeared in Japan in the 1960s was one consequence.

On the public front, present-day exhibitions of *shobu* often occur on baseball diamonds. These baseball *shobu* are duels between pitchers and hitters who put everything they have into the game, often ignoring instructions from their coaches and managers. There may be little hope for the pitcher to win the game, but giving up is never a consideration; instead, more effort goes into the game. As in earlier wars and sword fights, the participants and the spectators in a *shobu* duel forget that the original goal was to win a game. They get caught up in the form of the act and in not giving up and losing face. On such occasions, as long as the duelers show no lack of courage or effort, there is no dishonor in losing.

The bursting of Japan's "economic bubble" in 1990 and 1991 had a dramatic effect on the *shobu* syndrome among Japan's leading appliance and electronic goods manufacturers. A higher level of competition, the appearance of discount stores and cheap imports and plummeting sales forced manufacturers to cut back on their *shobu*-type battles in the marketplace. But this did not mean that the *shobu* approach to business was over. It resulted in greater efforts, which included moving additional manufacturing facilities overseas, and putting more emphasis on winning market shares abroad.

Westerners doing business with Japan and competing with the Japanese in their own home markets, as well as in other foreign markets, should keep in mind that much of the determination and energy that drives the Japanese is a manifestation of the *shobu* syndrome. To the Japanese, winning and keeping market shares is not just making profits, looking good, and feeling good. It is surviving in a do-or-die duel.

修行
Shugyo
(Shuu-g'yoe)

Training for Intuitive Wisdom

Most Westerners prize practical knowledge and hands-on experience above all other kinds of learning. They are also conditioned to approach work and other challenges directly, aiming for "the shortest distance between two points." It is therefore inevitable that Westerners in Japan, and those working for Japanese companies abroad, will be mystified and frustrated by a great deal of typical Japanese behavior, for to the Japanese the shortest distance between two points is not a straight line; indeed, both practical knowledge and experience can be a handicap in functioning well in a Japanese environment. Americans, in particular, are impatient for results once they begin any kind of training or enterprise. Novice foreign students of Zen Buddhism pester their masters, wanting to know when they are going to "learn something." The foreign employee newly hired by a Japanese company wants to put his experience to work immediately, almost always causing consternation.

In Japan the cultural element in training and work often takes precedence over results. This is particularly true in the early stages, but it generally applies in perpetuity. In the Japanese value system, the way things are done outweighs what is done. For example, young students practicing the ideograms used in writing the Japanese language are expected to learn more than just the mechanical strokes necessary to reproduce correct characters. They are also expected to learn form, order, aesthetics and harmony.

The first obligation of young employees of Japanese companies hired directly from school is not to learn work routines so they can immediately become "productive." Their first obligation is to learn the company philosophy and culture, so that their personal behavior and the work decisions they make in the future will be "correct."

One of the most important words in Japan's corporate world is *shugyo* (shuug'yoe), which is usually translated as "training," but *shugyo* has far deeper and broader implications than the English word implies.

Shugyo in its full Japanese context is better translated as "apprenticeship" in the old, traditional sense of the word, when it referred to a young person being apprenticed to a journeyman or to a master for at least ten and sometimes as many as 20 years.

The goal of *shugyo* in a Japanese company is for new employees to gradually absorb knowledge about the company and how it functions, and to determine intuitively what the responsibilities and duties of an employee are. Like apprentices of old, new employees get little or no direct feedback regarding their work performance for many years. Managers and supervisors do not stand over newcomers, instructing them about what to do and how to do it. The employees are expected to figure that out for themselves.

Things are not made easy for Japanese students or apprentice workers. The Japanese believe that the harder something is to learn and the more effort that is required to learn it, the more valuable the knowledge or the skill. Furthermore, the ultimate goal in Japanese training is perfection, which cannot be achieved, so theoretically there can be no end to training or to learning, and *shugyo* is seen as an ongoing process.

This Japanese attitude about learning is in sharp contrast to that of most Westerners, again, particularly Americans, who, after reaching a certain level, tend to either rest on their laurels or take so much pride in their learning that they do not open themselves up to learning more.

There is another important characteristic in Japanese training and employment that sets them apart and motivates them to continue learning and striving to improve. Because they receive no direct, explicit feedback about their work, they never know where they stand. In this atmosphere, peer pressure and the fear of bringing shame on themselves and their coworkers forces them to continuously strive to improve their performance.

就職指導
Shushoku Shido
(Shuu-show-kuu She-doh)

"Long Arms of Professors"

Large Japanese corporations traditionally hired all of their new employees directly from high school or college. They hired only in April, right after the end of the school year. Junior high school and high school graduates were recruited for blue-collar work, and college graduates were recruited as candidates for administrative or management positions.

Because of dramatic changes that began occurring in Japanese industry in the 1970s and 1980s, particularly the advance into computers and other high-tech areas, companies began to recruit middle-aged and older technicians, managers and executives as they were needed. This kind of hiring, known as "mid-career recruiting," contributed to the proliferation of employment agencies, which first appeared in the 1960s in response to the employment needs of foreign companies setting up operations in Japan. The bulk of all employees going into major Japanese companies, however, are still recruited directly from schools.

By law, the recruitment of college seniors on school campuses is not supposed to start until July of the year preceding graduation. However, most companies surreptitiously begin interviewing and making commitments, *naitei* (nigh-tay-e), or "secret, unofficial decisions," well before this legal starting date in an attempt to sign up the most desirable recruits. Some companies, in fact, make secret commitments to more desirable college students, and those with strong personal connections, as many as 18 months, and in some cases two years before they are due to graduate.

This system of early recruiting on college campuses is one of the reasons why it has long been common for many college students, particularly those seeking liberal arts degrees, to do little if any studying or class work during their junior and senior years in school. They already have jobs lined up, and they know that their grades and their studies are, at this point, irrelevant to their employment.

Generally, major Japanese corporations do not expect their new administrative employees to make any significant contribution to the company from one to three years, during which time they are expected to absorb the company philosophy, learn company etiquette, establish personal relationships with their superiors and peers, and then gradually begin to assume responsible duties.

Professors are especially important in hiring from universities in Japan. Most professors, especially those at the top universities, have long-standing relationships with a number of companies where former students occupy high executive positions. These professors use their connections with their former students to act as "job placement agents" for each new annual crop of students, a system referred to as *shushoku shido* (shuu-show-kuu she-doh), or "employment guidance."

At the same time, company managers and executives who graduated from elite universities invariably favor recruits from these schools. These managers are also typically active in maintaining contacts with their former professors, so the placement of students is an effort by both educators and business.

Generally speaking, *shushoku shido* in Japan is far more institutionalized than similar career guidance by professors in Western universities. *Shushoku shido* is one of the primary activities of most Japanese professors, and has a high priority on their time. The more students Japanese professors place with companies, the more influence the professors have with those firms, which results in more research grants and other contributions from the companies, as well as more consulting contracts for the professors. Some professors have such powerful connections with companies that they can arbitrarily parcel their favorite graduating students out to them.

Foreign companies in Japan generally have difficulty recruiting top-notch students from Japanese universities until the companies have established close relationships with a number of ranking professors, and until they become the benefactors of their *shushoku shido* prowess.

相談役
Sodanyaku
(Soe-dahn-yah-kuu)

The Quiet Advisors

Japan has traditionally had its shadow emperors, shadow shoguns, shadow prime ministers and other figures who stayed in the background but yielded enormous power—often, as the titles above suggest, the ultimate power. This custom is still alive and well in Japan today, particularly in politics, where the man out in front is almost always just that: a "front" for one or more people behind the scenes. But "shadow emperors" also exist in the arts, in entertainment, and in business.

During Japan's long feudal age, when the average life span of men was between 45 and 50, businessmen on all levels, including small-time shopkeepers, would often retire at around the age of 40, turning their businesses over to sons or sons-in-law. Some of these retirees continued to manage their businesses indirectly, but others took up hobbies, cultural activities, or traveled widely within Japan, seldom if ever concerning themselves with their former businesses.

In present-day Japan, the founders, chairmen and presidents of successful companies, especially those that are very large, often voluntarily retire early in order to free themselves from the daily routine of their offices and to devote themselves to some special project or long-term planning. They can afford to do this kind of thing because they continue to receive their salaries and benefits.

It is also common for high-level executives in Japanese companies, particularly chairmen, presidents and senior vice presidents, to voluntarily resign to take responsibility for mishaps or scandals involving their firms. In virtually all of these cases, the former executives are given the title of *sodanyaku* (soe-dahn-yah-kuu), which in these instances is translated as "senior advisor," thereby continuing to draw their salaries and benefits.

These *sodanyaku* are provided with offices, chauffeur-driven vehicles and secretaries. Some of them become "advisors" in name only, and thereafter have little or nothing to do with the management of their former companies. Others continue to play significant but usually very quiet roles in their new positions.

How active the *sodanyaku* remain is determined by many factors, including the circumstances of their resignation or early retirement; how politically sensitive the situations are; how popular the executives were before resigning; how aggressive they were in their management style; how their immediate replacements regard the ongoing value of their experience and knowledge, and so on. On the average, the change in the *sodanyaku* activities is significant. Most of them give direct advice only when they are asked for it. But most also keep in touch informally with the top executives in their former companies and are able to influence their thinking and decisions.

One of the key roles played by virtually all of these "honorary advisors" is to continue to use their political and commercial contacts on behalf of their companies. Japanese companies have traditionally been susceptible to scandals because of the ingrown, incestuous relationships that result from having only inside directors. There were so many company scandals in the 1980s and 1990s that some companies began bringing in directors from the outside—a practice that is expected to accelerate as time goes by.

In its usual sense, *sodanyaku* simply means "consultant" or "advisor," and refers to outside authorities who are retained, or are periodically called in, by companies that need their expertise. In normal usage, the word infers that the consultant or advisor is a person of considerable stature, and deals only with the highest executives in the client company. Large Japanese companies typically retain well-known professors and former government bureaucrats as *sodanyaku*—as much for their connections as their advice.

袖の下
Sode no Shita
(Soe-day no Ssh-tah)

A Little Something up the Sleeve

During the many centuries that the kimono and *yukata* (you-kah-tah) (a thin, cotton version of the kimono worn as a bathrobe or as casual outdoor wear) were the formal costumes of Japan, people used the voluminous sleeves of the garments as pockets for small items. The lower portions of the sleeves made ideal places to conceal things because there were no pockets on either kimono or *yukata*, and anything carried in a pouch or wallet on the outside could be seen.

This bag-like space in kimono sleeves was called *sode no shita* (soe-day no ssh-tah), which literally means "under the sleeves," and it was not long before *sode no shita* became a specific reference to something under-handed, secret and illegal, including bribes. Period films in Japan are replete with unscrupulous officials, wayward monks, and rogue samurai secreting bribes or payoffs of one kind or another into their *sode no shita*. Although most contemporary Japanese have had very little experience wearing kimono, and the expression may sound old-fashioned to the younger generation, the practice of *sode no shita* is probably more common now than in the feudal samurai era, and the phrase is still commonly used by older people.

Stories about bribery incidents are regular fare in the news media, particularly in connection with politicians and the various industries that depend upon government agencies as their primary source of business. There are several ways the expression *sode no shita* is used in connection with bribes: a *sode no shita no kiku hito* (soe-day no ssh-tah no kee-kuu) is "a person who will take a bribe"; *sode no shita wo tsukau* (soe-day no ssh-tah oh t'su-kah-oh) means "to bribe (a person)," and *sode no shita wo morau* (soe-day no ssh-tah oh moh-rah-oo) means "to receive or accept a bribe."

Japan's two huge gift-giving seasons, *ochugen* (oh-chuu-gain), in midsummer, and *oseibo* (oh-say-e-boe), just before the end of the year, are sometimes criticized as being *sode no shita* in disguise because many of the gifts given at this time go to government officials, bosses, school principles, professors, doctors, lawyers, gang bosses and others with whom people must stay on good terms.

Despite the public prominence of high-level *sode no shita* cases in Japan, there is remarkably little petty bribery in the country. In fact, as far as ordinary people are concerned, one is tempted to say that there is generally no bribery that involves the police, local ward office personnel, immigration personnel, or customs agents—the people most likely to abuse their power.

Unlike some countries where petty bribery has been institutionalized for centuries, the Japanese historically dealt with direct cases of *sode no shita* as serious felonies that more likely than not resulted in death sentences, especially if they involved public officials. This strict standard grew out of the ethics of the samurai, and since it was they who made and enforced the laws, there was no timidity when it came to dispensing their brand of justice. And it was because of these strictly enforced standards over a period of many centuries that the Japanese in all classes, and especially the lower classes, became amazingly honest and respectful of other people's property.

It is still common for the Japanese to ride bicycles to train stations, leave them unlocked and unguarded for hours and even days, and find them there when they return. Products of all kinds are routinely displayed on sidewalks outside of shops, because no one steals them. Soft-drink companies, such as Coca-Cola, say that one of the primary reasons why they have been so successful in Japan is because they were able to display their merchandise in hundreds of thousands of unattended vending machines in public places.

Foreigners who have been to Japan as visitors say that one of the greatest joys of traveling in Japan is that they are not forced to pay *sode no shita* to anyone for anything. While there were some demands for *sode no shita* by customs agents in the 1950s and 1960s, such behavior was an aberration remaining from the desperate days following Japan's defeat in World War II. Since that period, bribery has not been one of the many "barriers" facing foreign companies dealing with Japan.

相互依存
Sogo Izon
(Soe-go Ee-zone)

All in the Same Boat

Throughout Japanese history, one of the bedrock principles of the society was that every individual had to be a member of some group, and every group had to act more-or-less as a collective, with members cooperating and supporting each other for the benefit of the whole.

In this kind of social environment, the pursuit of individualism, personal ambition and entrepreneurship were taboo. In fact, groupism was carried so far that business and social groups, including shops and companies, were generally required to get permission from their competitors before they could initiate new enterprises or make changes in existing ones that might have an impact on others in the same line of business.

This philosophy and practice, known as *sogo izon* (soe-go ee-zone), or "mutual dependency," in Japanese, was changed somewhat when Japan industralized, beginning in 1870, particularly among the large manufacturing, wholesaling and trading combines known as *zaibatsu* (zigh-baht-sue). With government backing, these family-owned groups were able to ignore the semi-sacred principle of *sogo izon* and carve out huge commercial empires for themselves at the expense of other families.

The *zaibatsu* did continue using the mutual dependency principle within their own affiliated companies, however; *sogo izon* was maintained not only to bond their employees, but also to vertically integrate their affiliated firms into unified entities that were practically self-sufficient. *Sogo izon* in its original form has also survived down to modern times and continues to be a factor in the development of new businesses and in the growth of old ones—Japanese as well as foreign.

As is the case with many of Japan's culture-bound rules and customs, however, the *sogo izon* principle is not universal. It is applied selectively, both within Japan and in situations involving international interests. For example, small neighborhood stores selling toys were able to delay the entry of Toys R Us into Japan for several years by invoking the *sogo izon* concept and claiming that the practice of "mutual dependency" applied only to Japanese companies.

Japanese companies still base much of their personnel and business management on the principle of mutual dependency. This is most conspicuous in the interwoven relationships they develop with other companies and with various agencies of the government—all of which are designed to protect them from encroachers.

Generally speaking, the government and companies in Japan cooperate in an effort to make sure that Japanese companies do not become dependent upon anything foreign—especially technology—despite the fact that companies routinely promote the concept of mutual dependency on an international basis.

When pinned down, the Japanese say that international *sogo izon* is an ideal they believe in and are working toward, and intellectually that is no doubt true. But at an emotional and spiritual level mutual international dependence is something they are incapable of accepting, and it will not happen in the foreseeable future. Again, broadly speaking, the prevailing philosophy in Japan is that it is desirable for foreign companies and countries to be dependent upon Japan, but not the reverse.

損して得とれ
Sonshite Tokutore
(Sohn-ssh-tay Toe-kuu-toe-ray)

Losing to Win

Part of the historical legacy inherited by all Japanese is the concept that bending with the wind is better than fighting it—a philosophy that is derived as much from the authoritarian political system they lived under until 1945 as it is from the teachings of Buddhism.

The concept of allowing a superior force to have its way is an essential element in many of the arts, crafts and customs of Japan, from its traditional architecture and personal etiquette to a number of its most famous martial arts, such as aikido and judo. In both aikido and judo, the most skillful of the antagonists, and the ones most likely to win, are those who turn the force and energy of their opponents against them.

Even in kendo, the way of the sword, Japan's greatest masters were those who mastered the technique of letting their opponents attack them and then dealt them a fatal blow when they were in the midst of their attack and could not change their tactics.

This same philosophy plays a significant role in the way the Japanese conduct all of their affairs today, from politics to business. In virtually all situations, the standard Japanese approach is to draw the opponents or counterparts out, let them expose and overextend themselves, and then strike. Another characteristic of this philosophy and tactic is that the winning move is not always abrupt or obvious.

In fact, it almost never is, because that would be a contradiction of the technique. Except when they are obviously in a significantly superior position, the Japanese prefer to allow their opponents to believe and feel as though they are winning, while in fact the advantage and victory will ultimately be theirs. In a business context this philosophy and strategy is known as *sonshite tokutore* (sohn-ssh-tay toe-kuu-toe-ray), which literally means "lose, then profit."

Because of the nature of Japan's business culture, it has traditionally never been possible for companies to go out and attract new business with only better products, higher quality, better service, or lower prices; the right personal connections were necessary first, and then over a period of time a business relationship could gradually develop.

In virtually all cases, even when a company was able to establish the right kind of personal connections with a potential customer or source of business, it was still expected to *sonshite tokutore* for a period of time as a gesture of goodwill and gratitude. In some cases, the period of time that a company was expected to assume a loss could be quite long—as much as several years if it appeared that afterward it would earn substantial profits over a long period of time.

When American and other foreign businessmen started going into Japan in the 1970s and 1980s and encountered the *sonshite tokutore* concept, their reactions ranged from surprise to shock. Some strongly objected to the practice, saying that Japanese companies might grow their business that way, but they did not. Of course, the concept was not new to Western businesspeople, but the fact that this notion was institutionalized in Japan and that losses often went well beyond what they had budgeted for, set them back.

The *sonshite tokutore* approach to new business is still alive and well in Japan, although during the high-growth and high-profit years of the "bubble economy" (1970–1990), some foreign companies were able to get into Japan on their own terms because of the demand for their products or technology.

Generally speaking, Japanese companies that were not that wealthy have lived with the system by taking extraordinary measures to reduce costs and otherwise cover their losses during the time that they are paying "tribute" to the system.

There is another side to the *sonshite tokutore* coin. When the Japanese are obviously in a superior position, any diplomacy or pretense is generally dispensed with, and they become blunt, aggressive and demanding.

助っ人
Suketto
(Skate-toe)

From Heroes to Helpers

Few Westerners in Japan have experienced more culture shock than professional American baseball players. Movies have been made about their experiences, and best-selling books have been written about the differences between baseball in Japan and baseball in the United States.

Japanese baseball generally looks like American baseball, and Japanese baseball fans sometimes behave like American fans. But there are subtle as well as glaringly obvious differences between the players, the game and the fans in American and those in Japanese baseball stadiums, and these differences are illustrative of the cultural gaps between Japan and the United States.

Baseball was introduced into Japan in 1873 (when samurai warriors were still wearing their swords) by an American named Horace Wilson who had been hired as a teacher at Kasei Gakko, or "Kasei School," the present-day Tokyo University.

The first purely Japanese baseball team was organized by Tokyo's Shimbashi Athletic Club around 1880, and between 1880 and 1902, teams from the First Higher School in Tokyo regularly played—and defeated—teams made up of American residents of Yokohama. These highly touted games made baseball one of the most popular Western sports in Japan, and baseball clubs were formed at virtually all high schools and universities in the country.

A Waseda University baseball team played a number of exhibition games in the United States in 1905, and two years later, a semi-professional team of Americans in Hawaii went to Tokyo for a series of games, and between 1906 and 1936 the Waseda team played the University of Chicago team ten times. In 1913 Charles Comisky and John McGraw took a team of major leaguers on a world tour, stopping off in Japan for a series of games. Connie Mack took teams that included Lefty Grove, Lou Gehrig, Babe Ruth and Jimmie Foxx to Japan in 1931 and in 1934.

The first time an American was hired to play for a Japanese team occurred in 1936; Japanese teams began hiring American players again in the 1960s, a little more than a decade after the end of World War II.

Each of Japan's 12 teams—six in the Central League and six in the Pacific League—is permitted to have two foreign players on its roster, and all of the teams usually have their full quotas. However, because there are so many differences between the Japanese and American concepts of baseball—in the attitudes of the players, in how the coaches train, and in how the managers manage—that some American players on Japanese teams have left the country in disgust after short periods, convinced that Japanese baseball was not real baseball.

The lure of yen, however, has continued to attract American baseball players to Japan, where some adapt and some do not. One of the things that most upsets the American players is how they are "misused" by the Japanese teams.

Many American players who have gone to Japan were heroes in the eyes of both their American and Japanese fans. What few—if any—of the players realized, however, is that although they were being hired because of their "hero" image, they were going to be used in Japan as *suketto* (skate-toe), a word derived from *tetsudai* (tate-sue-die), meaning "help," or "helper."

In other words, these famous players were looked upon and treated as "helpers," not stars—and for the most part, Japanese managers naturally presumed that the *suketto* would not only follow traditional Japanese training practices, but that they would also play ball the Japanese way as well.

The connotations of *suketto* include someone who is temporary and is not a full-fledged member of a team or group: someone who is more-or-less like a hired gun, and who can be useful as long as he can be controlled. Generally speaking, the *suketto* concept applies to virtually all foreigners hired by Japanese corporations, professional organizations, schools, or whatever. It is still rare for a Japanese organization to employ any foreigner as a full-fledged team member.

But not all of the *suketto* concept that the Japanese typically apply to foreigners is necessarily negative. They point out that foreigners would not want to abide by the rules and customs routinely followed by Japanese employees, and that their foreign employees are extended special privileges that the Japanese do not get. Still, with few exceptions, the Japanese are culturally conditioned to the point that they cannot accept anything but *suketto* relationships with non-Japanese.

Foreigners who understand this from the start of their relationship with the Japanese are much less likely to suffer from culture shock.

素直さ
Sunao-Sa
(Sue-nah-oh-Sah)

The Meek Survive

There is an old and famous saying in Japan which warns that "the nail that sticks up gets hammered down"—a reference to the traditional Japanese custom of forcing conformity on anyone who stands out from the crowd—that is, individualistic persons, or those that were unique in other ways. This attitude toward anyone who was different, particularly if the difference illuminated the failings, weaknesses, or banality of others, was one of the many features of the Japanese social and cultural system that, within social classes, conditioned everyone to think alike and act alike, and left little room for variations in attitudes and behavior.

It seems to be a human characteristic that people who are locked into vertically arranged social classes, and who are not free to change their status, are more apt to be envious of people at their own level than they are of those above them. In any event, this was the case in Japan. People, in whatever class, who were smarter, more capable and therefore more successful than their social peers, had to be especially careful to avoid bringing the wrath of their own coworkers and neighbors down on them.

Women, regardless of their class, were in an especially sensitive position where their relationships with men were concerned. For more than a thousand years of Japan's most recent history—from around 900 to 1945—women were conditioned to be passive and subservient to men. From the sexist male viewpoint, this cultural conditioning made Japanese women into paragons of feminine virtue, instilling in them traits that early Western male visitors found totally captivating.

While the hammering down of women went to an extraordinary extreme, all Japanese were conditioned to maintain a demeanor of *sunao-sa* (sue-nah-oh-sah) or "meekness" when in the presence of superiors and toward the public in general.

Of course, there were exceptions to this strongly enforced rule; gang bosses, samurai warriors, clan leaders and others in leadership positions were notorious for being arrogant, aggressive and overbearing. But in general terms, all Japanese regarded *sunao-sa* as one of the most laudable of their character traits, and took pride in it.

As with most of the traditional traits of the Japanese, however, *sunao-sa* has suffered grievously from the onslaught of democracy, individualism and other peculiar Western concepts imported into the country since the mid-1900s. Yet, this trait survives because it is still the only acceptable standard of behavior in Japan's schools and workplaces. Despite growing calls for more individualism and aggressiveness in all areas of Japanese life, individualistic behavior at school or at work is still virtually unthinkable by most people, and when isolated cases do occur the hammers go into action.

What outsiders must learn and take into account is that the ongoing *sunao-sa* mode of most Japanese, although it may be played to perfection, is a role, an act, and particularly so in the case of high-ranking businessmen and government officials. Major Japanese figures traditionally wear Clark Kent masks of meekness, especially when meeting their foreign counterparts, but behind their masks they are superman, and woe to those who belittle or underestimate them.

And Japanese women are no longer the pushovers for men that they once were. By most criteria, Japanese women are smarter, more flexible, more durable, and often more talented, than Japanese men, and slowly but surely they are getting on top. It was Japanese women who led in virtually all of the social changes that took place in Japan following the real end of the feudal era in 1945, including dating, choosing their own mates, and setting up their own households.

It was also the women who fueled the growth of Japan's Western-style consumer market with their demands for new clothing, new foods, new kitchen and household goods and new gift items.

Foreign men who take the *sunao-sa* pose of young Japanese women as reality, soon have to come up with a new definition of the term.

摺り合わせ
Suri-Awase
(Sue-ree-Ah-wah-say)

Grinding off the Rough Edges

Cultural conditioning for over a thousand years made the Japanese extremely sensitive to any product that was not finely finished; there could be no rough edges or rough seams or anything else unfinished on a product.

Historically, virtually the only thing that the Japanese would accept that was less then perfectly finished was porcelain or ceramic ware that was not glazed on the bottom. To prevent the unglazed bottoms, of ceramic bowls, cups and other utensils from scratching the highly polished tops of lacquered tables, the Japanese would rub two unfinished surfaces together until they were smooth, a process that was known as *suri-awase* (sue-ree-ah-wah-say), which literally meant "rubbing-joining," "rubbing-uniting," or "rubbing and putting together."

In their usual way of creating colorful expressions to deal with human affairs, the Japanese began using the phrase *suri-awase* to describe discussions or negotiating sessions designed to reach consensus by achieving enough compromise from both parties to bring them together. A common idiomatic use of *suri-awase* in a business or political context may be translated as "adjustment of views," a term that prevents either side from regarding itself as a winner or a loser, while protecting both sides from loss of face or injured feelings.

Suri-awase is not used only during the initial stages of a business relationship or during negotiating sessions. It is, in fact, an ongoing process that the Japanese use constantly to keep their business relationships moving along as smoothly as possible. In their business affairs, the Japanese make a major point of emphasizing that circumstances change constantly, and that for two companies to work together in a mutually acceptable manner it is essential that their views, and often their operating procedures, be adjusted accordingly on a regular basis.

This is one of the reasons why the Japanese have always felt uncomfortable with very precise and very tight contracts that do not allow flexibility in a relationship, and why there is frequent friction with their foreign partners when they assume the right to "adjust" the terms of such contracts.

Anyone who has ever been involved in negotiating sessions with Japanese businesspeople and politicians can fully appreciate the concept of "grinding" away all the differences in viewpoints, goals and expectations. Negotiating sessions may go on for days, weeks and months, and oftentimes the ultimate "winner" is the side that was able to sit the longest, slowly grinding away at the other party's resolve. One of the ways to reduce the amount of time spent at *suri-awase* is to engage in separate sessions of *nemawashi* (nay-mah-wah-she), especially after hours during long eating and drinking bouts in restaurants, lounges, or cabarets.

Nemawashi originally referred to preparing a plant for transplanting. *Ne* means "root," and *mawashi* means "spin" or "turn." When used in the social sense, *nemawashi* refers to a combination of bargaining and subtle arm-twisting to win advocates for a cause, that is, turning roots around so they will "grow" they way you want them to.

When *suri-awase* sessions take place in Japan, the Japanese have an obvious advantage because they are on their home ground. When the first meetings are to take place in Japan, the foreign side should set a reasonable time frame for completion of the talks, and make prearrangements so that if additional meetings are necessary, they will take place at their offices.

From the viewpoint of foreign businesspeople it is better to have the final rather than the first meetings on their own home ground, in order not to be put in a position of pressure because of time constraints, or because of the expense involved in staying in Japan, or for other reasons.

大安
Taian
(Tie-ahn)

Waiting for Lucky Days

Geographically, Japan is about the size of the American state of Montana, but it boasts well over a half a million eating and drinking establishments, most of which are concentrated in the entertainment districts in the major cities. Tokyo, for example, has several hundred entertainment districts that range in size from two or three blocks in length to areas that are cities within the city; the districts are lit up at night like great Disneylands and draw nightly crowds of up to half a million people.

These districts draw not only diners, shoppers and revelers, they also attract huge numbers of people who go for the scene itself—for the lights, the sounds, the color and the people.

One of the minor but intriguing evening sights in most of Japan's entertainment districts are fortune tellers sitting on folding chairs behind tiny portable tables along the sidewalks. Some of these fortune tellers read palms, and others cast slender reed-like sticks and then interpret the future that the sticks reveal—a custom from the early days when much of life in Japan was ruled by superstitions and diviners.

Another holdover from the past is a persistent belief in *taian* (tie-ahn), or "great-luck days" and unlucky days, a superstition brought to Japan from China in the 1300s. *Taian* are a part of *rokuyo* (roe-kuu-yoe), or a "six-day cycle" of lucky and unlucky days. Generally speaking, three of the days in the cycle are good-luck days and three are bad-luck days, and some of the days are lucky in some respects and unlucky in others.

The unluckiest days in the cycle are known as *butsumetsu* (boot-sue-may-t'sue), which refers to the day Buddha died, and *tomobiki* (toe-moe-bee-kee), which means something like "trial day," when you never know what is going to happen.

The most auspicious of the days in the six-day cycle are called *taian*, which translates as "great luck." Most Japanese refer to the ancient Chinese calendar to select the most auspicious days for weddings, funerals and other ceremonies. Bad luck is supposed to befall anyone who attends a funeral on a *tomobiki* day, for example. A wedding held on a *butsumetsu* day is also believed to be inauspicious, and because of this superstition, professional wedding halls in Japan generally offer reduced rates on those days.

In the spring and fall, the most popular seasons for weddings, wedding halls and hotel banquet rooms that cater to wedding parties are usually booked on all *taian* days months in advance.

Ceremonies marking the beginning of construction on buildings, including private homes, are normally held on *taian* days if at all possible. Important business conferences are also generally scheduled to occur on auspicious days. Dates for elections and other such events are also selected with the *taian* days in mind.

When pinned down, most Japanese will say they really do not believe in *taian* or bad-luck days, but it is better to be safe than sorry, and they prefer not to dispute or disparage the feelings of those who are superstitious. Observing the rituals of *taian* may seem like a small and nonsensical thing to Westerners, but it is still meaningful enough to the Japanese that it should not be ignored. It is far better to have everyone feel positive about an event or ceremony than to risk offending people—or the gods of luck, who may just be lurking in the shadows.

待遇
Taigu
(Tie-goo)

Spreading the Red Carpet

Japan's Inland Sea, Seto Naikai (Say-toe Nigh-kigh), with its array of islands and islets and their varied coastlines, is so beautiful that a poetic viewer once described it as "A sight fit for the eyes of kings."

Over the centuries Japan's highly refined and stylized culture gave birth to manners and customs, particularly regarding the treatment of guests and dignitaries, that were also "fit for kings."

The customs and standards for treating dignitaries began at the emperor's court in the first centuries of Japan's existence as a unified country, and from there they spread to the courts of the provincial lords, many of whom were descendants of emperors. The class of samurai warrior families that arose during the 13th and 14th centuries helped to disseminate these customs and standards among the commercial and professional classes of Japan during later centuries. But it was a law known as *sankin kotai* (sahn-keen koe-tie), or "alternate attendance," passed in 1635 by Iemitsu Tokugawa, the third Tokugawa Shogun, that was to make Japanese hospitality a characteristic of all the people in Japan.

Sankin kotai required most of Japan's 270 provincial lords to spend every other year in Edo, the shogunate capital; this necessitated that the lords travel from their domains with a retinue of servants, aides and samurai warriors, and put up each night in special inns designed and operated for these special travelers. These lordly processions, known as *Daimyo Gyoretsu* (Dime-yoe G'yoe-rate-sue), or "Processions of the Lords," continued until 1862, just before the fall of the Tokugawa Shogunate in 1868. The lord of Maeda, the richest of the fiefs, was required to bring some 1,000 people with him on his biennial trips to Edo.

The provincial lords, or *daimyo*, and their chief retainers demanded the same style of behavior and the same level of service and hospitality from the staffs of these roadside inns as they did from their own servants when they were in their fief castles and Edo mansions. Thus, the *sankin kotai* system was a key factor in spreading the culture of the imperial, shogunate and clan courts among the ordinary people of Japan, and setting a standard of service and entertainment that came to be known as *taigu* (tie-goo), which might be translated as "service and entertainment fit for a king."

After the downfall of the Tokugawa Shogunate, the custom of extending *taigu* to guests and dignitaries was continued by Japan's political and military mandarins, by its business leaders, and, on a lower scale, by ordinary people.

It was not until the early 1950s, however, when the United States began pumping hundreds of millions of dollars a month into the Japanese economy to sustain its war in Korea, and Japanese manufacturers and traders began to entertain foreign importers who flocked to the country on buying sprees, that the custom of *taigu* came into its own.

By the end of the 1950s, Japan had the largest complex of bars, cabarets, clubs, geisha houses and massage parlors any country had ever seen. In addition, Tokyo, Osaka and other major cities had an unbelievable variety of world-class international restaurants.

Over the next four decades Japanese companies together spent billions of dollars each year on *taigu* for their suppliers and customers and for their own managers and executives, most of whom had generous monthly expense accounts for entertainment. Among my own circle of Japanese friends in the mid-1950s, one, a department manager in an oil company, had a monthly budget of 3,000 dollars for entertaining—an amount that was several times his monthly salary.

Taigu also has the meaning of "treating well," and the word also came to be used by companies as an adjunct to a managerial title that pertained to pay grade and prestige but not to duties or responsibilities. In other words, a person could be a *bucho taigu* (buu-shoe tie-goo), meaning he had been promoted to *bucho*, "general manager of a department," because of his long service, but he actually had no department under him because there were no *bucho* positions available.

The heyday of *taigu* entertainment in Japan ended with the collapse of the "bubble economy" in 1990 and 1991. But it is still a vital part of building and sustaining business and other professional relationships.

対人恐怖
Taijin Kyofu
(Tie-jeen K'yoe-fuu)

Fear of Getting Personal

During Japan's long feudal period, when the arbiters of social behavior were the authoritarian and often arrogant samurai warriors, morality was more a matter of following a very detailed and highly stylized etiquette based on hierarchical rank than abiding by universal principles of morality or proper behavior.

In this warrior-dominated society, it was necessary for the Japanese to exercise extreme care in how they spoke and behaved toward their superiors. When dealing with officials, any failure to use the right tone of voice and the right vocabulary, or to maintain the correct posture and manner, was regarded as a serious breach of morality that could have grave consequences. Living in this minutely structured and constantly monitored environment made the Japanese extraordinarily sensitive to all personal relationships and very uneasy when meeting unknown people for the first time—especially when the strangers were obviously their social superiors.

Over the centuries this situation resulted in the Japanese developing a pathological complex about meeting and interacting with strangers—something that present-day Japanese psychologists have recognized as a distinctive "Japanese thing." Japanese psychologists have labeled this neurotic reaction *taijin kyofu* (tie-jeen k'yoe-fuu), or "fear of personal relations," and say that it is the cause of many of the "complexes" that have traditionally afflicted the Japanese.

According to the psychologists, the *taijin kyofu* feelings of the Japanese began with having a poor or negative self-image, resulting from the fact that historically the people were generally not encouraged or allowed to develop strong personal opinions or to behave as individuals.

Another factor in the development of the *taijin kyofu* syndrome was the universal feeling among the Japanese that they were so different from others that non-Japanese could not possibly understand them, think like them, behave like them, or appreciate them. This exclusivity complex meant that the Japanese lived in a different dimension as far as foreigners were concerned because they were congenitally incapable of accepting outsiders into their inner circle, and they themselves could not step outside of their own cultural boundaries. They were therefore alone in the world.

All of these complexes made the Japanese compulsive comparers. Their very first reaction to new people and things was to instantly and automatically compare them with their built-in Japanese standards and expectations. Whomever they encountered was either regarded as inferior or superior to their culture. There was no in-between or equal class.

Japanese psychologists say that one of the strongest and most damaging of the inferiority complexes that have traditionally plagued them is their so-called *gaijin* (guy-jeen) complex, or "Caucasian foreigners complex," a complex based on the larger size of Caucasians, their superior physical strength, their white skin, their individual aggressiveness, and, until recent decades, their higher standards of living and superior technology. All of these attributes, the psychologists add, resulted in feelings of envy and anger, and produced uniformly negative feelings among the Japanese, both about themselves and about foreigners.

The psychologists say that Japanese men were more negative toward foreign men than toward foreign women, while the negative feelings of Japanese women toward foreign men were mild or nonexistent, and Japanese women were generally neutral or positive toward foreign women.

Japan's *gaijin* complex is still a major factor in business and in politics, where it continues to be discernible in virtually every company and government entity. But there are a growing number of Japanese who did not develop the complex as they grew up, or who overcame it after they reached adulthood, and these people are often in the group that is most likely to meet with foreigners as part of their work.

Taijin kyofu also continues to play a role in Japanese life. One of the biggest complaints of Japanese today is the amount of time and money they have to invest in nurturing "unpleasant" personal relationships that are essential to them and to their families' relationships with school authorities, doctors, government officials, their superiors at work, and so on.

Foreigners dealing with Japan should be aware that the very courteous reception and generous hospitality that the Japanese typically shower on visitors is a function of Japanese etiquette, and does not necessarily reflect their feelings or opinions. Before there is any possibility of getting beyond the etiquette barrier and divining the real feelings and attitudes of the Japanese, it is necessary to meet with them a number of times in completely informal situations, preferably over drinks—and there is no guarantee that this will work because they are masters at playing things close to their chests.

The good news is that the Japanese are very much aware of their negative feelings toward the outside world, and are striving to overcome them.

体験入隊
Taiken Nyutai
(Tie-ken N'yuu-tie)

Boot Camp for Company Recruits

Following the end of World War II, the lives of the Japanese began to change dramatically. The new American-imposed constitution that went into effect in 1947 eliminated the legal basis for the old feudalistic family system, and a variety of individual rights were guaranteed. The educational system was also reformed, with particular attention paid to eliminating its militaristic and nationalistic aspects.

These changes, combined with the influence of the seven-year occupation of the country by the victorious American forces and their allies, and the influx of American music and movies, were to have a profound effect on Japanese culture—an effect which is still unfolding today.

Japan's government was well aware of the cultural impact that these foreign influences were having on Japanese youth. When the country's postwar Self-Defense Force (SDF) was officially established in 1954, one of its mandates was to offer boot camp-style training to civilians who wanted to benefit from military discipline. The program was dubbed *taiken nyutai* (tie-ken n'yuu-tie), which can be translated as "personal experience enlistment." The government as well as parents and a number of companies actively encouraged young people to take full advantage of the SDF program.

But in the early years it was only nominally successful, because the idea of military training of any kind for any purpose was reviled by most young Japanese.

In the 1960s, larger Japanese companies began establishing their own recruit training programs to overcome the continuing breakdown in traditional values and behavior. Their programs combined psychological reorientation, group behavior, physical fitness, mental toughness and company loyalty. But by the end of the 1960s, the younger generation of Japanese were so different from their elders in their attitudes and behavior that they were called *shinjinrui* (sheen-jeen-rue-ee) or "new kind of people." Virtually all of the character and personality traits for which the Japanese had been famous for centuries—their passive obedience to all authority, their conformity in behavior, their group orientation, their tenacity in the face of all odds—had virtually disappeared.

In the eyes of many companies, the training that new corporate recruits received from in-house programs was no longer sufficient. By the mid-1970s, the Tochigi Bank had made it mandatory that its new employees would "enlist" in the SDF for a short but intense period of military "boot camp" training, prior to entering their own in-house training programs. Other companies in all categories of industry adopted the same policy. By the early 1990s the SDF was annually conducting some 1,600 boot camp programs nationwide for new corporate employees, training some 150,000 "corporate recruits" each year.

Also by this time, large numbers of Japanese companies had expanded and strengthened their own in-house training programs for new employees, often with extraordinary results. A visit to many of these companies today is like stepping back in time. Visitors are treated with the same traditional stylized etiquette that was characteristic of the Japanese for centuries.

However, the retraining of youth in the traditional etiquette and moral codes by corporate Japan involves less than one-fourth of the young people in the country. This surely means that all the in-house training and *taiken nyutai* combined will not be enough to guarantee that the old ways in Japan will be permanently preserved.

タレント
Tarento
(Tah-ren-toe)

People with Talent

Western-style entertainment is mostly a post-World War II phenomenon in Japan, and for the most part, it was introduced into the country by the American and allied military forces that occupied Japan from September 1945 to May 1952. During these years, all of the military and foreign civilian units in Japan had their cinemas and clubs, and most of the clubs featured live entertainment at one time or another. By the mid-1950s, live entertainment was one of the mainstays of a whole new, huge Japanese industry built around cabarets and nightclubs that catered to foreign residents, to foreign importers that began pouring into the country following the official end of the occupation, and to the large numbers of newly affluent Japanese manufacturers, traders and black marketers. The other mainstay of these nightspots was several hundred thousand hostesses, among whose numbers were some of the most intelligent, charming and beautiful women in Japan.

By the end of the 1950s, radio and television in Japan had progressed to the point that the broadcast industry needed large numbers of entertainers. But there were not enough show business professionals to go around, and most of those who had been working the nightclubs and cabarets did not fit the needs of the media. As a result, very few prewar veteran entertainers, such as Toni Tani, were on radio and TV for several hours every day, several days a week.

Finally, the lack of entertainers became so serious that it led to the appearance of large numbers of young boys and girls who had no professional training or experience, but who were packaged and offered to the public as *tarento* (tah-ren-toe), or "talent," whether or not they had any ability to entertain.

By the mid-1960s the selection, grooming and introduction of new *tarento* had become a major business. But out of the hundreds who debuted each year, there would be only two or three with real talent who went on to become true stars.

Among the *tarento* that appeared during the next several decades were a number of foreigners who had mastered, or mostly mastered, the Japanese language, including several former Mormon missionaries who had gone through the Church's excellent Japanese language training program and could now hold their own in the local language with ease.

At first, the use of the word *tarento* was confined to radio and television perform-ers, but it was soon applied to novice entertainers in other fields as well. Shintaro Ishihara, now known as one of Japan's most hawkish post-World War II politicians, was to broaden the scope of its usage. In the 1950s, when he was still in his twen-ties, Ishihara began publishing steamy novels about the sexual and other peccadil-loes of Japanese youth, and became rich and famous by the time he was 30. (His most famous book was called *Taiyo no Kisetsu* or *Season of the Sun*.)

In the 1960s, Ishihara followed this success by producing a number of highly pop-ular films starring his brother, Yujiro. In 1968 he ran for Japan's prestigious House of Councilors and received more votes than any other candidate in the election—giving rise to the use of tarento as *tarento koho* (tah-ren-toe koe-hoe), or "talent candidate."

In 1974 Teru Miyata, an NHK announcer, was elected to the House of Councilors, also winning by a landslide, and establishing a precedent that has since been fol-lowed by other entertainers and media celebrities.

Throughout the decade of the 1990s, Japanese television was monopolized by the few veterans that had emerged from the ranks of *tarento* who first appeared in the 1970s and 1980s. Joining these veterans was a continuous stream of fresh *tarento* drawn from huge numbers of teenagers who had responded to "talent searches" and "talent shows" sponsored by the television networks and other commercial organiza-tions. Well over 90 percent of the Japanese *tarento* introduced on television are in their mid-teens or younger, and 98 to 99 percent of them are out of the limelight and back in school within a few weeks or months of their debut.

Tarento is now also used in reference to movie starlets and would-be fashion mod-els who continue to flock to Tokyo from all over Japan and from around the world, seeking to have their moments of fame.Now it seems that virtually every situation comedy and game or quiz show on television must have its token foreign *tarento*, and their numbers come from the United States, Europe, Africa and Asia.

立役者
Tateyaku Sha
(Tah-tay-yahk Shah)

Finding the Kingpin

When Westerners first arrive in Japan one of the most awkward cultural dilemmas they experience is their inability to distinguish individual Japanese they meet from each other, unless the people concerned are distinguishable by a significant age dif-ference or some other striking physical characteristic.

The reason for this is that practically none of the physical characteristics that are commonly used in the West—such as the type of body build, hair and eye color, com-plexion, mannerisms, style of dress—are that useful in Japan, where everyone has black hair and black eyes, tends to have the same skin coloring, and shares many other physical and behavioral characteristics. Unfortunately, the hoary old cliché, that "they all look alike" is all too often true to an embarrassing degree, and over-coming the problem requires that newcomers focus much more carefully on every person they meet.

This particular problem can usually be resolved with a bit of conscious effort, but there is a related problem that is not as easily solved, and which can have far more than just embarrassing consequences. Historically, the Japanese have been forced to merge themselves into groups, to march in step with each other, and to be virtually indistinguishable from the crowd. This cultural imperative is illustrated by the old saying, *Deru kui wa utareru*, or "The nail that sticks up gets hammered down."

Theoretically, individualistic behavior is no longer taboo in Japan. In fact, since the early 1990s, the new conventional wisdom is that Japan cannot continue to survive and prosper in the increasingly complex world, unless people are unleashed from the old restraints and allowed to nurture their imagination and creativity as individuals.

The Japanese are now being encouraged by a growing number of social critics, independent economists, and a few maverick businesspeople to *suji wo tosu* (sue-jee oh toe-sue), or "act on principle," rather than follow the crowd. But such a fundamental change in Japanese behavior cannot occur quickly, especially in the business arena, where the old ways are so deeply embedded that it will take generations for them to gradually evolve into a more personal, individualistic approach to working together. In the meantime, the diffusion of authority and responsibility will remain the mainstay of Japanese management, and the problems that this presents to Westerners will remain an important and often critical issue.

However, despite all past efforts in Japan to homogenize the Japanese intellectually as well as emotionally and spiritually, there have always been significant differences in the intelligence and talents of individual Japanese. In virtually every business and professional group in Japan, of whatever size at whatever level, there is almost always a *tateyaku sha* (tah-tay-yahk shah) or "person who stands out as the key person" or the "kingpin of the group."

Tate means "stand up" or "stand out." *Yaku* means "office" or "position," and *sha* is "person." When used in a business context, *tateyaku sha* does not refer to the person in a group who has the highest title, but to the person who is recognized as being the most capable and the one everyone else in the group depends upon.

It usually does not take very long for other Japanese to recognize which person in a section or department is the *tateyaku sha* because their antennae are finely tuned to the verbal and nonverbal communication that takes place among group members.

Where Westerners are concerned, however, the challenge can be formidable. Most Westerners are not plugged into the same cultural wavelengths as the Japanese and cannot pick up on the right signals, so personally identifying a *tateyaku sha* ranges from very difficult to impossible. Westerners who have had in-depth experience in Japan and gained considerable insight into the Japanese Way often overcome the problem of identifying *tateyaku sha* by asking key Japanese contacts in the same company or in an affiliated company to single them out—something their contacts are invariably happy to do because they know how important it can be.

Foreign companies contemplating doing business with a particular Japanese enterprise should make a point of trying to identify in advance the *tateyaku sha* in all of the sections and departments that would be involved in the relationship.

多様化
Tayoka
(Tah-yohh-kah)

Going with the Flow

Throughout most of Japan's history, one of the primary goals of government, at both the national and local level, was to keep things as they were—to prevent fundamental changes that might disrupt the political status quo. Early contacts with Korea and China from around 300 to 700 were followed by long periods of virtual isolation from the rest of the world. Again in 1637, the government closed the country, and for well over 200 years (while the Industrial Revolution remade Europe and the United States), Japan practically stood still as far as technology and science were concerned.

Generally speaking, the policy of Japan's last shogunate dynasty, which reigned from 1603 to 1868, was to maintain the life-style that had evolved following the beginning of the shogunate system in 1185. During the exclusionary period of the last shogun, the government even banned the production and possession of guns, choosing to go back to the sword and the bow in a remarkable step that indicated the depth of its commitment to keeping things as they had been for centuries.

In this environment, there was no incentive for individual Japanese to innovate or invent. On the contrary, both custom and law actively prohibited change. Virtually the only thing the Japanese could safely do for hundreds of years was to improve upon things—and this they did with consummate patience and passion.

Following the final opening of Japan to the outside world in the 1850s, the Japanese used their extraordinary skills to copy and to improve upon Western products. And it was not until the 1950s, a hundred years later, that their world had changed to the point that they could begin to create new products and processes on their own. But even then, the fear that had built up over the centuries of any activity, including business competition that was not minutely structured and carefully controlled made creativity intellectually and emotionally taboo and continued to influence every facet of Japanese life.

It was not until the 1970s and 1980s that the Japanese were able to slough off most of the legacy of their sealed-in past and could begin to deal with the diversity that was being forced upon them. Within a relatively short period of time, the idea of *tayoh* (tah-yohh), or "diversity," went from being regarded as anti-Japanese and a sin, to being a new slogan for continued progress.

Today, *tayoka* (tah-yohh-kah), or "diversification," is a byword in Japan—but it is diversification within the ongoing Japanese context of things. There must still be structure and control for most Japanese to feel comfortable and safe in dealing with *tayoka*. Government bureaucrats and most businesspeople, in particular, are still very uncomfortable with diversity in thinking and behavior, and are not skilled in coping with them. Until they are, Japan will be at a serious disadvantage in dealing with the rest of the world.

Most diversification in Japan is therefore occurring from the bottom up—driven by maverick entrepreneurs and young people who are so different from their elders that they are known as *shinjinrui* (sheen-jeen-rue-ee) or a "new kind of people." This sea change in the economy and in the life-style of the Japanese is exactly the opposite of virtually all the other major changes that have occurred in Japan since the last days of the shoguns. Those changes were imposed from the top, by the government working in close collaboration with selected industrial combines.

Japan's ongoing weakness in dealing with diversity is one of the primary reasons for the successes the United States and other countries have had in competing with the Japanese in their home market as well as abroad.

手先
Tesaki
(Tay-sah-kee)

Putting Up a Front Man

As we have learned, there are a number of key factors that often make it difficult for outsiders to understand and deal effectively with their Japanese counterparts—or with the people whom they presume are their counterparts. One of these factors is that it is customary for Japanese businesspeople, diplomats and others to reveal as little as possible about their objectives when they engage in dialogue with others, while politely and unobtrusively getting as much as possible out of the other side.

Another aspect of Japanese behavior is their practice of concealing their true thoughts and motives behind facades, *tatemae* (tah-tay-my), and "clouds of smoke," *en maku* (enn mah-kuu), until they find out exactly what the other party is after—and sometimes even then they do not reveal their *honne* (hoan-nay), or "true intentions."

It is much easier than one might imagine for the Japanese to "control" most of their meetings in this manner. They almost always politely invite the other side to make their presentation first, thereby living up to Japan's famed courtesy and giving themselves an advantage at the same time. Just as significant is the fact that Westerners, especially Americans, habitually and gladly take the initiative in meetings with the Japanese, speaking first and in detail about their objectives.

A further aspect of Japanese behavior that is not common in the West, and which Westerners generally are not prepared for, is their custom of using *tesaki* (tay-sah-kee) in their dealings with others. The basic meaning of *tesaki* is "fingers," but its more common meanings include "pawn," and "agent," in the sense of "spy," and "cat's paw," in the sense of a person being used as a tool—all of which, of course, are negative connotations.

Probably the most conspicuous use of *tesaki* in Japan is in politics at its highest level. To hear some critics of the Japanese political system tell it, most of Japan's prime ministers in recent decades have been *tesaki*, put out in front by "shadow shoguns" who are the real power behind the office, another custom that has been common in Japan since the earliest times.

Political *tesaki* are, in fact, seen in Japan at virtually every level of government, from members of the Diet down to the mayors of cities, with those pulling the strings usually being a consortium of business interests in the area who provide the financing for their candidates.

In the area of business, one of the more common uses of a *tesaki* is to find out information about a rival company or a potential partner or acquisition without revealing the true identity of the interested party. Another use is for a large, well-known company to have a *tesaki* make purchases of one kind or another as a way of getting a better price than if a prominent company made the purchase.

There are also instances when one company is reluctant or refuses to do business with another company for some reason or other—something that has been fairly common in Japan—resulting in the use of a *tesaki* by one of the companies in order to conduct business without revealing its identity.

Japanese companies feeling out foreign firms will sometimes do so through a *tesaki* who is a junior member of their own staff. This is not done surreptitiously, but the low-level nature of the inquiry is deliberately done to prevent the foreign company from reading anything into the contact that the Japanese side does not want.

Foreign companies in Japan, as well as foreign residents, frequently make use of the *tesaki* ploy in order to stay behind the scenes. One of the more common occasions when foreigners use *tesaki* is when they are renting offices or residences. On these occasions foreigners use *tesaki* to prevent themselves from being gouged by landlords, and because the landlords sometimes refuse to rent to foreigners.

つーかー
Tsu-Ka
(T'sue-Kah)

Tuned to the Same Cues

To say that the typical Japanese on his or her first visit abroad is like a fish out of water is not as far-fetched as it may sound. One of the defining characteristics of life in Japan is that it is so programmed and marked with signs that it is totally predictable. Generally speaking, the Japanese know exactly what to expect when they go into a restaurant, a store, an office, or a home. They know how people are going to react to whatever situation that occurs, and the Japanese know how they are expected to act in turn.

One might say that there is nothing new or surprising in Japan, so people do not have to be on guard or constantly adjusting their thinking and behavior to accommodate the unexpected; this accounts for the befuddled look and lack of action when they are confronted with something different.

It is not that the Japanese prefer sameness, repetition and predictability. In fact, they are fascinated by new ideas and new things, but they do not accept new things or new ideas without going through a process of analyzing and Japanizing them—and at their own pace. It is because of intense, never-ending cultural conditioning in sameness and repetition that the Japanese are upset by surprises and prefer not to get involved with people or in situations that are unpredictable.

This is also one of the main reasons why Japanese manufacturers and exporters prefer to have their own distribution systems overseas, why Japanese tourists prefer that their travel arrangements abroad are handled by the branches or subsidiaries of Japanese travel companies, and why the Japanese are reluctant to do business with foreigners at all if there is a choice. They know how other Japanese behave, how meticulous and detailed Japanese businesses are, and how fastidious the Japanese are in maintaining personal and business relationships—all things that the Japanese need in order to feel comfortable and confident in any relationship.

Going abroad for the first time on their own, without any Japanese backup, therefore takes a great deal of courage for the average Japanese—and their concern goes much deeper than not being able to read signs or speak the local language. The *tsu-ka* (t'sue-kah), or "cultural cues," by which they have been guided in every aspect of their lives are no longer there. *Tsu* by itself means "being highly responsive to cues or hints," while *ka* refers to Japanese culture.

Once typical Japanese are outside of Japan, or in any strictly foreign environment, all of the expressions and posturing that have been the basis of their personal and professional relationships are gone. They tend to feel vulnerable, and generally react in one of two ways. They either become withdrawn and try to avoid interacting with non-Japanese, or they assume an arrogant, superior, insensitive stance and attempt to bully their way through everything. Many Japanese students who go abroad for short homestays become notorious for their insensitive, arrogant behavior—just the opposite of what is expected by their foreign hosts who have heard only about the extraordinary politeness of the Japanese. Japanese businessmen stationed abroad are also frequently accused of being arrogant and insensitive to the feelings of their foreign employees; Japanese employers are often not sufficiently open to questions, they offer few explanations, and sometimes they order workers around as though they were military commanders.

Of course, newly arrived foreigners in Japan suffer from the same inability to tune into the *tsu-ka* of the Japanese, and developing the ability to do so is not a casual thing that can be picked up easily or quickly. It takes a substantial amount of time and effort. However, there are times when doing things the Japanese way is the right thing to do, and there are times when the Japanese way can be a serious disadvantage.

Generally speaking, responding in the Japanese way insofar as personal etiquette is concerned is the courteous and thoughtful thing to do. But in business and political matters, and where clear, precise facts, complete understanding, and up-front decisions are essential, it is better to mix the "foreign way" with the Japanese way.

つき合い
Tsukiai
(T'sue-kee-aye)

Bonding with Your Associates

Years ago when I was the editor of a travel magazine in Tokyo, I was asked by one of the company's most aggressive Japanese advertising salesmen to go with him when he made calls on new prospects. I knew he wanted me to go with him so he could use my "foreign face" as leverage to get into the companies and see key *bucho* (buu-choe), or "department managers." At that time, Caucasian foreigners could get into the inner sanctums of almost any Japanese company without an appointment simply by presenting themselves and naming the person they wanted to see.

I also knew it was common practice for publications to solicit advertising from companies by offering to run articles about their presidents and their products.

But the advertising salesman was fully aware that I did not go along with that custom, so I asked him what kind of sales approach he was going to use, since our circulation was very small, and there was no legitimate business reason for the companies he had in mind to advertise with us. He said: "No sales approach! Just *tsukiai* (t'sue-kee-aye)!"

Tsukiai is still a magic word in Japan. It is sometimes translated as "friendship," but it goes well beyond the casual meaning this suggests, and is more like "social debt" or "social obligation." You "build" *tsukiai* with someone by associating with them, by helping them directly, and by doing favors for their families or close friends.

Tsukiai is the oil that fuels business relationships in Japan. Businesspeople and professionals go out of their way to create "debt" relationships with people within their own organizations and in other companies and government offices for the day they will need some kind of help, service or cooperation. Housewives work to build up a bank of *tsukiai* with school teachers, doctors and others whose goodwill and help they routinely need, primarily through gift-giving.

On the business front, the most common way of building *tsukiai* relationships has traditionally been after-hours drinking and dining in bars, cabarets and geisha houses, and in the 1970s, golf with business associates was added to this list.

In most companies, large or small, a sum of money is budgeted each month for *tsukiai* activities. In large companies the people authorized to spend most of this money are in marketing and sales jobs, but practically all managers have some kind of monthly *tsukiai* budget. Over the years I have palled around with Japanese friends who were authorized to spend thousands of dollars a month entertaining old clients and prospecting for new ones, and I benefited enormously from the custom.

Recently there have been opinions that Japanese-style *tsukiai*-building at eating and drinking establishments is losing its importance in the overall game of business in Japan. It is true that the number of cabarets is down from their heyday in the 1950s, 1960s and 1970s, when some of them, such as the great Mikado in Tokyo's Akasaka district, boasted as many as a thousand hostesses. But the night beat goes on. There are still as many bars and cabarets in Tokyo alone as in most countries, and the money spent *tsukiai* purposes amounts to several billion dollars yearly.

It is virtually impossible to do business with the Japanese without engaging in *tsukiai* activities because *tsukiai* remains an essential part of getting acquainted and building the personal trust that is the foundation for business relationships in Japan. The ability of businesspeople to function effectively in Japan can be virtually ruined if they become known as *tsukiai ga warui hito* (t'sue-kee-aye gah wah-rue-ee ssh-toe), or "a person who is not good at making and nurturing social relationships."

Fortunately for foreign businessmen, and younger Japanese as well, who do not relish spending two, three, or more nights a week out drinking for the purpose of *tsukiai*, it is now generally possible to achieve the same ends through breakfast and lunch meetings, or through golf or some other sports activity once or twice a month, with evening affairs limited to every other month or so.

During vital negotiations, however, it is often necessary to have after-hours drinking sessions two or three times a week in order to keep the negotiation process going forward, because it is often only during such gatherings that the Japanese are able to speak frankly and clearly.

腕
Ude
(Uu-day)

Having a Special Skill

Prior to industrialization in the last decades of the 19th century, Japan had a very sophisticated cottage-industry economy in which master artists and craftsmen abounded. The Japanese life-style had been refined to the point that the people were extraordinarily skilled in everything they did, from dicing foods and wrapping packages to constructing enormous wooden buildings.

It was also a tradition that every individual would develop a special skill of some kind, called *oiegei* (oh-ee-eh-gay-e)—especially an ability that could be used for entertaining others. People also took great pride in being able to play at least one group game with conspicuous expertise. This urge to excel in both professional pursuits and in at least one private endeavor not only survived Japan's transformation into an industrial economy in the 1870s, 1880s and 1890s, it was a key element in the transformation; it also played a major role in Japan's emergence a hundred years later as an economic superpower.

Probably the most common personal skill that the Japanese pursue today is singing, particularly in karaoke (kah-rah-oh-kay) bars. Karaoke is a compound made up of *kara*, meaning "empty," and the first syllables of the English word "orchestra." The word refers to an arrangement in which a person sings to recorded music—an audio or videotape player takes the place of a live orchestra. Many other Japanese make a special point of learning a foreign language, usually English. Others concentrate on photography, computer games, and the like.

The important point is that the Japanese have been culturally conditioned for centuries to develop a special *ude* (uu-day), literally "forearm," but the word is used colloquially to mean "ability" or "skill," in one or more areas, a factor that has contributed enormously to their economic achievements. In keeping with their cultural traditions of humility and maintaining a low profile, the Japanese by their very nature do not brag about their *ude*, and are very careful about when and how they demonstrate it, in order to avoid appearing arrogant.

Not surprisingly, the Western custom of emphasizing one's schooling, experience, and expertise is one of the things that grates on the sensibilities of the Japanese who associate with Westerners. Rather than brag about their accomplishments, the Japanese do not mention them at all, or they play them down—which is one of the reasons why Westerners so often underestimate the Japanese.

There are times, however, when it is appropriate for the Japanese to demonstrate their *ude*, and just one of these instances is the after-hours socializing in karaoke bars. These occasions are formally recognized as *ude no mise dokoro* (uu-day no mee-say doe-koe-roe), or "the time and place to show one's ability."

Besides karaoke bars, other *ude no mise dokoro* include singing at company parties, putting on entertaining skits during company trips to resorts, participating in sports events, giving a humorous speech at weddings, and acting as the master of ceremonies at a company or social function.

In addition to these more social occasions, it is also appropriate for some people to demonstrate their technical or professional *ude* by presenting papers at conferences or playing a role in negotiating sessions. Demonstrating *ude* in negotiating sessions has to be carefully timed and coordinated, however, in order not to reveal one's skill or expertise too soon and thereby putting the other side on guard.

Generally, the real experts in negotiations do not expound on the subject at hand—as Americans are wont to do. The experts sit and say nothing, taking in everything the other side has to say, or they may ask question after question. It is often not until after formal negotiating sessions, when the Japanese get together privately to debrief themselves and plan their strategy for the next meeting that the experts speak up.

Often, when the Japanese experts have someone else on their team ask the questions, foreigners conclude negotiations with Japanese groups without ever finding out who the experts are. When dealing with the Japanese, it does not always pay to show your *ude*.

初々しい
Uiuishii
(We-we-she-ee)

The Wiles of Naivety

There is something about the innocence of infants and the very young that brings out feelings of tenderness and protectiveness in the hearts of most people, including those who are generally not known for their sensitivity or kindness.

In Western societies, however, the innocence of young children is ordinarily gone by the time the children reach the age of six or seven—dispelled in large measure by the behavior of adults who see it as the antithesis of maturity. We commonly make fun of and criticize children who are slow in growing out of the innocence of childhood, and we sometimes abuse them as well. We see innocence and naivety as characteristics that are appropriate only for the very young.

In Japan, on the other hand, innocence and naivety had traditionally been regarded as highly admired traits in people of all ages, and something that was especially admired in adults. Both innocence and naivety were regarded as reflections of purity of heart, unselfishness, and a kind, forgiving nature. But as so often is the case in Japan's traditional culture, there was a dark side to this innocence factor. Men preferred that girls and young women be innocent as well as naive for the obvious reasons that it made them easier to dominate and use.

Even now in Japan, young women consciously as well as subconsciously frequently assume an innocent, naive mode when they are interacting with men, both for protection and to take advantage of the well-known weakness men have for such female behavior.

One of the most conspicuous of these occasions occurs in the so-called *mizu shobai* (me-zoo show-by), which literally means "water business," but figuratively refers to the country's famous nighttime entertainment trades. Cabaret girls routinely play the role of the naive innocent because they know it has a strongly seductive affect on most of their male customers.

But affectations of *uiuishii* (we-we-she-ee), or "charming naivety," are not limited to young Japanese females. Such role-playing is, in fact, a built-in feature of the behavior of most Japanese, male and female, and is a mainstay of the personality and manner they normally exhibit to others—especially to non-Japanese.

In addition to traditionally having been taught that naivety is an admirable trait, the Japanese were simultaneously conditioned to abhor the opposite kind of behavior. There was simply no normal place in Japanese society for know-it-alls, no matter how knowledgeable or talented they might actually be. This symptom remains a force to be reckoned with still. Dislike of such individuals is often so extreme that it results in some kind of behind-the-scenes action to bring the person down.

In addition to utilizing naive, innocent behavior to smooth their way within their own society, the Japanese became aware very early that such behavior works even better with outsiders, particularly Westerners. The Japanese learned that when typical Westerners meet an innocent and naive person, an automatic reflex sets in; they subconsciously presume that the person is child-like, and they then let their defense shields down, put most of their critical faculties on hold, and tend to fall all over themselves trying to help the poor innocent. Already masters at role-playing because of their highly stylized and demanding etiquette, Japanese businessmen and professionals are naturally adept at using an assumed innocence to put their Western counterparts at ease and to get extraordinary cooperation and help from them.

The more successful and older Japanese men become, whether businessmen, professionals, or yakuza gang leaders, the more they are inclined to assume a soft, gentle, innocent stance that perhaps can best be described as Buddha-like. How much of this Buddha-like character is make-believe and how much is real is often beside the point. Their image of virtuous selflessness gives them an aura of *uiuishii* that vastly increases their power because people look upon them as saint-like, incapable of evil, and, therefore, someone who can be trusted to say and do what is best for everyone.

Western businessmen, diplomats and politicians encountering such formidable figures should keep in mind that even Buddhas have agendas, and an unwavering will to win.

馬が合う
Uma ga Au
(Uu-mah ga Ow)

Harmonizing Your Horses

Horses have been familiar to the Japanese for at least 5,000 years. There is, in fact, growing evidence that Japan was first unified as a nation sometime around the end of the 3rd century by a group of horse-riding newcomers who arrived in Japan via the Korean Peninsula.

In any event, from this period on, horses became increasingly important in Japan as draft animals and as military mounts, and eventually they played a key role in the development and spread of Japanese culture and the Japanese empire. The civilian use of horses in Japan was primarily for pulling two-wheel carts and for hauling rice and other farm produce. Horses were not used for plowing fields because Japanese vegetable gardens were too small and the rice paddies, also small by Western standards, were flooded with water.

In 1870, two years after the fall of the Tokugawa Shogunate, two New Zealander brothers named Hoyt established a horse-drawn stagecoach service between Yokohama and Tokyo, and another company opened a stagecoach line between Odawara and Oiso, famous stops along the great Tokaido road that led to Kyoto. Shortly after the Hoyt brothers opened their stagecoach line, a number of Japanese entrepreneurs established stagecoach services connecting other remote towns— some of which continued until the appearance of buses well into the 1900s.

Japan's first horse-drawn streetcar service was inaugurated in 1882, and ran from Shimbashi to Nihonbashi in central Tokyo, a distance of about three miles. Because of the importance of horses in premodern Japan, many horse-related sayings referring to various social customs and Japanese characteristics became a part of the language. One of these sayings, *uma ga au* (uu-mah gah ow), which means more-or-less "the horses harmonize" or "the horses agree with each other," was a reference to people who got along exceptionally well. While the phrase itself is not likely to be heard in casual or business conversations today, particularly from younger Japanese, it is still a popular literary allusion and is especially meaningful to the Japanese.

All close and ongoing relationships in Japan, but especially business and political relationships, are based on the *uma ga au* or "harmony" concept, with a long list of reciprocal obligations that bind the parties to each other—just as a harness binds two horses to the same yoke. Businesspeople in particular are conditioned to go through lengthy get-acquainted periods before they commit themselves to important relationships. They must first determine if the other party can be depended upon, without reservation, to pull its share of the load and move forward in unison.

An even more important question is whether or not the two parties are stable and are compatible in their philosophy and policies.

Foreigners dealing with the Japanese should keep in mind that a great deal of this *uma ga au* approach to business and professional relationships is based on the fact that Japanese culture is far less forgiving than most Western cultures, and that individually the Japanese have far fewer options in their response to outsiders than do Westerners.

While Americans and others tend to regard mistakes as an expected part of life and as an educational experience, the Japanese are conditioned to regard mistakes as a failure in character, to dread them, and to do everything possible to avoid them— which accounts for a great deal of their slow, methodical approach in everything they do.

Of course, there are a growing number of "wild horses" in Japan today; those that buck tradition and try to behave like cowboys. But they are few, and they often get bucked off and stomped on.

裏方
Urakata
(Uu-rah-kah-tah)

The Hidden-Person Ploy

One of the aspects of Japanese culture that historically has been especially irritating and confusing to Westerners is the custom among the Japanese of diffusing power within a group; this makes it difficult or impossible for a single individual, no matter how senior in rank, to make decisions on his or her own. This diffusion of responsibility and authority was one of the sources of the "mystery of the Orient" factor that has long influenced East–West relations, and continues today to be an obstacle that helps to perpetuate the "East is East and West is West" syndrome.

At the same time, there have traditionally been individuals in China, Japan, and other parts of Asia who often had no impressive title, but who ruled with almost godlike power—not so much because of their talents, but because the people around them needed an absolute power to direct them and to keep them together.

Another feature of the culture that has traditionally played a key role in business and politics in Japan is the custom of keeping the most important figure in a negotiating session or other important event behind the scenes as an *urakata* (uu-rah-kah-tah), which literally means "back-side person." In its Japanese context, an *urakata* can be the most senior person in a group, or a person who has some special knowledge that everyone else depends upon. This special person is often kept in the background, more-or-less as a secret weapon.

One of the most fascinating examples of this kind of subterfuge occurred in the mid-1800s when the United States and other foreign countries were pressuring Japan to open its doors to trade and other kinds of intercourse with the rest of the world. When shogunate officials engaged in negotiations with America's Commodore Perry in 1853, they kept their interpreter hidden behind a screen during the entire proceedings and did not allow him to meet any of the Americans.

Generally speaking, there are *urakata* behind the scenes in virtually all of Japanese dealings. In some cases these unseen individuals are just ordinary people who do the "thankless" work involved in getting ready for and conducting meetings. In other cases, they are specialists of one kind or another who provide support for the main team.

The nature of the term *urakata* suggests that it relates to some activity that the Japanese do not want to do out in the open—an activity that will give them an advantage over the other side. And where negotiations with foreign businesspeople and government officials are concerned, this is often the case.

There may or may not be anything especially malicious about the *urakata* custom; that depends upon the circumstances and the individuals involved. But *urakata* is symptomatic of the Japanese custom of revealing as little as possible about their own intentions when engaged in negotiating, and of the custom of having knowledge and maneuvers that they can use to spring on their counterparts at the right time. Using this kind of strategy and tactics is not immoral or unfair as far as the Japanese are concerned. It is a matter of being smart and better prepared than the other side.

Because Western negotiators tend to be open and tend to depend upon facts logically and completely presented without any subterfuges, they often put themselves at a disadvantage when dealing with the Japanese by revealing their entire game plan and goals up front. Virtually the only effective way to level the negotiating table is to refrain from giving a complete summary of the arrangement desired during introductory comments, and then proceed with a point-by-point approach, getting everyone to sign off on each point as it is covered and agreed upon. At the same time, it is wise to always keep something in reserve for an unexpected move by the Japanese side.

See *Ihyo wo Tsuku*.

恨みを買う
Urami wo Kau
(Uu-rah-me oh Kow)

Buying into Trouble

During Japan's long samurai-dominated feudal age (1185–1868), the most common form of penal execution was beheading with a sword. Just before the fatal stroke, some executioners would order their victims to *kubi wo nagaku!* (kuu-bee oh nah-gah-kuu), or literally, "Make your neck longer!" The reason for ordering prisoners to stretch their necks was to provide the swordsmen with larger targets, and to make it easier for their swords to pass through the neck bones.

This practice led the Japanese to associate any risky actions with stretching one's neck out, and thereby making it easier for potential competitors or enemies to strike them a damaging or possibly fatal blow. The laws and very precise etiquette of premodern Japan were such that it was necessary to take extreme measures to avoid getting on the wrong side of anyone who could cause harm. While people had to be especially circumspect in their behavior toward arrogant warriors and authoritarian officials, virtually all Japanese were extremely sensitive about being shown proper respect, and when they felt they had been slighted, revenge of some kind was a must.

This syndrome led the Japanese to be extremely cautions about *urami wo kau* (uu-rah-me oh kow), which literally means "to buy (invite) jealousy, resentment, bitter feelings." Several generations have passed since the end of the samurai era in Japan, but the legacy of those many centuries remains evident in present-day Japan. People are still exceptionally sensitive to any perceived verbal or behavioral slight, and while they no longer literally take the heads of their targets, they do resort to both subtle and blatant measures to punish or eliminate them.

People are still frequently admonished to *urami wo kawanai de* (uu-rah-me oh kah-wah-nie day), which, paraphrased, means "don't invite rancor, jealously or revenge." The sensitivity of the Japanese to *urami* feelings has a direct, fundamental influence on their relations with all foreigners. It is symptomatic of the Japanese to feel that Westerners tend to look down on them and regard them as inferior. They are always on their guard for any indication of this belief, and they often see it when it does not exist because they are unable to judge foreign behavior.

Unfortunately, Japanese suspicions of the racial and cultural arrogance of many Westerners are all too often correct, and their age-old beliefs are reinforced again and again. Because of this factor, anti-foreign feelings are just below the surface in most Japanese, generally including those who have foreign friends. These individuals, who are numerous, avoid the bind of any dichotomy in their feelings by regarding their foreign friends as exceptions to the rule—and typically they say their foreign friends are not really foreign anymore, and that they have "become Japanese," which totally eliminates the contradiction.

Foreigners involved with Japan at any level, for any purpose, should keep in mind that the Japanese capacity for *urami* is limitless and unbounded, and can materialize in an instant over things that the outsider regards as neutral, benign and safe, or at least acceptable. More and more Japanese are developing the thick cultural skin that protects most Westerners from slings and arrows, real and imagined, but it will be some time in the future before this cultural change occurs in the majority of the Japanese population.

煩い
Urusai
(Uu-rue-sigh)

Hard to Please

When Japan industrialized during the last three decades of the 19th century, American and European importers were quick to take advantage of the remarkable ability of the Japanese to copy—and often make improvements to—Western products at costs that were substantially below that which prevailed abroad. These overseas importers constantly pressured their Japanese suppliers to produce goods for them at still lower prices, with the result that most of the things the Japanese made for export were of very low quality.

The attitude of the foreign buyers astounded the Japanese. They could not understand why people would buy such shoddy merchandise, and the Japanese referred to it derisively as *Yokohama hin* (Yo-koe-hah-mah heen), or "Yokohama goods," in reference to the fact that most of it was shipped out of the port of Yokohama.

The amazement of the Japanese came from the fact that over a period of nearly 2,000 years their own product quality standards had become so high that virtually everything they made was superior in both design and construction. Theirs had been a classic cottage-industry economy. Craft skills were based on a training system in which apprentices worked under masters for periods that lasted from five or six to 20 and even 30 years.

As a result of this system, all of the crafts for which Japan was later to become famous, including pottery, ceramics, lacquer ware, wooden ware and metalwork were raised to the level of art.

This long history of intensive training in work skills, combined with the application of a high order of aesthetics to their arts and crafts, imbued the Japanese with extraordinarily high standards and a built-in *urusai* (uu-rue-sigh) reflex to everything they were exposed to. The original meaning of *urusai* was something or somebody who was "persistently annoying," or "troublesome." Over time it also came to mean someone characteristically fastidious and fault-finding. Generations of cultural conditioning in aesthetics and in the manufacture and use of handicrafts that had been turned into works of art made the Japanese the most *urusai* people in the world.

Japanese consumers and shoppers carefully considered and examined every product they wanted to buy. They automatically scanned it with a built-in "cultural probe" that penetrated to its essence. If there was any flaw or any weakness in the material, the design, or the fabrication of the product, the fault registered instantly and the Japanese consumer rejected it. Thus, when they were first exposed to the quality of goods that were being demanded by American and European importers, they were both shocked and contemptuous of Western standards.

It was not until the early 1960s, however, that Japanese manufacturers were able to escape from the clutches of foreign importers, and then they began producing high-quality Western-style products. During the previous decade they had combined their own historical experience and standards with statistical quality-control methods taught to them by W. E. Deming and J. M. Juran, both American authorities on the subject.

Present-day Japanese are still among the most *urusai* consumers in the world, but as with so many other traits that they inherited from their past, their fastidiousness is being tempered by the new times. Still, it is common to hear the phrase, *shumi nado ni urusai* (shuu-me nah-doe ne uu-rue-sigh), meaning "fastidious in taste," "fussy," "meticulous," to describe Japanese shoppers, and they are still far more discerning and selective than run-of-the-mill consumers in other countries.

One of the aspects of the *urusai* character of Japanese consumers is that they expect the whole product to be "finished" and "detailed." That is, they expect the insides, the bottoms and other areas that generally cannot be seen to be "done." The Japanese also tend to want to buy accessories that may be used with products. They normally do not just buy a camera, for example. They also buy a case, additional lenses, a tripod, a light meter, and so on.

Foreign companies wanting to sell consumer products in Japan must contend with the "hard to please" eye of the Japanese.

Wakai
(Wah-kigh)

Making Honorable Concessions

In Japan, judicial decisions are not so much based on written laws as on the traditional mores of the society. Historically, Japanese judges have skirted and stretched laws in order to deal more fairly and with more common sense in their decisions regarding the public. During Japan's long feudal age, when town magistrates acted as judge and jury, and the laws of the shogunate tended to be harsh and unforgiving—death within hours of sentencing was a common punishment—some of the greatest heroes of the age were magistrates who used Solomon-like wisdom to resolve disputes and mete out punishment.

A key factor in the approach to law enforcement in Japan is an expectation that both parties to any dispute will compromise their positions to the point that they can reach a settlement before the case goes to trial—a process known as *wakai* (wah-kigh), which translates as "reconciliation" or "harmonious dissolution."

There were many reasons for the popularity of *wakai* in feudal Japan. One important reason was that it was the custom to treat both parties in a dispute as guilty, although one side was generally more guilty than the other. The rationale was simple. It takes two people to quarrel or fight. Making both parties subject to punishment was a powerful incentive for people to avoid confrontations that could come to the attention of the authorities.

Another reason for *wakai* was that guilt in premodern Japan also tended to be collective. That is, the family and sometimes the whole community of a criminal or a suspect were treated as equally guilty and subject to punishment.

Probably the most famous case of collective responsibility occurred during the early decades of the Tokugawa Shogunate (1603–1868) when a farmer named Sogo went over the head of an onerous local lord and handed the shogun a petition seeking redress from the high taxes imposed on farmers in his area. The shogun sent investigators to the fief, and subsequently ordered the fief lord to lower the taxes. But the local lord had his revenge by having Sogo, his wife and his two young sons beheaded for embarrassing him.

Another element in the propensity of the Japanese to avoid courts was the deeply ingrained custom for the offended party to take revenge against whomever brought the complaint against them.

Legal punishment in Japan is no longer collective. Plaintiffs are no longer legally regarded as bearing some of the guilt in a dispute. But the element of revenge has not disappeared, and the winner in a lawsuit often suffers as much, if not more than the losing party. The reputation of the plaintiff is invariably damaged because such an action is still regarded as "un-Japanese," and is looked upon as immoral and irresponsible. The feeling is that anyone who will resort to a lawsuit cannot be trusted.

Just as in feudal times, most Japanese courts require that the parties in a disagreement bring in substantial evidence that they have tried to settle the dispute themselves before the courts will agree to accept the case. As a result of these cultural factors, most disputes in Japan are resolved by mediation, either directly between the parties concerned, or through a mediator. There are professional mediators who belong to the Japan Association of Mediators, which publishes a guide called *A Handbook of Mediation*.

Another holdover from feudal times is the custom of asking local gang bosses to act as arbiters—a practice that is especially common in disputes involving construction and transportation companies, as well as politics, where organized gangs are powerful.

Foreign individuals and companies in Japan are well advised to make use of mediators and arbiters in any case they might become involved in, whether it concerns something as mundane as a dispute with a landlord, or one as serious as an accident that resulted in death or a criminal charge.

Americans and other Westerners are generally conditioned to think in terms of the letter of the law. The Japanese, on the other hand, regard the law as a last resort, and think of laws as suggested guidelines.

和気あいあい
Waki Aiai
(Wah-kee Aye-aye)

Living in Happy Harmony

There is something in the traditional cultural artifacts of Japan that appeals very strongly to the emotions, to the intellect, and to the spirit of aesthetically sensitive people. This special essence of things Japanese consists of a highly refined balance of materials, and includes the nature of the material and the forms contributed by the artists and craftsmen.

Japanese artists, craftsmen, designers and others who are skilled in creating this special essence say the secret of their art lies in working with the nature and spirit of the medium so that the person viewing the art can commune with that nature and spirit, and draw strength and feelings of harmony and well-being from it. Japanese arts and crafts, including utilitarian household articles, have therefore traditionally served as links between the physical world and the world of spirits, sentimentality and the intellect.

It is probable that this respect for and worship of the beauty of harmony in nature also contributed to the Japanese feeling that in a social system, harmony should also be the overriding rule in all personal relationships. *Waki aiai* (wah-kee aye-aye), which literally means "harmony/spirit/love/sharing," is one of the Japanese code words that refer to the idealized harmonious relationship between people—and especially between managers and workers.

While virtually the whole web of traditional Japanese morality was designed to encourage harmony, it was a hierarchical harmony based on the political imperatives of those in power, rather than serving on the individual needs and aspirations of the people at large. *Waki aiai* was, in fact, a tool used by those in power to exercise political, economic and spiritual control over all levels of Japanese society. In this context, *waki aiai* was given precedence over the welfare of the human spirit, and rather than enhance life, it was responsible for a great deal of suffering.

Although *waki aiai* exalted the spiritual side of life, it made rote obedience to higher authority and an ultrastrict physical etiquette the highest expressions of morality. Because of this denial of human nature on the one hand, Japan's culture spawned a series of contradictions that regularly brought the rational side of the Japanese into conflict with unnatural attitudes and behavior that ranged from painful to self-destructive.

The code of the samurai warrior class that ruled Japan for almost 700 years was perhaps the most far-reaching of these contradictions because it was based in large part on beliefs and practices that were anti-human. The ritual of ceremonial suicide by cutting open one's stomach was perhaps one of the more bizarre examples of the code's requirements.

In contemporary Japan the ideals of *waki aiai* would often seem to have gone with the samurai, but they remain an easily identified and significant part of the business and professional cultures. The prevailing system still requires its members to conform to age-old behavioral patterns that gloss over or totally ignore their feelings and their personal welfare. Few adults in contemporary Japan can escape the obligation to conform to the demands for a cooperative attitude and harmonious behavior, regardless of how unpleasant or harmful such behavior might be.

Waki aiai is also one of the many traditional Japanese cultural factors that continue to have an impact on Westerners involved in business or professional relations with Japanese companies and organizations. Westerners typically have difficulty interacting efficiently with the Japanese because the *waki aiai* factor requires that the Japanese give precedence to time-consuming consensus and group harmony, the latter oftentimes on a national scale, and frequently with strongly nationalistic overtones.

The fact that *waki aiai* practices regularly conflict with the Western way of doing things does not necessarily mean that they are always inherently irrational, or always wrong. But there is no denying that they constitute a cultural barrier that, not surprisingly, the Japanese themselves are finding more and more burdensome.

Because harmony has been the fundamental ethic in Japanese society for so many centuries, however, *waki aiai* is not going to disappear in one short generation. For a long time to come, Westerners will simply have to accommodate themselves to a different way of thinking and doing things.

和製英語
Wasei Eigo
(Wah-say-ee Aa-ee-go)

Made-in-Japan English

I once had an American friend who had lived in Japan for some ten years, but spoke only a few words of the Japanese language. What he could do with amazing facility, however, was speak "Japanized" English fluently, and be understood most of the time by Japanese who could not speak or understand "regular" English. The reason he could communicate fairly well with Japanese by pronouncing English with a strong Japanese accent was because that is the way the Japanese had learned English.

It is not recommended that other foreigners try to get by in Japan using only Japanized English. But it is necessary for students of the Japanese language to learn how to pronounce a great many English words that have been incorporated into Japanese—as well as pick up on new meanings that are part of the Japanization of these words.

Since 1945, the Japanese have been repeating a phenomenon that first occurred nearly 2,000 years ago—namely, importing thousands of words from a foreign country, Japanizing them, and merging them into the Japanese language. The first time this phenomenon occurred the foreign language was Chinese. This time it is English. More than 10,000 English words have become *Wasei Eigo* (Wah-say-ee Aa-ee-go), or "Made-in-Japan English," in the past several decades, and new ones are regularly being added to the list.

There are several reasons why the Japanese are such avid word importers. Some of the words that are imported do not exist in Japanese. In other cases, there are dictionary equivalents in the Japanese language, but the nuances or usages of the English are different enough from those of their Japanese equivalents that they are like new words. In still other cases, the Japanese take an English word or phrase and give it an entirely new meaning—so different from the original English that there is no way native English speakers can understand it without learning it as a "Japanese word" rather than an English word.

Most *Wasei Eigo* words are first introduced into Japan by the mass media, including newspapers, business publications, fashion magazines, entertainment magazines and comic books. Advertising agencies and businesses are also great creators of *Wasei Eigo*, especially words that are given a new spin in order to appeal to the emotional side of the Japanese by suggesting sophistication, something foreign, romance and happiness. If the words are really catchy and useful, they "catch on" and thereafter appear in the annual collection of new words.

I recall one example of *Wasei Eigo* that mystified the foreign community in Japan for a while. Someone in the restaurant business, possibly a Chinese restaurant located in an annex to the Shimbashi Daiichi Hotel in Tokyo, adopted a buffet format, and began promoting its new service as *baikingu* (by-keen-guu) the Japanese pronunciation of "Viking," no doubt in a take-off on the Swedish custom of serving many different dishes on long tables. In any event, the style became very popular, especially in the hotel industry. Diners paid a set sum and could refill their plates as many times as they wanted to, guaranteeing that *baikingu* would be integrated into the vocabulary of all Japanese.

Some of the more common examples of *Wasei Eigo* include *pasokon* (pah-so0kohn), "personal computer"; *eakon* (ee-eh-kohn), "air conditioner"; *supaa* (suu-pah), "supermarket" (A *supaa* usually refers to any market larger than a convenience store; the word also refers to subtitles on a film and is derived from "superimpose"); *reberuappu* (reh-bay-rue-ah-poo), "level up"; *fronto* (frohn-toe), "front desk" (the reception desk at a hotel); and *furita* (foo-ree-tah), "freelancer" (a person who does odd jobs for various companies instead of being employed full-time by one company; the word is derived from "freelance writer").

Foreign businesspeople are advised to carefully check any trade name or slogan they propose to use in Japan, whether it is a translation from English or a transliteration of an English word into Japanese, to be sure that the Japanese version of the English is accurate and safe.

役得
Yakutoku
(Yah-kuu-toe-kuu)

A Dangerous Perk

Among the most subtle facets of Japan's traditional culture are the attitudes and customs that developed to prevent official and commercial power from corrupting the society. Outright bribes of cash or kind have always been strictly taboo in Japan, and in earlier centuries were discouraged by a variety of sanctions that included banishment and capital punishment. But this did not mean that important positions in society did not require certain kinds of influence or that the powerless were left in a hopeless situation, unable to influence those in power in any way.

Japan's Establishment was fully aware of human weaknesses, the temptations that occur, the need for people to gain pardons and favors from those in power, and the benefits to be gained by the powerful; therefore, it sanctioned institutionalized forms of gift-giving and entertainment that made it possible for people from all levels of society to achieve a kind of balance of power by obligating those whose goodwill and cooperation they needed.

In present-day Japan gifts are given to family members and friends on individual occasions, and to others anytime that one needs some kind of favor. Twice a year, in midsummer and at the end of the year, virtually the whole population gives gifts to people on whom they depend for their livelihood and welfare, from bosses to teachers.

A special word, *yakutoku* (yah-kuu-toe-kuu), is used to describe the benefits that invariably flowed to those in positions of power in government, in commercial business, and in the professions. *Yaku* means "position," and *toku* means "benefit." The extent and value of the *yakutoku* offered to individuals depend upon their position and its importance in relation to others.

A bureaucrat whose approval is needed for a business license or for other important purposes, can expect to be offered a great deal of valuable *yakutoku*. Managers who are in charge of purchasing for their companies are also courted enthusiastically with *yakutoku* by people who want to get business from them.

Playing the game of *yakutoku* gifts and entertainment is not as simple as it might seem. It requires a great deal of insight into when such a benefit can be offered, how it should be offered, what its value should be, and whether it should be a gift, entertainment, or some other kind of favor. Any misjudgment could result in exactly the opposite effect from what is desired.

Government officials in particular are especially sensitive about receiving *yakutoku* from the public, because a smudge on their image could destroy their career.

It is always safer to offer entertainment than gifts, because the individual concerned can always decline an invitation to go out, and if he or she accepts, there is usually no physical evidence left to make anyone look bad. The most common *yakutoku* in Japan's business world is lunch, because it is usually the least expensive, the least intrusive on anyone's schedule, and the least likely to get anyone into any trouble.

The higher the rank of the businessperson or government official, the more delicate the *yakutoku* practice becomes. As a general rule, high-ranking people will not go to lunch or go out in the evening with anyone below their own rank, or anyone who is not capable of becoming a major benefactor. It is very dangerous for someone of low rank to offer someone of high rank an expensive gift because the ulterior motive is too obvious. People in some professions, such as lawyers, doctors and professors, may accept gifts without flinching, but businesspeople and government officials may not.

The best way for foreigners to deal with this custom when politicians or bureaucrats are concerned is to seek advice from their secretaries—usually men—about whether or not a gift is appropriate, or how to give it. Where businesspeople are concerned, an experienced Japanese friend can usually give valid advice.

やくざ
Yakuza
(Yah-kuu-zah)

The Honorable Gangsters

For most foreigners, Japan's famous yakuza (yah-kuu-zah), or professional criminals, represent one of the more conspicuous contradictions in Japanese mentality and behavior. The most common question asked by these foreigners is: how can the Japanese, from the highest echelons of the government down to corner policemen, as well as the public at large, countenance the existence of these criminal gangs?

This mystery is especially intriguing to outsiders who are familiar with the strong sense of law and order that prevails in Japan, and who are aware that Japan is rightfully known as one of the world's safest countries in terms of personal security. As usual, the explanation for this aspect of the Japanese character originates in feudal times, when the concept of "human rights" in the contemporary sense did not exist in Japan, and the general population was subject to the harsh dictates of the shogunate and to the often murderous whims of arrogant samurai warriors.

After clan lord Ieyasu Tokugawa became supreme in the country in 1603 and established the Tokugawa Shogunate, he created a system of strictly enforced laws that brought peace and an unprecedented period of prosperity to the country. By the 1700s there were thousands of rich merchants in the cities of Edo, Kyoto and Osaka, and a relatively affluent middle class. The traditionally small and inconspicuous courtesan districts, now patronized by the well-to-do, grew into virtual cities within cities. Arts, crafts and literature, much of it centered around the great red-light districts, flourished as never before. Gambling became a major industry, attracting the lower elements of the society, from petty criminals to *ronin* (roe-neen), masterless samurai.

As gambling expanded and professional gamblers prospered, they become increasingly independent and defiant of the shogunate authorities, particularly of the local, arrogant samurai who had traditionally used their elite status and ready swords to abuse and otherwise take advantage of ordinary people. As time passed, it became something of a custom for gamblers, who had to be brave and resourceful men to survive in an illegal enterprise, to come to the aid of people who were being harassed by samurai and local shogunate authorities.

In further defiance of the authorities, these "Robin Hood" gamblers began referring to themselves as yakuza, a word taken from the most popular card game of the day. The game, in which the sum of three cards determined a winning hand, was similar to blackjack, but with far fewer numerical possibilities for winning. The goal of the game was to come as close to 19 as possible without going over.

A hand that included an 8, *ya*, a 9, *ku*, and a 3, *sa* or *za* added up to 20-*yakuza*, and was therefore a losing hand. When a player drew this hand, the dealer would call out "*yakuza!*," which was the equivalent of "bad hand," or "loser." In adopting this name for themselves, the gamblers were literally warning authorities and others that they were tough men and not to be messed with.

As the decades passed, the number of yakuza gamblers grew. They gradually developed their own special argot and code of ethics that included taboos against attacking or fleecing ordinary people. They eventually became so powerful that they were able to influence, and sometimes control, local and regional shogunate authorities. Following the downfall of the Tokugawa Shogunate in 1868 and the subsequent industrialization of Japan, the yakuza moved into such industries as prostitution, entertainment, construction and transportation.

The yakuza not only survived Japan's defeat in World War II and the American military occupation of the country, they took advantage of the turmoil following the defeat and occupation to expand their numbers and their influence. By the end of the 1950s, there were more than 2,000 yakuza gangs in the country, with over a hundred thousand members.

With their increasing wealth, the large gangs began supporting political candidates. In the 1960s, yakuza gangs and members began buying stocks in major corporations, which put them in the position of being able to use pressure tactics to extort certain "fees" from the companies.

The activities as well as the individual leaders and members of the yakuza gangs were well known to the police. But generally no action was taken against them unless they committed a murder, and murder usually involved a turf dispute with another gang, or a personal run-in between members of different gangs.

Records of the National Police Agency show there were some 2,500 yakuza gangs and around 110,000 gang members in 1978. By the last half of the 1990s, the number of gangs had fallen to well under 2,000 and the number of gang members to around 70 thousand.

But during the intervening years, the operations of the yakuza had became increasingly sophisticated. In addition to moving into a variety of other industries, including tourism and drugs, and setting up operations overseas, the gangs continued to play an important role in the local, provincial and national politics of the country.

At any one time, anywhere from a few to dozens of yakuza chieftains, their aides and bodyguards can be seen in major hotels in Tokyo, Osaka, Kobe, and elsewhere, attending meetings and socializing just like other businessmen.

An unknown but significant number of foreign enterprises, joint ventures and other relationships in Japan involve yakuza elements that are generally known to the Japanese but not the foreign side.

Yakuza have traditionally been vehement nationalists, and are often very conspicuous during political protests and campaigns. Their ties go to the top of the political power structure.

Following an earthquake that devastated the city of Kobe and adjoining cities on January 17, 1995, Kobe yakuza mobilized their impressive forces to provide food, clothing and other essentials to dozens of thousands of residents who had lost everything. It was pointed out by the news media covering this extraordinary event that the yakuza were far more effective in helping Kobe residents than either the national or local governments during the first weeks following the disaster because they were organized.

The news media also noted that most of the items donated by the yakuza were obtained from local merchants and corporations "who dared not refuse their requests."

The city of Kobe has been the "corporate" headquarters of Yamaguchi Gumi, Japan's largest yakuza organization, for several generations.

やらせ

Yarase

(Yah-rah-say)

Beware of Intimidation

Juvenile delinquency, virtually unknown in predemocratic Japan, is now commonplace. Even more surprising to those who knew traditional Japan is the fact that young girls between the ages of 12 and 17 are just as likely to be involved in illegal activities and various forms of violence as boys of the same age.

Incidents of prostitution, bullying, beatings and extortion by young girls first began to appear in the national news in the 1970s, heralding a totally new phenomenon in Japanese society. These incidents were not random or independent actions by individuals. They were carried out by gangs of girls, and were meticulously planned and coordinated.

Japanese sociologists labeled this kind of youthful violence *yarase* (yah-rah-say), which literally means "coercion," "threat" or "pressure," and they explained this previously unheard of behavior by both young boys and girls as an irrational response to pressure put on Japanese children and youths; moreover, they maintained the educational system is chiefly responsible for the pressure because it emphasizes rote learning aimed at passing tests to get into the better universities.

In the summer of 1985, part of a TV Asahi newscast showed two teenage girls beating five younger grade school girls at a riverside barbecue party—a scene that created a public outcry. But it was later revealed that the scene had been staged by the TV program director, causing even more outrage. The president of TV Asahi fired the director, canceled the news program, and apologized to the public for the incident. The director, his assistants, and the two girls were arrested and fined. The director's excuse for staging the incident was that he wanted to emphasize the seriousness of the juvenile delinquency problem in the country.

Because of this incident, the news programs on all of Japan's TV networks came under closer scrutiny, and it was subsequently reported that such "rigging" of the news was in fact common, and from that time on, *yarase* took on the additional meaning of rigging a situation in an attempt to make a point or achieve a goal.

While it was the problem with juvenile delinquency and the scandal caused by the rigged TV show that made *yarase* a household word, *yarase* itself had, in fact, been an integral part of Japanese society since ancient times. Japan's traditional manners and ethics made open negotiations and debate taboo. This forced the Japanese to work behind the scenes by persuasion and *yarase* in their attempts to achieve their aims. The Japanese government in particular has historically depended upon *yarase* to implement its policies and programs, and enforce its laws.

The *yarase* element continues to play a key role in both politics and business in Japan today, although the government has lost a great deal of its power to control the people and industry through threats and legal sanctions. In business settings, large companies routinely use *yarase* to control or influence their suppliers. In fact, Japan's now controversial *keiretsu* (kay-ee-rate-sue) system was traditionally based on the use of *yarase*, and it was not until the early 1990s that some of these "aligned" firms began to resist being intimidated by their "patron" customers.

Japanese companies also automatically use *yarase* in their relationships with foreign firms whenever they are in a position to do so, because that is their standard way of operating.

Over the centuries, the Japanese in general have become extremely clever at disguising their use of *yarase* within the context of the culture, making it such an integral part of the culture that it was generally accepted as normal. It was not until the traditional Japanese way of doing things began to weaken, and in some cases break down entirely, during the 1970s and 1980s, that both ordinary people and companies began to resist government and corporate *yarase*.

But the use of *yarase* continues to be a built-in cultural characteristic of the Japanese when they are in a superior position, and is something that outsiders dealing with Japan should be aware of.

横並び
Yokonarabi
(Yoe-koe-nah-rah-bee)

The Copycat Syndrome

The copycat syndrome, for which the Japanese have traditionally been noted, has deep cultural roots, going back nearly 2,000 years to Japan's earliest contacts with Korea and China. Most of these early contacts involved Koreans visiting Japan and bringing with them artifacts and technology that were Chinese in origin, and which were far superior to anything known in Japan at that time.

In fact, according to substantial evidence in both Korea and Japan, there are strong indications that Japan's imperial house was founded by Korean horsemen whose weapons and methods of fighting gave them a significant advantage over the still primitive Japanese.

From around the years 300 to 800 virtually all of the new products that appeared in Japan were originally copied from Korean and Chinese samples, and then gradually Japanized to fit the already distinctive Japanese mindset. The next flurry of product copying occurred in the 1500s when the first Europeans arrived in Japan, bringing with them weapons, mechanical instruments, foods, clothing and other things the Japanese had never seen before.

One of the more humorous anecdotes dating from this period involved the cannons one of the Japanese clan fiefs copied from a European sample. The European cannon had a number of pits and other faults on its outer barrel that, of course, had nothing to do with its function. But the diligent Japanese cannon makers copied the pits and faults precisely.

The Japanese penchant for copying foreign products really came into its own after the fall of the feudal shogunate government in 1868. By 1900 the Japanese were major manufacturers and exporters of hundreds of Western-style toys, textiles, gift items and kitchen utensils—virtually all of them copies of items brought in by foreign importers. Any new product that was brought in and achieved any degree of success, quickly resulted in what the Japanese called the *yokonarabi* (yoe-koe-nah-rah-bee) effect, meaning that other makers rushed out copies of the new item.

Figuratively, *yokonarabi* means something like "lining up on the same side"; another meaning is copying any new product that appears in the market. The *yokonarabi* syndrome is still alive and well in Japan. In fact, it is one of the primary characteristics of the Japanese economy as a whole and the syndrome applies across the board to products made for the domestic as well as for the export market.

The more successful a product, whether in the local market or in the export market, the more other companies are likely to jump in with clones that are as close as possible to the original. Imitation is not restricted to products, however; Japanese makers copy names and logo designs as well.

Generally, the overall effects of the *yokonarabi* syndrome are negative as far as the manufacturers are concerned. The flood of copies results in excess production and lower prices, keeping extraordinary pressure on makers to cut their costs again and again, and to continuously introduce new products.

Practically all items imported into Japan face a *yokonarabi* onslaught that quickly dilutes the market and threatens their survival. Virtually the only products that succeed are those that have some attribute that cannot be copied or totally diluted, or those that are able to carve out a niche for themselves. Of course, this presupposes that the exporter-importer of the foreign-made product has the experience, financial resources and patience to persevere in the face of daunting odds.

Another aspect of the *yokonarabi* syndrome is that the companies that copy other people's products are well aware that they might be caught. They do it anyway, however, using the rationale that at worst they can make some quick money, and at best the original maker will not complain, or will agree to let them continue in exchange for a modest commission—something that has happened hundreds of times over the years.

湯舟
Yubune
(Yuu-buu-nay)

The Japanese and Hot Water

My old Japan-hand friend and colleague, business executive and writer George Fields, an Australian born and educated in Japan, once noted that if he had to pick the most unique aspect of Japanese culture, it would be the traditional Japanese way of bathing.

The Japanese may not have been the first people to adopt the practice of bathing daily, but they were at least among the earliest to make the practice a ritualistic part of their lives. In their case, the impetus for bathing every day was spiritual. One of the main tenets of Shintoism, the indigenous Japanese religion, advocated physical as well as mental cleanliness. Bathing daily not only ensured physical cleanliness, it also contributed to cleansing the mind of mental stress. And since the practice of

Shintoism in early Japan was a way of life for everyone, not a matter of choice, every Japanese without exception was taught to bathe daily if humanly possible.

From infancy on, families and neighbors bathed together, either in public bathhouses or in private baths that were shared with neighbors who did not have their own.

Another factor that contributed enormously to the Japanese fondness for bathing was the extraordinary number of hot springs in the country. Because of the volcanic nature of the Japanese islands, there are thousands of places in the country where hot water gushes from vents in the earth.

Traditional bathing practices in Japan differed significantly from those that developed in Europe. When the first Europeans arrived in Japan in the mid-1500s, they were shocked by these differences. To begin with, the Japanese bathed daily, while the Europeans thought that regular bathing was harmful to the health and avoided it most of the time. Anybody who bathed as often as once a month was considered touched in the head.

Another thing that was even more shocking to the puritanical Europeans of that time was the fact that mixed bathing was the rule in Japan. Like everything else in the lives of the Japanese, there was a time and a place for sex, and the bath was neither the place nor the time—an attitude that Europeans simply could not fathom. One of the first things that foreign missionaries in Japan did was to forbid their converts from engaging in mixed bathing, and to establish a rule that they could not bathe more than once a week—an extraordinary concession by the missionaries.

A third thing that the Westerners found weird about Japanese bathing was that people washed themselves totally before getting into the tub, or pool in the case of a hot springs. By the same token, when the Japanese observed foreigners soaping and washing themselves inside the tub they were astounded. They could not imagine that anyone could be so dumb as to both wash and soak in water soiled by soap and whatever dirt was scrubbed from their bodies.

A bathtub in Japanese is a *yubune* (yuu-buu-nay). *Yu* means "hot water," and *bune* means "boat." Together they make a "hot water boat." My friend George Fields suggests that the etymology of this term derives from the idea of visualizing the bathtub as a boat on a calm sea that allows one's mind and its cares to drift away.

Western-style bathrooms are now common in Japan, but the Japanese have not given up their traditional ways where *yubune* are concerned. Bathrooms in homes are designed with tile floors and floor drains so bathers can scrub themselves outside of the tub, and then soak in clean hot water.

The Japanese attitude toward bathing and the design of the *yubune* reveals a great deal about Japanese mentality that carries over into virtually all other areas of their life. To a Japanese Japanese, taking a bath is more than a simple physical practice. It is an emotional and spiritual experience that, according to George Fields, evokes feelings of contemplation, renewal and sensual pleasure. It is also a reflection of the neatness and orderliness that one sees in the typical Japanese factory, in their product displays, and in their concern for details and ritual.

Hot water occupies a special place in the mental construct of the Japanese. It is seen as something that washes away "sin" as well as ordinary psychological baggage, returning one to a virginal state.

I am reminded of the last night of General Hideki Tojo, who was the prime minister of Japan from 1941 to 1944, and who was tried and convicted as a war criminal by the Supreme Allied Powers following Japan's defeat in World War II. Before he was hanged early on the morning of December 23, 1948, Tojo asked to be allowed to take a hot bath and to change his clothing, saying, "We Japanese like to die clean."

財テク
Zaiteku
(Zigh-tay-kuu)

The High-Tech Investors

Most people outside Japan are familiar with the Japanese word *zaibatsu* (zigh-baht-sue), the term used to describe Japan's huge pre-World War II industrial combines—Mitsui, Mitsubishi, Sumitomo, Yasuda, Nissan, Asano, Furukawa, Okura, Nakajima and Nomura—and some have heard the term *zaikai* (zigh-kigh), meaning "financial" or "business circles," that came into use in reference to Japan's ranking industrialists in the decades following the end of the war. The chairman of Japan's prestigious *Keidanren* (Kay-dahn-ren), which is short for "Federation of Economic Organizations," is regarded as the nominal head of the *zaikai* (zigh-kigh) and is often unofficially referred to as the *zaikai sori* (zigh-kigh soh-ree) or "prime minister of the business world."

My favorite anecdote of the power and glory of the elite *zaikai* members during their heyday is a news story about one of their gatherings in the mountain resort city of Karuizawa, northwest of Tokyo. According to reports, one of the attractions arranged for the wives of the members attending the party were baskets of precious jewels set out on tables, from which the guests could take whatever they wanted.

It was during the heyday of the *zaikai* in the mid-1980s that another *zai* term, *zaiteku* (zigh-tay-kuu), became popular. *Zai* by itself refers to money or wealth and in a number of compound words it may be translated as "financial." *Teku* is the Japanization of the abbreviation "*tech*," from technology. When *zai* and *teku* are put together the word refers to investing in stocks and other securities, something that was practically limited to corporate and other institutional investors prior to Japan's sudden emergence as an economic superpower in the 1970s and 1980s.

Japanese corporations became heavy *zaiteku* players following the so-called "oil shock" in the early 1970s, when the price of oil shot upward. By the end of that decade, the interest and dividends many companies were making from their stock investments was a vital part of their bottom line. Some companies set up subsidiaries in Japan as well as overseas to handle their investments. A favorite investment in the United States—purchased with export earnings—were US bonds. A number of Japan's largest manufacturing firms, including Toyota Motor Corporation and Matsushita Electric Industrial Co., became so heavily involved in investing in stocks and bonds that the news media began referring to them as the Bank of Toyota and the Bank of Matsushita.

In the 1980s ordinary Japanese suddenly caught *zaiteku* fever. Large numbers of salaried workers began to use their household savings to play the stock market.

When Japan's "bubble economy" went flat in 1990, a number of the leading security houses reimbursed some of their large corporate investors for their losses—in amounts involving hundreds of millions of dollars. When this behind-the-scenes double-dealing became known to the public, the uproar from those who had invested their family savings in the then deflated stocks and bonds could be heard from one end of the country to the other.

The Japanese government subsequently passed new laws to bring the security firms under tighter financial control and to guarantee that they would not discriminate against small individual *zaiteku* players.

Interestingly, Japan's infamous yakuza gangs are also major *zaiteku* players, and are notorious for using the threat of physical violence to extort "special consulting fees" from the companies in which they own stocks.

前例
Zenrei
(Zen-ray-e)

Breaking the Molds of the Past

An American friend who first took up residence in Japan in the mid-1950s and soon became bilingual (unlike many other "old Japan hands" who speak little or none of the language), recently remarked to me, "The Japanese are not different from us! They are just 200 years behind us!"

My old friend—and favorite source of pithy quotes on Japan—was being a bit facetious and was letting off some steam. He immediately qualified his statement by explaining that, of course, he meant the Japanese were 200 years behind us in the everyday use of logical behavior—not in high-rise buildings and bullet trains.

There is perhaps nothing more frustrating to Westerners in Japan than the fact that the Japanese seem to behave in ways that defy Western logic and common sense, yet they are stunningly successful in business and in many other areas of human endeavor. To a great many Westerners in Japan, the apparent contradictions that are inherent in this situation are just too much to accept without a fight, even though they know there is more than one way of doing things.

There are also few things more irritating to Westerners in Japan than the inflexible behavior of government and business bureaucrats. It often seems that the prime directive in the mental software of Japanese businessmen and bureaucrats alike is that if a thing has not been done before, it cannot be done, and all too often their knee-jerk reaction is that it should not even be considered, much less attempted. To the outsider, this kind of behavior frequently appears to have been specifically designed to prevent foreigners from succeeding in the Japanese market.

But this seemingly deliberate ploy is not a contemporary invention. It is a deeply ingrained cultural trait that comes under the heading of avoiding *zenrei* (zen-ray-e), or "precedence." Throughout most of Japan's history, setting any kind of precedent was a dangerous thing, and doing things differently was often prohibited by law. Emphasis was on doing only things that had been done before, and in the way they had always been done, following forms and processes perfected over generations.

This philosophy and meticulously followed practice conditioned the Japanese to be wary of setting any kind of *zenrei* by themselves. Changes that did take place almost always occurred under the auspices of the local clan governments or the shogunate, and were the products of slow, consensus-building discussions over months, years, or decades.

Even the seminal political, economic and social changes that occurred following the fall of the shogunate clan system of government in 1868 were not spontaneous events. They had been debated and fought over for close to half a century, and were mostly decreed by the new government.

Japanese reluctance to set precedents was so deeply ingrained in the culture that it survived the American and allied military occupation of Japan from 1945 to 1952, as well as the new American-inspired postwar constitution which eliminated the feudal laws that had controlled Japanese behavior since the early 1600s.

And till this day, despite outward appearances, only a few Japanese are able to break with the past and set *zenrei*, particularly in politics and business. Virtually the only Japanese who dare to be different on a regular basis are artists, entertainers, the young before they finish school and join the Establishment, and maverick business owners who can afford to do things that are un-Japanese. Businesspeople and government bureaucrats are still restrained by a system that generally prevents them from deviating from the established way of doing things; this includes avoiding making exceptions to minor rules that do nothing but complicate matters.

Interestingly, the Japanese will set precedents for foreigners more often than they will for other Japanese, and this is one of the factors that makes life in Japan a little more tolerable for logical and expedient foreigners.